Mary of the Angels

12-7-2012
<u>Pearl Harbor Day</u>

Dear Truett & Diana,

It was Dec. 8th in the Philippines <u>and</u> Manila. We were in school when the Japanese bombed Pearl Harbor when the chaos began. It continued for over three years before MacArthur kept his promise. My book is a "promise kept" to our mother, whose strong faith and determination (along with God's Grace) kept us alive. So glad we are here and have such wonderful friends such as you two! God Bless You — and God Bless America —

Mary Jane

Mary of the Angels

MARY JANE HODGES VANCE

© 2012 Mary Jane Hodges Vance.
All Rights Reserved.

Dedication

I humbly dedicate this book to my children, their spouses, and my grandchildren, with the hope that this labor of love will provide them with a greater understanding of their rich family heritage. I pray they will never suffer the consequences of a military conflict or enemy oppression. May God Bless them and may God Bless America.

        John Charles (Chip) Vance Jr.
        Carmen Annette Eeds Vance
        Kelsea Danielle Vance
        Kacie Nicole Vance
        John Charles (Chase) Vance III

        Mary (Missy) Vance Spears
        Joseph Derek Spears
        Joseph Vance Spears
        John Kenneth (Jake) Spears

Author's Note

During World War II, our family endured over three years of the indescribable Japanese Occupation of the Philippines. The status of our American father, a civilian prisoner in Santo Tomas Internment Camp (STIC), was unknown to us for two years of that period. Our Spanish mother, Maria de los Angeles (Mary of the Angels), saved us from being interned by declaring us "Spanish Citizens." We remained under a "quasi" house arrest enforced by Japanese soldiers and their selected leader of a "Neighborhood Association." Their ever-watchful eyes and unannounced inspections kept us "in line," along with their loaded rifles, sharp bayonets, and gruff mannerisms. Our main support was our strong faith and the large band of angels watching over us…in both human and spiritual form.

Mary's story is crafted from her copious handwritten notes, family interviews and conversations, plus mounds of memorabilia collected during her lifetime. The process of piecing together the many parts of the puzzle required over ten years of sorting and matching each piece to a chronology of historical events. Mary's story of a rich Spanish heritage, her courtship and marriage to a Texan, their struggles in rearing a family, and providing for them during wartime, their hazardous journey through dangerous enemy waters to reach America, and her struggle to become a citizen of these United States…her ultimate goal, was a labor of love.

All historical data are accurate as reported. All names of individuals are as correct as one's memory can recall, and some are changed to protect the innocent or guilty. Most of the conversations were creatively constructed by the author to add interest and flow to the multitude of facts.

May angels guide your thoughts as you read.

Acknowledgement of Angels

My deepest appreciation goes to the following angels:

- The countless unsung heroes, both military and civilian, for their actions in the liberation of the Philippines—without you and yours, we may not have survived;
- The many friends and family contacts who gave their time, energy, and information as resources through phone calls, letters, or emails, especially our cousin, A. D. (Tony) Settember Jr. for unselfishly giving his time to help Allied troops, and his wife, Patti; cousin Maridel Gonzalez Beckman—daughter of Juaning, granddaughter of Consueling—for sharing precious family photos; Jerry Yrissary, a helpful friend from the S.S. Uruguay, who provided details and insights through his own accounts of WWII; David Poskey for providing photos of his father, Hubert Poskey;
- Our many friends, neighbors, former students, and coworkers for their interest, encouragement, and amazing support;
- Dr. Fred Tarpley, for providing guidance, instruction, and information through the auspices of Texas A&M University-Commerce and the Silver Leos Writers Guild;
- Vivian Freeman, Past President of the Silver Leos Writers Guild, for her sound advice, support, patience, encouragement, and professional typesetting;
- My older sisters: Emma Hodges Smith, for being "another set of eyes" and her recall of past events; and, Lucy Hodges Collins, for being our "other mother," and her husband, Cornelius "Buddy" Collins for his accurate accounts of WWII;
- My younger sisters: Joyce Hodges Barrow, for copies of family photos she collected; and, Linnie Hodges McCormack, for her love and caring support;
- Our daughter, Mary (Missy) Vance Spears, for graciously sharing her creative talents and inspirational thoughts through her poem, "Family;"
- Our brother, Jesse A. Hodges Jr., who is now with our family angel band; our brother, Robert Morris Hodges, wherever you are; and, finally,
- Our mother, Mary Gamero Hodges, for her determination and dedication to keep us together through impossible conditions before, during, and after World War II. Her strong faith, the triumph over adversity, and her positive attitude were the inspiration for this book. The family angels welcomed her on May 18, 1993.

Family

A family is like a multicolored rainbow

Etching impressions in the sky.

It is there, so fragile, yet so bold,

And the moment you reach out to touch it,

It disappears.

Its traditions are kept through memories

Its memories are locked inside each member

As a very special color

Spreading messages of sunshine to the world,

Yet, leaving all hopes waiting

For the next generation of rainbows.

Mary (Missy) Vance (1982)
Granddaughter of
Maria de los Angeles Gamero y Cucullu

PROLOGUE

Mary of the Angels

Mary gazed across the large Community Room in the CCD Building of St. Williams Catholic Church in Greenville, Texas. Many friends and family members were gathered on Sunday evening, February 17, 1985, to celebrate her eightieth birthday. *In two days, I will be eighty years old! Where have the years gone?*

As she collected her thoughts and counted her blessings, Mary said a silent prayer for the loved ones who were missing this party. Jesse Hodges, her husband, died almost eighteen years ago from a massive heart attack. She was left alone to rear two of their nine children. Robert, their eldest son, fondly called "Bobby," enlisted in the U.S. Navy at age seventeen prior to the attack on Pearl Harbor. He was later listed as, "Missing in Action," and was always on her mind. *"Missing in Action" was an empty answer to a heart full of questions.* Their second son, Jesse Jr., lived in Los Angeles with his ailing wife, Lucija, a refugee from Latvia. Rose, the youngest, lived in Spokane. She could neither leave her new job nor have her two sons miss school. Mary wished every family member could attend, however, she knew it was not possible. She felt her "angels" were watching.

The tinkling piano, played by Libby McNatt, spilled soft music across the room and combined with the pleasant hum of conversation. Peals of laughter jostled against the music, from time to time, adding staccato notes to the occasion.

Mary had been in this country for about forty years. It seemed like only a short time since she left her homeland, the Philippines, following its liberation by American troops in 1945. They left their familiar environment and many family members behind, including Bobby, her sisters and her mother. Mary felt she would probably never see them all again, and she was right. Her lifelong friends wished them well before leaving Manila to make a new home in Texas, her husband's birthplace.

What an amazing life I have experienced! I survived The Philippine Insurrection, World War I, and the Japanese Occupation of the Philippines during World War II. Many questions raced through her head. *How will I share all those memories? Who would help me? I barely managed to learn to speak English.* Her thick Spanish accent colored everything she uttered. She tried to understand the Texas lingo and practiced speaking "Texan," which often led to many comedic conversations! *Where will I find someone who understands me and will write my story?*

Monsignor John V. McCallum, Mary's priest, touched her elbow as he entered the room, bringing her into the moment. He took Mary's hand in both of his and greeted her warmly.

"My goodness, Mary," he teased, "You have so many friends! You must be so proud! I see you also have most of your family here!"

Mary's hand trembled in his as waves of emotion surged through her.

"Yes," she agreed, "I am truly blessed, as you can see. Many memories were swirling around like a whirlwind from the past before you arrived. I am glad to see you!"

They were chatting when her daughter, Linnie, approached to escort her to the refreshment table. She greeted Monsignor McCallum before speaking to her mother.

"Come on, Mother," Linnie said taking her by her left arm, "it's time to blow out your candles and cut your birthday cake!"

Those gathered clapped as she sauntered toward the well-appointed buffet table covered with twenty-four yards of pale yellow cloth crowned with a billowing stream of white Spanish lace and highlighted by a large floral arrangement with her favorite flowers. The beautiful cake, baked by Linnie, graced one end of the table. The other end sparkled with a large crystal punch bowl full of tropical fruit punch. Her children worked hard to make her birthday celebration perfect!

Once more, tears filled her eyes making it difficult to see. Another daughter, Emma, stepped to her right side, cupped Mary's elbow with her hand, and accompanied her across the room. Applause rippled throughout the crowd. Libby McNatt's nimble fingers launched into the introductory notes of *Happy Birthday To You*, and the crowd sang, with another daughter Mary Jane leading the group. The singing was followed by more applause. When it subsided, Jimmy, her youngest son, urged her to make a wish.

"Come on, Mom," he teased, "make a wish and blow out the candles before the fire department shows up!"

The group laughed as Mary took a deep breath and blew hard. She laughed and blew harder, when three candles were not extinguished. She knew one wish had already been granted. Her wish to bring surviving family members to the United States of America…to Texas…to a new life after all they had experienced during those terrible years under Japanese military rule. Secondly, that her husband, Jesse, would withstand the rigors of being a prisoner of war in Santo Tomas Internment Camp. The unresolved questions about their missing son, Bobby, however, hung like a mysterious cloud overhead.

"Here's your cake, Mother," Linnie said as she offered Mary a generous slice along with a small cup of fruit punch, "I'll take it to the table reserved for you. You can sit there and see everyone."

Mary moved slowly to the chair being pulled out for her. She offered a silent prayer of thanks for all who had made this celebration so memorable.

The evening stretched out into a haze of hugs, kisses, and handshakes as the guests stopped by her table to deliver their individual congratulations and wish her well. R. L. and Peggy Perser, Carlos and Ramona Wright, plus Jake and Paula Jacobs, Emma and Mary Jane's friends, offered their well wishes. Carol and Jack Ferguson were next. Carol appeared so festive with a lovely red felt fedora perked saucily to one side of her head. She and Carol laughed about being the pillars of the church. Many times, Carol, Mary, and Helen Mehmert were the only parishioners at evening services with Monsignor McCallum.

Mary was pleased to see Walter Harris Ford, retired superintendent of Quinlan Public Schools. With his encouragement, her children finished their education. *My Golden Tree holds all of their graduation photos.* Beside him were Hobart and Juanita Lytle with their niece, Glenna Wade Wilson. Mr. Lytle, Quinlan Postmaster for many years, was very helpful during her many struggles with the multiple forms and scheduled payments required to attain American citizenship. *The process was a long, arduous ordeal that even included a warrant for my arrest as an illegal alien!*

Beno and Edna Jean (Sissie) Smith's happy voices returned Mary to her celebration. The Smiths walked up behind Glenna Wade Wilson. Mary Jane joined them to share hugs and conversation. They walked away laughing as Aline Higdon Bagley, sister-in-law to C. N. and Linnie Higdon Hodges, came to share happy memories with her. Mary introduced Aline to Sue Jones, who was behind her. Hank and Helen Mehmert followed. Dr. Henry (Hank) Mehmert, Mary's physician, grabbed her arm as if to check her pulse.

"Wanted to see if your 'ticker' was doing all right with all this celebrating, Mary!" Dr. Mehmert teased as his eyes twinkled with merriment.

They chatted with Mary until Virginia Ewell, Mildred Trad, Polly Mullins, and Bea Phillips interrupted to offer their congratulations. Marie Heidmann and Eugenia Mehmert reached for Mary's hands. Marie came to America from Germany and was always an empathetic person. Marie understood about being away from her homeland. Close behind were Eva Lea Carter, Katie Hurse, and Charles Vance, Mary Jane's husband, with their mother, Mary Ellen (Bunt) Vance. They complimented Mary on her lovely turquoise dress and pink corsage before offering their congratulations. Bunt laughed as she noted she was five years older than Mary.

The voices of H. R. "Rooks" Epperson, a prosperous Quinlan businessman, boomed across the room as he, and his son, Jim, greeted Mary. Behind them were Lois Smith, Horace B. and Golda Marie Cooper, Alice Cooper, and Ruth Barbee. The line seemed endless.

Mary's face was frozen with a fixed smile as she graciously greeted each guest. The only ones remaining were family members, who made sure they collected their hugs and kisses before leaving for their separate homes.

Her daughters cleared the refreshment table and gathered her many cards and gifts. It was time to go home. Mary was ready. All the excitement and activity left her physically and emotionally drained. The peace and quiet of her home, conveniently located less than a block away on the corner of Stonewall and Pollard, would be a welcome respite. *Thank goodness I live nearby.*

Following the short ride home, Mary unlocked her kitchen door, stepped inside, and made room to store the remaining food and punch in her refrigerator. As her daughters unloaded the car, she cleared a place on her dining table for the gifts and cards. Goodnight hugs and kisses were shared. It was late, and Mary was tired, so they left her to prepare for a well-deserved night's rest.

Alone, Mary's thoughts returned to her celebration. Although she was tired, she was not sleepy. She readied herself for bed and crawled under the covers to stay warm on this chilly February night. Her thoughts raced about like cats frightened by a barking dog. She reached for her rosary and recited her prayers, hoping to calm her racing mind and help her sleep. When she had finished *The Lord's Prayer*, she once again thought about how to share her many life experiences.

Mary Jane urged her, several times, to write down as much as she remembered about her early life. She even provided several spiral bound notebooks for Mary to use. *I will ask Mary Jane tomorrow to help me.* A peaceful feeling engulfed her as she relaxed in the comforting arms of sleep.

Early the next morning, Mary awakened with a renewed vigor. She hummed as she prepared her morning coffee and decided her breakfast would be (what else) birthday cake.

As the water heated, Mary searched her desk area for those spiral notebooks. *I'll begin with the stories my mother told me about my grandparents coming to the Philippines from Spain. She and other family members recited them like a catechism. This will be enjoyable, fill my lonely days and give purpose to my life.* Mary found the spiral bound notebooks along with a pen, and placed them on the breakfast table. She was ready!

As she sipped her coffee and nibbled on the savory birthday cake, she jotted down facts she recalled about her parent's family histories. It was important that her family learn their heritage. She remembered the old family photos brought on that long sea voyage from the Philippines! *We did not know how dangerous it was until we had to wear our life jackets for three weeks in those enemy infested waters!*

Mary searched the closet in the front bedroom where she kept old family photos and letters. Those mementos survived World War II. They were packed, with loving care, for the long sea voyage to America in July 1945, and remained stored in the same silver-colored suitcase ever since. The hinges creaked as she gently opened the case and sorted through its contents. As she picked up the first album, a portrait of José Maria Gamero y Porras, her father, fell into her lap along with crumbled pieces of the album page.

"*Papá*," She murmured, "I'll begin my story with *Papá* and get Mary Jane to help me with the historic events during his lifetime."

Mary felt she was given a sign…a place to begin. She wrote diligently for three hours recording family history while sorting through the many photos before stopping to contemplate her next steps. Each photo sparked memories of people, places and events from her family's past. She had the beginning of her story and would write every day until it was told. Mary covered her writing table and the cherished photos with a clean white cloth and strolled into the living room to view her favorite soap operas. They were addictive and she dared not miss any episodes.

(left to right) Daughters Mary Jane Vance, Emma Smith, Lucy Collins; Msgr. John V. McCallum; Mary Gamero Hodges; Daughters Linnie McCormack, Joyce Barrow; Son James C. Hodges *(back)*

Maria de los Angeles Josefa Gabina Gamero y Cucullu (Mary of the Angels) celebrating her 80th birthday. The small cakes surrounding the tiered cake represented the eight living children of Jesse and Mary Gamero Hodges.

Spanish Angels

CHAPTER 1

Escape to Manila

In 1836, Don José Maria Gamero and his wife, Doña Maxima Porras y Gamero, made a critical decision about their lives in Spain. Several years prior to 1836, Spain was torn between King Ferdinand and the Roman Catholic Church on one side and the liberals on the other. In June 1833, Ferdinand swept aside the Salic Law, which forbade any woman to inherit the throne, so upon his death, his infant daughter, Isabella II, could succeed him, rather than his brother, Don Carlos. The Carlists, or Roman Catholic Church group, wanted Don Carlos as king.

King Ferdinand died in September 1833 leaving María Christina de Borbon, Isabella II's mother, to act as regent and hold the throne in her daughter's stead. The Carlists plotted and carried out many distasteful schemes against María Christina and Isabella II, causing María Christina to resign the regency in favor of a liberal, General Baldomero Espartero. In 1836, a bloody Civil War, between the Loyalists and the Rebels, ensued and raged fiercely throughout Spain.

Don José and Doña Maxima feared for their lives and for their only son, José Maria, barely one year old. Three years earlier, Don José found financial opportunities in the Philippines, since it was controlled by Spain, and became a stockholder in the Spanish bank, *El Monte de Piedad y Caja de Ahorros,* in Manila. The decision was made. They must emigrate or surely die!

Don José quietly made the travel arrangements. Gathering only those items and food supplies essential to sustain life on board their sailing vessel, Doña Maxima sewed their valuables inside the hems of her garments and took care to ensure they were unobtrusive, yet secure. Don José took money from their bank account, leaving a small amount, so the withdrawal would not be noticeable. With heavy hearts, they bade farewell to immediate family members and close friends. They would never see them again. Barcelona, Spain, was no longer their home.

In 1836, after a perilous sea journey through the Strait of Gibraltar, the enormous swells of the Atlantic Ocean, around the tip of Africa and amid the many small islands in the South China Sea, Don José Maria Gamero and his wife, Doña Maxima Porras y Gamero with their son, José Maria Gamero y Porras, arrived in Manila, Philippines. Exhausted after their long journey and weak from food deprivation, they set forth, with timidity and hesitation, to begin a new life in Manila. Unsettling stories about natives in the Philippines caused concern. The Gameros were unsure of many things. Once upon solid ground, they located the nearest Roman Catholic Church and offered prayers to St. Joseph, their patron saint. Help was sought from the local parish priest to find housing and assistance.

Mary paused with pen in mid-air. *My grandparents, Don José and Doña Maxima, were brave. Imagine, going to a strange, new country to start your life anew.*

Mary laughed to herself. She experienced something similar, except her voyage was to America through enemy infested waters before the end of World War II with her emaciated husband (released only weeks before from a Japanese concentration camp after thirty-seven months of hardship and deprivation) and their six surviving children. Only God knew about their eldest son, Bobby, who had enlisted in the United States Navy prior to the disaster at Pearl Harbor. She felt strongly connected to Doña Maxima and Don José, her paternal grandparents. They had survived...and so had she.

The doorbell interrupted her reverie. Mary Jane brought a large notebook filled with historical data for her use. Mary was delighted to have the data to make connections. These dates and facts would help her family have a better understanding of conditions in Spain and the Philippines.

Mary enjoyed the brief respite from her writing. More material to sort through and integrate into her family history waited on the table. The first item she spied was a chronology of historical events. She fixed a cup of hot cocoa and resumed her writing, while waiting for the cocoa to cool.

The news from Spain was alarming! Unrest seethed like a creeping fog among the Spaniards, and civil disorder erupted across Spain. Queen Isabella II tried to appease the Carlists, but they were not satisfied. The Roman Catholic Church supported the Carlists and spread the message of discontent across the land like a virus infecting all who listened. Chaos galloped across Spain, leaving death and destruction throughout the country.

"Dios mio!" Exclaimed Don José when he read the sad news of conditions in Spain. He held Doña Maxima's hand over his heart as tears filled her eyes. Their country was being destroyed from within. Invaders did not have to pillage the land...it was done by their own people and their own church. They made the right decision in coming to the Philippines to provide a safe haven for their son and a new beginning for their family.

The years passed swiftly. Don José obtained a position as bookkeeper at *El Monte de Piedad y Caja de Ahorros*. He and Doña Maxima managed to have a comfortable life, having bought a large home at the Rotonda Legarda in Manila. José Maria, their son, completed his first year of education at San Juan de Letran School for Spanish boys, under the management of the Dominican priests. He succeeded in his studies, much to his parents' delight!

After completing his studies at San Juan de Letran in 1851, José entered Ateneo de Manila College, also managed by the Dominicans, and completed his bachelor's degree in Accounting with a minor in Navigation. In 1854, upon graduation at age nineteen, he was hired as assistant bookkeeper to his father, Don José, at the Spanish Bank, *El Monte de Piedad*.

―――

Mary smiled knowingly as she recalled the fairytale beginning of her father's first marriage. Her *Mami* loved to tell the children stories about their *Papá*. He died when Mary was only three years old. These stories brought her father closer and filled the void in the life of a fatherless child. *Mami's* voice spun through her head like a phonograph record being played on the family Victrola.

―――

Being a healthy and inquisitive young man, José M. Gamero y Porras, didn't waste any time finding a young Spanish girl. Joaquina Saenz was a lovely intelligent person who attended their Roman Catholic Church. She had an angelic voice, a sparkling smile, and eyes that danced as she passed. She and José shared cordial greetings after morning mass and José wished for more. He spoke to his parents about Joaquina. As was the Spanish custom, the parents made the arrangements for the families to meet and obtained their consent for a "courting period." All these plans began by first consulting the parish priest. Don José knew the protocol. His parents set the proper example so he could court Maxima, and he would do likewise for his son.

Following Sunday Mass, Don José approached their parish priest and presented his proposal.

"Our son, José, seeks your blessings and the permission of Joaquina Saenz's parents to share Joaquina's company."

Father Domingo smiled and agreed to approach the Saenz family to obtain their approval. The stage was set. The rituals had begun.

CHAPTER 2

Joaquina

Miracle of all miracles…the Saenz family agreed to the marriage of their daughter, Joaquina, to José Maria Gamero y Porras. The wedding bans were announced and posted in their church for all to see. Eighteen hundred and fifty-four would be a glorious year!

As was the Spanish custom, the groom's family paid for all the wedding arrangements and expenses…including her wedding gown and all accessories. The best Spanish lace was purchased for the bride's *mantilla*. The exquisitely carved ivory rosary, which Doña Maxima carried at her own wedding, was her gift to Joaquina. Doña Maxima busied herself with the many preparations. José was their only child. The wedding must be perfect. Their friends and parishioners would recognize the Gameros as a prominent family in Manila. The Saenz family would be properly impressed with the wedding, and understand their decision to allow Joaquina to marry José was blessed by God.

José and Joaquina's wedding day arrived. Friends, relatives and parishioners were in awe during the celebratory High Mass with all its pomp and circumstance. When the couple knelt at the altar to receive their first Holy Communion as man and wife, Joaquina glanced lovingly at José while he lifted her veil to receive the host. José smiled at his new bride. A feeling of pride swelled within his chest. *She is so beautiful*.

Following their honeymoon in Cebu, a wealthy province of the Philippines, José and Joaquina returned to Manila to make their home with Don José and Doña Maxima. These would be temporary quarters until they found their own. Joaquina was happy to live with them, as the Gameros owned a large home and were kind and welcoming to her.

Joaquina busied herself with the household tasks and helped Doña Maxima. José was busy with his job as assistant bookkeeper to his father, Don José at the Spanish bank, *El Monte de Piedad*.

As the years passed, Joaquina became depressed. She had not given her husband a child. Two previous births were stillborn, and she felt unable carry a baby to full term. Her husband assured her God would provide. God knew best.

One Sunday afternoon, during their *paseo*, José and Joaquina admired a lovely home on the corner of Novaliches and Tanduay streets. They stopped to inquire. A Spanish gentleman, recently widowed, owned the home. In conversation, he discussed his desire to return to Spain and reconnect with his family. The couple expressed an interest in purchasing his home, which he felt was a sign from God. Time was his enemy, so he was willing to accept a reasonable price for his home.

After making the proper inquiries and arrangements for a bank loan, José decided this home would be perfect for them. Perhaps being alone in a new home would help them achieve their long-awaited miracle…the birth of a healthy child.

In 1864, they were still childless after losing a third baby to the Angel of Death. José talked with his father about using part of his parents' large home to offer classes in nautical engineering for Spanish boys from Manila and the provinces. José reasoned his evenings were free, and teaching navigation would be a way to improve financially in order to pay for their newly acquired home. The profits, after expenses were deducted from the tuition charged, would be shared equally. Don José agreed. *My son has thought this through and made a wise choice.* Preparations were made and enrollment began.

Professor Gamero, as his students addressed him, welcomed the Spanish young men from Manila, as well as sons of wealthy Spanish plantation owners from the provinces of Pampanga, Ilocos, Negros, and the Visayas. Abundant tobacco, sugar, and hemp crops made them wealthy. José was wise to provide living quarters for his students to board at his night school, for the provinces were quite a distance from Manila. Their parents were grateful and gladly paid the extra fees.

Meanwhile, Joaquina learned she was once again with child. She and José prayed daily. If it were God's Will, she would carry this baby to full term.

Time seemed to crawl by like a fat caterpillar missing several feet. Joaquina felt the first pangs of childbirth. The miracle of miracles was happening. Doña Maxima sent a servant to summon Dr. Guerrero. Another one was dispatched to tell her husband and José. Joaquina was in labor.

José bolted out the bank's front door upon being told the long-awaited news. Don José first made sure the accounts were in order before leaving. He was pleased but not as excited as his son, José.

Darkness fell upon the Gamero household. Joaquina was having difficulty with the baby's birth. The family doctor could only do so much. The hours of waiting for news felt like years to José. Dr. Guerrero, with Doña Maxima by his side, emerged from Joaquina's bedroom carrying his long-awaited child. José rushed toward them, but Dr. Guerrero's somber face and the tears in his mother's eyes caused him to stop. Dr. Guerrero placed the small bundle in José's arms, touched his elbow, and directed him to sit on the large overstuffed sofa in the parlor.

"José," Dr. Guerrero spoke, in a soft voice, "you have a lovely child, a healthy little girl. Your lovely Joaquina struggled hard to bring her into this world, but in doing so, she suffered greatly. Her life is in the Hands of God."

Tears welled in José's eyes, as he tried to comprehend. The joy of holding their first child in his arms was smothered by the knowledge his beloved wife had suffered. Wishing to provide him with a new life, his wife's health was compromised. His heart was broken. Don José approached his son and held his arms out to reach for his first grandchild.

"We shall name her Paz, Dr. Guerrero," Don José said with a calming voice. "She will bring the peace you have sought as a childless couple. *Our Father, which art in heaven, hallowed be Thy name, Thy Will be done....*"

José, his head bowed, rose from the sofa and took his child, Paz, into his arms. He gazed at her peaceful face and held her tightly to his chest. Joaquina had been given her wish. Although their prayers had been answered, sorrow filled his heart.

Joaquina, confined to her sick bed, cherished their only child, Paz, and lavished her with as much love and attention as her weakened condition would allow. José would bring them daily surprises and tried to find ways to bolster Joaquina's failing health. When Paz was two years old, Joaquina slipped away, leaving her pain and weariness behind. God's Will was done.

CHAPTER 3

Josepha

José buried himself in his work at the bank and teaching his students at his night school. He surrendered the care of Paz to his mother, Doña Maxima, a responsibility that gave her pleasure. Paz was their universe. Nothing interfered with their daily rituals. The growing unrest with Spanish control of the Philippines was ignored. Nationalism crept forth stealthily like a thief in the night. The sons of wealthy Filipinos were afforded opportunities for education in Manila and Madrid. The *ilustrados,* as they were called, opposed Spanish domination of the Philippines.

Doña Maxima was oblivious to these political movements. She was more concerned with finding a second wife for her son. A year had passed since Joaquina's death. José needed a wife, and Paz needed a mother.

I'm enjoying this portion of my story. Pascuala told me many details of her sister Josepha's marriage to my Papá, José. Pascuala never tired of its retelling…after all, Josepha and Pascuala, orphans at the time, finally had a family!

Mary adjusted her heavy eyeglasses on the thin chiseled bridge of her fine "del Valle" nose…one like her mother's. She smiled as she remembered details of Pascuala's tales.

Doña Maxima learned of several young Spanish orphans brought from Spain to the Philippines under the auspices of their church. Four of them were eligible young ladies. Josepha Boix, a tall dark-haired beauty, recently celebrated her eighteenth birthday. The parish priest made the announcement during the mass celebrating St. Joseph's Day, Josepha's patron saint. St. Joseph was also the Gamero's patron saint. Doña Maxima took this coincidence as a sign from God. She shared her thoughts, first, with Don José, and later, with her son.

José, at his mother's urging, observed Josepha while attending Mass. He paid particular attention to the way Josepha cared for her younger sister, Pascuala.

She kept Pascuala close to her side and instructed her throughout the Mass to provide understanding of the rituals. She was always gentle and never chastised Pascuala when she made a mistake, which impressed José.

José's conversations at the dinner table indicated he was interested in Josepha. Doña Maxima posed the question about his thoughts of Josepha, perhaps as a new wife. Surely he saw how Josepha cared for her younger sister, Pascuala. Perhaps she would be the perfect choice as a new mother for Paz?

José considered her questions. His mother dedicated herself to caring for Paz. He observed Josepha and her care for Pascuala on several occasions. Doña Maxima was right. He needed to share his life with another…to provide a mother for Paz. José agreed with his mother, much to her delight. Don José would, once again, speak to the parish priest, as Josepha had no family.

Following several prearranged meetings in 1872, José and Josepha married in a quiet ceremony attended only by the Gamero family and Josepha's sister, Pascuala. Doña Maxima provided guidance for Paz and instructed Josepha and Pascuala in household management. There was much to do and Doña Maxima wanted everything done correctly for Paz. Josepha followed instructions well and was pleased she and Pascuala had found a home.

During 1872 the influential Filipino intelligentsia, the *ilustrados,* fueled a major revolt in Cavite on Luzon. Over two hundred Filipino soldiers rebelled against their Spanish officers and murdered them. In retaliation, the Spanish government, executed the friars (Burgos, Gomez, and Zamora), three Filipino priests who joined this revolt. They dared to challenge the authority of Spanish officers and were publicly garroted, an act which strengthened demands for reforms.

José expressed his concerns to his young wife, but *Pepita,* as José called her, did not understand how this chaos in Cavite should matter to them, for Cavite was many kilometers away! *Manila was safe, wasn't it?* They would be safe; besides, she did not have time to concern herself with anything but Pascuala and Paz's care.

Revolution rumors spread across Manila in 1874 like a creeping fog, to be swept away by the dominating broom of the strong Spanish government. Josepha chose to ignore all this foolishness. She had much to do! Paz was enrolled in school and the time had come to bring her own child into the world. The seed planted in her was growing and stirring. Her hopes for her own family overshadowed all else.

Once again, Dr. Guerrero was summoned. Josepha was ready. Doña Maxima had prepared her for this event. Pascuala felt helpless as her older sister suffered through the pangs of childbirth. She cried and bolted from the room unable to witness her sister's pain. José reached for Pascuala as she ran by and put a comforting arm around her small shoulders. After all, she was too young to understand. He led her to the armchair beside the overstuffed sofa and gave her his handkerchief. The ticking of the large clock on the mantle pounded through her head like nails being driven through her skull.

The baby's loud crying as the bedroom door opened was a welcome respite from the ticking clock. Doña Maxima marched from Josepha's bedroom with a smile of gratitude on her face and a precious bundle in her arms. She presented this new life to her son, José. He glanced at his child and at his mother.

"Josepha?" He asked, with concern moving across his face.

"She will be fine, my son," she replied. "Dr. Guerrero said all is well."

Don José stepped closer to his son, José and reached for his new grandchild.

"So, we have another girl!" he exclaimed. "We shall choose a name for her."

Pascuala jumped to her feet to see her new niece. She reached out for the baby's hand and, immediately, felt the tiny fingers curl around one of hers.

"Mercedes," she said as she smiled, "for God has shown us His mercy."

"Mercedes," Don José announced…"Mercedes del Carmen."

Dr. Guerrero emerged from Josepha's bedroom and nodded toward José.

"You may see your wife. She is asking for you and the baby."

CHAPTER 4

The Cucullu Family

Conditions in Spain deteriorated. The banishment of the royal family led to Spain's leadership being placed under the rule of Amadeo, Duke of Aosta, from Italy. Amadeo ruled only two years and resigned in 1873, for he refused to serve as an absolute monarch. In 1874, a new constitutional monarchy emerged with Alfonso XII, Queen Isabella II's son, as the new king. Chaos reigned.

Mary propped her elbows on the kitchen table. She sorted through notes about her family's history. *Surely my grandparents, Don Angel Cucullu and Doña Amalia del Valle, were disturbed by this political dissatisfaction. No wonder they decided to migrate to the Philippines in 1877. My mother, Maria de la Luz, was fifteen months old. There were five children in all. Francisco was the oldest…followed by Herminia. Next were twin boys, Rogelio and Alfredo, then, Luz.* Her mother told these stories often.

Mary pulled her heavy sweater around her shoulders. She sipped the hot coffee to warm her as she continued writing.

Guernica, a town in the province of Biscay, Spain, was considered the center of Basque Country. Founded on a major river estuary as a center for trade, vessels had easy access to the port of Suso from the North Atlantic Ocean via the Bay of Biscay. Administrative districts governed the towns in the province of Biscay. By ancient tradition, representatives assembled under a tree, usually an oak, to discuss matters of importance to their governance. The Tree of Guernica, in the parish of Lumo, was located on a small hillock and became the seat of government for Biscay. The *Gernikako Arbola* was the symbol of the rights of the Basque people. Their laws were administered from this site until 1876, when King Alfonso XII changed the laws.

The many changes to their way of life angered Don Angel. He decided it was time to move his family away from Spain. His parish priest, Father Antonio

Guzman, was leaving within two weeks for his new parish in the Philippines...to the province of Ilocos Norte. He was excited about transiting the Suez Canal and spending less than half the time at sea, as earlier travel required, to reach the islands. Don Angel expressed his distaste for remaining in Spain, so Father Guzman planted the seed of traveling to the Philippines to find his fortune. The priest, who enjoyed a good cigar, was aware of those produced by *La Tabacalera*, the largest producer of fine cigars in the world. They had a large plantation in Ilocos Norte. Perhaps they could use a good businessman like Don Angel to manage their plantation. He would make inquiries as soon as he was established in his new parish.

Four months passed before Don Angel received a letter from Father Guzman. His news was exciting. Father Antonio had spoken with managerial staff at *La Tabacalera* and, based upon the parish priest's recommendation, they would welcome Don Angel as their new manager, if he would accept. Housing for their family would be provided on the plantation.

After sharing his news with Doña Amalia, Don Angel set his affairs in order to arrange for their departure and voyage. Within five weeks, arrangements were completed, and the Cucullus were ready for their sea voyage and transit through the Suez Canal. They prayed they had made the right decision.

The Cucullu family settled into their new environs apprehensively. Sanitary conditions were nonexistent in areas beyond the plantation where Spanish families lived. Going beyond the plantation was most unpleasant and dangerous. Dysentery, malaria, and cholera were prevalent in the area. The water supply was from shallow, mosquito infested surface wells or filthy canals. Other dangers existed. Warnings were issued. If caught off the premises at night by the native tribes, one might be captured and sold into slavery or, worse yet, be offered as a human sacrifice to appease evil spirits. The Cucullu children never wandered away from the plantation.

Doña Amalia Cucullu y del Valle, wife of Don Angel Cucullu—parents of Luz Cucullu del Valle, grandparents of Mary Gamero Hodges.

Mary recalled her mother's family came to the Philippines via the Suez Canal, rather than the longer route around the tip of Africa. The route was much shorter and less perilous. *Their passage through the canal took about forty hours and saved them many more days at sea.* Her father's parents traveled the longer route, as the canal did not open to ship traffic until November 17, 1869.

CHAPTER 5

The Angel of Death

José and Josepha's family increased. In 1876, they were blessed with the arrival of another girl, Maria de la Concepcion, whom they nicknamed, Concha. She was a quiet baby and gave much joy to Doña Maxima, Pascuala, Paz, and Carmen. Their home was filled with whispers and giggles. In 1878, Josepha was again with child. José hoped for a son, as most men would, however, when Maria del Rosario joined their family, he was grateful the angels guided her safe arrival. He lovingly called her Charing, for her cry was like the pealing of a tiny bell.

In 1879 the Angel of Death took José's father. His guide, mentor, counselor, and devoted father was no longer by his side. Doña Maxima leaned heavily on José's loving support. Her only child was now head of the family. He would make all their family decisions and be her sole support.

Wearing the title "Don" brought much responsibility; Don José decided his mother should come to live with them. Her home was still being used to house boarders attending his night school. He hired a supervisor to oversee the school and assist with classes in navigation. The recently titled Don José was promoted to chief bookkeeper, the position formerly held by his father. He would meet the challenge.

Doña Maxima eased into the supervision of servants and grandchildren's daily care, under Josepha's watchful eyes. Josepha was grateful for her knowledgeable assistance, as she was once again with child. In 1880, Maria de la Natividad made her entry into the Gamero family. Three years later, Maria de los Dolores bounced into their lives. They were blessed with five healthy girls, plus Paz, his daughter with Joaquina. Don José felt overwhelmed surrounded by yards of ribbon and lace! *Would God ever give them a son?*

In 1884 Don Angel Cucullu and his family relocated to Manila. He accepted the position as General Manager at the main headquarters of *La Tabacalera*. Their son, Francisco, was given a supervisory position. Doña Amalia was elated and the children were excited! They returned to a civilized area...they would not live in fear for their lives. The Walled City *(Intramuros)*, where most Spaniards lived in Manila, was safe. The children needed a proper education. Joining a large church with Spanish parishioners and making new friends, was important.

In 1885, Don José was granted his wish for a son. José Maria Gamero y Boix arrived...accompanied by the Angel of Death. Josepha struggled valiantly. She never knew how proud her husband was to hold his first son. Don José had mixed emotions. He was given a gift from God...his son, but Josepha, who gave him his only son, was taken away. The Angel of Death acted without compunction. He bowed his head, prayed for understanding, and dedicated his life to the Church.

On June 24, 1888, the Cucullu twins, Rogelio and Alfredo, wanted to venture beyond the walls of *Intramuros*. They begged Don Angel and Doña Amalia for permission to attend the *Fiesta de San Juan de Bautista* (Feast of Saint John the Baptist) in San Juan, Rizal province. They argued their years of confinement on the tobacco plantation in Ilocos Norte had stifled their youth. They were almost sixteen years old and had always been under the watchful eyes of their parents. They would soon be men. The Cucullus' soon tired of the twin's pleadings and gave them permission to go. They left quickly to board the first *caretela* beyond the massive walls of *Intramuros* to enjoy their first *fiesta* unsupervised by family. Part of the festivities included being "baptized" or dunked in the San Juan River, a token salute to St. John the Baptist. They were excited.

The native *caretela* driver tried to warn them during their ride to San Juan. He knew the two young men were courting danger. He told them not to cross the bridge from Santa Mesa into San Juan. The San Juan Bridge was the dividing line and he would leave them in Santa Mesa. The natives in San Juan hated white people, especially Spaniards. Most who dared to enter were executed. Rogelio and Alfredo laughed at his warnings. They were on an adventure and were not afraid. The twins were determined to swim in the San Juan River and join the festivities of the day. They thanked their driver and walked across the San Juan Bridge. They did not live to enjoy their decision...but their parents lived to regret theirs. The twins were reportedly caught and beheaded by natives as they were removing their clothing to swim. The Angel of Death was not to be denied.

⇝⇜

Mary knew the Angel of Death's touch. She felt the pain welling inside her. *Did my grandparents feel the same way? Don Angel and Doña Amalia, were devastated losing their twin sons, Rogelio and Alfonso...beheaded by natives.* Mary put her pencil down and rubbed her eyes. Her mother recalled the tragic loss of her twin brothers, Rogelio and Alfonso at age sixteen. Don Angel and Doña Amalia were never the same. *Why was God punishing them? What had they done to deserve this horrible tragedy?* There were no answers.

Mary felt sorrow in her heart for her grandparents. The painful loss of your child never goes away...it seethes like an angry sore deep within the core of your heart.

CHAPTER 6

Rescued by the Rochas

Following the deaths of his wife and father, Don José dedicated himself to filling his father's shoes at the Spanish bank. He entrusted childcare and household duties to his mother. Doña Maxima willingly accepted these tasks to fill a void in her heart left by her husband's death.

In 1886, a close family friend approached Don José. Miguel Bortas was embroiled in a lawsuit and needed to borrow money from the Spanish bank to secure a proper defense attorney. With no collateral, he pleaded with Don José to aid him in securing this loan by co-signing his note. Being a compassionate man, Don José co-signed Miguel's note. The loan was arranged and the court case went forward. To their dismay, the case was lost, and so was the money. With a heavy heart, Don José decided to sell their home plus his parents' home on Legarda Rotunda, which housed the night school and its boarders. Don José would have to find another home for his family and his night school. *Dios mio! What a foolish thing I have done! Everything dear to me is affected by my actions.* He dropped down to his knees, bowed his head, and prayed for guidance…for an answer…or a miracle.

Mary sighed as she recalled the many times her husband, Jesse, had allowed his gentle heart to rule his head in making similar monetary decisions resulting in financial losses.

My goodness, Jesse was so much like my Papá! I married my father! She shook her head in disbelief at this ironic realization and resumed writing.

Don José faced his students and advised them about the impending changes. He assured them the classes would continue, and lodging would be acquired. He was searching for the right place to accommodate his family and classroom space with lodging for them. José Rocha, a student, approached Don José after class.

"Professor Gamero," he said, "my sister, Rosario, owns a house in *Intramuros*

(The Walled City) on the corner of Calle Real de Palacio and San José streets. My sister and I live on the first floor apartment on the Calle Real de Palacio side, but the upstairs is presently vacant as are the living quarters on San Jose."

Don José's heart skipped a beat as he faced the handsome young man.

"I should like to see this house. Please ask your sister when I may call."

My prayers have been answered! Don José stroked his heavy, dark beard as he strolled through the rooms on the second and third floors of the Calle Real de Palacio Street side. *This will be perfect!* Rosario walked at his side as he discussed necessary changes. Her long dark skirt swished against the polished Philippine mahogany floors. Her ample bosom strained against the tiny mother-of-pearl buttons that marched like soldiers from the top of her white Spanish lace collar to the soft gathers around her sturdy waist. She reached for her small lace handkerchief tucked away in the cuff of her long sleeve and dabbed her forehead gently to blot the tiny beads of perspiration gathered around her dark hair. The day was unbearably hot and humid, and the exertion of walking up and down several flights of stairs dressed in mourning was stifling. Her husband died less than a year ago. She would be in mourning dress another two weeks, then she could reclaim her maiden name, Rocha.

"*Señora,* would you allow me to remodel in order to provide for classrooms and sleeping quarters for boarders?" he asked Rosario.

"Yes," she replied, as she fanned herself with her handkerchief. "You are an inspiration to my brother, José, I am pleased to have you make any changes in order to provide for your students."

"I also need housing for my family…for my mother, my seven children, and my sister-in-law, Pascuala. The San Jose quarters will be adequate."

"Your wife?" Rosario hesitatingly posed the question.

His face grew dark, and he bowed his head as he replied, "She died with the birth of my only son." Rosario bit her lip and was silent. She had intruded into his personal life.

Rosario's heart softened. She knew Don José was a man with a big heart. She asked for only half the usual rental fee. She would help him.

Don José worked tirelessly to ready the new quarters for his night school and its boarders. Within weeks the second and third floors on Calle Real de Palacio were ready for his students. No changes were made to the Gameros' living quarters, which faced San José Street. His landlady, Rosario Rocha, took care to see all was ready for his family to occupy those quarters.

Doña Maxima bustled about as she prepared for the move to their newly rented home in *Intramuros*. She was happy her son found a solution to his financial problem. The Gamero family homes sold within weeks. With sufficient funds, the loan at the Spanish bank was paid. They had money in a savings account, and his job was secure. She felt relieved and uttered a soft sigh as she wrapped her fine china in newspapers before placing them gently in sturdy boxes for moving day.

Pascuala, Don José's sister-in-law, led the parade of beribboned girls up the stairway to the *entresuelo,* in their new home. Paz, Joaquina and José's daughter, followed quietly as she was the eldest Gamero girl and must set the example for all the others. Carmen, who was thirteen, held Dolores, nicknamed Solita, by the hand. Solita, age three, stared solemnly at the large stairway with determination. She attempted the challenge of stretching her short legs to take each step while holding her soft white *sábana*. The little blanket dusted across the steps with each attempt. Concha and Charing giggled, as eleven- and nine-year-old girls would, while they watched Solita. They made a game of climbing the stairway by stepping on each tread with perfect precision, as if marching to the beat of a drum. Natividad, called Nati by Doña Maxima, held on to her grandmother's left hand as Doña Maxima pushed the carriage holding her only grandson, José, whom she called *Pépe*. As Doña Maxima reached the first step, she called to Pascuala.

"Stop and wait for all the children, Pascuala. Put Paz in charge, then come downstairs to help with the carriage."

José Rocha watched this parade with amusement. He was delighted to have Professor Gamero's family as neighbors. He became excited when his eyes rested upon Pascuala. So, this beauty was Don José's sister-in-law. She was angelic! His eyes never left Pascuala as she placed the younger Gamero girls under the watchful eyes of Paz. They followed her graceful descent to help Doña Maxima with the carriage. He bolted forward, stumbling on the cobblestones, in order to offer his services in lifting the carriage up the stairway.

"Doña Maxima, may I present myself to you. I am José Rocha, brother to Rosario Rocha, your landlady, and Professor Gamero's student."

Doña Maxima gave him a cursory inspection as Pascuala approached to reach for the carriage. Pascuala noticed the handsome young man. His dark eyes twinkled and he smiled as he spoke.

"Con permisso," uttered José as he smiled broadly at Pascuala and stepped toward the carriage.

Pascuala stared solemnly at this young man and took a step backward. She waited for Doña Maxima's instructions.

"Si, si, esta bien," spouted Doña Maxima as she lifted *Pépe* from the carriage and held him close to her generous bosom. *"Bueno, Pascuala, vamonos!"* She had seen the admiring glance José had given Pascuala as he lifted the carriage and carried it up the stairway.

≈≈≈

Mary laughed out loud. *Pascuala retold this favorite story often. Pascuala (Lola Lala, as she was lovingly called) enjoyed being surrounded by family on rainy Sunday afternoons and watched their admiring faces as she "performed!" Her embellished stories were easy to remember.*

A winter storm raged outside Mary's small white frame house on Stonewall Street. March was roaring in like the proverbial lion. *Oh, well...not much can be done outside today. I should have plenty of time for writing. Let's see...where did I put the notebook of historic events?*

CHAPTER 7

Sorrow and Joy

During 1888, resentment against Spanish rule of the Philippines erupted throughout Manila like a fiery volcano among the *illustrados*, the Filipino intelligentsia. They demanded the expulsion of the Spanish archbishop' and friars, plus confiscation of Augustinian and Dominican estates. Spanish families stayed within the confines of *Intramuros*...The Walled City. Only certified Filipino service personnel were allowed to enter. None were allowed to stay overnight.

Doña Maxima feared for her family's safety. She became acquainted with the Cucullu family, who also lived on San José Street, and found consolation in their warm welcome to the Gamero family. Doña Amalia, whose two sons were beheaded in San Juan, warned Doña Maxima about allowing any family members to leave The Walled City. A feeling of closeness grew between them. The Cucullu girls, Hermiñia and Luz, became fast friends with the older Gamero girls.

Caring for the entire Gamero family took its toll on Doña Maxima. She placed more responsibility on the older girls. She tired easily; after all, she was over seventy-two years old. The infirmities of old age crept in like a thief...robbing her energy, blinding her eyes, and maiming her limbs. She was forgetful and remiss in caring for her family. Don José observed her struggles to continue with her responsibilities. She needed help, but, with the growing tension among the Filipinos, he dared not bring Filipino servants into their home. He would discuss his dilemma with his landlady, Rosario. She was always ready to help.

Rosario was delighted Don José sought her advice and agreed to help. At first, Don José was taken aback at Rosario's generosity in offering to care for his family, but upon her insistence, he deferred to her. She assured him, since she lived next door, caring for his family would be an honor. He helped so many others; including her brother...she would help him.

Rosario assumed the care of the Gamero family. Don José noticed the exchange of love among them. Once again, he was alone...but not for long. He knew Rosario cared for him and his family. He would ask for her hand in marriage.

In September 1887, their parish priest recited the marriage vows for Don

José and Rosario Rocha. The Gamero children were the only ones in attendance. Although they missed their mother, they were pleased Rosario would be with them. She was so kind, generous and caring…to the point of spoiling the children. Pascuala felt a wave of relief, as she had major responsibility for the children's care during Doña Maxima's illness. She would now be free to make her own life choices…to consider her feelings for José Rocha, Rosario's brother.

As Doña Maxima's health failed, the gentle prodding of The Angel of Death pushed her toward life's end. In July 1889, Doña Maxima joined the saints and band of family angels in Heaven.

Mary paused in her writing. *When my paternal grandmother, Donã Maxima, left to become an angel . . . another angel was born . . . far away in Texas. My husband, Jesse, entered, and Doña Maxima exited, during July 1889. I was not aware of this coincidence between the two until now.*

CHAPTER 8

The Growing Family

José Agama, Don José's most promising student, held Professor Gamero in high esteem. Every time he stumbled, Don José set him on the right course. He was pleased Don José had remarried. Agama met Doña Rosario when she visited the school during the first months of their marriage. Although she was an older woman, she glowed like a blushing bride each time she visited the night school. *What a kind and gracious lady!*

When Agama and his wife, a lovely young Filipina, were expecting their second child, they discussed their choices for godparents. Agama surprised himself when he suggested they ask the Gameros. Since Don José was already their son's godfather, perhaps Doña Rosario would serve as the *padrina* for their second child. Agama would ask her the next time she visited his night school, after he asked Don José's permission.

"Doña Rosario, since Don José is my son's godfather, my wife and I would be pleased if you and Don José would also serve as godparents to our second child. If the baby is a girl, we would like to name her Rosario, with your permission."

"*Señor* Agama, I would be very pleased and honored to have your baby girl as my namesake," Doña Rosario smiled as she replied. "I will speak with my husband."

"*Muchísimas gracias, señora,*" he replied as he gave a small bow. "I have already spoken with Don José, and he said the decision was yours. We are very pleased."

Following the baptism of their second child, Rosario, José Agama's studies were one month away from completion. A promising interview guaranteed him a position to serve as apprentice to a captain with the major inter-island ferry from Manila to Cebu. Agama worked feverishly at his studies and day job. It was difficult to manage work, night school, and caring for his growing family. He was so close to his dream. It was not to be. Agama became deathly ill with yellow fever and did not survive. His widow, unable to cope with her husband's loss and the care of two young children, brought them to Don José and Doña

Rosario...leaving them in their care. She must return to the provinces, and could not take her children, as they were *meztisos,* and would be ostracized by her family and the natives. As *mestizos,* her children were also banned from living in *Intramuros* without their Spanish father.

The Gameros were overwhelmed and sought advice from their parish priest. They left the children in Pascuala's care and walked to the nearby church. The small weathered bell by the back door pealed its high notes, as Don José pulled the chain.

"Who is there?"

Father Angelo, who retired early, took caution before opening the door. He never opened it without checking. A month ago, some natives crawled over the thick wall of *Intramuros* to steal from residents.

"Father Angelo, my wife and I have come to seek your advice."

The elderly priest recognized Don José's low, bass voice, and opened the door. He apologized for his appearance, and invited them into his library...near his quarters.

After exchanging greetings, Don José explained the reason for their visit. Father Angelo was aware of Agama's death, but knew nothing of his wife's departure for the provinces. He was sad to hear she could not take her children, but understood how badly they would be mistreated among the natives. Mixed marriages were forbidden. He also knew they would not be accepted in *Intramuros* without their father.

"What must we do?" asked Don José, after completing the story of Agama's misfortune.

"Don José, you already know the answer. As their godparents, you made a promise to God to provide for their care and education. I believe you and your wife are aware of those responsibilities."

Don José nodded his head and asked, "I am already providing for seven children plus my wife and sister-in-law, Pascuala. We will need God's blessings. Will you pray for us to receive guidance and patience?"

They knelt on the polished mahogany floor and prayed for over an hour. Don José knew what he must do. Their *mestizo* godchildren, José and Rosario Agama, were legally prohibited from living in *Intramuros* unless adopted by a Spanish man.

The next day, he had his attorney draw the proper adoption papers so the children would legally be family members, live with them, but retain their father's family name. He smiled. *I have two more names to list in my Holy Bible! Remembering the two new names would be simple. Now they would be choosing another name, for Rosario was becoming heavy with their first child. Dios mio!*

Mary put down her pen and rubbed the stiffness from her hands. *With so many children, why would he take on two more? They already had seven children!* She laughed at herself. *I reared nine children!* Mary wagged her head in disbelief at yet another coincidence.

CHAPTER 9

Sorrow and Joy Revisited

The Walled City (*Intramuros*), the oldest district in Manila, felt like a prison to its residents, including the Gamero and Cucullu families. Their sanctuary, located on the southern bank of the Pasig River, was built by Spaniards in the sixteenth century, and served as a fortress with its thick, high walls and moats. Its Latin name, *Intramuros,* literally translates to "within the walls." Those *trace italienne* walls, built from eight-feet thick blocks of stone, rose twenty-two feet and surrounded sixty-four hectares of land. It was built to protect the Spaniards' seat of government from hostile natives and Chinese pirates. Only persons classified as *blanco* (white) were allowed to live within the walls, which once again, served to protect.

With the growing unrest and attacks by the *illustrados,* leaving *Intramuros* was dangerous. Security guards, hired to protect any Spaniards who were compelled to leave *Intramuros* to conduct business or travel to the provinces, were necessary. Women and children seldom left the fortress. Families relied upon each other for entertainment and a social life. The Gamero and Cucullu children became fast friends, as they found ways to occupy their time within *Intramuros* at each other's homes and their church.

Hermiñia, the Cucullu's eldest daughter, felt this frustration the most. Since her twin brothers, Alfonso and Rogelio, were beheaded in June 1888, her father, Don Angel, became terribly depressed and suffered a nervous breakdown. In less than a year, Don Angel experienced a major heart attack and was taken by the Angel of Death to join his twin sons. Hermiñia had more responsibility thrust upon her already tired shoulders. She visited her church and prayed for an escape from these tragedies.

A young Spanish sailor serving with the Spanish government observed Hermiñia as she devoutly clutched her rosary and knelt…her head bowed. Her soft, curving lips moved silently as she recited her prayers. Her beauty and the seriousness of her expression struck Armando Suarez, as Hermiñia knelt in reverence and supplication. *Why is she praying so fervently? Why does she seem so sad? What can I do to help her?* He waited at the church portal to see her after she finished.

"*Con permisso, señorita,* may I be allowed to escort you safely to your home?" he asked as she slipped her veil off her burnished hair and onto her gently sloping shoulders.

"*No, señor,*" replied Herminia, as she clutched her rosary close to her heart and prayed silently. *Dios mio! What a handsome man...do I dare encourage him?*

Armando noticed her hesitation as she spoke, and took it as a sign of encouragement. Flashing a brilliant and charming smile as he stepped toward her, he offered her his arm.

"Perhaps you would allow me this kindness," he said, "for I am away from my family in Spain and only wish to see you safely home."

"*Bueno, señor,*" she replied, "It is getting late. My home is close by and my mother will be worried if I am late."

After brief introductions, Herminia took his arm gingerly and took longer steps–trying to match his stride on the uneven cobblestone streets. The setting sun caused auburn sparks to dance across her burnished blonde hair. Armando felt powerful emotions surge within his body. She gazed quietly at him as he spoke about his service in the Spanish Navy and his recent adventures in coming to Manila. She smiled at his effervescent chatter. *I have made her smile! My mission is accomplished. I must see her again!*

"I will be coming to church for Mass tomorrow," Armando said offhandedly. "I miss my family in Spain, and being at Mass makes me feel closer to them."

Herminia did not offer a reply as they were nearing her home. *Is he the answer to my prayers? Was this a sign from God? Should I see him tomorrow?*

Maria del Herminia Cucullu y del Valle, older sister of Maria de la Luz.

Hostile conditions festered like an angry, infected boil in Manila. Spaniards moving about the city did so with the utmost caution, accompanied by security guards. Women and children dared not stray outside the protective walls of *Intramuros*. Doña Amalia wished she had never left Spain.

Following Don Angel's death, she received only a small widow's pension from the Spanish government. Her oldest son, Francisco, who supported the Cucullu family through his work at *La Tabacalera* during her husband's illness, decided it was time to marry. A lovely Spanish girl from Ilocos Norte waited patiently for him to get his affairs in order to return to her. She refused to live anywhere near Manila, as word had reached the provinces about the many dangers to Spaniards in the capitol.

Doña Amalia looked for other ways to meet family needs. She needed to provide for Herminia and Luz. Herminia, almost twenty-one, had no suitors. Luz was sixteen and still in school. She consulted her widowed sister, Doña Aurora Adriensen del Valle, who had a dressmaker's shop in *Intramuros*.

"*Por favor,* Aurora," she said, "I need to earn money as this widow's pension is but a pittance."

"*Seguro,*" she replied, "you and your daughters must join us and help with the dressmaking. Rita and I have much to do since families are afraid to shop in Manila, and native seamstresses cannot enter *Intramuros*."

The decision was made. Doña Amalia and her daughters, Herminia and Luz, would live above Doña Aurora's dressmaker's shop at #13 San Jose Street. They would be close to the Gameros, who lived at #19 San Jose.

Herminia was unhappy with the decision to live over the dress shop. She did not want to work as a seamstress. Luz, however, was pleased. She would be closer to her cousin, Rita, who was a year younger, and to the Gamero girls...her best friends. The days at work felt interminably long to Herminia. She neither had much time to attend church and pray, nor to visit the young sailor, whom she adored. She felt she must have more time to see Armando. She devised a plan.

One evening, when she knew Armando would be waiting at the church, she rushed to church, entered quietly, and observed him. She knew what she must do. She stepped into the pew where he was sitting and reached for his hand.

"Armando, I must find a way to escape. I cannot continue to work as a seamstress. I am so unhappy."

Armando quietly squeezed her hand...pulled it toward his lips and kissed it gently. He glanced around to see if anyone had seen his affectionate touch toward Herminia. No one was there.

"These hands shall never have to work so hard again. Here is what we shall do."

He quietly laid out plans for their elopement. Herminia was so happy. She would be saved from her detestable living conditions.

Herminia and Armando eloped within the month, but, alas...he was called into active duty. He left for Spain immediately. Herminia waited patiently for his return as she made plans for the birth of their first child.

Following her daughter's birth, Herminia lost all hope Armando would return to her. Inquiries were made as to Armando's disappearance with no results. He was missing. She needed help. Sadly, she had no other recourse except to return to live with her mother, Doña Amalia, and Luz, in that disgusting dressmaker's shop. She was so depressed, but she must provide for her baby, Pilar.

With no word from Armando for over two years, Herminia felt she would never see him again. Her cousin, Luis Cucullu proposed marriage. The widower with two daughters, Salvadora and Luisa, rescued Herminia from disgrace. She accepted. Marriage would be a way to provide for her child and to get away from dressmaking, which she abhorred. Following a quiet wedding, Herminia and Pilar moved into Luis' home on Magallenes street in *Intramuros*. She would be close to her family. She would be rid of that dressmaker's shop.

⸙

Mary's phone rang. She pulled her warm sweater around her ample abdomen and answered.

"Hello," she said.

A familiar voice spoke. It was Mary Jane.

"Mother? I called to see if you needed groceries. I knew you would not be getting out in this weather."

They chatted about items Mary needed. Mary Jane said she would bring them shortly and ended the call.

Mary heated water for hot chocolate. *Mary Jane will enjoy a hot beverage when she arrives.*

CHAPTER 10

Maria de la Luz

Mary stirred excitedly around the kitchen preparing her coffee, toast, and *lugao,* a Filipino rice dish to which she added grated coconut and dark brown sugar. Rain was pouring heavily outside and thunder occasionally rumbled in the distance. Today, she would write about her parents, José Maria Gamero y Porras, and Maria de la Luz Cucullu y del Valle. She guided her writing to this point to help family understand their rich Spanish heritage. Her parents' photos were placed on the table to inspire her. She gazed at her mother's photo. *Mami, I wish you were here. I have so many questions!* She picked up her pen, browsed through her notes, and began.

In 1890, two months following Don Angel Cucullu's death, Luz busied herself daily by helping her mother, Doña Amalia and her *Tita* Aurora with the daily chores in the dressmaker's shop. She also found time to visit the Gamero girls and had a special fondness for Carmen, who was about one year older than Luz. Carmen was helpful and supportive during the difficult period of her father's illness, death, and their ensuing change of living quarters. After Hermiñia eloped, Luz found herself busy with daily chores. Her only escape from the routine of sewing was to either go to church and be with her friends, or visit with Carmen Gamero in the Gamero's home. She truly enjoyed those respites. Luz loved playing with the Gamero's baby, Mercedes, whom they called Mercedita, because Carmen's first name was Mercedes, also. Sometimes she and Carmen would dress the baby and push her baby carriage around the bumpy cobblestone streets. The long rides soothed Mercedita, and Doña Rosario enjoyed having time to rest.

  Luz also enjoyed the company and attention given her by a young Spaniard during Mass. Antonio Perez had known and admired Luz for several months and sought permission to court her from Don Angel and Doña Amalia before Don Angel's death. Her parents stated since Luz and Antonio were still young they should be patient and allow time to become better acquainted. Luz and Antonio complied. Her mother had much on her mind with Don Angel's death, Francisco's marriage and return to Ilocos Norte, plus their hasty transfer to the quarters over the dress shop. Antonio and Luz knew they should not bother her mother. Herminia and her involvement with a young Spanish sailor hung over the family like a dark cloud.

The year following her father's death was filled with family crises. Luz thought... *Herminia eloped with her sailor... he left for Spain leaving her with child... Herminia's baby, Pilar, came into this world with no father present... Herminia returned to the apartment over the dressmaker's shop to provide for herself and her baby... madness controlled their lives.*

The madness spread. Antonio Perez was drafted into the Spanish Army on his eighteenth birthday, which required him to report for military duty in Spain. Luz felt alone. Antonio asked permission to be engaged to her before he left, but Doña Amalia felt they should wait until his return. Luz agreed and they promised to write often.

Seven months after Antonio left for duty in Spain, an acquaintance told Antonio that Luz was seeing another young man from their church in *Intramuros* while he was away. Antonio was furious and wrote a letter to Luz chastising her for being untrue to him.

Francisco Cucullu y del Valle (*Tio* Paco),
Maria de la Luz Cucullu y del Valle (*Mami*),
Maria del Herminia Cucullu y del Valle (Lola Miña)

She was shocked to read his accusations. *Why did he believe this lie?* Luz wrote a final letter to Antonio. He truly was foolish if he believed this tale. She told him to forget any hope for a courtship. She was never unfaithful, and he should not bother to return to her. Their relationship was finished.

Mami made the right decision. I would have done the same thing!

◈◈◈

Mary rose early to attend the first Mass at St. Williams Catholic Church. She whispered a prayer of thanks to St. Anthony. Her prayers to find a small home so nearby her church were answered. She dressed warmly, as there was an early morning chill in the air. Today, March 2, 1985, marked the eighteenth anniversary of Jesse's death. Before they married in 1923, he took instruction in Catholicism and signed official church documents so their children would be reared as Catholics. He kept his promise to her and her church, and she would continue being faithful to his memory.

Monsignor McCallum met Mary at St. Williams' portal. More often than not, they were the only two in attendance at early Mass.

"Well, Mary," spoke Msgr. McCallum gently as he took her hand, "I noted on my calendar we would be praying for Jesse's soul today."

Mary nodded as she covered her head with a lace veil, dipped her fingers in the Holy Water, made the Sign of the Cross, and followed him towards the altar. Msgr. McCallum had already lit a prayer candle for Jesse. Her priest stood at the altar and Mary knelt at her regular pew. She pulled out the tiny bell, which was brought regularly to ring at the designated times during the Mass, when the priest had no assistant. After Mass, Mary approached the table of prayer candles, and lit two…one for Jesse and one for Bobby, their missing son. She returned to her pew, reached for her rosary, and recited her prayers. Before leaving, she walked around the inside perimeter of the sanctuary, stopping before the stained glass window she and her children had donated as a memorial to Jess. *I miss you, sweetheart.*

Mary was in a pensive mood as she prepared hot chocolate to warm herself before returning to her notes. She was determined to write each day. Sometimes it was not possible, but she felt she must persist. Her life's clock was ticking. Jesse left many projects unfinished when he died. She was determined, with God's help; she would finish this project.

Luz answered a frantic knocking at the front door of the dressmaker's shop, which was already closed for the day. She was puzzled as to why someone was knocking so desperately. Luz eased downstairs and peered out to see who was being so demanding. One of the Gamero's servants continued to knock. Luz opened the door haltingly and the young girl was babbling and crying hysterically!

"Por favor, tienes que venir conmigo!" (Please, you must come with me!)

Luz tried to calm her by asking questions, but the poor girl was too distraught. Doña Amalia made her way downstairs and, after speaking with the girl, learned that Mercedita had suffered a fall and was in serious condition. The servant was sent to notify the Cucullus. Doña Amalia and Luz dressed quickly and accompanied her to the Gamero's home.

Don José's somber face told the story. The doctor was summoned. Her condition was serious. Mercedita's back was broken. Medication was given to ease her pain. They prayed for her soul and waited for the inevitable. Only the Angel of Death could release Mercedita from her pain. The younger children huddled together in the dining room. Each of the older ones held a rosary. The plaintive, prayerful chant rolled from their lips as the litany of prayers was recited.

Carmen embraced Doña Amalia and Luz. She burst into open sobs as she held onto Luz tightly. Her eyes were already swollen from the many tears she had shed. Luz spoke to her as she patted her soft, dark hair.

"Let us join the others in their prayers," Luz said.

The only sounds throughout the Gamero home were the hushed prayers being recited. The prayer vigil lasted all night.

As the early morning sun arrived, Mercedita, the tiny three-year-old angel, departed with the Angel of Death to join the family angel band.

CHAPTER 11

Salud

Don José burst into the *sala* with a magazine in his right hand. His face was filled with rage as he paced before Rosario, who was sitting quietly sewing lace on the new blanket for the baby she and José were expecting.

"José, que paso?" she inquired, trying hard to keep her voice calm.

"Los illustrados," he exclaimed, "are trying to ruin everything! This troublemaker, José Rizal, installed himself as the leader for the Filipino nationalist group and is writing dangerous propaganda about Spaniards in Manila! He lives in Spain as an expatriate. How dare he spread his poison in Spain and the Philippines!"

Don José popped the magazine repeatedly into his left hand as he paced vigorously. Rosario sighed. She knew how strongly her husband felt about the Spanish rule in Manila.

"Mi amor," she coaxed, "sit down by me and let us see what Rizal has written. Perhaps it is not as serious as you think."

Don José approached the large overstuffed sofa and perched gingerly on its edge beside Rosario. She had a calming effect on him as she took the magazine, *La Solidaridad*, and leafed through its pages to see what Rizal had written.

"Well, it appears Rizal wants to see the Philippines represented in Madrid as a province of Spain and not as a colony. It sounds reasonable."

"Rosario, all Spaniards might as well return to Spain if the Filipinos are given governmental control. We would all be in danger."

Rosario sighed once more. The excitement was too much for the child in her womb. Painful, contracting waves stretched across her back and into her abdomen. She tried to remain calm as she spoke.

"José, I think you should send for the doctor. Our baby has chosen this time to come into the world."

Don José jumped to his feet, dropped the offensive magazine, and called for his daughter, Carmen.

Maria del Salud Gamero y Rocha was welcomed into the Gamero family with tears of joy. Her half-sisters and half-brother laughed. Her face was red and wrinkled. She was a homely baby, but a blessing to Rosario, who still cried often when no one was around. Her tears were for Mercedita, her three-year-old angel.

Caring for her new baby, Salud, was hard for Rosario. She experienced a difficult delivery and was not recovering well. Fever consumed her body, and she had severe abdominal pains. José's children helped when they were not in school, but she needed more help. She would speak to José today.

Don José returned from work early, and slipped quietly through the house to not disturb Rosario and the baby. Silence filled the rooms. The children were still at school, so Rosario and the baby must be resting. He stepped into the nursery to take a peek at Salud. Rosario's body was crumpled beside the baby's cradle…motionless. Salud was sleeping but was beginning to stir. He knelt beside Rosario and pulled her shoulders forward, as he attempted to lift her toward him. Her head dropped back like a little rag doll…limp and lifeless.

Dios mio! Que paso!

Don José lifted Rosario gently in his arms and carried her to the nearby bed. He listened for her heartbeat. It was beating…faintly.

I must get help. I must get the doctor.

The front door closed followed by his daughters' chattering voices.

Thank God!

"Carmen,…hurry," he whispered hoarsely as he met the girls at the top of the stairway. They were still chattering as they removed their scarves. He returned to the nursery. Carmen followed.

"Papá, que paso?" asked Carmen as she stepped into the nursery. Rosario was laying on the bed…pale…her eyelids closed.

"I must get the doctor," he said hoarsely. "Keep the others away except for Charing. She must care for Salud, as she is beginning to stir."

Rosario waited too long to get medical attention. The doctor said she suffered a severe infection following Salud's birth. He was so sorry, but he could do nothing.

Gloom and misery settled over the Gamero household like a heavy, dark fog, choking all family members. Every breath Rosario took was labored. Don José kneeled with his children around him as they each held a rosary and gently fingered the holy beads to quietly recite their prayers. The Angel of Death took Rosario. She would be reunited with Mercedita, her firstborn.

Doña Amalia and Luz waited one week before visiting the Gameros. They took food and a simple bouquet of gardenias and *sampaguitas*…the islands' exotic white flowers. Perhaps these flowers and their delightful fragrance would soothe the sadness in their household. They kept their visit short as they knew the pain which sorrow brings. They would return next week and stay longer to help the Gameros. Luz wanted much to be with her dear friend, Carmen. She truly cared for the family.

⥈

Mary gazed at the kitchen clock. She was due at the women's luncheon at St. William's. She must hurry. She took the luscious caramel *flan* from her refrigerator and lowered the rich Spanish custard gently into a large Tupperware container. After closing the lid firmly, she gathered her purse and jacket before leaving quietly. Booger was asleep. She dared not disturb her dog

CHAPTER 12

Joy and Sorrow

Man proposes and God disposes. His father's voice echoed those words many times. Once again he was forced into a lonely period. His plans and God's plans had taken different directions.

Rearing a family weighed heavily upon Don José. He prayed God would lift this burden. The relentless wind from the Angel of Death's beating wings had stunned him many times, and this time was more difficult than the others. Don José also remembered The Angel of Mercy's gentle touch and knew God would provide. He uttered fervent prayers to have strength for the challenges he faced...his children needed him. They were in God's hands and God would provide.

Don José's first daughter, Paz, entered the *sala* quietly. Her father's pensive face as she approached, caused concern.

Should I tell Papá my news? He needed to smile. Would her news make him happy?

"*Papá,*" Paz murmured, "*podemos hablar un rato?*" (Papa, can we talk for a little while?)

"*Si, si, mi hija.*" (Yes, yes, my daughter.)

Paz perched beside him on the large brown overstuffed sofa she had loved since childhood. She reached across her father's lap and took his hand. Don José stared at her quizzically, noting this action was unusual for his daughter.

"*Papá, I have happy news to share with you.*"

Don José raised his heavy dark eyebrows and stroked his beard nervously as Paz patted his free hand. He nodded but said nothing.

"*Papá,* Antonio is paying us a visit this evening. He would like to speak with you if you would grant him this favor. Please, *Papá . . . por favor?*"

Don José had given his blessing to Isidorio Antonio del Valle, an employee at his bank, to see Paz. He had no idea this relationship had evolved so swiftly. He knew what this young man had in mind. Don José was emotionally drained by the deaths of Mercedita and Rosario. He lost touch with events in his daughter's life. He bowed his head, took her hands in his, and smiled knowingly.

"Of course, *mi hija,*" he said. "Of course."

"*Mil gracias, Papá,*" Paz said through pursed lips as she kissed her father gently on his cheek.

Paz scurried up the stairway to share the news with her siblings and prepare for Antonio's visit. There was much to do.

Doña Amalia and Luz were ecstatic with the news of the upcoming wedding in the Gamero family. They would make the wedding dress for Paz and attendants' dresses for all the girls in the family. Activity in the dress shop increased as the Gamero girls trickled in and out for their fittings. Each one flitted about like a butterfly trying out its new wings. Luz laughed at the younger girls as they tried to preen about like fully feathered peacocks on a sunny day. Luz was making a special baby dress for Salud, which would also serve as Salud's baptismal gown on her first birthday. The embroidered gown was perfect for Salud. The homely baby would be elegantly dressed.

The joys brought by the wedding celebration lingered in the Gamero household for several months. Another joyful celebration lay ahead. Plans were made for Salud's baptism on her first birthday. Don José invited the Cucullus, as he had seen the loving care Luz had given the baby during difficult times. He would pray for guidance from God during this celebratory Mass. He found himself drawn to Luz and her caring ways with his family. God would provide an answer.

Sounds like Jesse and me, thought Mary, as she put her writing away for the evening. *He was also much older than I. Perhaps my mother felt the same way.*

CHAPTER 13

José and Luz

In April 1895, angry waves of unrest crashed across the Philippines with the arrival of José Rizal, leader of the *illustrados*. They were spreading nationalist propaganda throughout Spain and the Philippines. Although Rizal stayed in the provinces, he exerted much pressure on political matters throughout the islands. Rizal, a well-educated son of an upper class Filipino family, had a vision...freedom for his country.

Don José read the news describing the civil unrest with much impatience. *Why are they unhappy with Spain? Was not Spain providing for their needs? They are not able to govern! Many natives, like the Moros, are wild and uncivilized in the faraway provinces. How can they possibly think they are capable of maintaining control?*

A gentle knock at the door disrupted his thinking. Don José strode angrily to the massive, hand-carved door and grasped the heavy metal doorknob. He was pleasantly surprised.

Luz brought a new dress for Salud and needed Carmen's help to try it on the little girl. She was always making clothing for the toddler from fabric scraps not large enough to use for anything else.

"*Buenos dias, Don José,*" she uttered as she modestly lowered her chin.

"*Buenos dias, Luz. Como estas?*" he said as he stepped back to allow her to enter.

"*Bien, bien, gracias. Y usted?*"

Following an exchange of pleasantries, Luz climbed the stairs to find Carmen, who would help hold the wriggling child to be dressed. She hoped Salud was not asleep.

Don José's eyes followed Luz as she gracefully climbed the long, curved wooden stairway leading to the girls' rooms.

She is so lovely and cares for my family. She does not appear to have an attachment to any man...perhaps I should speak to her mother. Yet I am so much older than Luz. I will speak with our parish priest first.

Doña Amalia was surprised to see the parish priest and Don José on the doorstep. *Men so seldom entered a woman's dress shop. Why are they here?* She hesitated before opening the door wider to allow them to enter.

"Don, José, is something wrong?" she inquired. "Please come in."

Don José, feeling uncomfortable about stepping into a woman's dress shop, was even more so when he remembered his reason for their visit…to ask Doña Amalia for permission to marry Luz. He was much closer to Amalia's age than to her daughter's. Luz was eighteen.

Doña Amalia ushered them toward the back to have privacy. Four small ladder backed chairs circled an equally small round table nestled in a corner. A tiny lamp flickered as she approached the far side of the table.

"Please, sit down," she said, motioning to the delicate chairs.

"How can I help you?"

Father Alfredo mentioned the closeness of the Gamero and Cucullu families and their seemingly warm associations in the church and neighborhood. He paused before he revealed the reason for their visit.

"Doña Amalia, Don José is a devout Catholic and a dependable man. He has provided well for his family but has suffered many sorrows. A year has passed since his wife, Rosario, died. Your families are close and have shown much kindness to each other. Don José would like your permission to marry your daughter, Luz."

Amalia was quiet. Don José cleared his throat, removed his gloves, and placed them inside his hat. He was impeccably dressed for this important occasion.

"I realize I am much older than Luz, but I have seen the way Luz loves my family," he started.

Don José pleaded his case as if he were in a court of law. He assured Doña Amalia he would provide for Luz and for

Maria de la Luz Cucullu y del Valle and Don José Maria Gamero y Porras (Mary's Parents) in wedding attire. The bride wore black as the Gamero family was still mourning the death of Paz.

her needs. If Luz were to agree, he would be forever grateful because he was lonely. He had seen the love and tender care Luz and Amalia had shared with his family. Amalia would not be left alone. She would also be a part of the Gamero family and live with them, if his request were granted.

Doña Amalia was silent for several minutes after Don José had stopped speaking. She bowed her head.

What would Don Angel have done? Would he allow this union? Would Luz be happy?

She raised her head and nodded to her guests.

"I will speak to Luz. She is an intelligent young woman and does care for your family. Let us pray together and seek God's Will."

With bowed heads, Father Alfredo prayed fervently, if it were God's will, José and Luz would make a new life together. Upon closing his prayer, they all made the Sign of The Cross. Father Alfredo arose from his chair, followed by Don José. Doña Amalia led them around the aisles toward the front door. Don José thanked her for allowing this visit, bowed in respect, and they left her, once again, alone.

Luz had no idea Don José wanted her as his wife, so when her mother talked with her about the visit from the parish priest and Don José and his intentions, she was taken aback.

"Mamá," she protested, "he is so much older."

Doña Amalia took her hand, and told Luz they would pray daily to seek God's will. God would provide an answer.

On July 6, 1895, Don José Maria Gamero y Porras and Maria de la Luz Cucullu del Valle were married in the Church of The Nazarene in Quiapo. Only family members attended the small wedding. Luz wore a black wedding dress made by her mother, as the Gamero family were still mourning the untimely death of Paz after giving birth to yet another angel, Pacita.

As she thought about events leading to her parents' union, Mary wondered. *What brought them together? The Gameros and Cucullus lived near each other. They attended the same church. The Gamero girls were close friends with Luz and her cousin, Rita. Doña Amalia was kind to the Gamero girls and acted as their chaperone when they visited parks and boulevards for paseos. Was it Fate or God's Hand? These facts were more than coincidental and led to their eventual marriage. Their age difference did not seem to matter.*

The wind was howling outside as Mary finished writing. She completed a most important chapter…the marriage of her father and mother. She was satisfied. Mary smiled. *I married a man almost sixteen years my senior because my mother, Luz, thought he was an honest man.* Her grandmother, Doña Amalia, was right about Don José, and *Mami* felt the same way about Jesse. She shook her head. She had so much more to write! Would she have the time to complete her story?

CHAPTER 14

Facing Uncertainty

The Filipinos revolted against the Spaniards but were swiftly quelled by Spanish troops. Rizal fomented rebellion and led more uprisings. The Spaniards arrested him in 1895 and charged him with treason against the government for leading a revolution. Rizal was sentenced to death by firing squad on December 30, 1896. His death only strengthened the Cry for Freedom. Others would take up his cause.

Luz did not allow this turmoil to intrude on her daily life. There was much to do after the birth of their first child, Maria de la Luz (Lucing) Gamero y Cucullu, on May 7, 1896. She was so thankful Carmen (Maming) cared for the older Gamero children, and Rosario (Charing) helped. *Pépe* continued his studies and looked forward to the day he would begin studying for the priesthood.

Luz barely had time to make arrangements for the Christmas celebrations before news of Rizal's execution reached *Intramuros*. Rizal's death created quite a reaction within the Spanish population of the Walled City. Employees at *El Monte de Piedad*, where Don José was chief accountant, felt Rizal's execution would make matters worse, and they were right.

Emilio Aguinaldo, a Filipino municipal officer, stepped into the leadership role vacated by Rizal's death. The following year, the Spaniards promised to provide reforms if Aguinaldo would end the revolt and leave the Philippines. He agreed, promptly took his chief aides, and left for Hong Kong.

In less than a year, April 1898, the United States declared war on Spain. Admiral George Dewey sailed into Manila Bay and destroyed the Spanish fleet. Two weeks later, Aguinaldo returned and recruited Filipinos to serve in his army. The Spaniards had not kept their promise for reform. Aguinaldo and his men fought alongside the Americans. He organized a revolutionary government and was named its president in June. American and Filipino troops captured Manila on August 13, 1898, and the Spanish-American War ended. A peace treaty was signed in December and Spain ceded the Philippines to the United States. Aguinaldo was angry because he believed his country would be under Filipino rule. He would have his revenge.

Meanwhile, Luz kept busy caring for her family. Doña Amalia took over the supervision of the servants and meal preparations. Don José was pleased all was in order in his household. He was concerned about the military activities and felt a deep contempt for the Americans for taking a stand with the Filipinos against his beloved Spain. He felt he must resign his position at *El Monte de Piedad*, as the Americans would control the Spanish bank. He would not work for anyone who did not speak his language.

Luz was once again with child. She prayed she would have a son. Don José cherished his son, *Pépe*. If God would grant her prayers, perhaps Don José would forget the many political distractions, which caused him to boil over like an overheated pot on the stove. Her prayer was answered when José Angel Gamero y Cucullu swept into their lives on the wings of the Angel of Mercy. *Gracias a Dios!*

Mary knew their joy would be short-lived. At the young age of eighteen months, Angel contracted smallpox from his older sister, Lucing, and was whisked away by the Angel of Death. Her mother had told the story many times. *Mami* shed tears for Angel each time she spoke his name. Mary always felt a tug at her heart for Bobby and whispered a prayer for him. She knew what it meant to lose a son. She never knew what had happened to Bobby. *Was he with the Gamero band of angels?*

CHAPTER 15

The Early Years

Although a peace agreement was reached following the Spanish-American War, battles erupted, much like the Mayon volcano. The Filipinos might have achieved their long sought independence, however, the timing was not in their favor. Following Dewey's successful rout of the Spanish Navy at Manila Bay, the Americans declared their control over all the Philippine Islands. Having captured the Philippines, President McKinley was cabled by Dewey. "Have captured the Philippines; what shall we do with them?"

McKinley's political position was precarious, so the decision was made to annex the Philippines in order to Christianize the natives. The Spanish tried the same approach three hundred years earlier. Since most Americans knew nothing about the Philippines and its people, they were ecstatic with McKinley's justification for claiming the Philippines. Those islands were another part of America's "manifest destiny" as was the annexation of Texas in 1845.

Less than one month after the annexation, Aguinaldo sought his revenge. He established the First Philippine Republic and named himself as president. Shortly after, an American soldier shot a Filipino soldier, and Aguinaldo declared war against the Americans.

Don José left his position with the Spanish bank, *El Monte de Piedad*. He would not work under American jurisdiction and wanted no part of this foolish war. He would stay home and tend to his family's safety and welfare. Their youngest child, Angel, died of smallpox, and his young wife, Luz, was with child once again.

On June 14, 1900, Maria del Consuelo (Consueling) joined the Gamero family while protesting her arrival at the top of her lungs. Don José was amused and thankful for a healthy child…another girl. Lucing, who was four years old, stared at Consueling solemnly and made no comment. She waited to see the expression on her father's face before she reacted to this baby. Don José laughed at all the noise Consueling was making; Lucing smiled quietly and patted the baby's tiny hand. Carmen (Maming) bustled into the room to take the children and give Luz time to rest.

Carmen's thoughts turned to Concha. *I wish Concepcion (Concha) were*

Angelita Bores y Gamero *(above)* daughter of Maria de la Natividad Gamero y Boix *(right)* and Capt. Carlos Bores.

here to see the newest Gamero. Concha left the family three years earlier to enter a cloistered nunnery at Santa Clara. Once in the cloister, she would remain until death. She was allowed visitors only twice a year. Her soft voice and shadowy outline behind a latticed window were all one could experience from a visit to her convent. Concha's name was changed to Madre Tecla de San Antonio. Carmen sighed. She wished to become a nun, but had promised her father she would care for the younger members of the Gamero family.

Her heart ached when she thought about Nati. *Natividad was also no longer in the Gamero household as she had married Captain Carlos Bores of the Spanish Navy in 1895. They were blessed with a daughter. Nati and Carlos asked Papá to select her name and he chose the name, Angela, in memory of his son, Angel, who had died from smallpox earlier. Sadly, Angela (Angelita) Bores y Gamero died from meningitis at age two. The death of Nati's husband, Carlos, followed during the Spanish-American War. The Angel of Death was busy.*

Enough! thought Carmen. *I have much to do with little help.*

~~~

The wind was blowing hard against the single-paned windows in Mary's dining room. Mary pulled her sweater closer around her. *Delicious hot chocolate is what I need.* "Just what the doctor ordered," as Jesse so often said.

She laughed to herself as she thought about her half-brother José. *The parrot at his rectory, which belonged to Rosario, spoke Spanish. Lorito would screech at her, "Quiero pan con chocolaté!" I'll have the same treat, except I'll dip tea biscuits in my hot chocolate.* After finishing her *merienda*, Mary thumbed through her family photos and gently stroked her father's cheek. *Why can't I remember touching him? I was only three years old when he died.* She tried hard to remember sitting in his lap, as *Mami* said she had often done. *I was his Nena...his baby girl.*

CHAPTER 16

Fortune Smiles

Change was in the air. General Aguinaldo, the self-proclaimed President of the First Philippine Republic, led battles against American domination until his capture in March 1901. In a show of force, President William McKinley appointed a five-man civilian commission, headed by William Howard Taft, a federal judge. Taft was inaugurated as the first American Governor-General of the Philippines on July 4, 1901.

Don José was still upset about Americans being in control, but resigned himself to tolerating their presence. He received notice from the Spanish bank to please consider returning to his position as chief accountant, as the bank would continue to function under Spanish management.

"Luz," he asked pensively, as she sewed the hem on a new dress for Lucing, "I was called to return to my work at the bank. The money from my nautical school is dwindling as fewer Spanish students are enrolling due to all the changes put in place by the new American governor. It would be better for our family if I returned to my job as chief accountant. What do you think?"

Luz finished her row of stitches before responding.

"José, it appears you have already decided. You are the provider for this family, so you must do what you think is best."

José leaned over, gently kissed her on the cheek, and smiled. Luz did not miss a stitch.

"It is decided. I will tell Carmen so she can arrange her plans for my daily absence."

As the family gathered around the dinner table, Don José announced his decision to return to work at *El Monte de Piedad*.

"Everyone in the family must work together to help with the work at home. I will be asking Carmen and your mother how you have been helpful. I expect everyone to do their share."

Carmen broke the silence, after his announcement.

"*Papá,*" she said, "perhaps we should consider enrolling *Pépe* in the Jesuit boarding school to study for the priesthood."

"Yes, *Papá!*" *Pépe* agreed excitedly. "I am anxious to begin my studies!"

Don José smiled as he thought about his only son entering the priesthood. Having a priest in the family was his fervent wish. He would be making enough money by his return to banking and could provide for those studies.

"I agree, Carmen. The time is perfect for *Pépe* to enroll at the Jesuit school. One less mouth to feed in this house," Don José said and laughed.

Pépe grinned broadly and complained *Papá* was anxious to be rid of him.

The earlier tension at the table became more relaxed as family members chattered about upcoming events. Luz observed all this quietly. *I hope these decisions are not hasty. Perhaps we should have prayed about hese changes.* She sighed as the children were dismissed from the table for their evening prayers. *She would join them shortly and pray for God's wisdom in these matters.*

Rosario Gamero y Boix (Charing) devoted her life to caring for her brother José Maria Gamero y Boix (Pépe) who became a Jesuit Priest.

With her husband returning to his job at the bank and still conducting matters at his nautical/boarding school next door, Luz prepared for the many changes to take place. Carmen would help with the registration for *Pépe* to enter the Jesuit boarding school. She would also take Consueling for smallpox vaccinations now required by the American government since the earlier outbreak had claimed many lives, including that of their young son, Angel. She knew Don José objected, but it was the law. Luz listed the chores and assigned family members to their various tasks.

Following *Pépe's* departure to the Jesuit school, Don José talked with Luz and Carmen about the future.

"I am no longer a young man and wish to have an understanding in place regarding my family's care should something, God forbid, happen to me. Carmen, as the eldest, you make sure *Pépe* completes his studies for the priesthood. You are responsible for managing the finances for this family. Luz will care for the younger children and manage the household. You will also manage the care for Salud. This house belonged to her mother, Rosario, and, rightfully, it belongs to her when she becomes an adult. Will you take charge?"

Carmen agreed. This was a huge responsibility for her.

"*Papá,*" she whispered, "when may I enter the convent? I am getting older and fear I will no longer be accepted."

"When *Pépe* is ordained as a priest, you will be freed from your promise," said Don José gently as he reached out to touch her face.

Carmen nodded and bowed her head. She was almost twenty-seven. *I will pray for strength and guidance. My younger sister, Charing, now twenty-three, will help me. I will put her in charge of Pépe and the completion of his studies. Charing enjoyed acting as Pépe's guardian angel. Salud will be enrolled in the Santa Catalina School for Spanish girls. I will keep my promise to Papá.*

CHAPTER 17

Maria del Pilar

On September 14, 1901, President McKinley died from bullet wounds from shots fired by an assassin in Buffalo, New York. In 1902, Theodore Roosevelt, his successor, declared the Philippines had been "pacified." Governor-General Taft commended Gen. Arthur MacArthur for quelling the insurrection. Major Manuel Quezon, leader of the insurgents, surrendered his sword to the general. *Years later, as the first President of the Philippines, Quezon would hand the baton of Field Marshall to MacArthur's son, Douglas.*

Luz and Carmen worked closely to manage the Gamero household while Don José worked days and most nights to provide for their family. Carmen was like a "second mother" to all the younger siblings. She took special pride in the care Charing was taking with *Pépe* and his studies toward the priesthood. About two years passed since he had begun, which meant she was much closer to becoming a nun. Soledad (Solita) begged their father for permission to enter the Dominican convent as a novice. *She will probably become a nun before I can enter the convent.* Carmen shrugged her shoulders as if to shake off these thoughts and scatter them to the four winds.

1903 popped into view much like the array of fireworks celebrating the New Year. By mid-February, Luz suspected she was once again with child. *Dear Lord, please let me have another son for José. Thy will be done. Amen.*

Don José was pleased they were to have another child. Perhaps this one would be another boy? He hummed with anticipation as he reviewed his students' paperwork.

On October 4, 1903, Maria del Pilar made her appearance in the Gamero household. Upon her arrival, she surveyed everyone solemnly, as if to inform family members the "queen" had arrived. She made her pronouncements loudly, which sent everyone scurrying to provide for her needs and demands.

Don José hid his disappointment but was pleased Pilar was a healthy baby and Luz had survived yet another rigorous childbirth. He summoned the family to their parlor to give thanks to God. Soledad (Solita), who was about to enter the Dominican convent, was named as Pilar's godmother. She offered the first prayer for the new child, Pilar (Pilachu). Solita would carry Pilar to the altar and present her to their priest for the ritual. She was extremely honored.

Following a festive baptismal service for Maria del Pilar, Solita entered the Dominican sisterhood as a noviate. As was the custom, she was given a new name. She was no longer Maria de los Dolores Soledad Gamero y Boix, but would be Dolores de San Expedito Gamero y Boix. Once again, Carmen sighed and prayed fervently for her turn to become a nun. *Pépe is eighteen and will soon be ordained as a priest!*

Pilar thrived as a baby and was a cuddly mass of dimples and blonde curls. Her laugh was infectious, and she brought delight to the household. Everyone wanted a turn to hold her or take her for a ride in her baby carriage. Her godmother, Sister Dolores (Solita), was ordained as a Dominican nun, and was filled with pride as she took Pilar to her convent so all the nuns would see her lovely godchild. Solita felt blessed. *I have achieved my goal of becoming a nun. I have a lovely godchild, and I will be going to China to serve my God as a Dominican missionary. All are God's blessings.*

Maria del Dolores Soledad Gamero y Boix (Solita) *(right)* entered the Dominican Order in 1905. Renamed Delores de San Expedito, she became a missionary to China.

CHAPTER 18

Maria de los Angeles

Mary clapped her hands! *Today is the day I join the Gamero family!* She worked hard to reach this point in her writing and felt she had earned a reward. *When I finish this chapter, I'll call Mary Jane and see if she will help me celebrate!* She grabbed her coffee, picked up a cookie, and resumed her writing.

In November 1904, "Teddy" Roosevelt was rewarded for his able service and elected as President of the United States. Excitement and celebrations spread in the Philippines as Governor-General Taft declared a holiday. He promised to work toward "self-government" for the Philippines. This announcement lifted the Filipinos' spirits and gave them hope they would be free to have their own government in place.

Once again, Don Jose paced around their *sala* muttering. The Americans were foolish if they believed the Filipinos were ready to govern themselves. *The Spaniards were the only ones who brought civilization to these islands!* He shook his head and waved his arms in the air as he continued pacing the floor in disbelief.

Luz entered the *sala* and observed his comedic exhibition. José was pacing the floor...scowling. He was not amused.

"José, que paso? Why are you walking around so furiously?"

"Those crazy Americans think the Filipinos can take control of the government! How ridiculous! Can you imagine Manila under Filipino rule?"

José glared as he ranted. Luz approached him and extended her arms to embrace him.

"Mi amor," she sighed, "you will only hurt yourself if you continue to allow these matters to upset you. Please calm down for your sake and for our children's. They will be coming to greet you before long."

Her calming voice soothed Don José, and he kissed her hands as she led him to the large overstuffed sofa. She gently rubbed his temples to soothe him.

"José, perhaps my news will bring you joy and cause you to forget this nonsense," she purred.

José gazed at her quizzically and smiled his one-sided grin making her heart skip a beat.

"What is this news?"

"We are having another child. Perhaps this one will be a boy…a gift, since we lost our little Angel."

He held her gently and was filled with the warmth of their love. *He was so fortunate to have found her. With all life's many sorrows, he somehow always was blessed with boundless joy.*

On February 19, 1905, Maria de los Angeles Josefa Gabina joined the Gamero household trilling the highest notes ever heard by the family. *She is bound to have the gift of music.* Luz spoke her thoughts and everyone laughed. José had wanted to name her, Angela, to honor the three angels they had lost, but Luz was adamant.

"José," she said, "all the children you named 'Angel or Angelita' went to Heaven. I want this child to remain here with us."

José was disappointed, so Luz compromised by adding *"de los Angeles"* (of the angels) to the baby's name. The name "Josefa" was added for her patron saint's name, St. Joseph.

"We shall call her 'Maria'," stated José.

"And I shall call her *'Nena'*," whispered Luz as she gently kissed her baby's brow. *She is my baby girl.*

A celebration of her baptism was held on March 5, 1905, with The Most Reverend Father Joaquin Adeva anointing her with the holy oils in the Santa Iglesia Cathedral Metropolitana de Manila with her godfather, Don José Cavanna Surab, and godmother, Doña Natividad Gamero.

Mary grabbed the phone, called Mary Jane and laughed while announcing: "Guess what? I gave birth to myself today! Let's celebrate!"

CHAPTER 19

A Boy!

Mary hummed a favorite tune as she prepared her breakfast. The long tree limbs, outside her kitchen window, swayed as a gentle breeze tickled its branches. She was going to accomplish her goal today…to write the chapter about Lorenzo's birth. Her baby brother's entry into this world made her *papá* happy. He had waited so long!

Two years passed since Maria's birth, and once again Luz had a special twinkle in her eyes. She was anxious to share her news with Don José. She was with child and was certain this baby would be the boy he wanted. Her fervent prayers to St. Anthony would be answered and her husband would be happy. He suffered through trying times at the Spanish bank. Cholera and diphtheria were rampant. Don José closed his School of Navigation due to the epidemic. He reduced his workload at the Spanish bank and only worked part time. In his early seventies, he was no longer able to work the ten hours required daily by the bank. He was deep in thought with his head in his hands when Luz entered the room.

"*Mi amor*," Luz began and hesitated to say more when she saw his face.

Don José noticed as she entered. His face broke into the gentle smile she had grown to love. His formerly dark beard was peppered with gray.

"*Si, mi angel*," responded José. He held out his arms as she drifted toward him. He was tired. She felt his shoulders sag as she slipped into his gentle embrace. *Should she tell him her news?*

They embraced quietly as he stroked her hair gently. Luz decided the time was right. Perhaps a new baby on its way would bring him cheer.

"José, you have always wanted another son. I have been praying and feel strongly my prayers will be answered. You will have another son," she stated adamantly.

José smiled broadly at her firmly delivered announcement. He cupped her chin in his right hand and kissed her cheek.

"Luz, you bring me much joy and happiness," he said. "What have I done to deserve having you as my wife? How can I make you see the joy you give me?"

Luz bowed her head and blushed at her husband's kind words.

"*O, mi amor,* seeing your smiling face is all the joy I need," Luz replied.

They savored these quiet moments before the children bounded up the stairs prodded from behind by Carmen, who carried Maria. Don José laughed at the comedic parade. His children…his family were his joy and his life. They gave him a reason for living.

On September 7, 1907, the lusty cries of a bouncing baby boy echoed throughout the Gamero household. Don José was elated. He called the children together and announced José Lorenzo Gamero y Cucullu had arrived! Another boy…another joy…added to his household.

"Come children, let us go to the *sala* and give thanks to God for granting this wish. Let us also give thanks because your *Mami* is doing well. We have so many reasons to give God our thanks. We have been blessed."

The children gathered around him and, with grateful hearts, recited the rosary. Luz sighed. She rested and gave her own private thanks to St. Anthony for granting her prayers. With God's help, she had given her husband his fervent wish…another son.

Mary sorted through her family photos and found Lorenzo's, her younger brother. Mixed emotions surged through her as she recalled his life. *I have written much, but there is more to tell. Please, God, give me the strength to continue and finish.* She would need strength to face the next challenge.

CHAPTER 20

An Angel Departs

Mary struggled with her thoughts as she sifted through the photos. She remembered little about her father. Her knowledge, gleaned from recollections shared by older family members and her mother, was imprinted in her memory by the retelling of stories. *Mami* had spoken about him often. Theirs was a marriage of convenience, but Luz had come to love and respect Don José. *Antonio, her first love, did not return from Spain. He was her* Corazon…*her heart. Years later, she would sing,* Donde Estas, Corazon? *as she completed chores around our home. We knew the story and understood.*

Don José knew his health was faltering. He suffered a serious case of intestinal flu and never fully recovered his strength. He discussed the family affairs with Luz and Carmen and reminded Carmen she was the administrator for the family and must see to their needs. As he rocked himself gently in his favorite rocking chair, he felt his time remaining with his family was measured and wanted assurances for their welfare. He enjoyed a full life and fathered a large family. He recalled the many hours he spent holding his children close to his heart as he rocked them gently to sleep. He was deep in thought when Luz entered the *sala* and ended his reverie.

"*Mi, amor,*" she scolded, "you should be in bed. You must rest and regain your strength."

Don José smiled at his wife. She brought happiness to him and the children.

"*Si, si,* I am resting well…perhaps in a while," he replied.

On November 14, 1908, Don José Maria Gamero y Porras suffered a massive heart attack and was found in the early morning hours…still sitting in his rocking chair. He left his earthly family to join his family's band of angels.

Although Luz was resigned regarding her husband's fate, she was not prepared for the raw emotions and heavy responsibilities, which followed. She was in shock. The tears would not flow. She appeared to be in a trance. The family doctor spoke to Carmen.

SR. D. JOSE GAMERO Y PORRAS
EN MANILA EL 14 DE NOVEIMBRE DE 1908.

Después de una penosa lucha con la enfermedad que venía padeciendo nuestro nunca olvidado y muy querido consocio D. José Gamero, Contador-Interventor que fué del Monte de Piedad y Caja de Ahorros de Manila, dejó de existir en la noche del 14 de los corrientes resignado ante la muerte, quién le arrancó del lado de los seres para el más querido; sembrando la tristeza, el dolor y la consternación en toda su familia y relaciones. Al sentimiento que hoy embargan á sus afligidísimos y desconsolados Esposa é Hijos, por tan rudo golpe é irreparable pérdida, LA ESTRELLA DE ANTIPOLO une su más doloroso pésame y ruega á sus lectores encomienden en sus oraciones al Tadopoderoso el alma de nuestro inolvidable y nunca bien llorado amigo.

Al honrar hoy estas columnas con el retrato del finado dedicamos
este pequeño recuerdo á su atribulada familia.

Señor Don José Gamero y Porras
IN MANILA ON THE 14TH OF NOVEMBER OF 1908

After a painful struggle with illness and unforgettable suffering, our beloved fellow member, Don José Gamero, Accountant-Auditor of the Monte de Piedad and Savings Bank of Manila, ceased to exist on the night of the 14th of this month, taken by death, who ripped him from the side of his loved ones and more, sowing sadness, pain and consternation around all family and relations. Our sentiments today go to the desconsolate Wife and Children afflicted by so rude a shock and irreparable loss. THE STAR OF ANTIPOLO, we believe, is most sad and encourages its readers, through their prayers, to entrust the soul of our unforgettable and well-lamented friend to the Almighty.

We honor him today through these columns with this portrait of the deceased,
and dedicate this little souvenir to his bereaved family.

A memorial honoring Don José Gamero y Porras and the Gameros
printed in Manila newspapers by El Monte de Piedad y Caja de Ahorros.

"Luz must release her emotions through tears, or she will suffer a deep depression. The family must help her."

Carmen called upon family members to join her in prayer for Luz. *Novenas* were set at their church and numerous candles were lit in their father's memory.

Don José was buried wearing the customary robe of a Franciscan monk. Maria, three years old, kept asking her mother, *"Mami, who is that priest who looks like my Papá sleeping in that box?"* Luz, still numb with shock, quieted her, bowed her head, and kept on reciting the rosary. The service was interminably long. The Catholic Church took pride in long rituals. The church was overflowing with many family members, bank coworkers, officials, friends, and a large number of Don José's former students...many of them captains of their own vessels. Their presence was a special tribute for a dedicated banker and educator who touched the lives of so many.

As her husband's casket was being placed in the family vault, Luz was stricken with waves of strong emotions. She burst into inconsolable sobs and wailed as she held her arms toward his tomb. Her husband's death broke her heart. She lost control of her emotions. Family members pulled the younger children away as they were frightened at their *Mami's* reactions. Older family members gathered close and held Luz until she became calm.

Carmen knew, with a heavy heart, she must begin her work as family administrator. She felt it would be difficult, but she had no idea about hardships that were to follow. Would she be able to shoulder this heavy burden, which her father put upon her? She realized she had accepted it willingly, but she was not prepared.

Mary recalled the many stories about her father and was filled with a sense of pride. He had instilled in them a dedicated love for family and a strong Catholic faith. These traits supported her through many trying times.

CHAPTER 21

Dealing with Change

During the year following Don José's death, no income was generated. Carmen, now the head of our family, knew the savings was depleted. The greatest worry was finding a way to pay the taxes. A serious discussion with Luz was required.

"*Mami*," she began thoughtfully, "since our home is so large and we need money to pay taxes, do you think we could sell the portion which *Papá* used for his boarding school? It lies vacant, and we need the money. Our neighbors, the Alcantaras, are interested in buying it and have made an offer. The other half can be remodeled to make additional rooms to rent. The extra income will provide for our living expenses."

Mami bowed her head and kept quiet. *Dear God, give me the strength to make the right decision. Angels in heaven, please help us.*

Mami nodded her head gently as she replied.

"I can tell you have been planning ways to provide for our family. Your father made a wise choice in putting you in charge before he died."

Carmen thanked her and took steps to put those plans in place. Thankfully, there was a large demand for rooms to rent. Many United States government employees were searching for prime locations in Manila. The Gamero's home was in the same block on Palacio Street as the Del Monico Hotel where many Americans lived. The U.S. government had also opened offices there. Her father's portion, the Navigational School, was sold to the Alcantaras. The Gameros lived in the remaining half, which belonged to Salud. Two first floor apartments, formerly used for domestic help, were prepared for renters. On the second floor, the large storage room and children's bedrooms were also remodeled into apartments to be rented. We resided in the remaining living space on the second floor.

Rosario (Charing) took charge of the older children and enrolled them in their respective schools as full boarders since they were considered orphans after Don José's death. The Spanish Sisters of Charity managed these Catholic schools and were supported by the Roman Catholic Church and the Spanish government. Salud was enrolled in Santa Catalina; Luz (Lucing) and Consuelo

(Consueling) boarded at Santa Rosa; Pacita Valle, their orphaned niece, and Pilar attended Santa Isabel; and, José *(Pépe)* continued in the Jesuit School to complete his studies for the priesthood. Only Lorenzo and Maria *(Nena)* remained at home. Natividad (Nati) was assigned as caretaker.

When the remodeling was completed, Pascuala, alone after her husband's death, decided she would live with our family, and rented the smaller first floor apartment. Her son, José Rocha Jr., married a girl from Cebu named Maria Noel, a Visayan. They, and their two sons, Arturo and José Juan Rocha y Noel, lived in Cebu. Pascuala (Lola Lala) brought her servant, a young man named Diego, to live with her. His family abandoned him, so Lola Lala took him and provided a home.

Luz's older sister, Herminia, and her second husband, Luis Cucullu, rented the larger apartment. Two of their four sons, Luis and José, ages ten and eight, were boarders at San Juan de Letran. They only returned home on the weekends. The other two, Angel and Alfredo, ages six and four, were not old enough to enter school. Salvadora, Luis' eldest daughter, married Don Juan Martinez, and lived in an apartment house owned by Don Juan's parents. Luisa, his second child, still lived at home. Herminia's daughter, Pilar, had died two years earlier. The Gamero's downstairs apartment suited their needs. We were delighted to have family members as neighbors.

The one-bedroom apartment on the second floor was rented to José Palmagil, a lawyer from Davao who worked for the U.S. government. In addition to his native language, he spoke English and Spanish. A model tenant, he offered free legal advice to Carmen when she expressed concerns about financial matters. He was helpful and never intruded. Palmagil was aware the Gameros needed more income and took steps to assist with the rental of the remaining two-bedroom apartment.

"*Señorita* Gamero," said Palmagil, "two American men, with whom I am acquainted, wish to rent a two-bedroom furnished apartment. They work in the same government offices with me. Shall I tell them about the remaining apartment for rent? I can vouch for them."

"Thank you, Mr. Palmagil, since I cannot speak English, would you bring them here so I can meet them?" Carmen asked. "I would be very grateful."

The next day, Palmagil brought the two U.S. government employees to the Gamero home to see the apartment and meet Carmen.

"*Señorita* Gamero, may I introduce my two friends, Mr. Charles Farnsworth and Mr. Mac McKinnon," Palmagil stated in Spanish.

Each American quietly nodded and waited for Carmen to speak first. The older man, Mr. Farnsworth, was in his early thirties, while Mr. McKinnon was much younger, perhaps in his early twenties. Carmen studied their features and demeanor before speaking.

"Welcome," she said, using the only English word she had practiced.

She turned to Palmagil and hurriedly asked him, in Spanish, to follow her and help show them the newly remodeled two-bedroom furnished apartment on the second floor. Palmagil was happy to be of service.

The two Americans were pleased with the rooms and agreed, via translation by Palmagil, to be renters. Carmen breathed a sigh of relief. *Thank, God, all the apartments are rented. God provides.* She thanked Mr. Palmagil for his assistance, as neither American spoke Spanish. Mr. Farnsworth carried a Spanish/English dictionary in his right hand, leafed through some pages, and mangled some Spanish phrases to convey thanks to Carmen before they left. She could hardly wait until they were gone before laughing at their attempts to speak Spanish. *They would probably laugh at me if I tried to use any English words besides "Welcome!" At least, they were sincere.*

Mary laughed out loud as she thought about the first time she tried to speak English. Mr. Farnsworth had been her first "teacher" and she was so grateful to him for helping her. Most of their Sunday afternoons were spent in comical one-sided conversations. She learned more English than he did Spanish. *What a gentle person he was. I wonder what happened to him?*

CHAPTER 22

Another Angel in Heaven

It was a dark, dreary day. The wind howled around Mary's small house on Stonewall Street and rattled the loose shutter on the north side near the Japanese persimmon tree. *I must get that shutter fixed before it falls off and breaks.* Mary pulled her shawl closer around her shoulders as she resumed writing.

Luz was slowly recovering from Don José's death, when her mother, Doña Amalia became desperately ill. The doctor was called.

"Pneumonia," said Dr. Fuentes as he shook his head. "Your mother is seriously ill. How old is she?"

"She is not old. She will be sixty-five on her next birthday," uttered Luz.

"Nevertheless," Dr. Fuentes stated, "she has had a difficult life."

Luz agreed with Dr. Fuentes. Doña Amalia made the long ocean voyage with her husband, Don Angel and their five children. They struggled to make a life in Ilocos Norte. His job transfer to Manila resulted in their twins being beheaded at age sixteen. The family never recovered. Her poor mother worked hard to provide for them. *How did she do it?*

Dr. Fuentes made arrangements for medicine and gave Luz instructions for her mother's care. Luz's heart sank. She knew the inevitable. Her shoulders slumped with another heavy burden dropped upon them. She knelt quietly beside her mother's bed and took her hand. She retrieved her rosary…the one her mother gave her at her First Holy Communion. *Let the vigil begin.*

Carmen tapped gently on the bedroom door and eased inside Doña Amalia's room. She found Luz asleep with her body resting against the bed…her hands clutching Doña Amalia's lifeless hand…the rosary still in place. Carmen touched Doña Amalia's cheek and its coldness sent a chill into Carmen's heart.

"*Mami*," whispered Carmen, "your mother is with the angels. She has joined *Papá*."

Luz stirred. One look at her mother's face and she knew Doña Amalia was dead. She kissed the cross on her rosary as she sobbed and prayed.

"You must be strong, *Mami*," Carmen said firmly. "The children will need your strength, especially the little ones, when we give them the news."

Luz collected herself and accepted a handkerchief from Carmen.

"You are right…you are right. We must decide what to tell them."

"I will gather the family in the *sala* and we will pray together for your mother's soul," said Carmen as she hurried out the door. It had been less than two years since Don José had died. She knew what to do.

༺༻

Yes, another angel left for Heaven while her angel arrived in the Philippines from Texas. Jesse arrived in 1910 to seek his fortune and changed her life. It's odd that Jess was born when my paternal grandmother died and arrived in the Philippines when my maternal grandmother died. Writing my story brought out connections I never knew.

The incessant ringing of the phone returned Mary to the present. Her mind was still sorting out details of the past.

"Hello. Yes, Father McCallum, I will be at church. I'll drive because it's raining hard. Sure! Goodbye."

The parish priest always called during inclement weather. Mary was usually the only parishioner who attended…rain or shine. More often than not, she and Father McCallum were the only ones at vespers. Sometimes, Carol Ferguson or Helen Mehmert would attend. *They take time to chat with me following the service and are so thoughtful.*

CHAPTER 23

A Time for Renewal

1910 brought more changes. After Doña Amalia's death, Luz relapsed into her former depression. She was quiet, listless, and hardly ever smiled…no matter what anyone did. Carmen, Rosario, and Natividad tried hard to ease their stepmother's burdens, but nothing seemed to help.

"It will take time," suggested Carmen. "She needs time to heal. Nati, you and Charing remember how much we suffered when our mother died. It is the same with *Mami*. She was still grieving for *Papá* when she lost her mother."

Her sisters nodded in agreement. They understood, and although they felt helpless, they took responsibility for the childcare and household duties.

All the apartments were rented. Carmen, who graduated with a degree in music, began teaching piano lessons to the young Spanish girls in the neighborhood. Nati and Charing embroidered beautifully. They took samples of their embroidery to Mrs. Fuller, who owned Fuller's Fine Designs…a nearby manufacturer of fine quality infant and children's clothing. She was delighted with their work and hired them to do embroidery by the piece. They could work at home and contribute to the family coffers.

Carmen searched for ways to cut expenses. For transportation, the Gamero family owned a coach, a spirited horse, and employed a coachman. Carmen felt they should sell the coach and horse plus dismiss the coachman. Nati had a different idea. She discovered that the German Benedictine nuns at Santa Scholastica College initiated a new Kindergarten program at the Singalong Street campus and were enrolling five-year-old girls. The Spanish Sisters of Charity schools accepted students only at age seven. She convinced Carmen she would find families from their neighborhood who wished to enroll their five-year-old daughters, and use the coach to transport them, since the Singalong Street campus of Santa Scholastica was not within walking distance. A fee would be charged for this service. Carmen had concerns, but gave her approval. *I was excited! I would be attending Santa Scholastica with my friends!*

Nati was successful in her efforts, so five other five-year-old neighborhood girls and I enrolled in Santa Scholastica, where classes included the teaching of

English. This "girls only" school was modern and attended by the daughters of well-known Manila families.

I studied English at Santa Scholastica and was anxious to get home each day to practice my "English" with our American renter, Mr. Farnsworth. He took a special interest in me. We spent many hours in the evening teaching each other. He would learn Spanish and I would learn English. Mr. Farnsworth enjoyed playing the piano and taught me an American song, *My Bonnie Lies Over The Ocean*. He was so funny and loved to make me laugh.

"Would you like to call me 'Daddy'?" he asked after several weeks. "'Mr. Farnsworth' is too formal for our conversations," he added. "I've always wished to have a little girl like you," he stated, "but I've been busy working."

I nodded my head in agreement but added, "I should ask my mother's permission first."

"Yes, you should. My sisters in Wichita, Kansas, would really like you. Perhaps you can come with me when I return to America."

Excitement surged through me! I rushed to find my mother to tell her about this conversation. When I found her in the *sala*, my words spilled from my mouth like water tumbling from a waterfall.

"*Mami! Mami!* Mr. Farnsworth wants to take me to America to meet his sisters!" I spouted.

"*Nena, quieta te,*" she scolded, "Lorenzo is taking his *siesta* and you may waken him. What is this foolishness?"

My heart sank at her tone of voice. I knew it was pointless to continue my argument. My hopes of going to America were dashed against the sadness in my *Mami's* heart like breakers on a rocky shore. *I will go to America, someday!* I made this promise to myself.

Charles W. Farnsworth from Wichita, Kansas, 1915.

CHAPTER 24

Bumps in the Road

My outburst about going to America with Mr. Farnsworth upset *Mami*, and she was ready to "throw those Americans out on the street!" Carmen tried to pacify her by assuring her she would keep a watchful eye on all the American renters. Before long, she discovered that Mr. Farnsworth's roommate, Mac McKinnon, was being overly friendly with Rosario (Charing). Carmen, as the eldest and the one responsible for her sisters, would not allow any relationship to develop. She called a family meeting.

"Do not become interested in any American renters. They are strangers to us. You know how our *Papá* despised the Americans during the Spanish-American War! Think about your *Papá!*" Carmen scolded her sisters…standing before them with her arms crossed over her ample breasts and a deep frown on her face.

Charing lowered her head so her eyes would not meet Carmen's. *Mr. McKinnon was so polite. He was always so respectful when they met in the hallway. I must honor Carmen's wishes. My Papá would be angry if I encouraged Mr. McKinnon.*

Mami agreed the girls should honor their father's wishes. Carmen was in charge and she must be obeyed. While the American renters appeared to be honorable, we had no guarantees. The subject was closed.

During September 1910, I became very ill with a sore throat. My mother called Dr. Cavana, a family friend. Dr. and Mrs. Cavana were Consuelo's godparents. Besides being the children's doctor, he also worked with the Health Department. I was diagnosed with "a touch of influenza." Medication was prescribed and instructions were given for my care. My condition worsened with each passing day. Mr. Farnsworth became concerned and asked my mother to call Dr. Lamm, an American doctor. Upon his urging, *Mami* agreed.

When Dr. Lamm arrived the next day, he told my mother I was seriously ill.

"She has diphtheria, Mrs. Gamero. She must be hospitalized immediately. I will arrange for her admittance to St. Lazarus Hospital so she can receive appropriate care. Everyone in this house must be vaccinated and put under quarantine," he said gravely.

Mami nodded. She felt overwhelmed and asked Carmen to accompany me to St. Lazarus Hospital. *Mami* stayed with Lorenzo, who was only three.

I was hospitalized for thirty days. Visitors were not allowed. After the quarantine was lifted at our home, my mother would come to stand outside my hospital window and Carmen would carry me to the window so we could see each other and wave. *Mami* stayed less than twenty minutes, as she came in the family coach and it was needed so Nati could transport the girls to and from Santa Scholastica.

Carmen stayed with me. She taught me how to make several items with paper. We cut paper dolls and made costumes for them. We made a single boat, a double boat, a hat, a ball, and a box…all by folding paper. She read many Bible stories to me in Spanish and I taught her the English I knew, as she wanted to learn.

On my return home from St. Lazarus Hospital, my family was delighted to see me. Mr. Farnsworth was pleased with my recovery. My bed felt wonderful.

The First Holy Communion for Maria de los Angeles Josefa Gabina Gamero y Cucullu (age 5) and her older sister Maria del Pilar Gamero y Cucullu (age 7). Rev. José Ma. Gamero y Boix, their half brother, conducted the rites in 1910.

Riding the family coach daily to Santa Scholastica with Nati, my friends, and our coachman filled me with excitement, or was it that Christmas was around the corner! My sisters, who were in boarding school, would come home for a two-week vacation for the holidays. We would sing carols, and receive presents on the sixth of January…The Day of The Three Kings. Perhaps the holidays would make *Mami* happy.

Shrieks of laughter ricocheted around our home and created much amusement for the American renters. They were away from their families and enjoyed our antics. Mr. Farnsworth admired my older sister, Lucing, who was mature at sixteen. I didn't get much attention from him while she was around. Lucing was not present for Carmen's stern warnings about the American tenants.

Many parties brightened our holidays. Neighbors were invited to join us in singing Christmas carols around the piano, played by Carmen. *Mami* joined the Christmas festivities, although we knew she was thinking about her mother and our father.

For Christmas, I received a small baby doll. I told Carmen my doll should be baptized. She smiled.

"Yes, we will have a baptism and a small party with your friends from Santa Scholastica," Carmen announced.

My sisters worked together to make this "baptism" a special event. They knew I had been quite ill and were happy to see me in a celebratory mood. Nati made a special baptismal gown for my doll and sent the invitations to those students who rode our coach daily. Carmen made arrangements for our brother, *Pépe* to come home from the Jesuit school to "conduct the baptism." Rosario prepared special cakes and the others prepared decorations. *I will always remember how helpful my family was to me. I thanked God for my sisters.*

We celebrated the New Year together by attending Midnight Mass. Everyone, including the children, shared the communion wine to usher in 1911. *Thank you, Lord, for* my *health and all the many blessings bestowed upon my family. Amen.*

CHAPTER 25

Bumps and Bruises

All was quiet once again in the Gamero household. The older girls and *Pépe* returned to their respective boarding schools. 1911 was beginning quietly, but changes were hovering, like the calm before a storm.

The first two weeks in February crept along like a sleepy turtle on a bumpy road. *Would my sixth birthday ever arrive?* Carmen promised to have a celebration and invite my school friends. Mr. Farnsworth was included. I spoke more English and was able to interpret sentences for my family. Carmen promised we would sing *Happy Birthday* in English. Mr. Farnsworth played the piano and led the singing. He and I were the only ones singing…the others clapped rhythmically.

The party was a success. *Mami* smiled, clapped her hands, and tapped her foot as we sang in English. I was so happy!

June pushed May aside and summer vacation dangled within reach like the heavy golden tassels on our brocade drapes…tantalizingly within reach. During the last week of school, we traveled in our family coach to Santa Scholastica as usual. Suddenly, our horse began racing, as if he were trying to win a derby. He was passing every horse-drawn coach we approached. Nati was alarmed.

"Sit quietly and pray," she instructed, trying to keep the panic from her voice as we clattered along.

The coachman struggled with the reins and tried to control the horse. The steed ran as if a bee had stung him! In an instant, the coach struck a utility pole in the median. The crashing noise was followed by silence. Darkness enveloped me. As I regained consciousness, a siren screamed in my head. A heavy weight lay across my chest. Through the fog in my head, men were yelling and girls crying. Nati's soothing voice was followed by her scream when she saw me trapped under the coach. The fog in my head became thicker and the darkness returned.

When the fog lifted, I was at home feeling the doctor's hands as he examined my head and chest. My ears were ringing and my head throbbed as if someone inside was beating a loud drum.

"She has a concussion and must be kept quiet for a day or so," Dr. Cavana whispered to my mother. "Make sure she has no other symptoms, like being sleepy, dizzy, or nauseated."

Mami sank into the nearest chair. Carmen took charge and took the doctor's instructions.

"*Gracias,* Dr. Cavana," Carmen whispered as she led him outside the bedroom door.

When Carmen returned, I asked about the other students in the coach.

"You must be quiet. The others had cuts and bruises and are home with their families. Nati is seeing to them, and I will care for you."

I smiled weakly, cuddled my baby doll, and fell asleep, only to be nudged awake by Carmen. She was following Dr. Cavana's instructions.

Mary raised her hand to her head. *It was quite a bump.* She remembered it well. She had to wait until she became seven to continue her schooling, as the coach was destroyed. She would never forget the experience!

Maria de los Angeles Josefa Gabina Gamero y Cucullu (age 8) with her younger brother, José Lorenzo Gamero y Cucullu (age 6), 1913.

CHAPTER 26

The Ordination

On March 19, 1912, José Maria Gamero y Boix was ordained as a Jesuit priest. Doña Luisa Campos, his baptismal godmother, sponsored his ordination at St. Ignatius Catholic Church in *Intramuros*. *A day of triumph and celebration for the Gamero family! Mami was so proud. She felt Don José's presence. His dream came true…his son was an ordained priest.* Days after his ordination he was assigned as coadjutor for the *Shrine of Nuestra Señora de la Paz y Buen Viaje* in Antipolo…The Virgin of Antipolo. The history of its location at Antipolo is retold each May during the annual festival.

> On March 25, 1626, Don Juan Niño de Tabora left Mexico on a Spanish galleon, *El Almirante,* to sail to the Philippines. Trade between Mexico and the Philippines had increased. As a gesture of good will, Governor Tabora's mission was to deliver the dark brown image of the Blessed Virgin Mother to the islands. Following three months on perilous seas, *El Almirante* arrived in Manila on July 18, 1626. Governor Tabora attributed their successful trip to the statue of the Blessed Virgin. An elaborate celebration was held which included a procession from the Church of San Ignacio in *Intramuros* to the Manila Cathedral, where it was first housed and named Our Lady of Peace and Good Voyage (*Nuestra Señora de la Paz y Buen Viaje*). When Tabora died in 1632, the sacred statue was placed under the care of Jesuit priests who were building a church in Antipolo.

Carmen busied herself with the arrangements while she and the family assisted their brother, Fr. José Ma. Gamero y Boix, with his assignment to Antipolo. She would enter the convent when her brother was ensconced at his parish.

Rosario (Charing) was studying opera under Professor Gambardela, but decided she would stop her studies and dedicate her life to her brother, Fr. Gamero. She would help him with his church at Antipolo. She and Carmen worked feverishly to attain this goal. They traveled with him to Antipolo and made sure he was settled comfortably in his new quarters.

Antipolo was a delightful place. The town, not far from Manila, was nestled in the mountains, which were lush with greenery. The convent was as large as Our Lady of Peace Church, which accommodated the many parishioners. After making sure her brother was comfortable, Carmen returned home. Rosario took responsibility for her brother's care. She dedicated her life to his wellbeing.

Father Gamero took pride in his responsibilities as coadjutor for the Blessed Virgin. Rosario (Charing) was equally as proud. Her brother was an excellent priest. She saw him through his studies and she would continue to help him as he served his parish. Her sister, Carmen, was now free to become a nun.

"My promise has been kept," said Carmen. "I will apply to enter the sisterhood, although I am no longer young. I pray they will still accept me, for becoming a nun is my deepest desire."

Within the year, Carmen was accepted as a novice with the Order of St. Augustine, and her brother, Fr. Gamero, hosted his first fiesta for Our Lady of Peace and Good Voyage as parish priest at Antipolo, in the Rizal province. The family celebrated both events at the fiesta in Antipolo, the Pilgrimage City.

Following the fiesta at Antipolo, Carmen

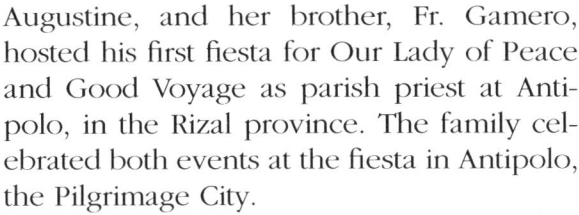

Fr. José Maria Gamero y Boix *(right)* during his Silver Jubilee Celebration of service to The Church of Our Lady of Peace and Good Voyage at Antipolo, P.I., where he served.

entered the convent as a novice in the Order of St. Augustine located on the banks of the Pasig River in Rizal. She was so pleased her brother, Fr. Gamero would be nearby and could visit her when he traveled to Manila on church business. *Thank you, God, for your many blessings and for allowing me to fulfill my life-long wish.*

Once more, the Gamero household settled into their daily routine, however, many changes had occurred. The empty spaces at the dining table reminded us of our missing family members. The atmosphere was quieter…solemn. We felt as if the heavy dark brocade drapes in our *sala* were wrapped around us. Our lives changed and more changes were on the horizon.

Mary held her rosary, the one her half-brother, *Pépe,* gave her after performing the rituals for her First Holy Communion at age seven. She and her sister Pilar were the first two to receive communion from him as he conducted his first Holy Mass. *A day of triumph and celebration for the Gamero family! Mami was so proud. She felt Don José was present.*

Sister (Mother) Superior Mercedes del Carmen Gamero y Boix (Maming)

CHAPTER 27

Disaster Comes Courting

In 1914, Salud, our youngest half-sister, decided to continue her education for another year to practice teaching at Sta. Catalina. She earned a bachelor's degree in languages and was proficient in Spanish, English, German and French. As she was homely, the family encouraged her to enter the teaching profession, for they felt she would never marry. She inherited her mother's home, where she and the Gameros now lived, and it would always be her home. Our father's portion was sold to pay taxes after his death. As Gamero's, we would continue to live together...or so we thought.

World War I erupted in Europe with the assassination of Archduke Francis Ferdinand, heir to the Austrian throne, and his wife in Sarajevo. German troops swallowed much of Europe with the ravenous appetite of a hungry wolf. Chaos reigned.

In May 1915, with World War I at full tilt, our American renters accomplished their mission in the Philippines and were returning to the United States. The rumblings of war spurred them to be with their families before hostilities reached the islands. Once again, Mr. Farnsworth approached my mother regarding my future.

"Doña Luz," he began, "would you reconsider allowing *Maria* to accompany me to the United States? My sisters would be delighted to have a little girl in our home. I have become so attached to her; I feel she is my child. I'll bring her home if she is unhappy."

I translated his request to her and waited silently for her response, hoping against hope her answer would be, *"Si."* I listened with a heavy heart, because I knew my mother would never let me go. I liked Mr. Farnsworth, and I truly wanted to go to America.

"*No,*" replied *Mami*. *"No puedes ir con el señor."*

I did not have to translate for Mr. Farnsworth. He understood. He shook her hand, gave my shoulder a quick squeeze, and returned to his quarters to finish packing. I ran to the room I shared with Lorenzo and cried myself to sleep.

Two months after his departure, my sister, Lucing, received a card from Mr.

Farnsworth from Wichita, Kansas, noting they arrived safely. He sent greetings to our family and noted he was sending a special present for me. Before long, I received the most beautiful doll I had ever seen! She was two feet tall in her black patent leather shoes and wore a crisp blue dress with a white organdy pinafore. Her perky straw hat was perched daintily on her long, curly, dark hair, and its brim was encircled by a matching blue ribbon. Her eyelids opened and closed as I moved her from a standing to reclining position…drawing attention to her piercing blue eyes. The enclosed card was signed by my adopted "Daddy," Mr. Farnsworth and his two sisters…my new "aunts." The girls at my school thought I was the luckiest girl in the world to have a beautiful doll from America.

Salud completed her studies and earned her teaching certificate. She returned to the family home and prepared the apartment vacated by the American renters, as her classroom. She would only teach girls and women, as our mother was opposed to any men coming into our home, unless the family knew them.

Neighborhood Spanish girls who wished to learn either English or French attended her classes. *Mami* was pleased with Salud's progress as a language teacher, until a young German businessman learned of her language classes from acquaintances at his hotel. He spoke only broken English and wished to improve his skills by practicing his English and learning Spanish, since a majority of the populace spoke Spanish. He was handsome and quite charming.

"Me Willi Kursweg. You help English?" He smiled as he spoke and took her hand.

Salud struggled to keep her composure and responded to him in fluent German. Surprise crossed his face as he smiled broadly. He uttered sentences in German to which Salud responded. He held her hand as they spoke.

Salud was stunned by his touch. His steel blue eyes penetrated hers. *She would help him.* She nodded in agreement. He would return the next day. He smiled, lifted her hand to his lips, and brushed them across her soft skin. Salud trembled.

Maria del Salud Gamero y Rocha

Mami stared in disbelief as the young German clicked his heels, bowed, and departed. She had a terrible feeling deep within her.

"*Que paso?*" *Mami* spoke anxiously. "*Dimé todo!*"

Mami wanted information about this foreigner, but Salud was not prepared to discuss her conversations she shared with Willi. She knew how her stepmother felt about strange men coming into their home. *But it is my home! I own this house!*

Salud braced herself for the long argument. She had already decided to teach Willi Kursweg. She would help this handsome German who stirred strange emotions inside her. She had never felt this way before.

As a realtor, Willi Kursweg knew what he was doing. His inspection of the property records on the Gamero house led him to discover that Maria del Salud Gamero y Rocha inherited the house from her mother, Rosario. He had come to the Philippines to escape the ravages of war in Europe and become wealthy any way he could. He found a ripe plum to pick in Salud. He would have his sanctuary and own her property. He smiled to himself. *That house will be mine to do with as I wish.*

Mary shook her head as she recalled the many times her mother repeated Salud's story. *Salud's tragic death was a dark moment. How could one man be so evil?* She shuddered as if to shake off those dark days. *I should pray. I should give thanks for my blessings.* Mary reached for her rosary.

CHAPTER 28

Disaster Moves In

World War I rumbled through 1916 wreaking havoc across Europe like a plague of locusts. The United States remained neutral but found ways to lend their support to the Allies. Uncertainty was affecting financial conditions in the Philippines causing an economic depression across the land.

Willi Kursweg played his cards deftly in courting Salud. Being young and inexperienced in relationships with men, she succumbed to his ploys and refused to listen to anyone in the family, as well as her friends, when they warned her about him and his cunning manner. *Mami* hired José Palmagil, the attorney who lived in our building, to investigate Willi. Mr. Palmagil made inquiries and told *Mami* and Salud about Willi's activities. Willi Kursweg was acquiring property in *Intramuros* and other parts of Manila to sell to rich Chinese merchants. Salud would not believe him.

"You don't know Willi like I do!" she shouted at *Mami* after Mr. Palmagil left. "I trust him. He is in love with me and has proposed marriage."

Her words poured forth like a tumbling waterfall. She was adamant. *Mami* knew she would not listen to anyone. She called her stepson, Fr. Gamero; to please come and counsel with Salud…perhaps she would listen to him.

Upon receiving the message, the young priest visited his family's home. The family gathered for his counsel.

"First, we must pray. We must ask God to guide us in our decisions so the right one will be chosen," Fr. Gamero said quietly.

His calm demeanor and serious approach in dealing with this family crisis spread across the room to quiet the anxiety seen on their faces. They prayed for over an hour and Fr. Gamero addressed his stepsister, Salud.

"Salud, do you truly love Willi and are you sure he is in love with you?" he inquired.

Salud rose from her kneeling position and faced him.

"I am sure he cares for me. He is so appreciative of my help with learning new languages. He needs me," Salud spoke firmly.

Her demeanor said it all. The subject was closed. There would be a wedding.

Mami's voice was trembling when she spoke, "If I were your mother, and not your stepmother, I would not allow you to marry him. All he wants is your property."

Fr. Gamero took his stepmother's hand. *Mami's* hand trembled in his as he offered assistance with the wedding plans. They could marry at Antipolo. Rosario would help with the arrangements, since Carmen was still at her convent. He assured *Mami* she would not have any responsibility.

"You are right, *Pépe*. I will have nothing to do with this horrible situation," *Mami* replied.

The arrangements were made. The disastrous day arrived. The family took the train to Antipolo. During the two-hour trip, *Mami* kept begging Salud to reconsider. Salud ignored her pleas.

"I will marry Willi and we will be happy. You will see!" Salud countered.

Following the wedding, planned by Rosario, the family stayed at the convent to spend time with her and *Pépe*. Many prayers were offered to God. *Mami* knew they were prayers of desperation.

Salud was married less than a month when Willi told *Mami* that everyone, including the renters, must vacate his home. They had one week to vacate the premises. If they were still in "his home" the next week, they would be put out on the street.

"I new owner. Salud only stay," Willi challenged forcefully and marched away.

Mami was in shock. No reply was needed. Willi had control. She could barely repeat his orders to us through her tears. The family was stunned. *Dear God, please help us!*

Willi Hertz Kursweg *(left)* and friend, Landsberg, Germany

CHAPTER 29

No Recourse

The only remaining tenant, who was not a relative, was the attorney, José Palmagil. *Mami* explained their dire circumstances. Not only would the Gameros have to vacate within a week, but also Mr. Palmagil. She asked his advice, but he saw no legal options open to the family. Through marriage, the property belonging to Salud became her husband's. According to local laws, Willi Kursweg was now the owner. Palmagil offered his sympathy and assured Doña Luz he would comply. He did not want to create more problems for the dear family.

Pascuala (Lola Lala) was the first family tenant to move. Her friend, Doña Sofia Barreto, was recently widowed. She and her husband, Ricardo, former president of La Tabacalera, owned a large home in Manila. Their children were grown and no longer lived at home. Sofia and her sister, Rosario Gorostiza, were once neighbors to Pascuala and the Gameros in the 1890s. Sofia married Ricardo Barreto, and her sister, Rosario, married Luis Elzingre Dumas. The couples were frequent visitors at the Gameros' home in *Intramuros* on San José Street.

Doña Sofia invited Lola Lala to live with her as a "companion" and would provide her with a salary, plus all the cigars she wished to smoke. Cigars were Lola Lala's weakness. They were cigarillos, not the large cigars smoked by most men. Lola Lala was happy to be Sophia's companion. Her prayers were answered.

Our aunt and uncle, Hermiñia and Luis Cucullu, were the next tenants to leave. They learned the Martinez apartment on Magallanes Street, that they previously rented, was available. They were familiar with the neighborhood, and were satisfied their prayers were answered.

After many pleas for help to family and friends to find lodging for our family, *Mami* found two rooms for rent on the second floor of a boarding house owned by Doña Petrona (Tonay) Gonzalez. She owned a large two-story building on Muralla Street in *Intramuros*, plus a large plantation with coconut and *abaca* crops in the Bicol area of Bulan, a neighboring province. *Mami* and Doña Petrona had known each other for many years since they attended the same church on Cabildo Street in *Intramuros*. Doña Petrona was widowed and had only one son, Juan Gonzalez y Bailon, who was attending college in London, England. She was delighted to rent to the Gameros and would help.

Another problem arose. What would we do with the many pieces of furniture from the large family home, when we only had two rooms? Our half-sister, Rosario, rescued the furniture. She and several parishioners from Antipolo transferred most of the furniture to the convent at Antipolo. Rosario also arranged to place several pieces in the convent of The Order of St. Augustine, where Carmen was a novice. Carmen was thrilled to have her own piano again and would use it to teach music at the convent. Another problem was settled.

We only had two rooms: one for our mother, *Mami;* and, the other for Natividad, our widowed half-sister. Rosario would share the room with Nati when she visited on her weekends off at Antipolo. All the remaining Gamero children were full boarders at schools operated by the Catholic Sisters of Charity, since we were all considered orphans. We shared two bathrooms and one large kitchen with about twenty tenants on the second floor. In spite of these problems, *Mami* still gave thanks that we and our furniture, were not thrown out into the street, as that devil, Willi, had threatened.

Our mother searched for better lodging for our family. It was crowded for us when we were home from boarding school on holidays. Lucing, Consueling, and Pilar stayed in Nati's room. Lorenzo and I stayed with our mother. There was barely floor space for sleeping and even less for walking, as the remaining furniture was squeezed into every space. We had to step carefully to avoid an accident.

Fifteen rooms on the first floor were rented to laborers of varied ethnicities and their families. It was like a small international village with various languages being spoken and pungent with the aromas of their many ethnic cuisines, which floated into our rooms on the second floor.

Over six months elapsed before other housing was found. Mother's cousin, Rita Swanson and her family lived on the first floor in the apartment house next door to the Gonzalez's boarding house where we now lived. Rita notified *Mami* that two large rooms were available in their building. *Mami* hurried to speak with Doña Socorro (Carito) Martinez, who owned the apartment building. A small apartment with two bedrooms, a small kitchen and bathroom was also for rent. Our mother decided the apartment would be a better arrangement for us. Once again, the upheaval was completed and furniture put into place. We had space for most of the furniture. Doña Carito allowed our mother to place the living room furniture in the hallway between two apartments on the second floor. *Mami* asked our landlady to advise her when she had another room or larger apartment to rent, as our sister, Lucing, would graduate soon and return to live with their family.

Everyone was happier with the change of housing. It was much quieter, and we were close to our cousin and her family. With her family settled into a better place, *Mami's* thoughts wandered to Salud. *How was she? Where was she? Was she all right? What had Willi done to her? She needed information.*

⊷⊶

Mary reached for her rosary as she thought about her mother's plight. *How terrible she must have felt. How did her frail mother survive these horrible events?*

CHAPTER 30

Salud's Sad Story

The war in Europe intensified in early 1917. The United States tried to remain neutral, but on April 6, the United States declared war on Germany. Europeans, fleeing the death and destruction in their countries, escaped to other lands. The Philippines experienced an influx of refugees. This influx brought about many changes to the nation's economic status with the demand for more housing, jobs, and food.

During this time, neighbors to our half-sister, Salud, brought the disturbing news regarding Salud's plight to our mother. Willi was observed beating Salud daily. While this abuse disturbed our mother, she was helpless to take action against Willi. Philippine laws did not protect against an abusive husband. They were considered "family quarrels" unless the wife asked authorities to intervene. Many times, reporting abuse created more problems for the abused spouse. Salud had made her bed. She would have to sleep in it.

On occasion, when Willi was away on business, Salud would slip away from their home for a brief visit with us. She never discussed her life with Willi. Sometimes she would start crying during her visits. When asked why, she offered other reasons.

"I am so happy to see you and miss you so much. I am so sorry you left our home. Willi told me you felt we should be alone as a couple…that you wanted to move because you did not approve of him."

Mami was surprised by her reply, but said nothing. Obviously, Willi never told Salud he had ousted her family. *Lies…all lies!*

Lucing's graduation created a need for new living quarters. *Mami* reminded Doña Carito of her earlier request. Within the week, Doña Carito offered a two-room apartment. Nati and Rosario moved into the new quarters, and their vacated room was prepared for Lucing and Consueling. School was over for the summer, and the family was together again.

Doña Petrona, who owned the boarding house next door, rented the two rooms we had vacated to a Russian, Luis Mazurofski, shortened to Mazur to not attract attention to his Russian Orthodox Jewish name. His sixteen-year-old sister, Anya (Annie), needed a place to stay during her visit to the Philippines, since Luis lived at the YMCA. Annie would be visiting for six months. Annie's parents sent her to Spain to attend boarding school to escape the atrocities being suffered in Europe. She could not return to Russia during her vacation months due to the revolution and war, so she came to see her brother, Luis, in Manila. He asked the landlady if she knew someone he could hire to care for his younger sister while he worked. She immediately thought about Nati, our widowed half-sister, who lived with us next door. Doña Petrona, with *Mami's* permission, brought Luis Mazur and his sister, Anya (Annie) to our building to meet Nati and Rosario. Luis worked as a clerk at I. Beck, a large department store in Manila. Annie barely spoke English but communicated fairly well in Spanish, which she learned at boarding school in Spain. Spanish was the Mazur's second language. Nati hesitated.

"*Sr*. Mazur, I take in piecework to embroider from Mrs. Fuller's factory to help pay our rent. I have some time, but do not think I will have enough time to attend to your sister."

"You will be paid well, *Sra*. Bores. I do not expect charity," Luis replied. "I can also help you find more work. I saw a notice at I. Beck's for a seamstress to do their alterations. I will be happy to speak with our manager, if you are interested."

It was agreed. Annie Mazur could stay with Nati during the day, and Nati would continue with her piecework from Mrs. Fuller's shop plus I. Becks' alterations. Luis made arrangements to bring the garments needing alterations from the store and return them when completed. Nati made sure Annie worked on her studies, and prepared their daily meals. The arrangements were satisfactory, and Nati's income increased.

Once again, Salud's neighbors visited our mother. Their news was disturbing. The Gamero home was sold to Chinese merchants. Willi removed the furniture and took Salud away. No one knew where. Rosario did not believe the neighbors' "tales." She wanted to see for herself and returned in tears. Rosario was worried. Salud had disappeared. No one had any information.

Two months dragged by with no news. Mrs. Fuller and Nati had become close friends and shared events in each other's lives. Mrs. Fuller knew the tragic story of the Gameros being ousted from their home. Nati also shared reports about her missing sister, Salud. Josefina Nasato, an employee at Mrs. Fuller's factory, lived in a nearby province. She was acquainted with Nati and Rosario, as she was responsible for the piecework they embroidered. She was also aware of Salud's situation, but was not acquainted with her. A German fellow and his pregnant wife had moved into her neighborhood two months earlier. Josefina noted he was unfriendly. She went to Mrs. Fuller and asked her advice as to whether or not to report this to Nati and Rosario, since they were looking for Salud. Mrs. Fuller suspected the couple to be Willi and Salud. She asked Josefina to get more information. Josefina agreed. When Nati arrived with the piecework the following day, Mrs. Fuller shared this information with Nati. On her way home, Nati decided to keep this information to herself until it was verified.

Around noon on the following Saturday, Josefina observed the German trudging toward the village, carrying a suitcase. She waited before going next door. She found a rather homely, pregnant woman sobbing. She lay crumpled in the doorway like a broken rag doll. Josefina helped her into a nearby chair just inside the front door. Josefina gasped when she saw the bruises on the woman's arms and face.

"I think my husband has left me," she sobbed. "What shall I do?"

Josefina was beside herself. She prattled about being her neighbor and her job at Mrs. Fuller's factory. She chattered on about knowing several Spanish ladies who took pieces home to do delicate embroidery.

"Perhaps Mrs. Fuller will allow me to bring embroidery work to you," Josefina stated.

The woman shivered as she stopped her crying. Josefina's chatter had a calming effect. She dried her tears with the hem of her apron.

"My sisters would bring piecework home from the factory to do at home. They sewed to help with the family's expenses."

"Tell me your sister's names and yours," Josefina said, encouraged she stopped crying. "I will ask Mrs. Fuller if they worked for her. She will surely let me bring work to you if she knows them."

"I am Salud Gamero Kursweg y Rocha. My sisters are Rosario Gamero y Boix and Natividad Gamero, Vda. de Bores. Natividad is a widow."

"I know them! I am in charge of the piecework for the factory and see them every week!"

Josefina assured her she would talk with Mrs. Fuller. She squeezed Salud's hand gently and gave her a smile as she left.

Josefina returned to work and told Mrs. Fuller about Salud. Mrs. Fuller left immediately to verify Salud's condition before alerting her family. When she arrived, Willi was nowhere around. Mrs. Fuller knocked, but there was no answer. She could hear a woman sobbing inside, so she walked through the open door. She found Salud on the kitchen floor. Her condition alarmed Mrs. Fuller. She needed medical help immediately.

"Salud, I am taking you to the hospital in Manila, now," Mrs. Fuller stated.

Salud was too weak to resist. Mrs. Fuller packed a small bag for Salud after she helped Salud to a chair and brought her some orange juice. As they prepared to leave, Salud murmured that a note should be left for her husband. Mrs. Fuller decided it was more important to leave than to write a note of explanation for Willi as Salud requested. Salud was taken to Manila and admitted to the American Hospital. Once Salud was under the doctor's care, Mrs. Fuller notified Nati and Rosario.

The Gamero sisters decided it was best to keep the information from *Mami* until they knew more, and rushed to the hospital to see Salud. They were shocked to see her in this terrible condition. Salud burst into deep sobs when they entered her hospital room. Her bruised face and body told the story. Nati and Rosario cried with her. When they stopped sobbing, Salud haltingly told her story.

"He threw a bucket at my stomach. He beat me, and then left me. I prayed to God someone would come by to help me. I felt weak. I thank God this neighbor and Mrs. Fuller helped. What will become of me?" Salud wailed.

"We will tell *Mami*. She will decide what to do," Rosario said as she and Nati gently touched their sister, Salud. "We will return tomorrow morning. You need to rest."

Mami's emotions exploded as Rosario and Nati retold Salud's story and described her terrible condition.

"You must call your brother, *Pépe,* and tell him to go immediately to the American Hospital. He must bring a small bottle of Holy Water and oils for the Last Sacrament. Hurry!"

They did as instructed. On their return to the American Hospital early the next morning, they found Salud dead with her stillborn child by her side. Nati and Rosario were shocked. They knew Salud was battered, but felt, with proper care, she would survive. Their brother, Fr. Gamero, arrived with the Holy Water and oils for the Last Sacrament. He knew what he must do. Two more angels joined the family band in Heaven.

The nurses were not aware Salud had aborted the baby and both died. They checked in on her after midnight, so the double tragedies must have occurred during the early morning hours. Salud had not called for help. She kept her promise to herself to not complain.

Nati and Rosario called Mrs. Fuller who arrived within the hour. She was a kind and generous person.

"I am so sorry your sister had to suffer this tragedy. Do not worry. I will pay the hospital and funeral expenses."

The Gamero sisters expressed the family's appreciation for her generosity. They could not afford to pay burial expenses for Salud and her infant. They made arrangements for their remains to be removed from the hospital.

Rosario and Nati took burial clothing for Salud and the baby to the mortician and gave instructions for their burial. Salud and her tiny angel were placed in the same coffin. Their headstone would bear only their family's name:

SALUD GAMERO Y ROCHA AND INFANT

The Gameros refused to allow that German's name inscribed on their sister's tombstone. Willi Kursweg would never be connected with Salud again. No one argued with them.

Two months after the funeral for Salud and her baby, Willi returned home. It was as he had left it, but Salud was not there. Willi decided to question the neighbors to see if anyone had seen his wife. He stopped at three different homes before he arrived at Josefina's. Willi was angry, so she decided to tell him the truth.

"Salud was taken to the American Hospital in Manila, by my employer, Mrs. Fuller. She desperately needed medical attention."

Questions were spouting from Willi's mouth. Josefina refused to answer any of his questions, stepped inside her home, and locked her door.

With anger surging through him, Willi drove to the American Hospital in Manila. When he arrived, he was told, regretfully, that Salud and her baby died, and the Gamero family took their remains for proper burial. Willi was stunned. He stormed from the hospital and sped to Doña Carito's apartments, where he knew the Gameros lived.

He arrived at Doña Carito's place and rushed to the second floor apartment where the Gameros lived. He shouted obscenities as he pounded on their door. A neighbor, disturbed by the noise, stepped from the neighboring apartment and confronted him.

"Sir, is there a problem?"

"Where are the Gameros? Willi demanded.

"Sir, the Gameros are at the church. They are making preparations for the wedding of their daughter, Lucing."

The angry German stomped downstairs without another word.

Willi had the nerve to return the next day. The only one at home was my mother, Doña Luz. She was startled by the loud pounding and shouting at their door. She recognized Willi's angry voice and reached for Don José's long heavy cane, which she kept by the door for her protection. She opened the door, stepped out and swung the heavy cane, striking him across his face and shoulder. As he stepped back to get away from the swinging cane, Willi tumbled down the stairs to the first floor landing. My mother returned to her apartment and locked the door.

We learned later Willi was taken as a prisoner of war, since the United States was at war with Germany during World War I. That devil deserved imprisonment.

Good riddance! Mary thought as she gathered her writing materials and prepared a bite to eat before going to church. Father McCallum would be waiting. She would light prayer candles for Salud and her baby.

CHAPTER 31

Lucing

The Gamero family found better living quarters in the Martinez apartment building on the corner of Magallanes and Victoria, where *Tia* Hermiñia and her family lived. Since the Gamero children were in school, they did not need as much living space. *Tia* Herminia had one room, plus a small den. The den served as our receiving room. *Mami* found a job to help pay the rent. The family routine slipped into its usual pace like an old pair of comfortable shoes. Much happened during the year with Salud's untimely death. The family hoped for a respite from preparations for funerals and weddings. There would be none.

With Luis Mazur's help, Lucing obtained a job as a clerk at I. Beck's Department Store in the ladies' department. Consuelo, now older and wiser, remained alone in their apartment, as the younger children were "farmed out" to various family members or godparents during vacation. Pilar and I stayed with Pilar's godparents, the Emilio Moretas. Don Moreta was still working at the Spanish Bank, *El Monte de Piedad*, and Doña Moreta was pleased to have her godchild, Pilar, as a guest along with me. Their daughter, Maria Lourdes, was about the same age as Pilar. Our younger brother Lorenzo, stayed with our aunt, Herminia and their four sons. Mami worked taking in sewing and cleaning apartments in order to provide for the family.

Lucing enjoyed her job as a sales clerk in the ladies department at I. Beck's and was thankful she was able to contribute toward her family's support. Her mother and older sisters worked hard to ensure she and younger siblings were educated. It was her turn to contribute.

El Zenith Jewelry Store, owned by Brimo Brothers, Inc., was located at the Escolta in Manila and was near I. Beck's where Lucing worked. Lucing enjoyed looking at expensive jewelry. She took pleasure in going to the El Zenith Jewelry Store during her lunch hour and pretending to select her engagement and wedding rings. Lucing became a frequent visitor. Cecelia Guiterrez, the young Portuguese assistant manager, greeted Lucing as she was poring over the jewelry counter.

"May I help you?" she inquired. "Are you looking for something special?"

"I am just browsing," Lucing responded truthfully. "I work at I. Beck's and enjoy coming during my lunch hour. I hope this does not inconvenience you."

Cecelia liked Lucing immediately and enjoyed her honest reply.

"Have you had lunch yet?" Cecelia inquired. "I was about to take my lunch break at the Japanese ice cream shop on the corner. Would you care to join me?"

Lucing hesitated, shrugged her shoulders, and nodded affirmatively.

"I am so grateful. I have not tried the ice cream shop before."

The two young girls hit it off immediately. Each was so busy they had no time for a social life. During the next two weeks, they met daily for lunch and became fast friends.

Cecelia's brother, Francisco Gutierrez, managed the jewelry store. She knew Lucing and Francisco would be perfect for each other. During a lunch meeting, Cecelia asked Lucing if she would like to come to work at El Zenith's as a cashier. Lucing liked the idea, but said she would have to discuss it with her mother.

That evening, Lucing broached the subject of changing jobs with *Mami*. She discussed the many reasons why she should take the job as cashier at El Zenith's with her mother as opposed to remaining at I. Beck's.

"*Mami*, at my present job, I have to stand all day long as a sales clerk. At El Zenith's, I could sit at the cash register. Although El Zenith's is a smaller place, the pay is the same," Lucing reasoned.

"If you feel you want to have more responsibility," *Mami* replied, "go ahead. Remember to give your current employer thirty days' notice. You must never burn any bridges behind you. You may have to return to I. Beck's if this job does not suit you or they are not happy with your work."

Lucing was delighted to tell Cecelia she would accept the job as cashier. Cecelia was more excited to tell her brother, Francisco, about hiring a new cashier.

"You will like her, Francisco. She is a lovely, young Spanish girl. I am glad she will be here with us."

Francisco smoothed his dark hair and nodded his head. *I hope my sister knows what she is doing. I wish she had let me do the hiring. Well, we will see.*

Thirty days passed and Lucing reported for her first day as cashier at El Zenith's. Cecelia introduced her to Francisco and it was love at first sight for him. Lucing felt an attraction, but, after all, he was Portuguese. *What would Mami think?*

Three months whirled by like swirling gusts of blustering winds. Lucing asked *Mami* about inviting her friend, Cecelia, for a visit.

"She is the assistant manager at the jewelry store. Although she does not speak Spanish well, I think you will enjoy meeting her. She has become my friend," Lucing stated.

Mami agreed. Cecelia was invited for a visit. Cecelia spent some time becoming better acquainted with the Gamero family. While her Spanish was not fluent, she spoke well enough to carry on a conversation. It was a pleasant and uncomplicated day, until Cecelia left to return to her home.

Mami noticed Cecelia's dark complexion and inquired about her background.

"She is a Portuguese woman who was reared in Hong Kong. Her brother, Francisco, is the manager of El Zenith's. Cecelia is three years older than her brother," Lucing responded while keeping her voice calm.

"Her brother?" *Mami* bristled.

"Yes, *Mami*," Lucing said calmly. "He is a polite young man and has become interested in me. He would like to come and ask your permission to see me socially."

Mami was not happy about Lucing's ploy to use Cecelia's visit as a way to tell her she was interested in seeing Cecelia's brother.

"I don't believe you should get serious about seeing her brother. He is not Spanish. You should be seeing Spaniards. I do not want him in this house," *Mami* said firmly.

Lucing was disappointed. She was fascinated by Francisco and he was infatuated with her. She did not want to go against her mother's wishes. *What must I do?*

Lucing continued working at El Zenith's. She and Francisco lunched together at least twice weekly. He would often see her home after work, but would come only as far as the corner to wait until her face appeared in the second floor window.

Francisco waited patiently, hoping against hope Lucing's mother would allow him to visit at their home. Nothing happened. In a desperate attempt to break the stalemate, Francisco spoke with the parish priest and asked him to intervene. After much discussion, our priest agreed to speak to *Mami* on Francisco's behalf.

The next week after church, our parish priest, Father Antonio, asked *Mami* if she would remain after services for a brief conversation. She agreed, but was uncomfortable, for she felt she had done something wrong.

"Doña Gamero," the priest began, "I have been approached by Francisco Gutierrez to speak to you on his behalf about your daughter Lucing. They are

Maria de la Luz Gamero y Cucullu (Lucing), oldest daughter of José Ma. Gamero y Porras and Maria de la Luz Cucullu y del Valle.

respectable people. As a daughter of Christ, you should treat this family as any other member of God's church."

Mami, although she was visibly not happy with this confrontation by the parish priest, consented to allow Francisco to visit Lucing in their home. Lucing and Francisco were elated. He wasted no time in arranging his first visit and did his best to put Doña Gamero at ease.

Once again, the Gamero family made preparations for yet another celebration. On May 27, 1917, Maria de la Luz Gamero y Cucullu (Lucing) and José Francisco Gutierrez were married by the Fr. José Maria Gamero y Boix at the Capuchin Catholic Church in Manila.

As Lucing was the primary breadwinner for the Gamero family, Francisco decided to provide the Gameros with a monthly check so Lucing would not have to continue working. This check covered the rent for the apartment in which our mother was living.

Mary recalled Lucing's wedding day vividly. *I was twelve years old. Pilar and I were her flower girls. What lovely dresses we wore! I felt like a princess that day. Nati and Rosario, the bridesmaids, made the wedding attire. The reception was at Francisco's home. An orchestra was hired and the feast was catered! We ate suman latic and suman ibus, wrapped in banana leaves and cooked in coconut cream; balut, duck eggs at the embryo stage boiled and served piping hot; and, the flan...and the bibinka malatkit! I'd better stop before I make myself hungry.* Mary reached for her rosary. Her nightly prayers would keep her mind off food.

CHAPTER 32

One by One

Consuelo was only sixteen but very well developed and would easily pass for nineteen or more. Her sparkling brown eyes, winsome smile, and "Dolly Parton" body caught the attention of many young men. She loved to flirt, however, she suffered from a bad case of "puppy love" after meeting Dr. Arturo Anguita, a young Spanish medical student at school. She did not want our mother to know, but Lucing told *Mami*. Her infatuation with the young medical student caused our mother to forbid Consuelo to continue seeing him. Although she promised *Mami* she would not see Arturo again, Consuelo secretly made plans with her young beau to elope. Consuelo made the mistake of sharing her plans with her schoolmates, and one of them informed the Mother Superior, who called *Mami* to tell her about the planned elopement.

"Consuelo will be expelled from Sta. Rosa," declared the Mother Superior firmly. "She has disgraced herself and set a poor example for the other girls."

Mami begged her to allow Consuelo to remain at Santa Rosa. Consuelo saw the pain in our mother's face, so she promised to dedicate herself to her studies.

The Mother Superior considered *Mami's* plea and Consuelo's promise before speaking.

"She will be allowed to stay provided she does not try to break the rules again. She must apply herself to her studies and do penance daily."

Consuelo agreed, but in her heart, she knew she would not keep her promise. Two months later, she tried to sneak away from Santa Rosa to meet her beau and was caught by the Mother Superior herself, who had been keeping a watchful eye on her.

Mami was called to come to Santa Rosa and take Consuelo home, as she was expelled. Consueling was within three months of graduating from high school. This event created a dilemma for our mother. She worked to provide for the family, and Consuelo could not remain at home by herself, besides, she needed to finish her education. Consueling required supervision and should not be left to her own devices. *Mami* sought the advice of Carmen, Sister Superior at the *Colegio de la Consolacion*. Sister Mercedes (Carmen) rescued us once again.

She had been responsible for the Gameros after her father's death and kept all her promises to him and to God. She offered to take personal charge of Consuelo. She would finish her education. *Mami* breathed a deep sigh. Consuelo remained quiet. She knew she had no other options.

Time for Consuelo seemed to crawl by like a fat caterpillar crawling up a tree with rough bark. She graduated, returned home and shared the apartment with Lucing until her marriage to Francisco. She knew she would never see her young doctor again. *Mami* watched her like a hawk. *I have a warden and a personal guard.*

Mr. Morales, who rented the apartment next to the older Gamero girls, noticed Consueling. Being a bachelor, he hired *Mami* to care for his apartment. Every evening, when he returned from work, he would walk through our "living room" (the hallway between our two apartments) and chat politely. Consuelo was flattered by the attentions of a handsome, older gentleman.

Meanwhile, Juanito, Doña Gonzalez's son, returned from his studies in London and was spending his vacation with his mother in the boarding house next door. As they were family friends, Doña Gonzalez hosted a reception as a "Welcome Home" event for her son, Juanito. Our mother, Luz, and all the older girls were invited.

Juanito's eyes were immediately drawn to Consuelo. Lucing, being four years older, told our mother about Juanito's attentions toward Consueling. She had two admirers, Juanito Gonzalez and Mr. Morales. Since Juanito lived next door, he visited quite often. Consuelo responded to his constant attention. Mr. Morales became a faint memory.

Maria del Consuelo Gamero y Cucullu and Juan Gonzalez y Bailon were married on February 2, 1918, by her brother, Fr. José Maria Gamero y Boix, at the Manila Cathedral. The reception was held at El Hotel de Francia in Plaza Santa Cruz

Maria del Consuelo Gamero y Cucullu (Consueling).

where Manila society feted their families. I was the flower girl, and Pilar, plus the groom's cousin, were maids of honor. Guests attended from Bicol, Bulan, and Sorsogon, where the Gonzalez family had their coconut and hemp plantations.

Following their honeymoon at a nearby resort, Juan and Consueling made their home in Bulan. Consuelo was lost. She was so unhappy being away from her family and Manila's social life. She was young and never learned to cook or do any housekeeping since her youth was spent in a Catholic convent to complete her education. They had servants to do the cooking and housekeeping, so Consueling was left to her own devices for entertainment. Most workers on the plantation were natives and did not converse with the owner's wife. Spanish families lived in the area, but none close enough to be considered neighbors, since they were many kilometers away.

Juan decided to take Consuelo to Spain to meet his extended family. Consuelo made the most of this trip and convinced Juan they must take more time to travel before starting their family. She threw a tantrum until he agreed. *Mami* breathed another sigh. *Traveling to Spain would not end Consuelo's wild escapades. Consuelo was a dramatic, strong-willed person. May God bless her and Juanito. Amen.*

Mary shook her head and agreed. Consueling was strong-willed and well built...sexy! She knew it, and flaunted it.

Oh, well, another story for another day. Mary hummed as she cleared her desk area and prepared to go to St. Williams. *Where is my rosary? Ah, there it is...on the nightstand. I must hurry and help Mickie O'Brien with the candles.*

CHAPTER 33

Love and Sorrow

Mary sorted through the family pictures she kept nearby to help spark, her memory. *Where is Lucing's wedding picture?* While searching, she found Natividad's, taken just before she married her second husband. *Oh, I forgot that Consueling, Lucing, and Nati married within months of each other. Yes, I was still receiving correspondence from Mr. Farnsworth from Kansas. I always answered his letters, but as World War I dragged on, I received only magazines containing current events and casualty lists, as well as news of the flu epidemic. Before long, the magazines stopped coming. I wrote, but my letter was returned..."Address Unknown."*

Nati was busy with her piecework from Mrs. Fuller's factory, her alterations from I. Beck, and being a companion to Annie, Luis Mazur's younger sister. Luis took more time to chat with Nati when he brought garments from I. Beck's to be altered, and when he collected them for return to the store. His sister's six-month visit in the Philippines would end in another week and he was desperately searching for a way to keep in touch with Nati after Annie returned to her boarding school in Spain. As the Fates would have it, the manager at I. Beck's decided it would be better for alterations to be completed at the store. He asked Luis to inquire if the widow Bores y Gamero would be interested in working at the store instead of altering the garments at her home. She would be offered more pay since the hours would be longer. Luis was excited as he explained the job offer to Nati. He was hoping against hope she would accept. Perhaps they could take the same carriage to work?

 Nati gave the job offer serious consideration, and, after discussing it with her sisters and *Mami,* she decided to accept. Luis tried to hide his elation and was anxious to inform the department manager about her decision. *Sra. Natividad Gamero Vda. de Bores will begin working at the store next week.*

 It took little time for the magic to work during the daily carriage rides to and from work. Luis was in love with Nati, and she thought she cared for him. His conversations were always questions about her and those around her. He hungered to learn all about her. Nati attributed this to Luis being lonely, as his sister, Annie, had returned to her boarding school in Spain in March following the long winter break. *Soon our family will be together enjoying their Easter holidays. Luis can meet them and not be lonely.*

The second floor of Doña Carito's apartment house filled with joyful noises as the Gamero family members returned home for their holiday. Pacita Valle, Don José's first grandchild, taught piano at Santa Isabel, where Pilar and I boarded, and was our piano teacher. She laughed as she corrected us, for we were her aunts, although we were much younger. She asked Nati if she might spend her vacation with her and the Gameros. She lived full-time at Santa Isabel and had no opportunities to leave unless she visited us. We were her only remaining family members. Nati did not refuse. She was more like Pacita's older sister than an aunt. Pacita was eight years younger than Nati.

When Pacita met Luis, she became infatuated with him, but he only had eyes for Nati. Pacita saw how much he cared for Nati, so she never told anyone until later.

Following Lucing's wedding, Nati told our mother she would be moving from the building to an apartment on San Marcelino Street. Since she and Luis were engaged, Luis offered to pay for her rent in the same building where he lived. They needed more privacy and time to prepare for their upcoming wedding. Rosario would stay with her on her weekends away from Antipolo.

Rosario and *Mami* were not happy Nati would be living in quarters paid for by her fiancé and would also be in the same building. Rosario was in Antipolo every week caring for her brother, Fr. Gamero. Nati would be alone in that apartment. She would be alone with Luis. Rosario bristled and later confronted Nati.

Seeing Rosario was visibly upset by the news, Nati confessed.

"Rosario, I have a secret which I must keep from *Mami* and the family. I am already married to Luis. Since Luis is not a Catholic and refuses Catholic instruction, we cannot be married in our church. We consulted Judge Manuel Camus, who performed the wedding ceremony at his office," Nati explained.

Rosario was appalled! The family would be crushed! What a terrible blow to her brother and sisters, who were all serving the church.

Two months afterward, Rosario decided she had to tell someone. Nati's secret burned inside Rosario's mind like a hot coal. She was distressed and irritated with Nati for making her promise not to tell. She would no longer stay with Nati and Luis on weekends. They were "living in sin" in the eyes of the Roman Catholic Church. She needed to see her family on weekends, but had nowhere to stay. She would have to tell *Mami*. It was wrong to keep this secret from her.

The next weekend, Rosario visited *Mami* and asked to stay with her for the weekend.

"Why aren't you staying with Nati? *Mami* asked and as she did, she noticed Rosario's gloomy facial expression. "What has happened? Have you and Nati quarreled?"

Rosario bowed her head and Nati's secret spewed forth like a fiery volcanic eruption. She was so shaken she hardly knew what she had done. She reached out to give *Mami* a hug, but *Mami* did not respond. She was like a statue...horror and disbelief carved into her face. *Mami* spoke quietly.

"We must tell Lola Lala. She is Nati's aunt and the oldest and wisest family member," *Mami* said without ever changing her facial expression.

At Pascuala's apartment, they poured Nati's secret out like a hot beverage into a delicate teacup, slowly and carefully. Pascuala listened in disbelief. She was visibly upset and insisted *Mami* accompany her to confront Nati while Luis was at work.

Nati was surprised to see *Mami* and Lola Lala at her door.

"Come in, come in," she uttered as she opened the door wider.

The older ladies marched in like troops ready to do battle. Their faces were grim with no smile in sight. Nati steeled herself for a confrontation.

"What brings you here for this surprise visit?" Nati probed, feeling a gnawing fear growing inside her.

"What have you done?" Pascuala spouted, "You must have this marriage annulled immediately. Our church does not recognize it and to continue to live in sin would humiliate your brother and your sisters who have dedicated their lives to the church. Your mother and father would be horrified! God rest their souls."

Nati bristled. She disliked being disrespectful to her elders, but Luis was a Russian Jew and would never convert.

"I will not have our marriage annulled. I love Luis. We have been married by Judge Camus and are legally married. We cannot be living in sin," Nati said stiffly.

Mami and Pascuala rose to leave, stopping at the door to deliver an ultimatum.

"Nati, you are no longer welcome in our homes until you see the mistake you have made. You must have this marriage annulled. You have brought shame on our family," Pascuala spoke with her head held high...her chin lifted.

During Christmas vacation, all the younger children were home from school and enjoying their holidays. Nati and Luis knocked on our door. *Mami* would not allow them to enter.

"But Maria is my godchild. I have brought her a present," Nati insisted.

"She can come out to your *calesa* to get her gift. I will send her out shortly," *Mami* affirmed. "Do not come here again...not even to see your godchild."

I ran all the way down the stairs and to their horse-drawn rig where they were waiting. I was afraid. *Mami* had told me I must never see Nati again. I cried as she greeted me. She gave me a hug and handed me a beautifully gift-wrapped box.

"Open it, *Nena*," she said. "You will like it. I bought it for you, my godchild."

With fingers trembling and tears still flowing down my cheeks, I opened the gift. It was a special dress from I. Beck's. I had always worn homemade clothing, so this gift was truly special. I thanked her and, after giving her a hug and kiss, stepped away from the *calesa*, waving as they drove away. *Mami* was watching from the second floor window.

※
A tear slid down Mary's cheek as she thought of Nati. *I slipped away one day to see Nati, but she was not home. On my way home, Mami and Lola Lala drove by in their calesa and saw me. I never left home again without permission. To do so would result in a whipping. I remember Mami's face. She meant every word. I never saw Nati again.*
※

Maria de la Natividad Gamero, Vda. de Bores, and Luis Mazur were married less than one year when Nati, who was with child, lost her baby and became yet another statistic of the 1918 flu epidemic along with our niece, Pacita Valle. Pacita would be playing the piano for the family's heavenly band, but according to the Roman Catholic Church, Nati and her baby were banned, for she had married outside the Catholic faith.

CHAPTER 34

The Killer Flu

From October 1918, and for months to follow, the flu epidemic raged throughout the islands like a huge typhoon…tearing families apart and washing away hundreds into a crevasse of despair. Like a force of nature, the killer flu spread death and devastation across the Philippines. All schools were closed. Every hospital was filled with those seeking treatment, but for many, the treatment was either insufficient or late. Hospital hallways were filled with the dead and dying. Most victims perished within three weeks or less following the onset of flu symptoms.

We were sent home from our boarding schools. Windows stayed closed for fear the air would carry the deadly disease. We stayed inside our crowded quarters and prayed no one else in our family would become ill. We saw what the flu had done to poor Nati, her baby, and Pacita, only in her twenties.

Mami was thankful *Pépe's* church at Antipolo sent him to Rome for six months to visit The Holy Father and discuss his plans for opening a new parochial school in Antipolo. Fr. Gamero was charged with persuading The Pope and his Cardinals that a school was necessary and would need financing from The Vatican. She was also glad Lucing and her husband Francisco were in Hong Kong on business for El Zenith's Jewelry Store. The buying trip would keep them away for five months, and, perhaps, they would be spared this flu epidemic.

Mami was concerned about Consueling and Juanito in Bulan. Consueling was pregnant, and, if she contracted the flu, it would be an immediate death sentence for her and her baby. She prayed they would be spared.

Her cousin, Rita and her husband, Charles Swanson, had separated. Charles had custody of their daughter, Aurora, and needed a place for her to stay. All the boarding schools were closed. Their son, Arturo, was staying with his mother, Rita, since Arturo was too young to attend school. Charles was beside himself. He knew only one person to entrust with the care of Aurora, so he called on *Mami*.

"Doña Luz, your quarters are crowded with your own children since the schools are closed, but I need somewhere for Aurora to stay until this deadly flu passes and the schools open once again," Charles posed. "I will pay well for her room and board."

Mami thought about his request. He sounded desperate. She also knew extra money would be helpful at this time. Charles Swanson was an American businessman with several successful business ventures in Manila and the provinces. He would pay well.

"Charles," she replied, "You are a dependable man. The problems you and Rita have are yours to solve, not mine. I will help you only because we can also use the money. I left my last job as housekeeper for *El Barbudo* because he wanted more than a housekeeper. His advances were disgusting. Aurora can stay with us. We will make room for her. She will be close to Rita, and must be allowed to visit her mother. A daughter should never be separated from her mother. God would not approve."

Charles thanked her effusively, agreed to her terms, and prepared to bring Aurora's luggage into the Gamero's living quarters. Charles would remember her generosity far into the future.

Mary remembered every detail. *Pilar, Lorenzo, and I were glad to have a new face in the house. We were indoors for so long, due to the flu; it felt as if we were in quarantine again. Aurora brought in a breath of fresh air...outside news...new games...fancy ideas...and welcome conversation at the dinner table.*

CHAPTER 35

Return from Rome

By January 1919, the flu epidemic waned and limped away as it stepped over the damage it left behind. Schools were in session. We felt as if we were released from our "cells" and were now free to play outside. We visited friends and classmates without fearing the killer flu.

Rosario (Charing) lived with *Tía* Hermiñia since Herminia lost her husband, Luis, to the flu. Rosario felt she should not stay at Antipolo while her brother was in Rome. Her aunt, Herminia, wanted help during those trying times and Rosario needed a place to stay, as the Gamero house was filled with children during the epidemic.

The children returned to boarding school. Charing felt she should spend more time with *Mami* before returning to Antipolo to prepare for her brother's return from Rome. She was surprised to learn that Pilar, who was fifteen, was keeping company with a young medical student, Dr. Juanito Goitia. Since he was Spanish, he received *Mami's* approval. In order to have a proper courtship, the Gameros needed larger living quarters. A parlor was needed for Dr. Goitia's visits during school holidays. Another room was necessary for Charing's weekend visits. *Mami* felt Dr. Goitia would be the perfect match for Pilar, since she had expensive taste. She would allow Pilar and Juanito's courtship. *We would have a doctor in the family!* Perhaps.

Doña Encarmita owned a large apartment house across the street from the Gamero's present living quarters, and had an apartment, which was perfect for them. Additionally, Doña Encarmita had an American tenant, Mr. John Duncan, a widower with two children. He lost his wife during the flu epidemic and needed someone to care for his young children plus do light housekeeping. His job at the U.S. Government offices kept him busy working long hours on occasion.

"You would be perfect for this job, Doña Luz!" Doña Encarmita exclaimed. "Mr. Duncan has two children, a girl, Jeannie, who is about five and a boy, Johnny, who is two. By living in this building, you would not even have to leave the building to work. Mr. Duncan will pay well, for he desperately needs help."

After prayerful thought, *Mami* agreed and arrangements were made. We had better living quarters and *Mami* had a job as housekeeper/nanny for the two young children. Jeannie was so cute with her chubby round face, pink cheeks, blonde hair and blue eyes. Johnny looked like a cherub painted by Gainsborough. *Mami* thanked God for her blessings and Mr. Duncan gave thanks for our *Mami*.

Fr. Gamero returned from his successful trip to Rome and began work on the new parochial school. Father Fernandez, a Filipino priest, was in charge of the parish during his absence. There was much to do to get the school ready for the coming year. May had arrived and the fiesta for the Virgin of Antipolo, known as Our Lady of Peace and Good Voyage, was beginning. Construction would have to wait until those festivities ended, for his parish was deeply involved in the celebration.

Fr. Gamero asked Father Fernandez to remain until the fiesta for the Virgin of Antipolo closed, then he could return to Manila. The Filipino priest was disturbed…many native parishioners wanted him to stay. Native parishioners threatened to kill Fr. Gamero. Their attitude puzzled our brother. What happened in the short six months while he was in Rome? He hired a watchman as security to guard against the possible threats to his life. He questioned his faithful chauffeur, Diego. At first, Diego remained silent, but when told about the threat on Fr. Gamero's life, he fell to his knees and confessed.

"Father Fernandez was using the rectory as a place to let his friends gamble! They threatened to kill me if I told anyone! You must protect me!" Diego shook while the words tumbled over each other as they rushed from his mouth.

"Have no fear, Diego, for God is on our side," Fr. Gamero said soothingly as he helped Diego to his feet. "We shall address this matter immediately."

Father Fernandez was confronted and confessed his sins. He was banished from the church at Antipolo and returned to Manila to face the Diocese. They would decide his punishment. Father Fernandez's friends were furious. They plotted revenge.

Besides his car, Fr. Gamero owned an exquisite white horse. The steed was used to pull his buggy when he visited parishioners living in areas where his car could not travel. A caretaker, who also served as groundskeeper, was responsible for the spirited steed and buggy.

Late one evening, the security guard alerted Fr. Gamero. Men's voices drifted from behind the convent, where a deep, narrow, underground cistern…the convent's water supply, was located. He and the guard crept around the building and discovered, to their dismay, his white horse had been shoved backwards into the deep water and was struggling and snorting. Rescuing the poor animal without help was impossible, so they ran to the constable's office to get help, but their pleas fell on deaf ears, as those men were Father Fernandez's friends.

"The horse probably fell inside the cistern. Nobody would push a horse into that narrow opening," one man jeered.

"Explain how the horse entered the cistern "rear first" rather than "head first?" Fr. Gamero countered.

"Stranger things have happened," was the reply.

No help came from the constable's office. Fr. Gamero, Diego, and the security guard tried valiantly to extricate the horse from the cistern, but it was deep and narrow. The decision was made to shoot the steed to end its suffering.

The growing resentment of the native parishioners against Fr. Gamero was quelled when the tragic news of the handsome steed spread across the parish. Many were chagrined to learn about the gambling, which Father Fernandez allowed to take place in the rectory in Fr. Gamero's absence. Taking their revenge out on an innocent animal was a cowardly deed. Six months passed before the cowards were exposed. They left the parish of Antipolo in shame.

As a result, the parochial school was late in its completion, but was a huge success. The initial building was an elementary campus, which became the pride of the natives. Classes were taught in *Tagalog,* the main native dialect, and Spanish. The school building was also used to host plays, native celebrations, and pageants. All was for the glory of God and the Roman Catholic Church.

Mary recalled *Pépe*'s face when he told *Mami* and the family what had happened. *I will never forget his sad expression.*

CHAPTER 36

Pilar's Philandering Physician

During vacation, Pilar's boyfriend, Dr. Juanito Goitia, visited her often. Since he was Spanish, he was quite the romantic, however, Pilar was not impressed with him. She was beautiful, and she knew it. Her soft curly blonde hair framed her face and caressed her creamy cherub-like complexion. When she smiled, two most adorable dimples decorated her cheeks and her crystal blue eyes twinkled with merriment. She was always turning heads when in public, which made her smile and her eyes twinkle…adding more charm and charisma to her demeanor. At sixteen, she was in command.

We spent our vacation at our aunt's beach house in Pasay. Our mother was working, so we were invited to the beach and would be supervised by *Tia* Hermiñia.

During the first week, a pimple appeared on Pilar's face, near her nose. She wanted to get rid of the pimple, so she squeezed it, covered it with powder, and forgot about it as we all ran to the lovely beach to enjoy the sea. We were enjoying ourselves splashing, swimming, and playing with our friends. No one noticed Pilar's face was swelling. A reddish tinge spread across her face. She became frightened when her eyelids began to swell shut.

We were taken home immediately and *Mami* called Dr. Goitia for advice. After he arrived and examined Pilar's face, she was rushed to the hospital. She was treated and Dr. Goitia brought Pilar home. The seawater had irritated the pimple. An allergic reaction caused her face to swell. Two weeks passed before her face returned to its normal size. Dr. Goitia tended to Pilar daily and showered her with gifts and flowers.

Our vacation was ruined. It was time to return to school. Visiting days were on Thursdays and Sundays. Dr. Goitia visited each time and our mother served as *dueña*. No young men could visit without an adult chaperone being present. Pilar was flattered, but still did not encourage the young doctor. She enjoyed flirting.

Lucing gave birth to her second child, Antonio (Tony). They needed more living space, so a second floor apartment in Santa Mesa was rented. Since they had an extra bedroom, Lola Lala moved in to help Lucing with the new baby.

It was vacation time again and Lucing and Frank were leaving for another buying trip to Hong Kong for El Zenith's. Since Lola Lala was charged with the care of Francisco Jr. and Antonio (Tony), she asked our mother if Pilar and I could stay with her, as she needed help. Pilar was seventeen and I was two years younger. We were old enough to be helpful and responsible. I was excited about being treated as an adult. Pilar chose to stay with *Mami*. She was still keeping Dr. Goitia dangling like a puppet on a string, and he did not seem to mind.

Lola Lala ruled the roost. I did what she asked in her prescribed manner. She was strict, but also quite entertaining. I learned much about caring for a home and children under her tutelage.

While busy with my duties with Lola Lala, Dr. Goitia made a surprise announcement. He would be leaving for Mexico to complete his internship in medicine, but he wanted to ensure Pilar would be waiting for his return from Mexico. He gave her the most exquisite engagement ring, which took Pilar's breath away. She was so surprised and, although she was not in love with him, agreed to accept his ring and wait for his return. *Mami* was pleased. She smiled like the Cheshire cat. *It was worth the extra effort to have larger quarters so this young doctor would have a suitable place to court Pilar.*

With Dr. Goitia away in Mexico, Pilar concentrated on completing her last year at school. She wanted to get this year behind her, and plan her future as the doctor's wife. *I will be wealthy. I will buy all new clothes. I will live in a large house. I will have many servants. I…I…I…*Her thoughts were a reflection of her wishes.

Letters arrived from Dr. Goitia often. They were mailed to our mother, as the school censored any mail received by students. *Mami* felt his letters should be seen only by Pilar. Each Sunday she would visit us and bring the letters to Pilar. She did not reply because he would be moving around to different places and the mail would probably not reach him.

A family acquaintance visited our mother about five months after Dr. Goitia's departure. She learned he was involved with another woman in Mexico. This woman was pregnant with his child. *Mami* was upset, but was silent. She wanted to investigate the matter further before repeating any rumors to her daughter. The letters from Mexico continued to arrive and were delivered, as usual, to Pilar.

Before long, *Mami* decided to pay a visit to Dr. Goitia's mother, Doña Sofia, and quell the rumors. Doña Sofia was astonished to see Doña Luz on her doorstep. She was rather haughty and not accustomed to having callers who did not present their calling cards first.

"Doña Luz, what a surprise! What brings you to my home this afternoon?" queried Doña Sofia. "Come in, come in, please."

Mami entered their spacious *sala* and waited for Doña Sofia to invite her to sit.

"I am busy, so I cannot ask you to stay for *merienda*. " Doña Sofia said icily.

"I will come straight to the point," *Mami* spoke briskly. "Since my daughter, Pilar, and your son are engaged, I need to verify if rumors about his escapades in Mexico are true. Is he seeing another woman? Is she carrying his child?"

Doña Sofia paled, reached for the back of a chair and bowed her head as she spoke, "Yes, Doña Luz, I am afraid they are true. He does not love this woman as he loves Pilar. Young men stray when they are away from home."

Mami reached the door and stopped. Anger was in her voice as she spoke. "Pilar will be told. The engagement is broken. Your son must never come to see her again. It will not be allowed. Any letters sent from him will be thrown away."

Mary recalled Pilar was more upset about returning the engagement ring than she was in losing her doctor. Christmas vacation was different that year. *Mami* was in no mood to celebrate.

CHAPTER 37

Pilar Rebels

The Manila Tribune touted a new vaudeville show playing at The Savoy during the Christmas holidays. Everyone who was anyone would attend. Our sister Lucing and her husband Francisco recently returned from Hong Kong and were ready to celebrate with us. Francisco bought tickets for the new show and would take us the day after Christmas. This special holiday extravaganza, which everyone wanted to see, included magicians, comedians, singing troubadours, and noted Filipino radio celebrities. We were excited about seeing this extravaganza, but also because Francisco and Lucing brought many fine and exotic presents from Hong Kong. We would have to wait for the Day of The Three Kings to receive our gifts.

The show was spectacular! With so many different acts, we laughed, cried, and clapped until our hands hurt. Francisco announced another surprise. Arrangements were made for us to go backstage and meet the entertainers. We were so excited!

"Follow me," Francisco ordered, as he guided us toward the stage. "Be careful. We cannot stay long. The troupe has to prepare for another show tomorrow night."

We followed dutifully and excitedly. We had never met professional entertainers before, so this was a new experience.

After meeting the entertainers, we said our "thanks," wished them a "Merry Christmas," and floated on air on our way home. We were strolling and chatting about the show when I missed Pilar. As I turned to look, I noticed an entertainer walking beside Pilar at least one block behind us. I walked toward them, raised my eyebrows, and shook my head in a disapproving manner.

"*Nena,*" Pilar said, "I want you to meet Manuel Infante. He is the one you thought was so funny."

Manuel, a thin, tall person with dark hair and dark piercing eyes, flashed a charming smile.

"With your permission, I will walk with you to your home," Manuel said pleasantly.

(left to right) Maria del Pilar Gamero y Cucullu (Pilachu), Maria del Rosario Gamero y Boix (Charing), and Pascuala Rocha y Boix (Lola Lala)—sister of Josepha Boix, second wife of José Ma. Gamero y Porras. Pascuala married José Rocha, brother of Don José's third wife, Rosario Rocha.

I stared at his face and wondered what *Mami* would say, but I already knew. She told us many times "vaudeville people" were not respectable people. Manuel was not a decent man in her eyes.

As we approached our apartment building, Pilar warned me with her eyes to not tell our mother. I tiptoed to our second floor apartment, but Pilar stayed behind. She remained on the doorstep chatting with Manuel. I waited. When she did not come upstairs, I tiptoed downstairs to check on her.

"Go away!" Pilar spouted as I motioned for her to come upstairs. "I will come in when I am through talking with Manuel."

Manuel was holding her hand, chatting, and making her laugh with his clever witticisms. She was mesmerized.

"Pilachu, you must come or *Mami* will be wondering where you are," I said hoarsely.

There was no reply...just Pilar and Manuel's laughter.

Sadly, I returned and *Mami* met me at the door.

"Where is your sister?" *Mami* asked with arms folded across her chest.

"She is talking with a comedian from the vaudeville show," I replied knowing what the result would be.

She shot down those stairs like a bullet being fired from a pistol. Within seconds, Pilar was running upstairs, tears streaming down her face, with our mother closely behind. Pilar was holding her hand to her cheek for she had been slapped by our mother.

The next day, Pilar gazed out her window. Manuel was waiting at the corner.

Our cousins arrived for a visit and we were all in the *sala* singing Christmas songs as I played the piano. Pilar slipped out the door, unnoticed, to meet Manuel. After we finished our caroling, *Mami* went to the kitchen and prepared special *tapas* for the holiday celebration. Pilar and I were to serve our guests.

"Where is Pilar?" I asked my cousin, Aurora.

"She left while we were singing. Was she meeting someone?" Aurora responded.

I shuddered and imagined horrible things happening to Pilar. *Was she safe?*

"I'll check to see if she is outside getting fresh air," I told Aurora as I slipped out the apartment door to find Pilar.

I searched beyond the doorstep. Pilar and Manuel were huddled together chatting and laughing.

"Pilar, you must come inside or I will tell our mother," I threatened. "Our guests are waiting to be served."

"No, no, please," Pilar begged as she rushed toward me. "Please don't tell *Mami*."

As she spoke, our mother appeared in the doorway. The "look" on her face would have killed an elephant at ten paces. She did not have to utter a word. Pilar rushed past her in fear she would be slapped again. *Mami* walked behind her. As I reached the doorway, Manuel was running toward The Savoy.

Mary laughed as she recalled the many times the "look" crossed her mother's face. Words were not necessary. The "look" conveyed a strong message. She tried the "look" on her children. *I wonder if it is genetic? It must be, because it worked.*

Mary put away her writing materials for the weekend, as she was helping Mary Ann Bracken and Audrey Eichner with the church rummage sale all day tomorrow. She would start anew on Monday.

CHAPTER 38

The Teen Years

An elaborate hand-written invitation was delivered by a uniformed coachman to the Gamero's apartment. Their neighbors, Mr. and Mrs. Ramon Ortigas, a successful attorney in Manila and his wife, Lucita, were hosting another exciting New Year's Eve party. *What better way to celebrate a new year than with a splendid party?* Our family was excited to be invited. On the invitation, Lucita requested that I play the piano and, with my sisters, lead the group in singing to welcome the New Year. Lucita admired my high soprano voice. I was thrilled! My mother responded that I would be happy to help usher in 1920.

The Ortigas, "upper crust" of Manila society, invited only the finest Spanish families in Manila and *Intramuros*. Our aunt, Carmen Cucullu, had recently married Captain Carlos Camus, and they would attend. His brother, Judge Manuel Camus, was married to Matilde, sister to Lucita Ortigas…so, they would join the festivities. I became nervous about performing for those important people, but *Mami* assured me all would go well. They were all friends and would be appreciative of my efforts.

New Year's Eve, 1919, was spectacular. My new dress, for this special performance, was made from yards of shiny green taffeta. The fitted bodice, with long, tapered sleeves, accentuated my small waist. The tiny mother-of-pearl buttons trailed down its front in orderly fashion, surrounded by a ruche of white Spanish lace. The full gathered skirt fell to mid-calf, showing my white silk stockings embroidered with tiny flowers near my slender ankles.

The Ortigas' home was specially decorated for the festive event with fresh flowers in ornate vases adorning each serving table and tall tapers cradled in silver candlesticks acting as sentinels beside each vase. Guests, dressed in the latest fashion, mingled and chattered while sipping on tiny crystal glasses filled with Spanish sherry. Platters of *tapas* and rich pastries were judiciously placed inviting guests to select a delicacy or two. Six uniformed servants carried platters with assorted hot *tapas*. Two servants collected empty glasses and replenished the delicate glasses. Everyone was in a festive mood as the midnight hour approached.

Promptly at 11:00 p.m., Mr. Ortigas asked me to gather the young girls around the piano.

"When you get all the singers together, go ahead and begin playing. The sound of your music will alert the guests to prepare for the approaching New Year," Mr. Ortigas said.

I signaled to those who were helping with the singing. They approached and gathered around the piano. As I settled myself onto the piano bench, the guests noticed and became quiet. *God, please help me be calm so I do not make mistakes.* This silent plea was uttered as I struck the opening chords of *"O, Solo Mio."* The adults listened quietly at first, then joined in lustily on the chorus. I hurried into *Torna Sorrento.* My uncle, Carlos Camus, asked his son, Perico, to sing *Vivo Para Amarte* with me. Following our duet, *Vagamundo* was requested. Everyone joined the singing. Luisito Cucullu, another cousin, sat beside me on the piano bench.

"Maria," he whispered, "it is time to welcome in the New Year."

Precisely at 11:58 p.m., I began playing *Himno Nacional,* the Spanish national anthem. Everyone joined in the singing with glasses held high. As the tall grandfather clock chimed the midnight hour, hugs, kisses, and well wishes for the coming year rippled across the room like waves lapping at a sandy shore. I stared at Perico standing by my side. He had kissed me on the cheek while everyone was busy celebrating!

We only had five days to wait before opening our gifts. As is the Spanish custom, presents are shared on *El Dia de Los Tres Reyes Magos,* the day of The Magi or Three Kings, on January 6. We gave thanks for our many blessings as we attended church together. As I nestled in my bed, I drifted to sleep wondering what it would have been like to have our father with us for these celebrations. *Would he have been proud of the way I played the piano? I prayed he would.*

A whole year rushed by like a typhoon…blowing the months away so swiftly. I would complete my education at Real Colegio de Santa Isabel. Pilar was already through and was helping *Mami* at home. She had not decided what she wanted to do next, but I had. I would go to business school and become a secretary. In the meantime, I wanted time for fun and a social life before ending my stay at boarding school. Lucing and Francisco made sure to include Pilar and me in their outings. We were always ready to attend dances at their dance clubs. I discovered I liked to dance and did well at ballroom dancing. Before long, the young men at the dance clubs sought Francisco and Lucing's permission to dance with us. *Why didn't someone tell me how much fun dancing would be?*

During our next vacation from school, our aunt, Carmen Camus, rented a beach house at Pasay near the Ortigas' beach house. She invited Pilar and me to stay, as her daughters, Carolina and Mercedes, were about our ages and would enjoy our company. Her son, Perico, would be there also. Perico was handsome and popular with the girls. He was two years older than I and attended LaSalle College in Manila. We were delighted to be included.

Our first day at Pasay was exciting. We readied for the beach and rushed to play in the water. As we were wading and allowing the gentle waves to lap around our legs, Perico called to a friend who was walking toward us. They greeted each other. Perico introduced us to his college classmate, who lived nearby.

"Maria, I want to introduce my friend and classmate, Louie Lewinson. His family emigrated from Germany. I was in awe. Louie was so tall, with blond wavy hair, steel blue eyes, a charming smile, and a well-muscled body. I mumbled something unintelligible and stared.

"I built a small boat for two which I brought today if anyone would care to go sailing," Louie grinned as he spoke.

I asked for a boat ride. *Was that my voice? I could hardly swim!*

"I am an excellent swimmer," replied Louie. "The boat is down this way."

My quick response did not go unnoticed by Perico. As Louie and I ran toward his boat, Perico chanted a song in Spanish to tease me about going with Louie. *"Y alli viene la banca, la banca, y ali untitos los dos, gracias a Dios, y una Linda chulapa y remando Lewinson!"* I was mad at Perico. *What would Louie think?*

We spent two delightful months laughing, playing, swimming, and enjoying each other's company at the beach. It was time to go home and return to school. *Mami* came for the weekend to help us pack. We had one last day at the beach.

While we were playing and splashing in the shallow water, a motor launch with several young Spanish acquaintances stopped beside us. They invited us to go for a boat ride before the day's end. *Mami, Tia* Carmen and Mrs. Ortigas watched us from the long beachfront porch. I was not a swimmer, so I did not want to go. They had a long, thick rope hanging from the side and told me to hang on and let go when I became tired.

"Come on, Maria," urged Louie. "I will hold on to you.."

I agreed to go, if he were by my side. That was a mistake.

I held on tightly. Louie held onto the rope with his left hand, while his right arm encircled my waist. The launch eased ahead gently at first, then lurched forward, as if a madman had taken over the controls. The boat sped toward the deeper water…increasing its speed, and I panicked. I screamed only to have seawater splash into my open mouth and choke me.

"Release the rope, Maria," Louie commanded. "I will help you swim to shore."

When I let go and floated beside him, the shore seemed miles away. I began sobbing. Louie did his best to be calm and encouraged me to swim. When I tired, he would swim on his back and pull me through the water. I thought we would never reach land.

Once on the beach, I lay still to catch my breath. When I rolled over, *Mami* was standing above me…her arms across her chest and the "look" on her stoic face. I knew what it meant.

~~~

My goodness! I shall never forget my boat ride. It was my "puppy love" for Louie that caused me to be so foolish. I wonder what ever happened to Louie?

Mary covered her writing materials and prepared to attend the church Chili Supper and Bingo Night. *Maybe I will win the prize tonight!*

CHAPTER 39

Graduation and Change

In December 1921, my long-awaited graduation day arrived. Our graduating class members wore white dresses with matching white accessories. The Sisters of Charity provided each of us an eighteen-inch square of white Spanish lace to wear on our heads for the church service, as all Catholic females must have their heads covered for any religious service. The day was one of mixed emotions. We were anxious to graduate, but we knew graduation meant we would no longer see our classmates daily. At age sixteen, I was on the bridge to adulthood. We would no longer be carefree, young girls. We must either continue our education or find employment.

Thankfully, I received a scholarship to attend the Cosmopolitan Business College near the Santa Cruz Bridge in Manila. John Danon, cousin Perico's American friend, was already a student at Cosmopolitan. Perico introduced me to John during our last vacation at the beach. I was pleased to know someone already attending college to show me around. John lived nearby and offered to provide transportation to Cosmopolitan, once I was enrolled. My venture into higher education was launched.

Change was in the air. Change…change was everywhere. The Roman Catholic churches all over the world were mourning the death of Pope Benedict XV in Rome. The cardinal dean verified the pope's death by touching the pope's forehead three times with a silver mallet and calling the pope by his baptismal name. My brother, Fr. José Gamero, explained the process. The conclave of the Sacred College would meet in the Sistine Chapel between the thirteenth and eighteenth day after the pope's death to select a new pope, but the news was "leaked" from The Vatican.

A new pope was named. In early 1922, Cardinal Achille Ratti was heralded by the Cardinals, who had elected him during their meeting of the Sacred College, as Pope Pius XI and visionary of the future. The church's work would thrive under the Holy Father's guidance.

In order to continue my studies, I found part time employment at our church helping the nuns prepare the linens used during mass, and only attended evening classes. John attended evening classes also. Our schedules allowed me to ride with him at four-thirty each afternoon and take the streetcar home at seven-thirty in the evenings. I was enrolled for a seven-month course in shorthand and typing. By mid-May 1922, I had completed five months of business school when Lucing's husband, Francisco, told me about an excellent employment opportunity. His uncle, Arturo Silva, was manager of the jewelry department at The American Bazaar, formerly known as I. Beck's Department Store. They needed a sales clerk they could trust with the sale of loose diamonds and fine jewelry. Since I was his sister-in-law, he felt he could recommend me for the job and would have his uncle arrange an interview for me with his boss, Mr. Robert Thomas. Money was scarce and I felt it was my turn to help fill the family coffers.

Francisco suggested I dress more conservatively, wear my hair in a bun, and wear high heels…due to my youthful appearance. He told his uncle, Mr. Arturo Silva, and Mr. Robert Thomas, general manager at The American Bazaar, I was eighteen. I was sixteen and needed to appear older.

My nerves were jangled and my palms perspired. Before I left home for the interview, I asked *Mami* to pray that my interview might go well. She promised to pray to St. Anthony.

Mr. Robert Thomas was rather short, bald-headed, and had a large stomach, which hung over his tight belt like an overstuffed pillow. He had a round face and a pleasant smile. Although he was pleasant, I was uncomfortable. I kept shifting my handkerchief from one hand to the other. Since he was an American and only spoke English, I listened to his questions and responded hesitantly in my broken English. *I wish I had worked harder to speak English correctly. I could read it and write it quite well, but my Spanish accent colored its pronunciation.*

"Mr. Silva says you are eighteen years old," Mr. Thomas stated.

I waited without speaking. Francisco's lie to his uncle about my age hung in mid-air. Mr. Thomas must have taken my silence as agreement with his statement.

"Since Mr. Silva is the one who has recommended you for this position, and since he will be your boss, it will be okay with me to employ you for the jewelry department," Mr. Thomas concluded.

I was elated and smiled broadly. *I did it! I have a job!*

"Thank you, Mr. Thomas. You will not regret your decision. I shall work hard to meet the requirements for The American Bazaar," I said as I continued to smile.

I left his office to tell Mr. Silva my news.

"*Bueno, Maria,*" he said. "You can begin working right away. I will have your paperwork ready and you can report in the morning at seven-thirty. Your lunch break will be from noon until two, and the store will close at seven-thirty at night."

At the streetcar station, I bought a monthly streetcar ticket booklet, discounted for working people, and rode the streetcar home. I was glad to have a job to help my family with expenses, but sad I no longer enjoyed a leisurely lifestyle. No more walks on the beach with Louie.

The next morning, my sister, Pilar, and cousin, Aurora, were leaving for vacation days at the beach at Pasay. I would not be joining them this week, or maybe ever again.

"Pilar, please tell Louie why I'm not swimming with you and Aurora," I begged. "Tell him where I am working."

Pilar agreed. She and Aurora grabbed their luggage and laughed all the way down the stairway to meet our aunt. My regretful sigh followed them out the front door like wispy smoke. *I have probably lost Louie.*

Louie did come by the store a week later to tell me he missed me. I was glad to see him, but felt uncomfortable talking with him at the store. Spending time conversing with friends while working was strictly forbidden, unless they were customers, which Louie was not.

"You will be at the university, Louie. We can meet on Sundays at the beach," I whispered.

Absence makes the heart grow fonder…for someone else, thought Mary as she put her writing materials away. Mass would start in thirty minutes. She must be early to light her candles.

Mary thought about the many pontiffs who led the church during her lifetime. She liked Pope Pius XI the best, perhaps because she met him when he visited her brother's church at Antipolo. He had blessed her Saint Anthony statue, her patron saint. Her prayers to St. Anthony were usually answered. She had many religious icons, but she treasured St. Anthony the most. Msgr, McCallum called on her many times to pray to St. Anthony in his behalf, as had many parishioners at St. Williams.

When Mary arrived at church, Cynthia Beacom was placing lovely flower arrangements near the altar. Mickie O'Brien finished preparing the candles. Mary Jackson helped her prepare for the service. *Where is Mike Rivera? He said he would be here tonight. I brought the lyrics to songs I sang at Santa Isabel. I wanted him to learn how to play them on his guitar. I hope he can, so I can sing them once more.*

CHAPTER 40

Dealing with Change

Going to work daily consumed my life. My small amount of social life was connected to work. Remedios Navarro, the cashier at the jewelry department, who was about one year older, became my friend. At closing time, I waited for Remedios to balance the accounts before taking the streetcar together each evening. My social life consisted of chatting with her on the streetcar.

About two months after I was employed, a sign "Apartment for Rent" appeared in the window of the drugstore across the street from The American Bazaar. During my lunch hour, I made inquiries. Fate stepped in. The owner was a former neighbor who delighted in the prospect of our family as her tenants. The apartment had two-bedrooms, a large living room, dining room, kitchen and large bath. The rent was reasonable. Being close to work would save streetcar fare. I was anxious to tell *Mami* about my discovery.

The apartment suited our family just fine. Aunt Pascuala (Lola Lala) selected the smaller bedroom, which accommodated two beds. Rosario could use the second bed in Pascuala's room when she visited on weekends. Our mother, Pilar, and I would share the other large bedroom. My younger brother, Lorenzo, would sleep on the living room sofa when home from boarding school.

Charles Swanson, cousin Rita's estranged husband, paid us a visit. His daughter, Aurora, completed her education at Santa Scholastica and needed a place to live. He lived at the Y.M.C.A., where females were not allowed. He asked *Mami* if she could board with us. He would gladly pay for her room and board. The only bed remaining was one Rosario would use when she visited on weekends.

"Doña Luz, I need your help. The best place for Aurora is with your family. I am prepared to pay a generous amount, for I am desperate," Charles Swanson implored.

Mami noticed his desperate tone and worried look on his face.

"Aurora can stay with us, but I am afraid she may not be comfortable here, as she would have to share Lola Lala's bedroom," *Mami* responded.

"Aurora will be happy being here with Pilar and Maria. She will be much more comfortable here as she has lived with you before and is familiar with the family," Swanson said. "Besides, she loves your piano and can continue her lessons."

Once again, Aurora became a member of the Gamero household. Her father would visit weekly, which delighted me, as it gave me another opportunity to practice speaking English with this American. During his visits, Aurora would play small concerts for him, much to his delight. She had majored in music at his insistence, and played only when asked. Playing the piano was not enjoyable for her…it was her duty.

Two weeks after I began working, my sister, Lucing, and her husband, Francisco, traveled once more to Hong Kong and Shanghai to purchase jewelry for El Zenith's Jewelry. Upon their return in mid-June, they joined Manila's premiere dance clubs. The Bohemian and El Circulo Social were two clubs where younger members of Manila society gathered to dance and mingle once a month. Francisco and Lucing obtained permission from our mother to take us. *Mami* insisted Aurora, Pilar and I return home by midnight and Frank and Lucing must serve as chaperones.

Social life brightened our dull lives. On our first visit to El Circulo Social, the club president introduced us in front of the band. We danced every dance. I can't remember sitting down once. Raphael Reyes, a young meztiso, asked me to dance.

"Don't you work at The American Bazaar?" Raphael asked.

"Yes, I work in the jewelry department as a sales clerk," I replied.

"I thought I recognized you. I work on the second floor also," Raphael said.

He was an excellent dancer and had won several dance contests at El Circulo Social. We danced several more times before leaving just before midnight. We did not want to get that "look" from *Mami*.

The next day, Raphael stopped by the jewelry department and invited me to have lunch. I declined graciously. He smiled and left for lunch on his own. As I left work, he was waiting outside the door.

"May I walk you to the streetcar?" Raphael asked.

"I live across the street, over the drugstore," I laughed as I replied.

"Oh, well, allow me," Raphael said as he extended his elbow for my arm.

We strolled across the street to our family's apartment. *Mami* was observing this whole process.

Once across the street, we said our goodbyes. I hurried upstairs, for I had seen the lace curtains pulled to one side. *Mami* was waiting. The inquisition would begin.

CHAPTER 41

Dealing with Differences

Mary recalled the barrage of questions spilling from her mother's mouth... faster than she could answer. *Who is he? Why was he walking with you? Where did you meet him? His skin is dark. What is his nationality?* The inquisition lasted about thirty minutes. *I told her Francisco knew him, and I had met him at El Circulo Social.*

Doña Luz summoned her son-in-law, Francisco, to explain why he allowed a *mestizo* to dance with her daughter. Wasn't he the chaperone at the dance clubs? Who was "this" Raphael Reyes?

Francisco responded by offering to bring Raphael for a proper introduction. She agreed and a date was set. I was beside myself and did not speak to Raphael when he appeared at the jewelry counter. He was puzzled, for I acted busy.

The next week, Francisco brought Raphael to meet my mother. I observed from the corner of the room while Raphael and Francisco sat stiffly on the large overstuffed sofa. *Mami* stationed herself on a ladder-back chair directly across the large sofa. She held her best accordion-type Spanish fan in one hand and a white handkerchief in the other. She obviously had her hands "occupied" so she would not have to touch the visitor or offer her hand in welcome.

Raphael and Francisco left after the niceties of genteel conversation were exchanged and *Mami* was satisfied with the answers to her questions. I waited for her pronouncement.

"He seems to be a decent young man, but since his mother is a native, he can only be considered as a friend," *Mami* spoke firmly. "You are not to get seriously involved with him under any circumstances, as he is of mixed blood."

I did not have to explain to Raphael the next day at work. He understood our mother did not accept him. Her decision was final.

I kept busy with my job and attended club dances with Francisco and Lucing. I danced with many young men, but none piqued my interest. At least we had a social life away from the monotony of work.

In August 1922, a young American gentleman, probably in his early thirties, visited the store often. He usually stopped at my jewelry counter to browse. Sometimes he would purchase a small item and make small talk with me. I was glad to have someone with whom to practice my English. One day he bought a pen, a Parker Duofold, and chatted about relatively unimportant topics. I wondered about him and considered asking him questions, but felt it would be an intrusion. He wore a uniform unfamiliar to me...a khaki suit with leggings. *Was he in a branch of the military unknown to me?*

The American appeared again the following day. This time he bought a different pen, a Waterman made by Parker Pen Co., and walked to the men's department. Later, he approached my counter to chat. I was not interested in what he had to say, so I did not encourage further conversation. He was probably in the army. We were not allowed to be friends with military men, as they were only in the Philippines temporarily.

He visited the jewelry department on a daily basis to chat with me, before going to the music department located next to my area. I avoided him by going into the vault pretending to take inventory. He would go to the music department, until I would emerge from the vault. In a flash, he would be at my counter. I lost my patience with this customer.

"Sir," I countered with my nose in the air, "we are not allowed to have extended conversations with anyone unless they are shopping in our department."

He was chagrined as he smiled and asked, "Would you help me with the selection of records in the music department?"

"No, sir," was my immediate reply. "That is not my department. I must stay at the jewelry counter."

"I'd like to see the floor manager," he requested...still smiling.

I contacted Mr. Arturo Silva and told him a customer would like to speak with him. After conversing with the American, Mr. Silva called me over where he and this American were standing.

"Maria, since you are not busy, this gentleman would like your help in selecting records in the music department. He is an excellent customer, so I have agreed to his request," Mr. Silva stated.

The nerve of this man! I can't believe he is so stubborn. I wish he would go away!

"Why don't you pick out your favorites," he suggested as we walked toward the music department.

I politely led the American to the record section and selected two recordings...the latest hits being played around Manila: *Three O'Clock in the Morning* and *Fate*. He listened, not uttering a word, nodded his head, paid for the two records and left smiling.

Remedios, the cashier, observed this interchange from her perch behind the cash register.

"Who is he?" Remedios asked.

"I have no idea, and I don't care," I retorted...still miffed. "I think he wants a girlfriend. Are you interested?'

Remedios Navarro, co-worker of Mary's at the American Bazaar (Jewelry Dept.).

Remedios, a lovely Spanish girl, had sparkling green eyes, a creamy complexion, and soft light-brown hair. Her well-endowed figure turned many heads.

"Sure," Remedios replied. "Tell me when he comes in again!"

Two days later, he stood at my counter. I was ready for him.

"I see you come here often," I stated. "My friend, Remedios, the cashier noticed you also. If you will return around noon, I will introduce you to her. Perhaps you can have lunch together to get acquainted."

He was quiet...solemn, as he replied, "I am not interested, thank you. How about going to lunch with me?"

"I'm sorry, sir, you are a stranger, so having lunch with you is not allowed," I sputtered.

"Well, my name is Jesse Hodges, but my friends call me 'Jess'. I am in the construction business and new to Manila. My three partners and I own a lumber-yard and make custom-built homes," Jess recited, trying to impress me.

"Oh," I responded. "I thought you were a military person since you are wearing a uniform."

"No, I ride a motorcycle and need to wear these leggings," he said. "The motorcycle is convenient transportation because I ride the ferry to Olongapo to check other businesses I own with my partners. We have a pawn shop; The WaWa Dance Hall; and, The Post Exchange Sanitary Steam Laundry on Santa Rita Road near the Naval Reservation. I had not planned to remain in the Philippines, but these three Americans I met convinced me I would do well by becoming their partner."

"Who are your partners?" I asked just to make conversation, because my head was whirling.

"They are J. E. Grant, John Gallagher, and O. E. Hart. I felt I had nothing to lose as I was prepared to return to Texas. We have done well so far and have hired more workers to help us. We also bought a dance hall in Cavite called The Dream-land Cabaret. That one, plus the one in Olongapo, The WaWa Dance Hall, do

> For and in consideration of the sum of five thousand pesos (₱5000) received on November 13, 1916, I hereby turn over to J. Hodges all my rights, titles and interests in the following property in which J. E. Grant of Olongapo and the undersigned of Subic are equal partners:
>
> Post Exchange Sanitary Steam Laundry situated on Santa Rita Road, Naval Reservation, Olongapo, P.I.
>
> Saloon and Dance hall and all appurtenances situated in Subic, Zambales, P.I.
>
> One-fourth interest in business in Olongapo under the firm name of J. E. Grant & Co. embracing places of business designated as "Cabaret" and "Wa Wa Dance Hall".
>
> Henry Barton
>
> Olongapo, P.I.,
>   Nov. 18, 1916.

well because they are near U.S. naval bases. Mr. Hart and Mr. Gallagher manage the dance halls and Mr. Grant handles the pawnshop and laundry in Olongapo. I have the lumberyard and construction business, with my own crew and truck driver, Tony Settember, to deliver materials."

Remedios gave me a "look," so I told Jess I must return to my duties. I did not want to lose my job. He gave me another disarming smile and said he would return tomorrow.

⌇⌇

Mary thought how different her life would have been if Jesse had agreed to take Remedios to lunch. Fate had stepped in and pushed her in the right direction. *The song* Fate *became our song, and I taught Jess to waltz to* Three O'Clock in the Morning. *Once again, she must give thanks for her many blessings.*

Let's see, I think I'll sip a glass of the blackberry wine Lucy and Buddy brought. Dr. Mehmert said I needed to sip wine before breakfast and at bedtime. I believe in following the doctor's orders. I'll watch Lawrence Welk while I sip.

CHAPTER 42

The Deception

All through September 1922 Remedios and I carried out our plan to avoid Jess. We drew Raphael into our plans without Raphael's knowledge. Each evening Raphael and I would wait for Remedios to complete her duties as cashier, then take the streetcar, get off near Remedios' home and walk to her place. After a while, Raphael and I would take the streetcar returning to The American Bazaar, and walk across the street to my family's apartment above the drugstore. On several occasions, Jess followed the streetcar's route on his motorcycle, but never stopped when we arrived near Remedios' home, because we three were walking together. Jess was bold, but not that bold.

Jess was polite and had a sincere face, but was short and chubby. He was not tall and handsome like Raphael. Although *Mami* told me Raphael could not be a suitor, he was allowed to be my friend. Raphael and I had an understanding to be dance partners and "partners in the deception of Jess." We laughed at our devious plan.

December was just a hop, skip, and a jump away. The holiday season was "high season" for the dance clubs. They held dance contests to name the Dance King and Queen for each club. The first competition was at El Circulo Social, the next at The Bohemian, and, finally, at *El Tiro al Blanco,* the Spanish dance club. The winners competed at a marathon dance held on New Year's Eve to become King and Queen of Dance for Manila. These were scheduled for consecutive Saturday nights and contestants competed in their specialty.

As was our usual routine, Aurora, Pilar and I went to dance clubs with our sister, Lucing and her husband, Francisco. We would meet our dance partners and enjoy the evening socializing or dancing in competitions. Raphael and I entered the One-Step competition at El Circulo Social and won easily. We were excited with our success but knew this news must never reach *Mami's* ears. Aurora, Pilar, Lucing, and Francisco were sworn to secrecy.

While at El Circulo Social, Pilar received a gift from the club's president, Mr. Limm. He was impressed with her beauty and sought to get her attention with a gift. Pilar did not tell anyone until we were on our way home. She opened the small jewelry box and displayed an exquisite gold bracelet.

"Pilachu, where did you get the bracelet?" Lucing asked.

"It was a gift," Pilar murmured.

"Who gave you this gift?" Francisco spouted.

"The president of El Circulo Social," responded Pilar.

"*Dios mio!*" exclaimed Lucing. "He is a married man. Why is he giving you an expensive gift?"

"I have no idea…he just did," replied Pilar, as she shrugged her shoulders.

"You cannot accept it. The bracelet must be returned. *Mami* must not see it," stated Lucing emphatically.

"Well, I'll wear it until then," laughed Pilar.

The ride home was quiet. We knew Pilar was facing disaster. I had no idea it would spill over on me.

Mami was waiting at her usual spot by the window. The *calesa* stopped and chattering voices floated in the night air. She glanced out the window. The gold bracelet gleamed brightly under the streetlamp as Pilar turned it on her wrist…admiring the way the light from the streetlamp made it sparkle.

Mami's first words were about the bracelet. We faced the inquisition. Pilar burst into tears, told her about the bracelet, and threw herself on the mercy of her mother's court. The verdict was final. We were not allowed to go to any more dances.

My heart fell. I did not believe the verdict. *Why was I included? I did not accept a gift from anyone.*

At work on Monday, I told Raphael what happened. He was shocked.

"Maria, we have to compete the next two Saturdays. We will win the marathon competition easily. You must convince your mother to let you go. You did nothing wrong," exclaimed Raphael.

"If my mother found out we are dance partners, she would not allow me to attend a dance again. I cannot tell her," I explained.

While we were talking, Jess approached the jewelry counter. Raphael ducked out as Jess arrived.

"Say, young lady," Jess said, "I've been trying to find out where you live. Would you please tell me so I can come by and meet your parents?"

I gave him a fictitious address near Remedios' home on Manga Avenue. I wanted to discourage him. *Maybe he will stop bothering me, and I won't have to take the streetcar anymore.*

Jess returned the next day. Although I had tricked him, he still displayed an engaging smile.

"Say, I couldn't find the address you gave me yesterday. I waited for more than an hour after the streetcar left…you never arrived. I also waited this morning, hoping to see you before work. Would you mind telling me again?" Jess asked.

"Oh, that was my aunt's house, but I did not stay with her last night," I lied. "I cannot give you my address. No one is allowed to visit without being properly introduced to my mother. It's a Spanish custom."

"Well, I will see what I can do," Jess spoke and waved as he left.

The next week, an older Spaniard asked for me at the jewelry department. Remedios stepped into the ladies room, where I was brushing my hair, and told me I had a visitor. When I approached the counter, he introduced himself and explained his mission.

"*Srta*. Gamero, my name is Juan Segin, and Mr. Hodges is my employer. I am here to speak on his behalf. He is a dependable man...a fine man. If you will introduce me to your mother, since I am Spanish, I would, in turn, introduce him to her," Mr. Segin stated.

"No, *Señor* Segin. You are a stranger to us. Being Spanish, you should understand that proper introductions would be through a family friend or relative," I replied.

Mr. Segin agreed, apologized for the inconvenience, and left the store promptly. *That should be the end of Jess Hodges and his attempts to meet my mother!*

By mid-week, Jess was in the store. I was transferred to the ladies department, as they were having a sale. Jess met Mr. Silva, the manager, and asked where I was. Mr. Silva explained I was needed at the ladies' department, as a year-end sale was in progress. Jess thanked Mr. Silva and left.

The weekend was approaching and Raphael was sad, because I could not attend the dance and be his partner for the competition. He would have to find another dance partner. I spoke with Maria Serra, a friend, who agreed to attend the dance as Raphael's partner. He was pleased, as he knew Maria and had danced with her previously.

Saturday night, Aurora, Pilar, and I entertained *Mami* and Lola Lala at home, but our thoughts were at The Bohemian Club. Aurora could have gone, but decided it would make us feel worse, so she stayed home. Lucing and Francisco attended and returned the bracelet to Mr. Linn. They gave their regrets for our absence. Raphael and Maria Serra won the One-Step dance competition and were named the King and Queen for the club. They would compete in the marathon against all the other Kings and Queens at the Spanish dance club on New Year's Eve. We could not attend, thanks to Pilar.

As she put her writing materials away for the day, Mary heard a knock at the back door. *I wonder who is there?* It was her daughter, Joyce.

"How about lunch? I don't have to return to the Tax Office this afternoon, and I'm hungry for Chinese food. What about you?'

Mary never refused an offer to go to Yen Jing's. It was always a delicious treat.

"Just a minute. I'll get my sweater and comb my hair," Mary replied.

CHAPTER 43

A Relative Strategy

New Year's Eve was fast approaching. Pilar, and I really wanted to attend the New Year's Eve dance at *El Tiro al Blanco* followed by the New Year's party at the Santa Ana Cabaret. Lucing and Francisco had purchased the tickets for us three months ago for the party at the cabaret…long before the gold bracelet incident. Aurora was free to attend.

Lucing brought her sons, Francisco and Antonio for a visit with their grandmother. While *Mami* was enjoying her grandsons' amusing antics, Lucing broached the subject.

"Francisco bought the tickets for the New Year's Dance a long time ago and has already reserved a table for us at the Santa Ana Cabaret," posed Lucing. "It would be a shame to give those tickets away to someone else. Aurora plans to go with us. Don't you think Maria and Pilar have been punished enough?"

Mami was quiet, as she observed the boys at play.

"I suppose they have learned their lesson. You and Francisco must be more watchful than before," *Mami* stated emphatically. "They must be home by two o'clock."

Lucing and the boys stayed until I returned from work. She wanted to see the reaction on my face. Pilar and Aurora had already been told and were sitting there with smiles on their faces.

"What is it?" I quizzed, as they stared at me and grinned.

"We can go to the New Year's Eve dance at *El Tiro al Blanco* and Santa Ana!" Pilar and Aurora cried in unison, as they rushed to hug me. "We can stay until two!"

We all hugged *Mami* and Lucing. They laughed at our antics as we danced around the room for several minutes. Our prayers were answered. *I can't wait to tell Raphael! What will I wear?*

Raphael was delighted with my news. He told me the plans for New Year's Eve.

"I will meet you at *El Tiro* and we will dance every dance. Later I can meet you at Santa Ana. What an exciting New Year's Eve this will be! Goodbye, 1922…Hello, 1923!" Raphael shouted.

I laughed and shushed him. I did not need trouble at work. Nothing must happen to cancel our New Year's Eve plans. It was, indeed, a Happy New Year.

In mid-January, Raphael pressured me to talk to my mother again. He wanted more than friendship. He wanted us to become engaged.

"If you talk to my mother about an engagement, she will not allow me to attend any more dances. We must only be friends."

Raphael left…dejected. I was sorry to turn him down because he was an excellent dance partner, but I knew how my mother would react to his request for an engagement.

Jess was not coming by the store as often. His construction work had grown. He had over ten employees working on several custom homes in the area and visited the store twice weekly. He usually bought small items while there, and insisted I assist him with his purchases. *I later learned he would ask his partners what they needed at the store and would buy it for them to save them a trip into Manila.*

February 19, 1923, my eighteenth birthday arrived with a flourish. A Chinese messenger delivered a large box of chocolate-covered cherries to me at the store. *What a surprise! Who besides my family knew it was my birthday?*

The card was inscribed: "For Mary Guerrero." I pointed this out to the messenger boy.

"My family name is Gamero," I explained. "Who sent this candy?"

The young boy shrugged his shoulders and said, "I no know."

"This candy is not for me. Return it to the sender," I stated, and returned the box.

He took it and started toward the exit. Mrs. Beck, the store's co-owner and manager of the ladies department, observed this exchange. As the messenger turned to leave, she summoned him, read the card on the box, and told him to give it to me.

"You are the only 'Mary' in the store, so this is yours. The family name has been misspelled," Mrs. Beck stated.

During lunch, I called Raphael and thanked him for the chocolate candy. I wanted to get his reaction.

"What chocolate candy?" Raphael asked. "What are you talking about?"

"I thought maybe you had sent it to me for my birthday," I teased.

"Your birthday! I am sorry. Happy birthday," Raphael said.

I put the candy away. *I guess I will take it home and share it with my family.*

That was a mistake. The minute my mother saw the chocolates, I knew I was in trouble.

"Who gave you the candy?" *Mami* demanded. "Was it Raphael?"

"No, *Mami*," I replied. "I called him. He had no idea."

Pilar spied the candy, took it from me, and opened the box.

"What does it matter?" Pilar said as she popped a piece into her mouth. "We can be thankful someone remembered your birthday. Let's start the celebration!"

I'm not sure if my mother believed me, but at least the candy was not mentioned again.

By February's end, Jess stopped by my jewelry counter and surprised me with his news.

"Mary (he discovered the English translation for Maria)," he started, "I have found a friend of your mother's. He will take me to your home and introduce me to her. He is an American."

"An American?" I questioned. "An American knows my mother? I can't believe it!"

"Yes. One night, when I was standing outside your house, a man exited your front door. I realized I knew him as he is also in the construction business. His name is Charles Swanson," Jess stated excitedly.

"My Uncle Carlos!" I exclaimed. "He has been in the family so long I guess I forgot he was an American citizen, although he was originally from Denmark. He joined the United States Army during the Spanish-American War when he was nineteen and later was granted citizenship for his service to your country. His daughter, Aurora, lives with us since he and my mother's cousin, Rita, have been separated. Oh, my goodness!"

I was babbling and hardly knew whether or not I was making any sense. What a surprise! Jess stood quietly…overwhelmed by my prattle. He waited before speaking.

"He has already made arrangements for my visit to meet your mother," Jess announced.

I was stunned. The visit was to take place during the coming weekend.

Saturday arrived and I was so nervous. Pilar and Aurora teased me and did their best to make my life miserable. *Do I want this man to court me?*

Uncle Carlos and Jess arrived promptly at the appointed time. *Merienda*, consisting of tea, coffee, small pastries, and tiny sandwiches had been prepared and the *sala* was ready for guests. *Mami* wore her best black lace dress with her hair pulled tightly into a bun. A delicate Spanish decorative comb was pushed into the bun at an angle. She was dressed to impress.

Jess was invited to sit on the large overstuffed sofa beside our Uncle Carlos. After the introductions were made and niceties were exchanged, tea and coffee were offered, along with the various accompaniments.

"Cousin Luz, Jess has been visiting the store where Maria works and has taken an interest in knowing her better, with your permission. He is dependable and is successful in the construction business. I have worked with him. He is a fine businessman and an honest person in his dealings with me. Until he told me he was interested in your daughter, I considered introducing him to Aurora," Uncle Carlos spoke convincingly.

Following a brief visit with *Mami*, Pilar, and Aurora, Jess asked my mother if he may come to visit me the next day, Sunday. She replied the family would be at church on Sunday.

"If you don't mind, I can take the family to church and bring you home after the services," Jess offered.

"I suppose it would be all right," *Mami* responded. "We attend the ten o'clock services."

Jess agreed. He and Uncle Carlos left after everyone finished their *merienda*. We waited quietly for my mother's opinion on Jess.

"Well, I like the young American. He has a sincere face. He is not handsome, but he has a sweet smile," *Mami* stated as she carried out the tray with the remainder of the pastries and sandwiches.

Pilar waited for our mother to retire for the evening. When *Mami* closed her bedroom door, she pelted me with her opinions about Jess.

"He's not handsome. He's not tall. He's quite chubby," Pilar kept chattering. "Do not get serious about him or you will not be able to go to dances with us if he is your boyfriend."

I told Pilar I would think about it. *What should I do?*

Mami entered the room to kiss us goodnight, and suspected we had been exchanging opinions.

"We will pray to St. Joseph. We will not make any decisions until we have been to church for seven consecutive Sundays. We must take Holy Communion each of those days and dedicate our prayers to St. Joseph, for he is the patron saint of our family. We will begin next Sunday as it is March 19…the Feast Day of St. Joseph.

The rituals of attending Mass for seven Sundays with Jess escorting our family began. He arrived promptly each Sunday, attended church with us, and brought us home for Sunday *merienda* or took us to *Los Baños* for picnics (if the weather permitted). These rituals mattered to my mother. Jess was happy. He bought a Spanish/English dictionary and studied phrases to help him converse with the family.

Mary giggled as she remembered those early days of their courtship. *He was a determined person. He wanted to marry me. I'm so glad he did.*

CHAPTER 44

The Courtship of Maria

By mid-April 1923, our family became comfortable having Jess around our apartment and taking us to church, followed by light lunches at our place or picnics at various sites in and around Manila. I was still unsure if I wanted him as my boyfriend. Yes, he was decent, polite and tender, but not what I imagined in my "girlish" dreams.

He took the family for a picnic at his favorite place in *Los Baños*. We finished our lunch and remained chatting around the picnic table…enjoying the pleasant weather. The picnic basket was repacked for our return trip. Jess faced me and asked if I would like to become engaged. I was surprised, and then I recalled my mother's rituals.

"I'm sorry, Jess, I cannot give you an answer until after we complete our seven Sundays of prayers to St. Joseph," I sputtered. "I have promised my mother. She would expect us to wait at least one year."

Jess was disappointed. He was quiet and hardly spoke all the way home.

I thought about my words to Jess. *What must I do? He was almost sixteen years my senior. He is an American, and I have always wanted to go to America.*

My thoughts were whirling around like a cyclone. Pilar's question returned me to the present.

"Are you going to the club dance with us next Saturday, Jess?"

I froze. I knew he did not dance, so I never thought about inviting him.

"No, Pilar, I don't care much for dancing," Jess replied. "Go ahead and enjoy yourselves. I know how much you and Mary like dancing."

Our usual group attended *El Circulo Social* on Saturday and enjoyed the evening. On Sunday, Jess arrived, as usual, to take us to church. After church we went for a picnic at The Luneta, a broad boulevard surrounded by a park filled with tropical flowering plants. After our picnic, Jess excused himself to buy a box of cigars to send his father. After about thirty minutes, I noticed someone in Jess' car. It was parked in the designated parking area close to our picnic spot. Thinking Jess had returned to his car to store the cigars, I approached his car. To my surprise, the man was not Jess.

"I'm sorry. I recognized Jess' car and I thought he was waiting here," I said.

"No, this is our company car, and I am waiting for Jess. My name is Grant, Jess' partner," he said, nodding his head in greeting. "How do you like this car?"

"It's a beautiful car. I've never seen another like it," I responded.

"This Packard is a one-of-a-kind vehicle. It was built to specifications for a millionaire who changed his mind about buying it. The dealer lowered the price since other customers did not want all the 'extras,' so we bought it for our partnership."

I smiled, realizing I had probably intruded on something that was none of my business, and began walking away to find Jess, but Mr. Grant stopped me.

"Wait a minute, young lady. I'm here to meet you." Mr. Grant smiled. "Jess talks about you often. After meeting you, I understand why he spends so much time away from work."

By then, Jess was walking toward me with a grin on his face.

"I see you have met Mary," he said. "I hope you didn't scare her."

Mr. Grant laughed. He and Jess chatted a while before Jess told him it was time to take my family home.

"Okay, Jess. I'll see you later," Grant said as he crawled out from under the steering wheel. "Take care of her."

Our seven consecutive Sundays of prayers to St. Joseph were completed on the last Sunday in April. Jess waited patiently until afternoon before he asked me about becoming engaged. I told him I needed more time. Once again, the drive home was quiet.

Jess did not come to the store at all the next week. On Saturday, when he was to make his usual visit to our home, Jess was absent.

"Have you seen Jess this week?" *Mami* inquired.

"No, *Mami,* he has not come to see me at work," I replied.

"I am worried he may be sick. He is usually prompt every Saturday. You should go downstairs and ask to use their phone," *Mami* stated.

I did as I was told. When Jess' phone rang, it was answered by someone else.

"Hello, may I speak with Jess?" I inquired.

"Mr. Jess is not feeling well," was the reply.

"Can he come to the phone?" I asked, and waited several minutes for a response.

"Hello?" A thick scratchy voice croaked.

"Jess? What is wrong? Are you sick?" I chattered.

"Yes. I have a cold and sore throat. That's why I have not come to see you. I didn't want you to catch my cold," Jess responded.

We chatted about five minutes, before he said he should probably stop talking, as his throat was sore.

I rushed upstairs to tell our mother Jess was sick. To my surprise she rose from her chair and hurried to the kitchen before she spoke.

"We must call a *calesa* and go to see him. I will prepare hot soup and fresh fruit. Hurry!" *Mami* ordered.

I gave the *calesa* driver his address on Dakota street. Once there, we took the basket containing the hot soup, crackers, and fruit to the second floor apartment and knocked.

An American gentleman opened the door

"Is this the apartment of Jesse Hodges?" I asked.

"Yes, how may I help you?"

"Just tell him Mary and her mother are here to see him," I replied.

Our voices wakened Jess, who emerged from his room wearing a robe. His hair was tousled, and his usually smoothly shaven face was covered with stubble. He was embarrassed and surprised.

After introducing us to his partners, he invited us to sit, however, we felt he was not comfortable hosting us in his condition. After about ten minutes, we deposited the basket on a side table and wished him a speedy recovery.

"Your visit has made me feel better. I will come by for church next Sunday," Jess announced. "Sorry about tomorrow. I should probably stay in."

The following Sunday morning, Jess arrived as promised. He was smooth shaven and wore his Sunday best. Following the services, he took us to lunch, and later, to a movie. After taking us home, Jess asked me to sit in the car with him before going inside. He said he was about to give up on my ever becoming his fiancé. When we visited him the week before, he and his partners were trying to decide whether or not to continue the partnership because Jess told them he wanted to sell his part and return to the United States and be a hermit.

"Your visit changed my mind. I hope your answer will prove I made the right decision. Mary, will you ever consider becoming engaged to me?' Jess pleaded.

"I just wanted to be sure. Yes, Jess, I will be engaged to you," I murmured.

He was surprised and happy. His face beamed with a grin from ear-to-ear.

"I can't wait to tell my partners," Jess shouted.

Jess gave me a brief kiss on the cheek and escorted me to the door.

"Goodnight, my love," Jess whispered. "Sweet dreams."

Mary quietly recalled those special moments. She surprised herself when she agreed to marry Jesse. It was as if someone else put those words in her mouth. *Was it Fate?*

CHAPTER 45

The Engagement

Jess hurried to his apartment and told his partners the news. He parked the long Packard in the usual place in the alley, grabbed the keys, and bounded up the stairs. His partners were still playing poker when he swung the door open and announced his news.

"Mary has agreed to the engagement!" Jess shouted.

"Whoa, not so loud," Grant said. "Bring it down a notch or two. Congratulations, by the way."

Gallagher and Hart stepped forward to shake his hand.

"Well, well, well," laughed Hart, "I guess it means you won't be selling your part of the business…guess you'll be staying in the islands for a while."

"Did you buy a ring for her, Jess?" Gallagher asked.

"No, I was kidding her about becoming engaged, and she surprised me by saying she would! I had no ring for her, but plan to get one. She deserves a perfect diamond," Jess stated.

"You might check out what we have at our pawn shop," Grant suggested. "I think we have three or four beauties for sale."

"Her engagement ring must be perfect," Jess noted.

Tony Settember, their truck driver, was sitting at the table holding his cards.

"Hey, Jess," he teased in his thick Italian accent, "Spanish women are supposed to be jealous types and don't make good wives."

"Not Mary and her sisters," Jess stated. "They are more like American girls."

Grant agreed. "Aw, Tony, I met Mary and her mother. I also met Mary's sisters at The Luneta. Jess is right. They are all okay."

"Well, in that case," Tony kidded, "maybe I should come with you the next time and see for myself."

"All right," Jess grinned, "I'll take you next Sunday, if you'd like to go."

During that week, *Mami* called a family meeting. She told the family Maria had agreed to an engagement, however, it was not official until she had an engagement ring. In order to avoid any embarrassment, the engagement would be kept secret by the family until it was made official with the ring. If and when a ring was provided and accepted, the engagement would be officially announced. All were agreed this procedure would be the best for all concerned.

It was the first Sunday in May. Tony stood by the Packard waiting for Jess. Antonio D. Settembrini (Tony D. Settember) was impeccably dressed. His swarthy skin glowed against the trim white suit he wore so well on his tall, lanky body. With his hat perched at a jaunty angle, he was rather dashing, and when he smiled, he charmed the ladies.

"I'll drive," Jess said. "You don't know the way."

At the Gameros place, Jess strode upstairs to knock on the door. Tony remained with the car. As the family filed out the doorway and approached the car, Tony stepped out and introductions were made. After greeting us with a gracious bow and flashing smile, he opened car doors…making a smashing first impression.

Rosario (Charing) was visiting from Antipolo, and once they were all moving down the road, she made a comment.

"*Que hermosos ojos tiene mi compadre.*" ("What beautiful eyes my friend has!")

She had no idea Tony, being Italian, would understand Spanish. He turned to Rosario and flashed his most charming smile.

"*Gracias, Señorita Gamero.*" He nodded his head and tipped his hat.

We laughed and teased her. She put her lace *mantilla* over her head and was quiet the rest of the way to church. Pilar was truly impressed by Tony. She flashed a smile at him and waved as the car pulled away, with Tony at the wheel.

Jesse A. Hodges in the Packard, leaving his bachelor's home to move to Santa Mesa before he married in 1923.

The first Sunday in May, Jess took *Mami* and me to Antipolo for the Fiesta of Our Lady of Peace and Good Voyage. Pilar, Aurora, and Rosario were already there. People from all walks of life would congregate to celebrate, enjoy the fresh mountain air, and splash in the waterfalls at *Hinulugang Taktak*. I was excited. Many friends I had not seen in a while would attend.

Following Mass, celebrated by my brother, Fr. José Gamero, Jess drove to the open picnic area near the falls. Pilar, Aurora, Jess and I met our friends. Among them were my "puppy love" Louie, his brother Ernest, and Raphael. I introduced Jess as my American friend, as agreed by my family, since I had not yet received an engagement ring. Our relatives were also there, so they met Jess. Since they were not our "immediate" family, Jess was introduced as a friend.

After lunch, we girls changed into the Filipino native wear *barong Tagalog*, and were joined by the fellows for a stroll. Jess was to my left and Raphael on my right, followed by Pilar, Ernest, and Louie. Jess was talking with me.

"Pilar," Raphael asked, "why is Maria talking so much with the American?"

"It's because she can speak English so much better than we can," Pilar replied.

It was time to return to Manila. I had to work the next day, so Jess took us home. Pilar and Aurora stayed with Rosario at Antipolo so they could continue to enjoy the remaining feast days. Before we arrived home, Jess asked my mother if she would prefer to go to *Los Baños* after church next Sunday, instead of returning to Antipolo. He would make arrangements for lunch. She agreed to his plans and thanked him for being so thoughtful.

The following Sunday, Jess came for our Sunday rituals. On the way to *Los Baños*, Jess asked me if I enjoyed the chocolate-covered cherries he sent me for Valentines' Day. I laughed uncontrollably.

"*Mami*," I giggled. "Jess is the one who gave me the chocolate candy."

Mami smiled and was quiet, but I could tell she was pleased Jess had been the one who sent the chocolates.

"Jess, I received those chocolates on my eighteenth birthday, February 19. I never thanked you, because the sender was a mystery. They were delicious, by the way. We all enjoyed them."

We enjoyed a good laugh. Jess made a mental note about February 19.

"Guess I'll have to call you 'The Candy Kid'," Jess joked.

We arrived at *Los Baños* and received a surprise. Jess had made all the arrangements for a special meal at the area's finest restaurant, The Springs Cafe.

"Are you surprised?" Jess asked with an impish smile on his face. "You have worked hard all week long and deserve a special meal."

Jess escorted us, one on each arm, into the restaurant, where we were seated at a well-appointed table. He signaled the waiter, who poured the beverage Jess had pre-selected…champagne!

"Here's to the most beautiful girl in the world and her lovely mother," Jess said as he raised his glass.

We touched our glasses while he gave us a charming smile. For the meal, he had selected chicken *adobo, baduya* (coconut and sweet potato patty), *achara* salad, and a choice of *gina ta-an* or *bibinca* for dessert. We also had *chicharon bulaklak* on the table for munching. He knew all my favorites!

After lunch, we took a short walk near a tree-lined lake across from the restaurant while *Mami* remained to sip her hot tea and finish her dessert. As we approached a park bench, Jess and I stopped to rest. After quietly contemplating the scenery, Jess broke the silence abruptly.

"Mary, will you please marry me?" Jess asked while holding out a small jewelry box he had pulled from his pocket.

I was so surprised! I took the velvet-covered ring box and opened it. An exquisite diamond ring sparkled in the sunlight! I must have stared at it for more than a minute.

"Well, do I get a 'Yes?'" Jess asked.

"Oh, yes, Jess," I replied.

He took the ring from its box and gently placed it on my finger and kissed my hand. I cried.

"Mary, we don't need tears. Your mother may think I've mistreated you," Jess said firmly.

We returned to the restaurant…walking arm-in-arm. Jess was amused as I held my left hand in front of me to see the sparkling diamond. I was anxious to show my ring to *Mami* and see the look on her face. *Mami was so pleased! She could now "officially" announce our engagement.*

After we arrived home, Jess stayed until ten o'clock. *Mami* remained in the *sala* while I played the piano to accompany Jess, who was playing his violin. He brought two pieces of sheet music with him. One was *Melody of Love,* and the other was *Fate,* the song I had selected on the records he bought at the store. Following our brief recital, Jess decided to leave as we

Maria de los Angeles Josefa Gabina Gamero y Cucullu, engagement photo, 1923.

both had work the next day. I accompanied him to the door and stepped into the hallway. Jess hugged me and gave me my first kiss on my lips. He left immediately. I was shocked. On my way upstairs, I saw *Mami* in the hallway. I'm not sure she saw the "kiss," because it happened so swiftly. I was worried. The only time I had seen someone being kissed on the lips was in the movies. Before long, the couple in the movies had a child. *Will that happen to me?*

≈≈

Mary shook with laughter as she recalled her first kiss. *Married life was a mystery. In those days, women were told nothing about what to expect. How did I ever manage married life?*

She laughed at herself on her way to the kitchen to fix hot chocolate. The banana bread Mary Jane brought would go well with the hot beverage. She sipped, snacked, and collected her thoughts. *I can't believe I was so naïve!*

CHAPTER 46

Wedding Preparations

So much had occurred during the weekend. I was in a daze as I stood at the jewelry counter at work, admiring my ring. My boss, Mr. Silva, broke my reverie when he noticed the ring.

"Maria, let me see your ring," Mr. Silva said, as he took my hand and pulled it closer. "It's not one of ours. Where did he purchase your ring?"

"I have no idea where it was purchased," I responded honestly.

"You should have told your fiancé to buy your ring here," he stated.

"My ring was a surprise," I replied.

Mr. Silva was miffed. He returned to his office without another word.

When Jess entered the store later, I told him what my boss had said.

"Mary, I'm sorry, but the diamonds offered for sale in this store are not as high quality as the diamond I wanted you to have," Jess stated. "I have dealt with jewelry since my partners and I have a pawn shop."

I lifted my hand closer to compare the diamond to one on display.

"You are right, Jess," I replied, "My diamond is much clearer and more brilliant."

"We need to talk to your mother about setting our wedding date," Jess said. "I will come by for a visit tonight."

Jess arrived as promised, and my mother, Jess, and I discussed a possible wedding date. Jess wanted the earliest possible date.

"We have so much to do before Maria can be married," *Mami* countered. "First, we must prepare her trousseau; then we must decide on her wedding gown and dresses for her attendants; and before you can marry her, you must talk with my step-son, Fr. Gamero, and sign the documents to promise the church your children will be reared as Catholics."

Jess and I listened to her from our perch on the overstuffed sofa. She listed details to be completed before setting a wedding date.

"I can buy all the clothes for her plus all the items for her trousseau," Jess stated before *Mami* interrupted him.

"It is the Spanish custom for the bride to provide all her new clothes except for her wedding gown," *Mami* stated firmly. "The groom will pay for the wedding gown and the wedding expenses. We are not ready to set the date."

Jess prepared to be married by dissolving his partnerships. He kept the lumberyard and sold his motorcycle. His shares in the Packard, the pawnshop, the WaWa Dance Hall, and the laundry in Olongapo, plus the Dreamland Cabaret in Cavite were sold to his partners. He rented a house on Altura Street in Santa Mesa owned by family friends…Doña Rogelia and Don Pio. Since it was unfurnished, he bought furniture and hired a houseboy, DacDac, who also cooked. A used Cleveland touring car was purchased at a bargain, to continue taking our family to church and Sunday outings.

Business improved for Jess as he built homes for a new development in San Juan Heights. They were reasonably priced for quick sale, as he needed to generate income to establish his business. Many homes were designed and built for Americans, who were pleased to deal with another American.

Jess suffered a setback when thieves broke into his lumberyard, located on the outskirts of Manila, and stole equipment and building materials. The watchman was in on the plot and was not found, according to police. Since nothing was insured, Jess suffered a large financial loss, but he did not let the loss dissuade him.

In August, Jess asked my mother again about a wedding date. She set the wedding for November 26…the Feast of the Betrothal of the Virgin Mary to Joseph.

"It seems like a long time to wait," Jess said. "Mary is working long hours. I would like her to stop working. I will give you the same salary amount she is receiving to help with family expenses."

"No," *Mami* said firmly. "No, we cannot allow you to do that."

Jess left…feeling dejected. *I must be more patient.*

(left to right) Jesse A. Hodges and W. W. Pate, manager of their pawn shop in Olongapo, P.I.

In mid-September, Lucing called to say the house next to hers was being vacated. She thought Jess and I might like its location better than the home he had rented. Jess investigated and agreed. It was a much larger home. He thought I would be happier living next door to Lucing. Perhaps I would not be lonely there since Lucing was nearby.

Once more, Jess asked my mother about changing the wedding date. He had a better home next door to Lucing, and she could help me with the transition into married life. I could help care for her children.

My mother agreed to change the date to November 10 rather than the twenty-third. A small concession, but she knew Jess was becoming impatient. Jess was happy to have won one small battle with my mother.

With the wedding date less than two months away, the Gamero family sewed furiously. Lucing was making my wedding gown. Jess gave me money to purchase the materials. Lucing, *Mami*, and I shopped during my lunch hours. The Escolta, which had the best stores, was near The American Bazaar. We found a bolt of luxurious, heavy white satin, called Baronette, for my gown and fifteen yards of Spanish *Tulle de Ilusion* for my veil. I was so excited when we found the crown encircled with apple blossoms. We also bought tiny apple blossoms to sew onto my gown. Lucing found white silk stockings with apple blossoms embroidered on the front, plus a pair of white, high-heeled shoes. My aunt Adelaida was making my bridal bouquet from white tea roses and another flower called "love chain" or in Spanish, *cadena de amor. Our wedding will be perfect!*

The whole family was involved in making arrangements for our wedding. As part of my trousseau, my mother sewed all my lingerie. Rosario made all my sheets and pillowcases which Luisita, my cousin,

Jess and Mary Hodges wed on November 10, 1923.
Photo by Sun Studio, Manila.

embroidered with the initials "H-G" for Hodges-Gamero. My aunt Rita Swanson made six embroidered satin and lace nightgowns. They also hired a catering service to provide food and beverages for the wedding reception at Lucing and Francisco's home. Fifty guests…family and close friends, would be invited.

The designated wedding date arrived. Rosario (Charing) and I decided we should probably prepare extra tea sandwiches to ensure we had enough food at the wedding reception. We purchased the bread and other ingredients and took them to Lucing's home. I was shocked to see Raphael waiting at her door, talking to Francisco. I handed the groceries to Rosario, who took them inside to prepare sandwiches. Raphael rushed toward me.

"Maria, I'm so glad to see you. I wanted to invite you to come to the club tonight. We can enter the dance contest again!" Raphael said excitedly.

I was stunned. Francisco waited a minute to see if I would respond before he spoke.

"I'm sorry, Raphael. I thought you knew today is Maria's wedding day," He said quietly.

Raphael was shocked…as if he had been struck by lightning. He ducked his head and was quiet for a minute before he wished me well. He did not wait for a reply but left immediately.

I was so embarrassed. I forgot to tell Raphael. He knew I was engaged to Jess, but had no idea today was my wedding day.

Lucing hurried down the stairs.

"*Nena,* hurry. You need to try your wedding gown on one more time," Lucing urged as she bustled around the room.

In their *sala,* the display of gifts and decorated tables for the reception filled me with awe. I was grateful to my family for all their hard work.

On Saturday, November 10, 1923, Francisco and Lucing, my sponsors, and I were thirty minutes late in arriving at the church. November is monsoon season in the Philippines. A typhoon was threatening, and we waited for a passing rainstorm to diminish before leaving for the church. I could not get my wedding gown wet.

Finally, we were all in place. Francisco was to give me away, so he offered his arm as the organ music heralded my entrance. Lucing, my matron of honor and Pilar, my bridesmaid were already at the altar. Charles Swanson, the best man, and Jess were handsome in their tuxedos and stood…waiting patiently. Family and friends filled the pews of the beautifully decorated sanctuary of Saint Ignatius Catholic Church in Manila. Waiting at the altar, was Father Hogan, an American priest, and my brother, Fr. José Gamero, who would assist. Jess was nervous. He smiled as I neared his side.

The wedding vows were read in English by Father Hogan and repeated in Spanish by my brother, Fr. Gamero. The ceremony was perfect. Months of preparation for this wedding resulted in only thirty minutes of wedding rituals. We were pronounced man and wife…Mr. and Mrs. Jesse Allen Hodges.

In those days, photography was done only in the photographer's studio. We could not keep the eight o'clock appointment to have our wedding photos taken at Sun Studio after the ceremony, as the rituals were not completed until that time. Sun Studio closed at 8:30 p.m., and it was already 8:00 o'clock and still raining. The photographer had told us to come to his studio after noon on Sunday, if we were unable to come after the ceremony. So we hurried to Lucing and Francisco's house for the reception. Jess drove his Cleveland touring car close to the doorway, as the weather was still threatening.

What a day! It is as vivid to me today as it was sixty-two years ago! Mary raised her left hand and stroked her rings. She did not learn until much later that Jess bought them from her brother-in-law, Francisco, manager at El Zenith's Jewelry. Francisco knew her ring size, so Jess did not have to guess. She gazed at their wedding portrait. They were a handsome couple. She had kept Jess' tuxedo for him all through World War II and packed it for the sea voyage to America after they were liberated. He insisted that he would be buried in that tuxedo…and he was. *Goodnight, my love…till we meet again.*

ST COLUMBAN'S SOCIETY
MALATE CONVENT
1016 M. H. DEL PILAR
MANILA, P. I.

CERTIFICATE OF MARRIAGE OF
<u>JESSE ALLEN HODGES AND MARIA GAMERO</u>
11-10-23

This is to certify that according to our Marriage Book, Volume 6, page 9, <u>JESSE ALLEN HODGES,</u> single 34 years of age, born in Quinlan, Texas, U.S.A. and resident of Manila, son of Robert Hodges and Malissie Pierce contracted marriage with <u>MARIA GAMERO,</u> single, 18 years of age, born and resident of Manila, daughter of José Gamero and Maria Luz Cucullu.
The witnesses to the marriage were Francisco Gutierrez and Maria Luz Gamero.
The officiating priest was Rev. José M. Gamero.

(REV.) PATRICK KELLY, S.S.C.
Parish Priest
Roman Catholic American Congregation
of Manila

September 21st, 1942

CHAPTER 47

The Reception and Honeymoon

Everyone was in a celebratory mood! The caterers provided delicious dishes and champagne plus other assorted offerings. Pilar and Rosario took turns playing the piano and took requests from the guests. Laurentino Gamez took my mother out on the "dance floor" in the center of the *sala*, and danced *La Jota Aragoneza,* a lively Spanish number. *Mami* and Laurentino received a rousing round of applause. The guests insisted I play the piano. In my excitement, all I remembered was one Jess had been singing lately, *Yes, We Have No Bananas!* Everyone laughed and sang along, including myself. I should have played *Melody of Love* or *Fate* for they were the two songs Jess bought for me.

After about two hours, I slipped away from the festivities and changed into my "going-away" outfit...a lovely white silk dress Lucing had made for me with a special design embroidered near the left shoulder of two white doves flying across the center of a red and blue moon. Lucing also sewed a red bow at the neckline plus a red sash around the dropped waist, which was the latest style. We hurried because it had begun to rain again and we wanted to make sure we would get to our honeymoon site in *Los Baños*.

We were halfway there when the monsoon rains started and the wind blew with a vengeance, causing the curtains to snap open on the Cleveland. We were soaked. Jess decided we should return to Manila because the weather was getting worse.

As we entered our new home, we surprised Lucing and her sister-in-law, Cecelia, who had brought our wedding gifts from Lucing's house next door, and were placing them on display in our *sala*. They were not expecting us to return until the next day. As they left, she told me she would return another time to help me put the gifts away.

The next morning, Jess took me to early Mass because we wanted to be at the photography studio right after lunch and have our wedding photos taken. Afterward, we drove to *Los Baños* and salvaged our honeymoon. We stopped at The Springs Café, where Jess had surprised me with my engagement ring, and enjoyed our first meal together as man and wife until five o'clock, before deciding to drive home, because the weather was becoming unstable again.

While we were away, Lucing arranged our wedding gifts and had a light snack prepared for us on the breakfast table. I immediately called to thank her for all she had done.

When Jess opened the back door the next morning to leave for work, he encountered a problem. The yard was flooded. Since he was already dressed for work, he asked me to drive the car from the garage to the back stairway so he would not get his pants and shoes wet, as the water was over a foot high.

"Jess, I've never driven a car before! I don't think I can!" I yelped.

"Sure you can," Jess said in a soothing voice. "I'll tell you what to do. It's a short distance. You can do it!"

He explained the process, and I followed his instructions given from his perch on the steps. I inched the car along, sloshed through the receding water, and surprised myself by successfully bringing the car around to him.

"I'm so proud of you!" Jess said. "You can do anything you really want to do."

On the following Sunday, he gave me driving lessons. We did this for three Sunday afternoons, until I became comfortable with driving. Jess took me to apply for a student's license so we would not get into trouble if we were stopped or had an accident.

I was the first female in my family who learned to drive a car and the first one to learn English. It all happened because I was determined to marry an American. She sang, *Yes, We Have No Bananas* to herself as she put her writing materials away. The ringing phone interrupted the chorus. It was Mary Jane.

"Well, I was married today," she laughed as she replied to Mary Jane's query about her day. "Would you like to read it?"

CHAPTER 48

Adjusting to Marriage

The monsoon season struck with a vengeance. Life came to a standstill with the severe flooding. It was dangerous to ford the deep waters as one might easily be swept away by the strong current. If the swift current did not get you, a large snake seeking higher and drier ground might. Pigs, cattle, horses, and *carabaos* floated alongside the ducks and geese. All were struggling for their lives. Santa Mesa was noted for floods more than any other area of Luzon due to its low elevation.

Jess decided we should not live in Santa Mesa. He would search for a house on higher ground. His construction work was in San Juan, in the foothills, making it further inland and away from the sea. We needed to live in San Juan, so Jess would be closer to his work. We had our first New Year's resolution for 1924.

Christmas was approaching, and Jess needed the perfect gift for his new bride. *Mary should have an excellent piano...only the best.* He set out to find one and was successful. Her piano would be delivered on Christmas Eve as a surprise.

Thankfully, the rains eased enough on December 24 so the new piano could be delivered. Jess made sure he would be home in time to witness its delivery. When he spied the delivery truck from the upstairs window, Jess called downstairs.

"Mary, someone is at the door. Would you answer? I am still shaving."

He waited about one minute before he peeped around the stairway to catch the expression on her face. He was glad he did.

"Oh, my goodness!" I exclaimed with mouth and eyes wide open. "Is the piano for this address?"

When the deliverymen read the address on the invoice, I laughed and tears of happiness trickled down my face.

"Oh, Jess, it is the most beautiful piano I have ever seen!" I cried and slid my fingers gently across the polished, upright piano.

"It's your Christmas present, dear," Jess said, as I rushed into his arms.

"But it isn't the Day of The Three Kings!" I spouted.

"The day of what?" Jess asked while scratching his head. "What do three kings have to do with a Christmas gift?"

"Oh, it is our custom that gifts are given on January 6, the Day of The Magi," I explained.

"Well, I can always return it," Jess teased.

"Don't you dare," I said. "The piano is staying right here."

When the piano was in place, I began running my fingers over the polished ebony and ivory keys. I played *Yes, We Have No Bananas,* because I knew Jess liked it.

"Well, we may have no bananas, but you have a piano!" Jess teased and laughed.

After a while, I stopped playing because it was time to have a light supper before attending Mass with my family. We were expected at Midnight Mass. I was anxious to brag about my special early gift...my new piano.

Following Midnight Mass, Jess drove us to Frank and Lucing's home for *tapas y copas*...small snacks and wine. I excitedly told everyone the news about my piano. They were all happy for me for they knew how much I loved to play. Pilar changed the subject.

"Will you and Jess be joining us at the Santa Ana Cabaret?" Pilar asked. "Francisco and Lucing have reserved a table for New Year's Eve."

Jess was quiet and so was I. New Year's Eve once meant going to a dance club, dancing all night and welcoming the New Year. My thoughts were racing. *My life is different. I am married. I really want to go dancing. I always have so much fun at the Santa Ana Cabaret, but I hate to ask Jess to go. Jess does not like to dance. What should I do?*

"I'll have to discuss it with Jess, Pilar," I replied and glanced at Jess.

Later, when we were at home, Jess knew I was thinking about New Year's Eve, so he broached the subject.

"Mary, I have a proposition for you. We can be with your family, but just before midnight, I want us to come home and receive the New Year together....just us," Jess said quietly. "Everyone gets so crazy at the dance hall on New Year's Eve, and many get drunk."

Jess would drink wine on special occasions, but never touched hard liquor. He had seen its effects on others.

I agreed to his proposition. *At least I would be with friends and family and enjoy the evening.* I chided myself for having these thoughts.

We arrived at the Santa Ana Cabaret around 10:30 p.m. and the music was playing so loud, we had to raise our voices to be heard. The large dance hall was divided in half by a latticework wall so the public was on one side and the servicemen, their dates, and/or paid dancers used the other half. Separate outside doors assured one group did not enter the other's designated area.

Francisco knew I loved to dance so he escorted me to the dance floor. Raphael spotted me on the dance floor and hurried to see me.

"Maria, I'm so happy to see you!" Raphael exclaimed.

I told Francisco I needed to return to our table, thinking Raphael would walk away, but he followed us. When we arrived at our table, Jess rose to greet us.

"Jess, you remember Raphael." I averted my eyes as I spoke.

Jess and Raphael shook hands, while Raphael congratulated him on our marriage. The lights dimmed for the next dance and Raphael asked Jess if he might have one dance with me. Jess had no choice but to agree. As we danced, I became disillusioned. It seemed I didn't care anymore about dancing. It was so different before, when I was single. Our conversation was stilted and not interesting.

"Your husband must be a dependable man, Maria, or you would not have married him," Raphael offered.

"Yes, Raphael," I replied. "Would you please take me to our table?"

Well, we won't be coming to any more dances. Much has changed.

Raphael wished everyone a "Happy New Year," thanked Jess for allowing me to dance with him, and left.

"We can go home anytime you are ready, Jess," I said. "I don't care to stay any longer."

We expressed our thanks, bid them all a "Happy New Year," and slipped away. A quiet celebration at home would be perfect. We would ring in 1924 in our own way.

The phone rang. It was Linnie. She wanted to bring photos by for her mother to see. She had baked a cake to share, as Emma and Lucy would be with her. Mary always enjoyed having her daughters drop by for a visit. She removed a box of receipts and cancelled checks from the dining table. Audrey Eichner, a dedicated member of St. Williams, was coming this afternoon to help with her annual tax report. Mary put the kettle on to make instant tea, coffee, and, of course, hot chocolate!

CHAPTER 49

Making Changes

February tiptoed into our lives quietly…full of secrets to be disclosed. I said nothing about my upcoming birthday to Jess. I wanted to see if he would remember. On the fourteenth, Jess arrived with a beautiful bouquet of white roses and a large box of chocolate-covered cherries. He smiled, gave me a hug and a kiss while he whispered in my ear.

"Happy Valentine's Day, Mary. I love you."

"I have no gift for you," I cried. "Is it the American custom for the wife to give her husband a gift?"

Our family never celebrated Valentine's Day before. Yes, he was a saint, but we prayed to saints. We never bought gifts or cards on St. Valentine's Day.

"You are my gift," Jess said smiling. "I don't need anything else."

The next day Jess announced we were going shopping. I was rather puzzled.

"Why are we going shopping?" I asked. "I don't need anything."

"Ah, yes, you do," Jess explained. "You will need a birthday gift, and since I don't do well selecting gifts, you may purchase anything you like for your birthday."

I was surprised and happy. I grabbed my purse, pulled on my hat, and followed Jess to the car.

Jess drove to The Escolta where several high-end shops were located, parked the car, and escorted me into the finest dress shop. I found two dresses I liked and tried them on for Jess' approval. If I had tried on a sack, he would have said he liked it. He paid for the dresses and we continued shopping. A men's shop caught my eye.

"Let's go in here," I said.

"What for? You already have a man!" Jess teased.

"Well, I want you to have a new suit for church. It's my birthday and you said I could have anything I wanted. I want you to have a new suit. You also need a new hat," I informed him.

He selected a suit similar to his old one and showed it to me.

"Oh, no, Jess. You are going to have a different color and style this time," I insisted.

He settled on a smart navy blue suit and tried it on. While he was busy with the alterations clerk, I saw the display of men's hats and found a white Stetson. *This hat would be perfect for a man from Texas!*

The alterations were completed and Jess approached me. I pointed to the white Stetson. Jess laughed.

"Are you trying to make me a cowboy?"

"No, I think a man from Texas should wear a Texas hat!" I laughed.

He tried several on before he selected a light gray hat. He felt the white one would become soiled with daily wear in his business.

We were through shopping so we left, collected our clothes from the Chinese laundry, and were returning home, when Jess noticed the signs for the Manila Exposition.

"What is the Manila Exposition?" Jess asked.

"Well, it is like a fair," I explained. "There are many exhibits, shows, rides, and food vendors."

"Why don't we see what it's all about?" Jess asked.

We walked around viewing some of the exhibits displayed in the large halls. Later we sampled some of the tasty food offerings at several booths before sitting outside to enjoy a beverage and watch the people drift by. We enjoyed being at the fair, but decided we had seen enough, so we went home. We were so tired from the walking and excitement that we did not take time to put our packages and laundry away. Our houseboy, DacDac, would handle those chores on Monday.

Jess awakened early on Monday morning and noticed his new suit, which he had hung over the door, was missing. His hatbox containing the new Stetson was also gone. He stepped into the hallway and discovered the hall mirror was missing.

"Mary," he said as he nudged me awake. "Did you put everything away last night? I thought you were going to let our houseboy take care of it. Did you have DacDac remove the hall mirror?"

"What are you talking about, Jess?" I said, as I began stirring from the bed. "What do you mean?"

"We've been robbed, Mary," Jess said. "We were robbed last night while we were sleeping. I'm calling the police."

I was in shock. I rushed into my dressing room. My jewelry, Jess' watch and cufflinks...all were stolen. I thanked God I was too tired to remove my rings last night. I usually removed them when I prepared for bed. Jess and I made a list for the police. I dictated and he wrote.

The police made a thorough search and discovered someone had gained access through the open window in the kitchen downstairs. I guess our houseboy had forgotten to close it before leaving for the weekend. *Was the thief already in their home when they returned last night?*

I was frightened and did not want to be by myself. I visited my mother and stayed with her until Jess returned from work.

"That settles it. I am finding a place for us to stay in San Juan tomorrow," Jess announced. "Get help and start packing."

Mary recalled moving to a different place before the end of February. *I was so happy to be out of there. I still get nervous when I think about being robbed as we slept!*

The front doorbell rang. Mary went to investigate. *Who is ringing my front doorbell? My family uses the kitchen door.* She peeked out the side curtains. Two young girls and an adult were waiting.

"Yes, who is it?" Mary asked.

"We're from the Girl Scouts of America. Would you like to buy a box of cookies?"

Mary smiled, unlocked the door, and removed the safety chain. *I can't turn down Girl Scout cookies! They are so delicious with hot chocolate!*

CHAPTER 50

Building Together

In early March 1924, many changes were taking place in my body. Since my sister Lucing lived next door, I asked her questions about these changes. She gave me a hug and asked several pertinent questions. After listening to my answers, she patted my tummy.

"Your body is preparing for a baby," Lucing said and hugged me again.

"Oh, what must I tell Jess?" I asked, as I knew nothing about having a baby.

"Tell him, if God wills, he will be a father in about seven months," Lucing smiled knowingly.

I was anxious for Jess to get home to give him the news. I put on my best dress and brushed my hair until it sparkled. *We are expecting our first child!*

When Jess entered our bedroom, he noticed I was dressed in my best outfit.

"Are we going somewhere?" Jess inquired. "Have I forgotten an important date?"

"No, Jess," I said with a smile. "I have news for you."

Words poured from my mouth spilling over each other like water rushing through a rocky stream. Jess was quiet. He reached for me and gave me a tender embrace.

"I guess this is what happens when you spend New Year's Eve at home together instead of at a dance hall," Jess teased. "I am so happy, Mary. We have to find a new place to live right away!'

March bumped right into April and pushed it into May before Jess found another house for us to rent. In May, he located a house at #84 Blumentritt Street in San Juan. It was fairly close to his job site so he could return daily for lunch. Having Jess nearby pleased me, as I was nervous about moving, living away from my family, and having a baby. I was also happy to learn our new residence was next door to family friends…the former mayor of Manila, Felix Roxas, and his wife, Doña Carmen. They had two girls, Maria and Florencia. It was comforting to have a Spanish family nearby.

Our houseboy, DacDac, did not want to live in San Juan. On the first of June, we hired a young couple, Florensio and Teresa. Since I was expecting our first child, the arrangement would work out well. Teresa was to do the housework and Florensio would do the marketing, cooking, and yard work.

The house was a large two-story building. The kitchen, dining room, and office were located on the first floor. A sunroom, large living room, and three spacious bedrooms with baths were on the second floor. The floors were polished wide planks of Philippine mahogany *(narra)*. Wide windows allowed daylight to dance across the shiny floors. The backyard was large, peppered with fruit trees, and landscaped with native shrubbery. A two-car garage was attached to one side with an entry into the kitchen.

We were settled into our new home and Jess was building a home for the Hickock family when he was approached by a wealthy Spanish farmer, Felico Suarez, about building a home on a hilly lot in San Juan. He had seen the work being done on the Hickock place nearby and was impressed with the quality of the construction. Mr. Suarez described what he wanted, and met with Jess and his draftsman to prepare the building plans for approval. The plans were approved and construction started. Mr. Tom Weeks, manager of San Juan Heights Development, came to see Jess about being in charge of the development. Six lots were ready for homes with many more lots included in the plans. He had seen homes Jess had already built and was impressed. Following a long discussion, Jess agreed to manage construction of the development and to build six homes. Jess had two prefabricated homes already built…the first ones in Manila. These could be relocated to the lots. A contract was signed to accept those two, plus four others. Jess made sure he did not overcharge, as he wanted their business. Only a small margin of profit was built into the contract.

All was going well and Jess was about halfway through the project when construction costs escalated. Reconstruction after the 1923 earthquake, which destroyed the centers of Tokyo and Yokohama, spilled over into 1924 and created a high demand for building materials from the Philippines. Lumber doubled in price. It was impossible for Jess to build those contracted homes for the prices he had quoted. Jess approached Mr. Weeks with his problem, but Mr. Weeks was unyielding. He had already sold many homes using the base price quoted by Jess and would not budge.

When Jess explained the situation to me, I advised him to get an attorney, but Jess was not an aggressive person and chose to continue with the building although it would mean a huge financial loss. The Philippine Trust & Company Bank loaned Jess enough money to pay the laborers and cover expenses. We were broke and in debt.

Jess became depressed. I tried to comfort him and repeated my mother's favorite Spanish saying, *"No hay mal que por bien no venga."* Thank goodness Jess listened to me. He was still building the two-story home for Mr. Suarez so Jess approached him about getting a draw to pay his employees. Mr. Suarez liked Jess so he provided the partial payment.

Mr. Suarez took interest in Jess' personal life and inquired about our family.

"Well," Jess replied, "I am married to a Spanish girl and we are expecting our first child in September."

"Really?" Mr. Suarez responded. "I am acquainted with many Spanish families, as I was educated in Manila. What is your wife's family name?"

"Her family's name is Gamero," Jess stated.

Mr. Suarez became excited.

"Would you ask her if she is related to Don José Gamero, the professor of nautical engineering who taught in Manila? I was his student," Mr. Suarez said.

Jess said he would. That evening, Jess told me about his chat with Mr. Suarez.

"Mr. Suarez asked me about your maiden name. He got excited when I said it was 'Gamero.' He asked if Don José Gamero was a relative," Jess said.

"Don José was my father," I replied. "I was only three years old when he died so I don't remember much about him. *Mami* and my older sisters have told me many stories about him."

"Well," Jess continued, "Mr. Suarez was his student. He will be glad to know you are related."

Jess met Mr. Suarez the next day and told him Don José was my father. He was delighted and surprised Jess with his generosity.

"Jess, I am so pleased you are married to Don José's daughter. I will be happy and honored to help my professor's family in any way. I can start paying for all the building materials myself, so you will not have to cover those expenses," Mr. Suarez stated.

While Jess was finishing Mr. Suarez's home, Mr. Weeks was fired as manager of San Juan Heights and Mr. Sam Myers was named as the new manager. After he found out what Mr. Weeks had done to Jess, he called and asked Jess to come to meet with him.

Jess promised to come after he finished the Suarez's home. Mr. Suarez was anxious to relocate his family from Iloilo to Manila. His children were preparing for their university studies. Jess met the Suarez family and was amused by the names they selected for their children…Jesus, Maria, and Joseph. Mr. Suarez was proud of his family and insisted, once they were settled in their new home, we come to visit them and become better acquainted.

Funny, how I am remembering my life so clearly. It seems like these events took place only yesterday. Times were tough, but toughness helped us become closer.

Mary covered her notes, photos, and other writing materials with a clean cloth. She was becoming tired and ready for *merienda*…a Spanish custom. *I think I'm ready for blackberry wine. Salud!*

CHAPTER 51

News from Texas

While Jess and I shopped for my birthday present in February 1924, Jess found a box of cigars to send his father, Robert Wesley Hodges, who lived on the family farm west of Quinlan, Texas. Jess wrote a brief note to enclose with the package. He knew his father would enjoy those cigars for his birthday in March.

Jess thought about his home in Texas. He left when he was almost seventeen. Jess was about twelve when his mother, Malissie (Lissie) Pierce, died in 1901. His life was never the same after her death. His father, Robert Wesley (R. W.) Hodges, was left to care for the three children: James Wesley (Jim), Jesse Allen (Jess), and Emma Ethel. Not long after Malissie died, R. W. married his stepsister, Mary Andrew (Terry) Mann. To this union were born: Lois Eleanor (who died in 1916), Thelma Alberta, and Dorothy Pauline. Mary and R. W. divorced in 1911. On May 19, 1912, R. W. married Della Baker. Their children were: Robert Newton, William Glen, Margaret Edwina, Helen Passatta, and Benjamin Eugene (Gene). Gene, the last child, was born four months after Jess and I had our first child.

Jess and I received the following letter acknowledging receipt of the cigars along with a touch of news from Hunt County, Texas:

Quinlan, Tex. 3-3-1924 R-3
Mr. J. Hodges
1429 P. O. B. Manila, P. I.

My Dear Son,

The 2 Boxes Cigars arrived last week. Many Thanks they are fine Smokers. I have only Smoked 3. I half to Smoke at my Leisure. I Cant Smoke and Even Gear up a horse. Every time I draw Smoke I half to take Out my Cigar and let the Smoke Out. It would make my head Swim. We have had a wet cold winter. So far it is fair and nice today. All is well with us. On the 16th of March, this month, I will bee 61 years old. Cant bee hear many more years. So wee must Live in a waye that wee Can go to Heaven Where there is no Sorrow no Weary. Jim is at Lubbock, Tex. All well far as I no. Josh and

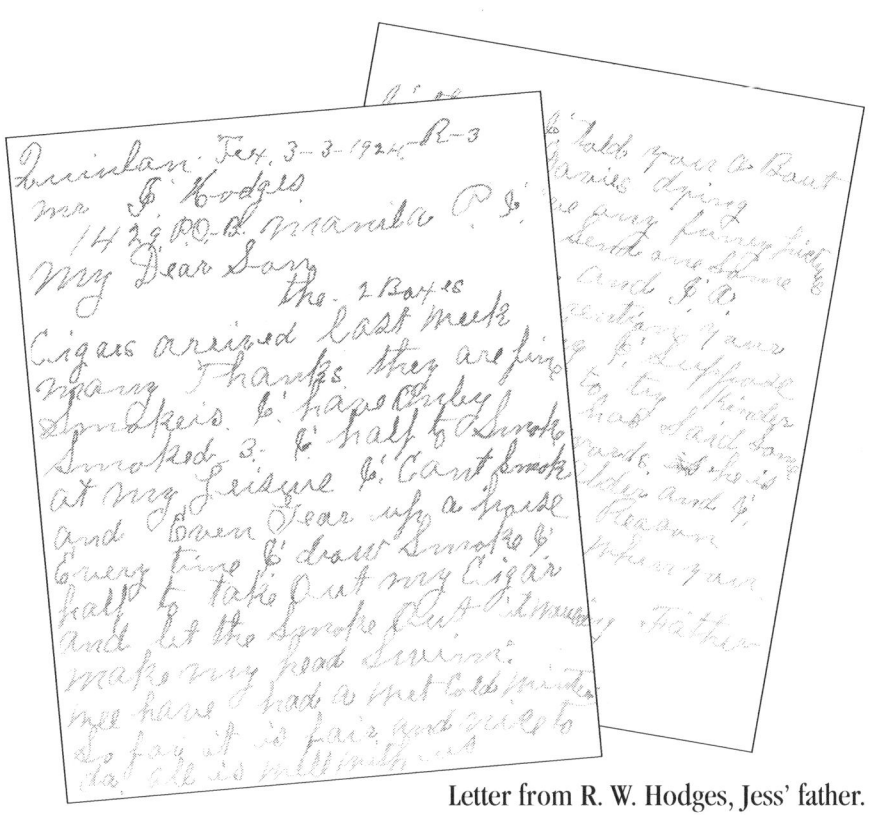

Letter from R. W. Hodges, Jess' father.

Family are well. Jim Pierces people are all Stirring. Charley Mings Still unmarried and live with his mother he plays the Fiddle for parties 2 and Some time 3 a week. $5 per night. He is making a Small Crop last year and this - well Jesse, I hope you are well and doing nicely. I think I told you about Miss Pear Davies dying. If you have any funny pictures or verses Send one Some time. C. N. and J. A. have not mention your name lately. I Suppose C. N. Decided to try kinder treatment. He had Said Some awfull hard words. He is getten Some Older and I Suppose Better Reason however. So Rite when you can.

                                              Your Loving Father
                                              R. W. Hodges

Jess explained about his Uncle Charles Newton (C. N.) Hodges. He was unhappy with Jess because he wanted Jess to come to work for him in Iloilo. C. N. and his wife, Linnie Higdon Hodges, found ways to make money in Iloilo with pawn shops, stores, and rental property. He reinvested his profits by purchasing sections of land in Texas and Oklahoma, plus real estate in New York. C. N. was a successful entrepreneur. He loved his money more than anything else. Jess' uncle had no compunction about taking advantage of relatives in order to turn a profit. Jess learned this trait about his Uncle C. N. after working for him. Jess knew he would have to go into business for himself in order to make money. Jess had not spoken to or seen his uncle since he left Iloilo.

    About a month after we had received the letter from Jess' father, someone rang the bell incessantly at our front gate. Our servants were in their quarters, so Jess left the bed, dressed, and checked to see who was so insistent at this late hour. I was already in bed and did not plan to get out because I had been on my feet all day and my ankles were swollen.

Before long, I heard men's voices in our living room. Whoever was at the front gate was invited into our home. I heard a booming voice, heavily "infected" with a Texas accent arguing with Jess.

"I'm here to meet your bride, Jess, and I'm not leaving until I do."

"She's already in bed and really needs to rest, as she is expecting our first child," Jess stated.

"All the more reason I need to see her. I got a letter from your dad, and he asked me to do him the favor of coming to see you and meet your wife, since he can't come himself." The Texas twang resonated into our bedroom.

Jess was reluctant to ask me to get out of bed and meet the man.

"I'm sorry, Mary," Jess said apologetically. "My Uncle C. N. has come from Iloilo at my father's request and says he will not leave until he has met you. Please put on your robe and come into the living room. Maybe he will go after he meets you."

When I entered the living room, Jess' uncle was standing near the piano admiring our wedding portrait, which hung above the piano. He turned, glanced at me and smiled.

"By golly, you're like your picture. You've changed, though!" C. N. laughed. "I guess you and Jess are going to grow before long. I'll have to report the news to my brother, R. W., in Texas."

"I am pleased to meet a member of Jess' family," I said.

"Well, I've done my duty. It's late and I need to make the midnight ferry to Iloilo," C. N. stated.

"We hope you will come again and, perhaps, have dinner with us the next time you are here," I said as I held out my hand.

He gave me a firm handshake, picked up his hat, gave Jess a smile, and headed for the front door.

"I'll walk with you," Jess said. "I need to lock the gate."

My mother and Rosario were weekly visitors at our home each Saturday as we made preparations for my baby's arrival. Rosario prepared the baby's layette and arranged for the nuns at Antipolo to make several hand-embroidered pillowcases for the baby's two tiny pillows. *Mami* selected several items at Fuller's Fine Designs, a factory for children and infant's wear, and had family members embellish them with fine embroidery. My baby would be the best-dressed baby in Manila.

Mary smiled as she remembered the items prepared by her family for her baby's layette. Her mother was so proud to have an American grandchild. Her father, Don José would have felt quite the opposite. *It is amazing how events and experiences can change the attitudes and emotions entrenched within us. What a difference Jess made in our lives.*

CHAPTER 52

Pilar and Tony

Mary switched the small oscillating fan near her writing table on "Low" so the breeze would not scatter her writing materials, notes, and photos. She pulled Pilar and Tony's photo from the family album and recalled their romantic story. *What a handsome couple...Pilar with her fair peachy complexion and blonde hair and Tony with his swarthy olive skin and dark brown hair. How opposite they were! No wonder they were attracted to each other.*

When Tony Settember came with Jess to escort my family to church, Pilar noticed his handsome appearance. An affable gentleman and a snappy dresser, his winning smile flashed "Hello" before he said the word. His dark eyes twinkled mischievously as he spoke. Tony and Pilar each admired the other. She kept hoping he would come to church with Jess again, but Tony was busy with his work.

After Jess and I became engaged, Jess dissolved his partnerships, and Tony searched for new employment. The remaining partners continued their businesses. Tony was hired by the City of Manila as a motorcycle traffic policeman. He thoroughly enjoyed wearing his snappy uniform, and racing around the city on a motorcycle. Catching speeders was a game. Tony could issue a speeding ticket and present it in a such charming way. It would have been poor manners to object or not accept the ticket.

At our wedding reception, Tony paid special attention to Pilar, and she enjoyed his attention immensely. They danced several numbers. Tony turned on his Italian charm. Pilar was truly impressed. He made sure to also be attentive to our mother, Doña Luz, and curried her favor. The dashing Italian easily charmed anyone within range of his flashing smile.

Mami noticed a Manila policeman driving by their apartment daily. She also watched Pilar rush to the window to catch a glimpse of him as he passed.

"Why are you so interested in that policeman driving by on a motorcycle, Pilachu?" *Mami* inquired.

Pilar replied, "Do you remember the young Italian with Jess? He chatted with you at Maria and Jess' wedding reception."

"Ah, *si, Tony,*" *Mami* noted. "I remember him."

Pilar left the room to avoid further questioning. She was not ready with answers.

Tony asked us in December if we would accompany him to the Gamero's apartment to speak with *Mami* about courting Pilar. He asked at least three times, before we gave in to his request and made the arrangements just before Christmas.

The visit with my mother did not go well. Tony arrived still wearing his uniform, which startled *Mami*. Having a policeman enter your home meant something was wrong…perhaps a crime had been committed. She was upset because the neighbors might see a uniformed officer entering her residence and start ugly rumors. Tony apologized for wearing his uniform. He felt it was a badge of honor, not something to cause disgrace to Pilar's family.

"Doña Luz, I will not wear my uniform when I come to call on Pilar," Tony offered.

"No, Tony," *Mami* stated flatly. "As long as you are a policeman, you cannot come into this house."

Tony left feeling dejected. *What am I to do? I love this job! I need this job! I love Pilar!* He continued to drive by Pilar's window…hoping to see her.

Fate stepped in. In January 1924, Tony was chasing a speeder when his front tire hit a large water puddle, causing him to lose control. An ambulance rushed him to the hospital. Tony had several broken bones and external injuries. The motorcycle was demolished, and his career as a motorcycle policeman was over. He would be hospitalized for at least two weeks and needed two more for recovery and therapy.

Jess and I told Pilar what happened. She was upset and wanted to see him. We plotted a ruse. The first Sunday after Tony's accident, Jess told *Mami* we were going to the park (Luneta). He asked permission to take Pilar with us, as it was a beautiful day for a walk. *Mami* agreed. Instead, Jess drove us to the hospital to see Tony. When we arrived, we discovered he was in a men's ward with several other patients. As Jess stepped inside the ward, Tony waved from the first bed. From the doorway, we could see an attractive native girl, with long black hair spilling over her shoulders, perched on his bedside. Pilar refused to go in, because Tony was talking with *that* woman. Tony noticed Pilar and me in the doorway and asked the girl to please step outside. She swept by us, ignoring our presence as she passed.

Pilar was blushing as we stepped into Tony's ward. She did not say a word…just listened and smiled. Jess and Tony talked about his work, until Jess decided it was time for us to drive to the Luneta. My mother might ask questions. Jess knew her well.

The following week, Tony was dismissed, and began his search for another job during his recovery period. Within three days, he was hired as car salesman for Luneta Motors in Ermita. He would earn a smaller salary than he did as a police officer, but it was adequate, plus he could make commissions on sales.

The main motivation for accepting the job was to obtain permission to court Pilar. Surely, Doña Luz would accept him as an industrious salesman.

Once again, Tony asked Jess to accompany him to talk with Doña Luz. Jess agreed and the date was set for the following Sunday. Tony would go with us to escort my mother, Pilar, and Lorenzo to Mass. Lorenzo, seventeen, had finished his education, and returned home to make plans for his future. Fr. Gamero, our half-brother, offered to take Lorenzo to train as a Jesuit priest. *Mami* did not want him to be a priest. She wanted him with her. She was hoping, since Lorenzo was her only living son, he would be the one to provide for her after Pilar married.

After church, we returned to my mother's apartment for *merienda*. Everyone enjoyed the delicious *tapas y postres* along with tea or coffee. Jess and Tony remained in the *sala* to talk with *Mami* while we went to the kitchen to wash the dishes. Once again, Jess spoke on Tony's behalf. *Mami* listened to what Jess had to say. She respected his opinion. After Jess explained Tony had a fine job as a salesman with Luneta Motors and was no longer with the Manila Police Department, *Mami* agreed to allow Tony to call on Pilar, who was listening intently from the kitchen doorway. She smiled and hugged me. *Tony would be courting her!*

Tony became a regular visitor in the Gamero home and shared the responsibility of taking the family to church each Sunday, as I was becoming rather large with my pregnancy and could not attend on occasion. Tony was happy to take them to church. He was Roman Catholic, spoke Spanish, Italian, *Tagalog,* and English, and made every effort to charm Doña Luz. He had already charmed Pilar.

In June 1924, Tony proposed to Pilar and she happily accepted his ring. They needed a year to make the preparations for their wedding. Once again the women of the family gathered to prepare her trousseau, as they had done for me. It became a dual project, as we were also preparing baby clothes for our baby due in September.

Mary smiled as she remembered how long it took to prepare for those events. Everyone concentrated efforts to complete the baby's layette, as Pilar's wedding date was set for July 25, 1925, and our baby was due in September 1924. *I was her matron of honor, and still nursing when they wed!*

CHAPTER 53

And Bobby Makes Three

In August 1924, one month prior to our first child's birth, all was ready for the baby's arrival. Teresa, our cook's pregnant wife, and I were chatting while she was darning clothes when she screamed and shook spasmodically. I grabbed her shoulders and tried to hold her but her convulsions were severe. I lowered her to the floor to keep her from falling from her chair. Unsure of what to do next, I yelled for help. Doña Carmen, our neighbor, heard my cries. She hurried over, and looked at Teresa in dismay.

"Maria, your servant is having epileptic seizures," Doña Carmen said. "Get a small towel…hurry."

She folded the hand towel and put it between Teresa's teeth to protect her tongue.

"All we can do is keep her from harming herself and wait for the seizures to stop," Doña Carmen continued. "Where is her husband?"

"Florensio is at the market," I said, after I caught my breath.

I was so afraid Teresa might lose her baby because her convulsions were so violent. The seizures abated. Teresa was exhausted and could not recall what happened.

"I will get a pillow and blanket so she can rest there," I said.

"What happened? Why am I on the floor?" Teresa asked in a weak voice.

"You have had seizures and should lay quietly until you are feeling better," Doña Carmen ordered.

As I adjusted the pillow and blanket, Florensio entered the room. He was shocked to see his wife on the floor and shouted questions as he rushed to her side. Doña Carmen explained and told him Teresa should not be moved until she felt stronger.

"Is she having our baby?" Florensio asked.

Doña Carmen said, "You need to talk with the doctor about her condition."

When Teresa was feeling better, Florensio helped her to the servant's quarters. He returned to say he would not prepare the evening meal. Teresa should not be by herself. The next day, he announced they should return to their province to be with her family. He gave us one week's notice.

Jess arrived home from work tired, hot, and dirty. He hurried past the kitchen door announcing that he needed a shower before touching anything or anybody. I continued preparing a small supper while he showered and rested. I stepped into our bedroom, where he was stretched out on the bed, to tell him supper was ready.

"Where are the servants? Why aren't they serving our meal? You shouldn't be doing all this work!" Jess spouted as I served the meal.

I explained what had occurred earlier and told him we would have to find someone else to help with the cooking, housework, and yard work. We needed to train servants regarding our daily routine before our baby arrived. Jess patted my hand and assured me he would take care of matters.

After helping me clear the table, Jess visited the servant's quarters while I was putting food away and washing dishes. Before long he returned wearing a smile.

"Florensio and Teresa will stay until after our baby is born. She won't be much help, but at least we will have someone here we can trust while you are in the hospital. This will give us more time," Jess beamed, feeling proud.

I felt better. Our trusted servants would be in our home while we were away. I did not want to be robbed again!

On September 22, my first labor pains began. I was frightened. Jess helped me into our car. We stopped by *Mami's* apartment to get her, and drove to St. Paul's Hospital in Manila. Dr. Benito Valdez, my attending physician, had made all the arrangements. I was admitted and taken to the maternity ward where the sisters of St. Paul's attended to my needs before calling Dr. Valdez. He arrived within the hour and checked my progress regularly. *Mami* and Jess were by my side giving me encouragement and attention.

By late afternoon, I had not progressed sufficiently, so Dr. Valdez decided he would go home to have his evening meal and return for his rounds afterward. Jess was restless and decided he would go home as well and eat, since he had not eaten since breakfast. *Mami* stayed with me.

Dr. Valdez returned as promised. After checking me at nine o'clock, he decided to stay at the hospital. By eleven o'clock, he checked again and felt I was ready to deliver. During the delivery, Dr. Valdez kept telling me to take deep breaths, while he worked with moving the baby's head for the delivery. Our baby was delivered just before midnight. The umbilical cord was wrapped around his neck. *The navel cord was strangling my poor baby!*

I prayed aloud for God to help Dr. Valdez. He worked hard to keep my baby alive. After cutting the umbilical cord, the nurses had two pans of water ready…one with cold water and the other with warm water. The baby was immersed first in cold water, then in warm water. Between immersions, he would strike the baby with a wet towel. I kept my eyes on my baby and prayed the entire time. *Please, God, spare my baby!*

Jess was called when I was taken into the delivery room, but was not allowed to enter. *I'm glad he does not have to see this. He would be devastated. He counted the days till the baby's arrival. Our "blue baby" was hanging between life and death!*

When our baby uttered his first cries, tears of joy sprang to my eyes and I sobbed. *Thank you, God, for granting life for my baby! Thank you, God, for helping Dr. Valdez! Thank you, God, for our baby boy!*

Mami brought the pink silk baby shirt that I had worn as a newborn. She asked the nurses to dress the baby in the "girly" diaper shirt, after the baby was cleaned. She wanted to play a joke on Jess.

Jess entered the maternity ward with a wide grin on his face. He was so excited that the baby and I were all right, because he was told it was a difficult birth. When the nurse brought the baby dressed in pink, he was puzzled and stared at the baby, whose face was as pink as its shirt. *Had he been so excited he misunderstood Dr. Valdez about the sex of the baby? He thought they had a boy!*

Mami noticed his confusion. She laughed and explained her reason.

"*Nena* said your friends bet the baby was going to be a girl, but you insisted your first baby would be a boy," *Mami* said. "I requested the nurse dress your baby in *Nena's* first baby shirt to trick you."

Jess grinned, but was not sure what to say. He kissed me and told me he would see me in the morning, as *Mami* wanted to stay. He was excited, proud, and anxious to hand out cigars to his friends.

Early the next morning, I had a visitor. Luie, my first "puppy love" visited the maternity ward. His sister was having surgery in the same hospital. When he learned I was there, he came to give us his well wishes. I thanked him for coming and sent my best wishes for his sister's full recovery.

Jess stopped by the hospital on his way to work to bring a new book about infant care, since I would be hospitalized for ten days. He was still beaming about his bouncing baby boy. As soon as he left, I began reading the baby book to learn more about nursing my baby, as I was having difficulty nursing. The nurses began using a bottle to feed him, which concerned me. My breasts were becoming distended and painful.

Sister Adrienne, my nurse and friend of my deceased sister, Natividad, noticed my breasts were hard when she gave me a sponge bath. She was concerned about

Mary and Jess Hodges with their first born son, Robert Morris Hodges (Bobby) at Blumentritt, San Juan, P.I., 1924.

mastitis. Another patient in the next ward, who was nursing her child, was having an emergency appendectomy. Her three-month-old baby was under Sister Adrienne's care, since the woman had no family. Sister Adrienne suggested I allow the three-month-old baby to nurse my breasts to relieve distension. She felt it would be beneficial for both of us. Her patient would not be able to nurse her baby due to the emergency surgery. Her baby refused the bottle and would soon become dehydrated. Sister Adrienne assured me that, although the woman was destitute, she had no contagious diseases. I needed help to relieve the pain in my breasts, and her baby needed to be fed, so I agreed. Her baby and I would help each other. Once I finished nursing her baby, the pressure in my breasts was relieved, and Bobby nursed easily. I nursed both her baby and mine until I left the hospital. I was thankful for Sister Adrienne's help and guidance.

The Sisters of St. Paul's came from France and enjoyed a rare sense of humor. They teasingly called our baby Maurice, since we had not yet named him. Jess and I decided to name him "Robert," after Jess' dad with "Morris" as his middle name, although his birth certificate listed his middle name as "Maurice'." The teasing nuns would not be denied their "Maurice." We never changed the birth certificate.

"Robert is a such a formal name for a little baby," Jess said. "Let's call him 'Bobby'."

The ten-day hospital stay was over. Now we faced the reality of being parents, all alone with our first baby. We were terrified.

CHAPTER 54

So Many Challenges

October 1924 through September 1925 was a period of challenges. Mary rummaged through her notes and photos making sure the major ones were included. The chronological list was checked against the historical events Mary Jane had provided. She sipped her coffee, took two more bites of Malto Meal, and resumed writing.

By October 1, the Hodges family settled into their routine of working, caring for the new baby, and hiring new servants. Florensio and Teresa would leave in two weeks to return to their province to be close to her family when their baby arrived. We interviewed several domestics and hired a native, Aquino, who was older than our previous cook. He would do the cooking and serve as houseboy. His employment was on a trial basis. *Mami* would help care for the baby.

Mami was anxious to schedule an early date for Bobby's baptism, so October 7 was set, since it was also her birthday. My half-brother Fr. Gamero would perform this ritual at The Manila Cathedral in *Intramuros*; however, the date and place were changed, as riots spread in San Juan.

The Filipinos fought with Chinese merchants and created havoc in the area. The police warned the public to stay in their homes until the fighting ceased. In a week, the situation calmed down and, although the issues had not been resolved, it was not as dangerous to travel in the area. The Chinese merchants kept their businesses closed.

The baptism was rescheduled for October 20. Fr. Gamero and Rosario (Charing) met us at our home for the trip to The Cathedral of The Immaculate Conception in Manila, instead of The Manila Cathedral in *Intramuros*. Scheduling conflicts occurred after the date was changed. Jess, Bobby, *Mami,* and I were in one car, and Fr. Gamero, Rosario, and my brother Lorenzo followed in the vehicle provided by the church at Antipolo. A small family gathering in our home followed the rituals, conducted by The Rev. H. J. McNulty, S. J., assisted by my half-brother, Fr. José Gamero, so both English and Spanish rituals could be heard. Jess invited Mr. Suarez to meet Don José Gamero's family. He was so pleased to meet more family members of his beloved Professor Gamero.

"*Srta*. Gamero, how is your aunt, Pascuala?" Mr. Suarez inquired.

Rosario was surprised this relative stranger knew Lola Lala. "She is doing well, *Señor* Suarez," Rosario replied. "Are you acquainted with her?"

"Yes, I met her at the wedding of your father, Don José and your step-mother, Rosario Rocha," Suarez responded. "Pascuala visited our classes at the nautical college to bring messages from your step-mother to Don José. She visited the classrooms often and paid much attention to one student, José Rocha."

After enjoying the *merienda* and the conversation, my half-brother and half-sister left to return to Antipolo so they would not have to drive in the dark. *Mami* was pleased Bobby's soul was protected with his baptism.

Once more we settled into our family routine. Jess worked longer hours on the San Juan Heights development. Caring for Bobby, with help from my mother, kept me busy. I spent more time than necessary reminding Aquino about his household duties. His lazy attitude could not be tolerated. I told Jess we should find someone else. Although Aquino was a better cook than Florensio, he left other chores undone. Jess was puzzled because Aquino refused to live in the servant's quarters. After he finished the supper dishes each evening, he would go to his nearby home and be with his family. Jess never complained.

We made it through the busy holiday season with Aquino. I wished we had someone else, perhaps a couple to live in the servant's quarters. I needed help.

Final preparations for Tony and Pilar's wedding in July 1925 consumed my time and energy. I was doing my best to prepare for being her matron of honor.

On July 15, an unusual noise emerged from under Bobby's crib where Willie, our dog, usually slept. Jess pushed the crib aside, only to have Willie rush past him, stumble down the stairway, and collapse at the foot of the stairs. Willie had suffered a convulsion.

"Willie's been poisoned," Jess stated.

I rushed to the kitchen, poured a cup of milk into a bowl, and beat two eggs into the milk. I set the concoction by Willie's head. He lapped up less than a fourth of the mixture, collapsed, and lay still. Jess took him to his downstairs office, and fixed a place for the dog to rest. Willie made it through the night and rested quietly during the next day. We decided to keep him there until he improved.

Our fox terrier stayed in our bedroom. I needed a watchdog by my side ever since we were robbed in a former residence. We had not yet installed bars over the windows on this home, so I felt vulnerable.

Two days later, Aquino completed his kitchen duties and stopped by the *sala* to tell us he was leaving for the evening. He held a small bundle in his hand…a black handkerchief or small headscarf wrapped around something. Sometimes he would take leftover food home with him, so I dismissed it as being unimportant.

As we prepared to retire, the sounds of Willie's growls from Jess' downstairs office startled us. Jess checked, but found no reason for his growling. He felt Willie was having nightmares. The nightlight was on so I could nurse the baby without waking Jess. After we dozed off, I felt something near my face. When

I opened my eyes, a man's masked face was close to mine. I screamed and the intruder bolted. Jess jumped, grabbed his shotgun and fired a shot. The fox terrier had not uttered a sound. So much for having a watchdog.

All this commotion wakened Bobby, and he began crying. I was shaking as I rushed to his bedroom. After changing him and letting him nurse, I put my sleeping baby in his crib, returned to our bedroom, and checked my dresser for my jewelry box. It was missing.

The next day, Aquino gave notice he would be leaving our employ. He said he and his family were moving from San Juan. I was glad he left, as I never had trusted him.

Mami and Lola Lala arrived later, and were told of the robbery. I told them I suspected Aquino. Jess reported to the police, but Aquino was no longer in San Juan. Lola Lala called her friends with servants to find someone as a replacement. By afternoon, she found a cook named Felix and a house girl named Petra. They were Visayans, had excellent references, and could begin their duties in two days. We were relieved as preparing for Pilar and Tony's wedding on July 25 took priority.

Jess suffered with a cold ever since we left Santa Mesa. We wondered why he did not improve. He was unhappy. He wanted to hold his son, but feared Bobby would catch his cold. I asked Doña Carmen, our next-door neighbor, about the last tenants in this house to see if any suffered any illnesses.

"Maria," she said, "the only one who lived here was the original owner. He had tuberculosis and, instead of going to a sanatorium, he hired special nurses to care for him at home until he died."

I was shocked with her news. *What if Jess has contracted tuberculosis? It is a contagious disease!*

"Jess, you have to see a doctor, and we have to find another house," I announced as he walked in the door.

He was surprised as I retold the details given to me by Doña Carmen.

"I will not live here anymore," I said adamantly. "What if you have already caught tuberculosis! What if our baby gets this horrible disease!"

Jess spoke soothingly and tried to calm my anxiety.

"Mary, I think it's necessary to have direct contact with the infected person to catch the disease," Jess stated. "But, if it will make you feel better, I will see my doctor and look for another place tomorrow."

The medication prescribed for Jess, with instructions to drink plenty of fluids and get more rest, took care of his cold. I made sure he had plenty of eggs and chicken soup.

Within a week, Jess found a home on the corner of Riverside and Salvador. Number Four Salvador was a large two-story house with a kitchen, dining room, and office/den on the first floor; four bedrooms and two baths on the second floor; a double garage; and, ample servant's quarters. It would be perfect for us. We would have room for *Mami* and Lorenzo to live with us after Pilar and Tony's wedding. Only two months remained to complete all the preparations for Pilar and Tony's wedding.

On July 25, 1925, Anthony D. Settember and Maria del Pilar Gamero y Cucullu were married at the Manila Cathedral. Fr. José Ma. Gamero was the officiating priest. Pilar was stunning in her exquisite white brocade wedding dress. The long train, which was delicately embroidered with tiny seed pearls and wisps of Spanish lace, matched the Spanish lace *mantilla* she wore as her veil. She carried a bouquet containing fresh orchids, white roses, and sampaguitas interspersed with lacy greenery and trailing white ribbon. Tony, the handsome groom, was impeccably dressed in his tuxedo with long tails, white high-collared starched shirt, and white gloves. His boutonniere was a single white rose. *Mami* was happy her last daughter was married and would be living nearby. *Don José would have been pleased.*

Following their honeymoon, Tony and Pilar rented a home near his workplace, Luneta Motors, in Ermita on St. Luis Street. The two-story house had two bedrooms, kitchen, dining room, living room and bath on the second floor and a small apartment on the first floor, which Tony rented to his friend, Mr. Long. They used the company car so they did not need a garage.

Mary rubbed her eyes and noted she had missed the nine o'clock news. *Oh, well, I'll fix myself some hot chocolate and, eat a slice of Puddin' Hill fruitcake during the ten o'clock version. The news will be the same.*

Gamero Family Portrait *(L-R):* Mary and Jess Hodges; Consueling and Juanito Gonzalez; Luz *(Mami)* and son, Lorenzo; Pilar and Tony Settember; Lucing and Frank Guiterrez. Photo taken in 1925.

CHAPTER 55

Mami's Secret

In August 1924, *Mami* discovered a lump in her breast and kept her discovery to herself. The family doctor advised her to have the lump removed. Doña Luz told him she would wait until she finished her family responsibilities. She wanted to make sure I survived the delivery of my first child and provided care for my baby. She also needed time to make plans for Tony and Pilar's wedding. She and Lorenzo would be moving in with Jess and me after her surgery. Pascuala (Lola Lala) needed another place to live. These family events were more important to her than her own health.

In August 1925, after discussing the situation with family, Doña Luz entered the hospital to have her long-needed surgery. The lump had grown in those months and her breast was removed. The surgery was devastating. Surgeons cauterized the open flesh with a hot iron rod to kill any remaining roots from the tumor. Compared to our modern procedures, it was barbaric. She took cobalt treatments every two weeks to assure eradication of any malignant cells…considered a preventive measure. She was hospitalized for one month in order to assure recuperation and to complete treatment.

When released from the hospital in September, Jess and I brought my mother and brother, Lorenzo, to live with us. I felt so relieved to have *Mami* and Lorenzo close. They would no longer have to pay rent and would be helpful. Jess hired Lorenzo as his timekeeper to record the working hours for his building crew, as Jess was currently working on building a new home for the Cuzners.

Harold Cuzner, employed by the government as Professor of Agriculture at The Philippine Agricultural College in *Los Baños*, visited San Juan on the weekends to view progress on his new home and visit his wife and seven-year-old daughter, Mary. Their new home was in the same subdivision as the home of Judge and Mrs. Manuel Camus, a relative of our Aunt Carmen.

Jess felt we should entertain the Cuzner and Camus families. He recalled my telling him about playing the piano for the Camus family at several parties when we lived in *Intramuros*.

"Jess," I protested, "I have not had time to practice playing the piano. I have been so busy with moving, our baby, my mother, Lorenzo...."

"Stop," Jess ordered. "Not another word. Do what is necessary to get ready."

"I have not bought any new music pieces or had piano lessons in a long time," I stated, hoping he would not want to add more expenses to our lean budget.

"Find a piano teacher tomorrow and take lessons," Jess stated flatly. "Mary, I enjoy your music. Your mother and Bobby will also enjoy having music in our home."

I checked with my friends about a piano teacher and they recommended Concha Cuervo, a music professor at San Juan University. Arrangements were made. She would start the next day and come once a week to our home. She was demanding and challenged me to try a new piece every week to improve my sight-reading. Lessons were expensive, and I was not happy with the challenges of piano lessons, childcare, and tending to Jess' needs.

Mami sensed my developing frustration. She was fully recovered from her surgery, so she took over the childcare duties and supervised the servants. I was relieved and enjoyed my music lessons much more. Jess was pleased we had worked out the difficulties. We would entertain in our home.

In October, we invited the two families, my Uncle Carlos and Aunt Carmen Cucullu Camus, plus Pilar and Tony for a light supper and entertainment. Jess was the perfect host and made sure everyone was introduced to our young son, Bobby, before I took him to his room for the night. Everyone enjoyed the evening as they laughed, supped, sang, and danced. Jess gave me a hug after the last guest departed. *Although it was an enjoyable evening, I was glad it was behind me.*

Mary shook her head as she remembered. *Jess was trying so hard to impress the Cuzners. We endured extra expense and effort, but it paid off. Word spread about the quality of his work and dedication to his family. Business was booming. He knew what he was doing.*

CHAPTER 56

Dealing with Fate

In late October 1925, Tony was named as top salesman for Luneta Motors. We celebrated his success with a dinner at our home. In early November, the new models were delivered, and he took pride in demonstrating their many features. By November's end, Tony was close to breaking his own record for sales. An important customer asked Tony to bring the Marmon's latest model to his place of business. Tony jumped at the chance. Mr. Alicante bought a new car every year. Tony would break his own record for sales.

As Tony drove the shiny new vehicle away from Luneta Motors and onto St. Luis Street, a streetcar rounded the corner and crashed into the driver's side injuring Tony seriously. A fellow employee rushed him to the hospital. Arriving at the emergency room in an unconscious state, Tony was placed in intensive care and diagnosed with several broken ribs, internal injuries, and a concussion.

Once Tony was admitted, a secretary at Luneta Motors called our home and informed *Mami* of Tony's accident and serious condition. The secretary felt a family member should notify Pilar. We called my sister Pilar to tell her we were coming by to get her, giving her no reason. She should not hear the sad news over the phone.

We arrived at Tony and Pilar's home, gave her the news, and allowed her to collect herself before taking her to see Tony. She was devastated. She had just learned she was pregnant with their first child. She had not told anyone…not even Tony.

When we arrived at the hospital, Tony regained consciousness and acted the part of the "macho Italian" by shrugging off the accident. He was mad at himself for not making a record-breaking sale. He would miss his opportunity, as he was hospitalized. The doctors felt he would be there at least three weeks.

"I will stay with Pilachu while you are in the hospital," *Mami* stated. "She should not be alone."

Her offer had a calming effect on Pilar. She was still distraught, but she had stopped crying. Tony was glad Pilar would have her mother in their home.

"Thank goodness the new cars are fully insured," Tony said. "I'm happy my hospital expenses will also be covered by my insurance with Luneta Motors."

During Tony's hospital stay, our Uncle Carlos (Charles) Swanson decided to accept Pilar's offer to have his daughter, Aurora, live with them. Aurora was happy to be in the Settember's home. The rent was reasonable, and she would be helpful as a companion to Pilar until Tony was released. She wanted to help with the housework when Tony returned. Aurora was happy. She could resume her social life, as her father did not allow her to go out at night or have friends in to visit. She had Pilar's permission.

Mr. Long, an American in his mid-twenties, was renting the downstairs apartment from the Settembers. He noticed Aurora. After Aurora was there about a week, he came upstairs to pay his rent…early. His intent was to meet Aurora.

When Tony returned home to recuperate, Mr. Long visited often to chat with him, but always found time to engage Aurora in conversation. Tony and Pilar watched this budding romance developing. *Should they tell Aurora's father?* They decided to wait and let Aurora tell him when she was ready.

∽∘∾

Mary pulled out a photo of Aurora and remembered what a quiet and private person she was. She did not tell her father about her young man until she was sure her beau was the right one. Aurora suffered emotionally when her mother and father separated. She wanted time to be sure she had chosen wisely. She waited a year before introducing Mr. Long to her father.

CHAPTER 57

Boom or Bust

1926 pushed 1925 aside like a big bulldozer shoving dirt. Jess was swamped with building new homes for the San Juan Heights subdivision. Mr. Myers, the manager, complimented his work. Word spread to a Spanish company, La Urbana. Since Jess had only two more homes to finish for the San Juan Heights job site, he agreed to build houses for La Urbana, also located in San Juan. He finished one small house for La Urbana and was asked to start building a large two-story home for another client, Mr. Montelibano, a wealthy farmer from Negros who wanted his children educated in Manila. Jess was close to finishing the two-story home when Mr. Montelibano decided he wanted the long front stairway covered with a narrow sloping roof for protection from the elements. This roof was not included in the plans or in the pricing for the home. Mr. Montelibano was adamant.

"If La Urbana does not pay you for building the roof, I will pay for it myself," Mr. Montelibano stated. "I will talk with the manager at La Urbana myself."

So, with only a verbal contract between Jess and Mr. Montelibano, Jess built the requested addition. It cost twelve hundred *pesos* more, which was about the amount of profit Jess had figured in his estimate to La Urbana.

Jess informed the inspectors at La Urbana that Mr. Montelibano's home was completed. During their inspection, they noticed the additional roof, but found it was not included in the original plans. The inspector would not approve the building, which delayed the closing process.

"I'm sorry, Mr. Hodges," said the inspector. "You should have spoken with a manager at La Urbana before making those changes."

"Well," Jess offered, "Mr. Montelibano said he would talk with the manager and get approval. He also said if La Urbana did not pay, he would."

The inspector stood his ground. La Urbana would not pay.

Jess became worried, so he visited Mr. Montelibano to explain the situation.

"Well, Mr. Hodges," Mr. Montelibano said, "You are out of luck, as we did not have a written contract."

Jess never collected the money owed to him by Mr. Montelibano. Another lesson learned the hard way...not everyone was to be trusted.

After Jess told me his sad news, I told him my happy news. I was pregnant again. We would be welcoming our second child in August! Pilar and Tony's first child was due in July. Our sister, Consuelo, who lived in Bulan, was pregnant with her fourth child. Her children were Estephania (Fanny, born in 1920 and fathered by M. Reyes); José Maria (Peping or Bull, born in 1922); and, Juan (Juaning, born in 1924). Our oldest sister, Lucing, was pregnant with her fifth child and was due to deliver in July. She already had Francisco Jr. (Frankie, born in 1916); Antonio (Toning, born in 1919); Carmen (Nena, born in 1921); and, José Luis (Peping or Pepito, born in 1923). We were having more babies for our mother to enjoy.

Consueling traveled to Manila to shop for her family, and asked to stay with us. *Mami* and Lorenzo were also there which allowed Consueling more time to visit with them. The Gamero sisters decided to accompany Consueling to The Escolta…the finest shopping district in Manila. We must have been a sight…four pregnant women…giggling and chatting as we waddled down Avenida Rizal.

Mami knew Jess had suffered financial losses and was concerned, since another child was on the way. She was discussing Jess' problems with her friend who told her about Mrs. Cavana, recently widowed, who needed someone to take over her husband's successful enterprise…a luxury car rental business. Mrs. Cavana was not able to continue its operation and the business was for sale. *Would Jess be interested?*

It was May and time for the Fiesta of the Virgin of Antipolo. Rosario visited our home to collect Consueling, her children, and *Mami*. They would stay with Rosario at the convent and wait for the family to

Jess Hodges and crew at the La Urbana construction site.

join them for the annual celebration of *Nuestra Señora de la Paz y Buen Viaje* in Antipolo. Our annual pilgrimage was always a special event in our lives. Our brother Lorenzo stayed behind because he was working for Jess as timekeeper. Lucing, Francisco, Pilar, and Tony would go the following weekend as would Jess, Bobby, and I.

Mami told me her news about the car rental business before leaving for Antipolo. We needed money, so I decided to tell Jess *Mami's* news about Mrs. Cavana's business. Jess was not sure, either, but said we would talk with Mrs. Cavana.

CHAPTER 58

More Texas Visitors

1926 was filled with many surprises. In early June, after Jess and Lorenzo returned to the construction job site following lunch, I received a phone call, and was surprised to learn Jess' brother, James Wesley (Jim) Hodges, and his cousin, Charlie Simpkins, just arrived from Texas. They were calling from a printing office in Santa Cruz, and wanted to speak to Jess.

"Jess just left for work, but I will come to get you," I offered.

There was a pause at the other end. I was a foreigner and a stranger to Jim.

"Yes, that sounds fine," Jim finally replied, and gave me the address.

I drove to the printing shop about ten miles away. When we arrived, I honked the horn and waved at two American men waiting in front. Introductions were shared, but Jim appeared hesitant about getting into our car. We were quite a sight. I was in the driver's seat with my pregnant abdomen touching the steering wheel. Bobby, my two-year-old was squirming beside me. Petra, our Filipina maid, filled the remainder of the front passenger seat.

"The back seat is all yours. Jess will be coming home for *merienda* about mid-afternoon," I stated.

"Mir-what?" Jim asked, seeming confused.

"*Merienda,*" I replied. "It's like a coffee break. By the way, I couldn't reach Jess to tell him you were here, as he was on a job site. He will be so surprised to see you! How long has it been?"

"Oh, I think it was 1917," Jim replied, as he opened the car door.

After Jim and Charlie settled in the back seat, I drove to San Juan and our home. I chatted on the way, describing the sights during the ten-mile return trip, as if I were a tour guide. We arrived after about twenty-five minutes. I showed Jim and Charlie Jess' office, which adjoined our dining room, downstairs.

"We'll wait for Jess in his office," Jim said.

"Have you had your lunch yet?" I inquired.

"No, Mary," Jim replied. "We were hoping Jess would meet us in town for lunch, because we have to catch the boat for Iloilo this evening."

"Come upstairs and relax in our living room, and I'll have our cook prepare a light snack for you," I said.

I showed them upstairs and offered them a beverage while they waited. Returning downstairs, I asked Felix, our cook, if he could prepare a light lunch for our guests. He just finished cleaning the kitchen after the luncheon meal.

"I can make a *tinapa* salad and dice fresh fruit for dessert," Felix offered.

"Thank you, Felix," I replied, and returned to the *sala*.

Before long, Felix served the salad, that included smoked fish, greens, salted duck eggs, chopped scallions, and diced tomatoes topped with a vinaigrette dressing. Jim admired the large, blue, lavishly decorated Chinese salad bowl. After eating their serving, Jim and Charlie asked for more of the delicious Filipino salad. Felix removed the empty salad bowls, replenished their beverages, and served the dessert. He had prepared chopped mango, papaya, pineapple, guava, and sprinkled freshly grated young coconut on top. The men were pleased they had come to see Jess at his home.

Jess arrived around four in the afternoon. I called from the second floor.

"We have company. It's a surprise."

He took the steps two-at-a-time. The expression on his face, when he entered the living room, was priceless. After all the hugs and handshaking, they settled in for a chat.

"Jess, I'm glad your wedding picture was over the piano," Jim teased. "Until then, I was not sure whether or not I was in the right house!"

Their conversation trickled through family news and events. Jim was married to Charlie's sister, Mary (also his cousin). They had four children, James, David, Howard and Mary Kathryn. His family lived in Lubbock.

"I had to sell my grocery business in Quinlan as we went broke selling groceries on credit," Jim said. "Uncle C. N. paid my debts. I relocated the family to Lubbock to work for Uncle J. A., but Uncle C. N. wanted me in Iloilo to work for him, so…here I am!"

Mary recalled Jess had started the same way. He arrived in the Philippines in 1910 to work for his Uncle C. N. with his numerous business ventures. He had a movie theater, a pawnshop, plantations with various crops, and cattle. Uncle C. N. usually brought his Texas relatives to Iloilo to work for him as it gave him control. They were indebted to him for their travel expenses and would have to work at his rate of pay until their fares were repaid, plus living expenses. Jess got out from under his uncle's thumb and opened his own pawnshop in Olongapo.

Jim and Charlie left around seven. Jess took Bobby along for the ride and took them to catch the Inter-Island steamship to Iloilo. Jess was pensive on the drive home while Bobby slept.

Jess completed all contracted jobs at San Juan Heights and collected his pay. He had decisions to make. He headed for home for a decision-making chat.

After our evening meal, I was getting Bobby ready for bed, when Jess popped his head into Bobby's room.

"Mary, when you're finished, please come to the living room. We need to talk."

After singing two lullabies and settling Bobby in his bed, I tiptoed from his room to meet Jess in the living room. He was sitting in his favorite rocking chair and rubbing his chin.

"Well, what is it?" I asked, as I eased into the large overstuffed sofa we had transferred from *Mami's* apartment.

"Mary, the construction business isn't doing well. We need to decide whether or not to stay in the Philippines and start our own business or relocate to Texas and live on my part of the Hodges farm," Jess proposed.

I sighed. We had not been able to save enough money to build our own home. We paid rent and made improvements to houses we were renting, only to have them sold out from under us or to have rental costs escalate.

"I don't know, Jess," I responded, "Our second child will arrive in less than two months. It would be difficult to travel."

Circumstances had dictated our decision. We would be staying in the Philippines.

If we had come to America then, we would have been spared the hardships of World War II. We might still have Bobby. "If" is a small word with far-reaching consequences.

CHAPTER 59

A Time to Deliver

Our lives continued in our usual pattern as we approached July 1926. In June, Aurora decided to live with a girlfriend, Charing Olves. She knew Pilar would need a nursery for her first child due in July. After Aurora left, I helped Pilar to prepare the nursery for the new baby. Our nursery for our second child, due in August, was already prepared. Pilar had not prepared hers because Aurora occupied the bedroom, plus she was busy with Tony's care after his accident.

After Tony returned to work, he continued to do well and was provided a company car driven by a chauffeur. He joined The Elks Club, a prominent social club for businessmen, where he met many prospective clients. Tony also developed his skill at playing bridge and would take Pilar to The Elks Club and various venues to enter bridge competitions. Pilar used the car and chauffeur at her discretion. Often, Tony would be dropped off at The Elks Club and she would come to visit us. She left in the chauffeured company car in time to pick up Tony by seven in the evening.

July was upon us and the stork had several deliveries to make. Of the four Gamero sisters who were pregnant, Pilar's baby would arrive first. She entered the hospital early on July 9, 1926. Dr. Benito Valdez made the preparations for the

Maria del Pilar Gamero y Cucullu with spouse Tony Settember holding their only child, Anthony D. (Tony) Settember Jr., Manila, Philippines, 1926.

delivery of the Settember's child. After about eighteen hours of hard labor, Pilar experienced difficulties. A Caesarian section was being considered by Dr. Valdez, because she was bleeding profusely. Dr. Valdez decided to use forceps to help the baby along and was successful. Anthony Dennis (Tony) Settember Jr., weighing ten pounds, arrived on July 10, 1926. Prayers were offered for the rest of the day.

Mami and Tony were by Pilar's side. Tony was ecstatic about having a son! He beamed, bragged, and marched around the hospital handing out cigars to all he knew as well as complete strangers. He hurried to Luneta Motors with another box of cigars and shared his news. His boss surprised him by giving him a raise and increasing his commission. Since Pilar experienced a difficult delivery, she stayed in the hospital for ten days to make sure she would recover without complications.

When Tony took Pilar and Anthony home, they barely had time for their new baby to become accustomed to the newly prepared nursery when Francisco took Lucing to the hospital to deliver her fifth child. Rosario was called in from Antipolo to help Pilar, and *Mami* took her vigil at Lucing's side. From past experience and knowledge, Lucing felt she would have another easy delivery. She probably would not need Dr. Valdez. She had been in labor for several hours before she arrived at hospital and felt something was different. After Dr. Valdez's examination, he decided the baby must be delivered by Caesarian section. Instead of a howling entrance into this world on July 23, 1926, Ramon (Pacquito) Gutierrez was lifted from his mother's womb. The umbilical cord that provided life-giving sustenance was wrapped around the infant's neck. Dr. Valdez knew what to do and the baby survived. Francisco was delighted with his fourth son. His daughter, Carmen, would never have a sister, as Dr. Valdez stated that another pregnancy would cost Lucing her life.

The maternity ward should have installed revolving doors for the Gamero sisters. When one gave birth, another was waiting in the wings for her turn.

On August 15, 1926, labor pains spread across my abdomen at two in the morning. These pains made me hungry, so I eased downstairs to find something to eat. A whole *penca* of bananas hung from a hook in the kitchen. I ate two bananas, trudged upstairs, and returned to bed. Within the hour, my labor pains increased. Once again, I crept downstairs to eat more bananas. This process was repeated at least six times before I decided to waken Jess.

Mami was spending the night with her sister, Herminia, so he told Petra we were leaving for the hospital. She would need to go with us to care for Bobby. Jess picked Bobby up gently from his bed, wrapped him in a blanket, and put him in the back seat with his head on Petra's lap to continue his slumber.

Dr. Valdez was called once I was admitted to San Juan de Dios Hospital and was checked by the head nurse. He returned around eight, as the head nurse told him it was not urgent. Petra stayed in the car with Bobby. After thoroughly checking me, Dr. Valdez suggested I stay nearby. The baby would arrive before long. Jess and I took this opportunity to take Bobby and Petra to Herminia's house and tell my mother what was happening. *Mami* prepared to go with us. I called Pilar and Tony to give them the news. They wanted us to come to their home in Ermita.

Since it was Sunday, August 15, the day of The Feast of The Assumption of The Virgin, we stopped by our church to attend the celebratory eleven o'clock Mass. Afterward, we visited Tony and Pilar's home and ate a light lunch. Rosario was still at Pilar's…helping care for Anthony. Around three in the afternoon my labor pains intensified. It was time. My mother would stay with me during the delivery. Jess returned to Pilar and Tony's. *Mami* would call him with any news.

At 3:45 p.m. on August 15, 1926, Luz Asunción (later changed to Lucy Ann) Hodges made her quick entrance into this world. Tony was surprised when *Mami* called with the news. It had taken Pilar about two days to deliver their child. Lucy arrived within thirty minutes of my return to the hospital. They told Rosario and Jess the news. They hurried to the hospital, while Pilar stayed with her baby.

Rosario was enchanted with our baby girl, Lucy…our baby doll with dark hair swooping across her forehead as if she had bangs. *Mami* was so proud to have a namesake. She preferred girls.

Jess stayed for a while longer and decided he should rescue Petra and Bobby from Herminia's and give them the news about Lucy before taking them home to rest. *Mami* decided she would go with them, pack a small bag, and return to our home to care for Bobby.

Jess arrived early every morning to visit us. On the third visit, he put his face close to our baby's and noticed Lucy's ears.

"Her ears are pierced," Jess said unhappily.

He did not believe ears should be pierced period, much less when they were newborn babies.

"Dr. Valdez said it was the best time to have their ears pierced as they feel less pain and sleep most of the time," I replied with authority.

The deed was done. The subject was closed.

I stayed in the hospital one week before Lucy and I were dismissed. I was so ready to go home, and so thankful my mother was taking care of Bobby and supervising the servants. I sent prayers of gratitude to the Virgin Mary.

One more Gamero sister was waiting in the wings. Consueling would be the last one to deliver in November 1926. Dr. Valdez could take his vacation afterward.

CHAPTER 60

Growing Together

Toward the end of August 1926, we settled into the household routine with our baby girl, Lucy. Judge Manuel Camus and his wife, Mathilde, gave a burnished copper baby bed, since Bobby was still using his crib. Mathilde Camus fell in love with Lucy. She visited often and enjoyed holding her. Jess and I decided Judge and Mrs. Camus would be the ideal godparents for Lucy, so we asked them if they would honor us by accepting this role. They accepted immediately.

We selected September 22, Bobby's second birthday, to hold Lucy's baptism. Her baptismal rituals were held in the morning, and we celebrated Bobby's birthday party in the afternoon. We busied ourselves with plans. *Mami* asked an old family friend, Father Pedro, to conduct the rites for baptism at the Manila Cathedral, which pleased him.

Following Lucy's baptism, Judge and Mrs. Camus gave a baptismal gift of ten American gold dollars, valued at over ten *pesos* each. Our home was filled with family members and friends who brought gifts for Lucy and Bobby. As the guests arrived, the five-piece string band we hired for the baptism/birthday party, played "Happy Birthday to You." Everyone clapped and formed a large circle in the *sala*. *Mami* held Bobby's hand and led him to the center as her dance partner. We laughed to see him jumping up and down as he feigned dancing with his grandmother. Following their performance, the guests were invited to sample the generous buffet while servants carried trays with various beverages around the living areas and porches.

After finishing lunch, the small children were called once again to form a large circle in the center of the living room. We were ready to celebrate the *Agua Madrina* (Godmother's Shower). Dozens of coins were tossed onto the floor within the children's circle. The children scrambled to gather as many coins as possible. Laughter, shouting, and calling of children's names filled the air as they scurried to collect them.

During October, Mr. Meyers asked Jess to build two large garden chairs. He and his wife were large persons, so the chairs must be sturdy. Jess used hardwood and completed them in about one week, which pleased Mr. Meyers. As he and Jess loaded the finished garden chairs, he asked Jess about building one more house in San Juan Heights.

"I'll start within the next three weeks," Jess said.

"Before you do, I have a problem to solve and was hoping you would help," Mr. Meyers stated. "I go deep sea fishing and need a strong rod and reel…one strong enough to support the 'big one'."

Jess laughed. "I'll give it a try, but there are no guarantees! What if you catch a whale?"

Both men laughed as they strolled outside to admire the new lawn chairs Jess had built.

November 1926 was knocking at the door and Consueling was preparing to deliver her fourth child. Once again, *Mami* was called into action to her bedside. Maria del Pilar (Pilachu) Gonzalez entered this world squealing, to the delight of her older siblings, on November 26. Estephania (Fanny), José (Bull/Peping), and Juan (Juaning) were happy to bring home their new baby sister.

Jess finished the last house at San Juan Heights in December. No job prospects were in sight, so we considered starting a new business. We had spoken with Mrs. Cavana about the rental car business…a possible venture. We needed cash.

My purebred fox terrier had five pups, so I sold four pups for twenty-five *pesos* each. Jess had given me a pair of canaries in a gilded cage. (He thought I might want to raise canaries.) I did not care for those birds.

Mary Gamero Hodges, holding Luz Asunción (Lucy Ann), Robert Morris (Bobby), and Jess Hodges, 1927.

A neighbor, who owned a pony, was moving into downtown Manila and did not have space for the pony. He asked me if I would exchange the remaining pup for the pony. Nothing would convince him he should take the canaries; even though I pointed out they would make less noise in an apartment than the pup. He was adamant. He wanted the pup, so we exchanged. I decided the pony would be a special Christmas gift for Bobby. *Would one of my sisters want the canaries?*

Petra, our nanny, was heavy with child in early December. She gave notice she would return to her province to stay with family. She helped us find two girls, Tokia and Trinidad, who would work for the same salary Petra was receiving, if I would allow them to attend night classes. I agreed. They took care of Bobby and Lucy. Six months passed without practicing the piano, so more help was welcome. When I tried to practice the piano, Bobby rushed to my side to bang on the keys. Now Tokia could distract him.

I stopped taking piano lessons and practiced on my own, since I had more help at home. The piano lessons were expensive and we needed to save money. The family coffers were slim, so we had a quiet holiday season. The four Gamero sisters were busy nursing babies and enjoying a blessed Christmas and a peaceful New Year.

Although I missed the dancing, the happy crowds in the cabarets, and welcoming in the New Year with confetti and horns, 1926 was a busy year for the Gamero sisters…each with a new baby. I doubt that will happen again. My sisters and I will miss Rudolph Valentino…he died after filming The Son of the Sheik. *I cuddled Lucy and hummed* One Alone, *my favorite song from* Desert Song. *As I gazed at Bobby curled up in Jess' lap, I blew him a kiss and wished him a Happy 1927!*

CHAPTER 61

The San Miguel Garage

Bobby, thrilled with his new pony, wanted to ride every day. Tokia, his new *tota,* caught the pony daily, put its harness and saddle on, placed Bobby astride, and led the pony around the yard by a rope tied to its harness. The pony was not allowed to run, as Bobby could not hold on by himself. Two weeks after receiving the pony, Bobby fell and struck his head as the pony bolted. Tokia carried the screaming child into the kitchen to wash the wound. His cries sent me dashing downstairs to investigate. The wound was superficial. After it was dressed, he lay with his head in Tokia's lap while she held a small ice pack over his bandage and soothed him as we listened to music on our small radio.

The music stopped and the announcer spouted the news of changes in Japan made by Emperor Hirohito, who succeeded his father, Yoshihito, following his death in 1926. The young Hirohito was building a stronger, larger military force to impress neighboring China. Overshadowing that announcement was news of the release of *The Jazz Singer* starring Al Jolson. The film world presented its first "talkie." We paid little attention to this historic event, as we were preoccupied with our own problems.

The construction business dwindled to a slow crawl. We needed income and needed it fast. Jess and I decided to open a rental car business and provide chauffeurs. Jess had worked with Mr. Parsons, owner of The Overland Company, so he inquired about start-up costs.

"Well, Jess, you will need about four new small cars and two larger used cars," Mr. Parsons said. "I can give you a loan. You will need a down payment and can repay me monthly."

Jess became excited at this prospect. We found a site for the business. An old building in an excellent location on General Solano Street, in the San Miguel district, was for rent. The large stable would house at least five cars. The buildings needed repair, but Jess and Lorenzo could make them presentable. Our new business was named "The San Miguel Garage." We signed a contract for three four-cycle Whippets, a Star; one used six-cycle Durant, and a used six-cycle Maxwell. We hired five chauffeurs. Jess would be the mechanic. We bought white, removable seat covers and covered the spare tire, mounted on the back, with a red leather cover emblazoned with "San Miguel Garage."

We needed a chauffeur for the Durant, so Tony, Pilar's husband, sent a driver he recommended. The first time this driver took the car out on a job, he never returned. We called the authorities before dark to report the missing vehicle, which was found the next day, abandoned in a nearby province. Jess took our old Cleveland and another driver to tow the Durant to our garage.

Business was booming for about a year and a half, but wear and tear on the vehicles soon resulted in numerous breakdowns. We also discovered our drivers were causing the breakdowns. They would take passengers to their destinations; pick up more passengers for other destinations, deliver them, then return to the original site for the first passengers. Money collected from their interim passengers was pocketed. Odometers were adjusted so the extra miles would not register. Honest drivers were hard to find.

Mr. Parsons, who held our loan, asked Jess to design and build an outside elevator for moving heavy items to the second floor of The Overland Company. Jess jumped at the chance to work, since our garage business was becoming defunct. After taking measurements and drawing the plans, Jess built the elevator. Everyone at The Overland Company was impressed. Jess' design and construction made their jobs much easier.

Mr. Parsons visited Jess at our garage and found Jess working on a car with Lorenzo's help.

"Where's your mechanic, Jess?" Mr. Parsons asked.

"We don't make enough money to hire a mechanic," Jess replied. "Mary's brother and I do all the work here."

"How would you like to work for me? I need a new assistant manager at Overland. I can pay an excellent starting salary plus a commission."

"Sounds great to me, Mr. Parsons," Jess said. "Let me talk it over with Mary, and I will call you tomorrow."

We decided this job offer would stop our downhill financial spiral. Lorenzo would take over as mechanic and Jess could work for Mr. Parsons.

Mr. Hedges, manager at Overland, was not happy Mr. Parsons had hired an assistant without consulting him. He gave Jess a hard time at every opportunity. Jess took the verbal abuse for a while, but later offered his resignation to Mr. Parsons.

"What's the matter, Jess?"

"I'm sorry, Mr. Parsons, but Mr. Hedges and I are having trouble adjusting to each other. I believe you should find someone he likes better." Jess did not mention the verbal abuse.

Mr. Parsons could tell Jess was being polite.

"How do you feel about traveling for Overland? I have several customers who owe payments on cars. I will pay you a better salary plus a commission on the number of cars you repossess or payments you collect."

In October 1927, Jess acted as collection agent for Mr. Parsons' Overland Sales Company. Jess was away from home from two to three weeks at a time.

Meanwhile, Lorenzo and I kept the San Miguel Garage open and operating. Credit was no longer allowed. We operated a cash business only. I met with the drivers and told them the care of the cars was their responsibility. If the car they were assigned to drive had a breakdown, they should fix it, otherwise, they would lose their job.

"If any of our vehicles are seen in areas outside Manila, you will be fired. The city limits are our boundaries. Do you understand?" I stated firmly.

Heads nodded, either in assent or disbelief. They were more careful, and we had fewer repairs to make following my speech. I got results.

Our financial picture was improving, as Jess earned a salary plus commission, and we operated a "cash only" business at the garage. My spirits lifted, then I discovered I was pregnant again. I was not prepared.

In March 1928, while Jess was sailing to one of the provinces, a typhoon struck the Philippines. News on the radio reported two crew members' of an Inter-Island ship were found washed ashore in Sorsogon. Jess had left Manila on the ship to Sorsogon. I became distraught and thought to call my Uncle Carlos, who piloted for Inter-Island Ship Company.

"Maria, do not worry. I will get in touch with the main office, and will call with any news."

I was pregnant with my third child and facing another disaster. *Mami* and I prayed to *San Expedito*, patron saint of Impossible Causes, and I promised to wear the habit of Our Lady of Sorrows for one month, if my husband had been spared from death or injury during the storm.

After four days, Uncle Carlos called with news.

"Maria, the two men found on the beach at Sorsogon were the only ones from the inter-island ship hit by large waves during the typhoon. They have accounted for everyone else on board. Jess will be in touch with you soon...you'll see."

I told *Mami* the news. After a celebration during *merienda,* she retired to the drawing room to sew the habit of Our Lady of Sorrows. By noon the next day, she finished. I uttered a prayer of thanks as I donned the habit, which I would wear for one month. Strains of *Blue Skies* danced across the room, followed by *Let a Smile Be Your Umbrella. Perhaps our future will soon be brighter.*

Jess wrote a letter after they landed, which arrived two weeks later. He had to stay in Sorsogon longer than planned, since the typhoon delayed his arrival. There was much work to do for Overland.

Mary felt tired as she pushed the writing materials off to one side. *I had no idea writing was so hard. It's not just the writing; it's remembering events in their correct sequence. I started over several times because I recalled more events that must be included. Oh, my back hurts from sitting in this chair.*

She fixed a cup of hot chocolate and rescued the last cookie from the cookie jar. *I must bake cookies tomorrow.*

CHAPTER 62

A Namesake for Jess

The morning news blared the collapse of Brazil's economy due to coffee overproduction, followed by the song, *You're the Cream in My Coffee,* as an ironic punctuation mark. I kept myself busy getting the paperwork completed from closing The San Miguel Garage. *Closing the business was another big bump in the road.*

Strains of *Sonny Boy* sung by Al Jolson made me smile as I sipped my morning coffee. I rubbed my hand slowly over my expanded abdomen as the baby moved actively. *Is this child in my womb another boy?* Jess would like another one. He was finishing his last job for Mr. Parsons and wrote he would be home before long.

On June 8, 1928, I experienced abdominal contractions. *Mami* gave instructions for the children's care, while I finished packing for my hospital stay. Lorenzo would drive us. Within the hour, I checked into San Juan de Dios Hospital, the oldest one in the Philippines. Dr. Valdez was notified.

In the wee hours of the morning on June 9, 1928, Jesse Anthony Hodges Jr. was born. We gave him the middle name "Anthony" in honor of St. Anthony, my favorite saint. It was customary to have part of one's full name include a saint. If the birth was not on a "Saint's Day," a patron saint of a family member, or one's favorite, was used instead. He was a sweet, quiet child with soft brown eyes and a pleasant expression. He resembled Jess.

Jess arrived from the provinces the next day. He was thrilled to have another son. This delivery was much easier than the previous two, so my stay at the hospital was only five days.

"Mary, I have a few more trips to make for Mr. Parsons. I'm sorry I was not here when you left for the hospital. I'm glad everything went well. I will begin looking around for construction work, besides, I want to be home for my birthday," Jess stated.

"Let's have a big celebration and christen Junior on your birthday. We need something to lift our spirits," I said.

Jess agreed, so plans were made and arrangements were completed for the combined celebration to include Jess' birthday and Junior's baptism on July

31, 1928. My half-brother, Fr. José Gamero served as godfather; and, my half-sister, Rosario as his godmother. Fr. Angel Fernandez conducted the rituals for the baptism of Jesse Anthony Hodges Jr. at the Manila Cathedral in *Intramuros*. The entire family attended and joined us for the double celebration at our home.

Two days later, my mother received a huge disappointment. Lorenzo was missing. When *Mami* questioned the servants, they reported the sad news. Lorenzo told the servants he would not be returning to our home. He had eloped with one of the older, female servants…a native. They would live with her family in one of the provinces and await the birth of their child. She had entrapped Lorenzo by giving him sexual favors. *Mami* was beside herself. Our servants knew about the sordid affair and never reported it to any of us.

"I will find him. We will send notices to all the parish priests in the vicinity and give them Lorenzo's name. If he tries to marry that *puñetera* in a Catholic church, they will notify us and not perform the wedding rituals," *Mami* said angrily.

Three days later, we had a surprise visit from Jess' brother, Jim, who was working for Uncle C. N. in Iloilo. He was homesick and disgusted with working for his uncle. Jim needed to find a way to return to his family in Lubbock. He did not "get rich" as was promised and needed to work for his return passage. Jim was almost broke and needed a place to stay, until he found employment on a ship returning to America.

Our spare bedroom was now a children's bedroom for Bobby and Lucy. Junior, the baby, was in the nursery. Jim did not mind where he slept. He would sleep on the overstuffed sofa, if necessary.

"No, Jim, Jess and I can put a small bed in his office for a makeshift bedroom. I have a bamboo screen to use for privacy. You will be more comfortable there," I said.

The next day, Jim left for the shipyard and applied for a job on a cargo ship, The U.S.S. Wasp. It would sail within ten days for the United States. Within a week, he was called to report as a painter on The Wasp. He had never painted a ship before, but he was desperate and would take any job. He was so happy to take what little money he saved from working for Uncle C. N. and return home. His family in Texas needed the money.

Before he left, he gave us the picture he carried of himself and his wife, Mary. He was so eager to see them. He hardly talked about anything else except his wife and four children.

Jess was glad he had the opportunity to have a longer visit with his brother. The last time Jim was in San Juan, he stayed a short time before taking the Inter-Island ship to Iloilo.

Two days after Jim left, he surprised us by having a half-gallon of ice cream delivered to us before his ship sailed. Jim wrote a long letter after his arrival in Texas. He truly appreciated our help and hospitality. Jess read the letter several times.

Mami became very depressed with no news from Lorenzo. Her only living son had deserted her for a native woman who tricked him into marriage. None of the parish priests reported sighting Lorenzo. He was a disgrace to the family and was disowned. Lorenzo's name was no longer spoken aloud in our home.

The local radio announcer reported on George Eastman's exhibition of the first motion pictures in color. The second breakthrough announced was the installation of a "moving" electric sign around The New York Times building. *I wonder if we will be able to see a colored motion picture soon?*

CHAPTER 63

Setbacks and Decisions

Since the San Miguel Garage business was a disaster, we looked for other ways to make money while Jess was still with Parsons Overland Sales Company. We sold the cars and equipment, paid off debts, and began cutting living expenses.

We needed to find another place to live with lower rent. A small house was rented in the country on the outskirts of San Juan at #10 Salvador Street. Our servants, Trinidad and Tokia left our employ. Lola Lala helped us locate an older couple, Santos and Christela, as our cook and maid. They had worked for Captain Zagabarria, a family friend of Lola Lala's. The children had trouble saying, "Christela," so they called her *"Tota,"* a *Tagalog* word for nanny.

In July 1929, while still working for Parsons Overland Sales, Jess found out The Manila Electric Company needed a foreman to build a new hydroelectric plant in the mountains of Botocan, Laguna. Jess was unhappy as a collections agent and really wanted to return to construction, so he applied for the job. He received excellent references from Mr. Parsons and was awarded the job as foreman. This construction was estimated to take at least two years to complete. After giving Mr. Parsons two weeks notice, Jess prepared for his job at Botocan.

While waiting for delivery of supplies and equipment to Botocan for construction of the hydroelectric plant, Mr. Myers asked Jess if he would build a hardwood double bed frame. Since he had built other furniture for Mr. Myers, Jess completed this project to make money before leaving for Botocan.

In September, the bulk of supplies and equipment was delivered to the plant's mountainous site, so Jess left for this new project. He could return only once a month, which was difficult for our family. *Mami* moved into the small house with us, to help.

My mother settled into one bedroom. The second bedroom housed Jess and me, plus Bobby and Lucy. The baby bed for Jesse Jr. was in the living room. Santos and *Tota* lived downstairs in a small room beside the kitchen and small dining room.

I enjoyed staying at home with the children and not dealing with the problems connected to operating a business. I did the marketing chores while *Mami* and *Tota* handled childcare. Santos was happy to have help in menu planning. He felt the children were eating better with the meals I planned.

Four months later, Jess completed his living quarters in Botocan…a two-bedroom shack. He only worked on it when not busy with his job as foreman. He hoped we would come to Botocan for a short vacation, so we could see his project.

"Mary, I'm anxious to see you and the kids. I think the shack is ready," Jess stated, with urgency in his voice. "You can bring Bobby and Lucy. Your mother and the servants can care for Junior and the house. When will you come?"

"Jess, as much as we would all like being with you, I don't think it's a good idea. I am about seven months pregnant," I countered. "The long, winding, mountainous, rough road to Botocan would be difficult to drive. If I had car trouble, there would be no help. There are only large, isolated coconut plantations in the area."

"You are right. I wasn't thinking," Jess said, disappointedly. "I wanted to see you and the children. We'll wait until after this baby arrives, then decide."

Jess built a screened-in kiddie-coop for the new baby during his time off in the evenings. The work progressed well, but costs were rising. To save money, Jess replaced the Japanese workers with less expensive Filipino laborers. This action provided for more workers at less expense. MERALCO (Manila Electric Railroad and Light Company) bosses were impressed. *The hydroelectric plant at Botocan was the first of its kind in the Philippines, and would be hailed as landmark construction.*

Six months passed since Jim left for his home in Texas. Jess' uncle from Iloilo, C. N. Hodges, paid a surprise visit. He was amazed to see Bobby and Lucy playing in our front yard. The last time he visited, we were newlyweds. Now we had three children.

C. N. was on a mission. His visit was more than a social call.

"Jess, have you seen Jim?" C. N. asked.

"Well, he was here about six months ago waiting for a job on a ship going home," Jess responded.

"Home? He said he was coming to see you," C. N. replied.

"Yes, he did. He stayed with us until a job opened for him," Jess said.

"Well, I'll be…guess I didn't understand he was leaving for Texas," C. N. said, as he scratched his head.

Uncle C. N. dropped the subject and chatted a while about conditions in Iloilo. We invited him to stay for dinner, but he declined because he was taking the next Inter-Island ship to Iloilo.

My goodness, I am so tired. I should have taken a break from my writing. I think I'll call Rosie and see how she and the boys are doing.

Mary called and chatted with Rose about Shawn and Ryan. Lyle was working out-of-town, so not much was happening, other than her job at the music store, taking the kids to school and other activities, plus housework.

After she finished, Mary decided to eat a small snack before taking her medicine and retiring for the night. *I will pray for Rosie and her family tonight. I wish she lived here and not in Spokane.*

CHAPTER 64

Another Girl

News of the day in 1930 heralded change: Constantinople would now be called Istanbul. *All Quiet on the Western Front* was playing in theaters as the last Allied troops left Germany. The song *Georgia on My Mind* was climbing the charts, and *I Got Rhythm* was close behind. I could still sway to the first song as it played on my radio, but was too pregnant to even try the second one.

We formed a pattern in building our family. Our first child was a boy named Robert (Bobby) for Jess' dad; our second, (a girl) Luz (Lucy) for my mother; our third, another boy, was named for Jess; and, if we had a girl, I wanted to give her my name (Maria de los Angeles). I decided on the name, Marie Angela. At the time, Caruso, the handsome Italian baritone, had a popular song, *Angela Mia*. *What a perfect middle name for our girl…an adaptation of my middle name.* Jess thought differently. He had a younger sister, Emma Ethel, whom he adored. She died in 1919 after Jess left Texas. He really wanted to use his sister's name. I gave in, and on March 1, 1930, Marie Emma Hodges popped into our lives at 12:50 a.m. at The Chinese Hospital in Tablante. She was called by her middle name to honor Jess' sister.

About one month after Emma's birth, I told Jess we would go with him to Botocan for a visit. Emma

Emma Ethel Hodges,
younger sister of Jess Hodges.

needed to be christened before leaving, so plans were made for those rituals. *Srta*. Maria Luisa Elzimgre was delighted to serve as her godmother, and my godfather, Don José Cavana served as her godfather. Once again, my half-brother, Fr. José Gamero did the honors. *There are benefits to having a priest in the family!*

Jess returned during early May. The rituals were conducted and a small reception was held at the Elzingre's home, as our home was too small. Most family members attended, which gave us a chance to share news on our ever-expanding families. In 1928, Consueling had given birth to another son, Juan Carlos, whom they nicknamed "Carlitos." We did not see them often as they lived in Bulan. The more our "tribes" increased, the less time we had to visit each other. *Mami* was delighted to have most of her children and grandchildren together, but in the back of her mind and in her heart, she was thinking of Lorenzo.

Following the festivities, we packed for the trip to Botocan. *Mami* and Junior were hugged and kissed before we left for a month's vacation. Junior held onto his maid, *Tota*. He was perfectly happy staying with her. Jess did the driving, and I held Emma in my lap, so she could nurse. Bobby and Lucy rode in the back seat alternating their time sleeping, talking, or hitting each other during the trip.

Once we arrived at Jess' shack, we unpacked for our stay. Jess had built a wooden bed for us, small bunk beds for Bobby and Lucy, and, a screened-in bed for Emma, the baby. We had a kerosene lamp, wooden dining table, and long benches. He also prepared a wood stove for cooking. Two ingeniously constructed four-gallon water tanks stood conspicuously in the kitchen. One beside the icebox held cold water and the other for hot water stood behind the stove. As fire blazed in the stove, the water was heated as the meal cooked. "Birdbaths" with warm water were taken before bedtime.

The shack's location concerned me. Jess built the shack near the edge of a deep precipice. The shack, surrounded by coconut trees, was in an isolated area. Jess' job site was over two hundred yards away. The closest habitation was over a mile away…a nipa hut with three natives, one man and two women. Their curiosity drew them to our shack. We were unable to communicate for they spoke a different dialect. They entered the shack without being invited, pointed at our baby, Emma, and called her *calamay* (sugar), because she was inside a screened box. Their gestures indicated they admired the children. *I later learned many children born to natives in the area did not survive the dangerous and unsanitary conditions.* After touching the furniture and running their hands across the beds and table, they left abruptly. *I discovered later they had no furniture. They slept or sat on mats woven from either palm or coconut leaves.*

Emma stayed in her screened-in "coop." Gnats, flies, mosquitoes, and other disease-bearing insects were plentiful. I created two small individual "covers" from mosquito netting for Bobby and Lucy to wear over their heads to protect them from insects as they played. The two "little ghosts" were able to play outside wearing their protective covers.

Jess built a seesaw from a long board centered over a barrel for Bobby and Lucy to use. I thought it was unsafe, but Jess disagreed. Two days later, while Bobby and Lucy were attempting to use the seesaw, Lucy was bumped off. Her forehead was badly cut. I screamed and held a towel over Lucy's wound. A native woman, on her way to the job site, saw the accident and ran to get Jess. Within minutes, Jess arrived with the physician at his side. Lucy's cut required two stitches, sterile bandaging, and astringent solution. She cried the entire time while being treated. Jess took the seesaw apart. I was thankful a resident physician was on the job site, as we were many miles from medical care.

There were no grocery stores, so we had to depend on the natives from the job site to bring us eggs, fish, and chickens, for which we paid dearly. I continued nursing Emma, as milk was scarce. I planned meals around whatever was available.

My days were spent caring for Emma and watching Bobby and Lucy play in the front yard. They were not allowed to play behind the shack. One misstep would cause a fall into the deep crevasse costing them their lives.

It was not an enjoyable vacation. Discomforts were tolerated so Jess and the children would have time together during his days off.

One day, a drunken native on a horse, rode to our shack accompanied by another man, who was walking. The drunk gestured to me as I stepped outside to bring Bobby and Lucy inside. I did not understand his gestures or dialect. He spoke something other than *Tagalog*. He urged the horse forward, as I backed inside the shack, and could not close the door as the horse's head was inside the doorway.

"No! No! Get out!" I shouted.

The other man grabbed the horse's mane and pulled the horse backward…away from the doorway. The drunk grabbed his *bolo* from his waist and hit the rescuer's head with its flat side. The kids were screaming and crying. The rescuer stepped back, slapped the horse on its left flank. It bolted and sped away. *Good riddance!* I despised this horrible place.

The next morning, Bobby wakened…swollen from head to toe. He was unable to open his eyes. The poor child was terrified. Jess took Bobby to the physician at his job site. The doctor said it appeared Bobby had developed an allergic reaction to eating too many eggs. Often, all we had were eggs. He gave Jess medication for Bobby and told him to not eat any more eggs.

The days seemed to crawl by like a lazy snake. My only adult conversation was chatting with Jess. Knowledge of their dialect was limited to "*eh, eh, marikit*" (market) and "*calamay.*" I had not learned their dialect, as the natives' pronunciation involved a "sing-song" effect in their rhythmic language. I counted the days until Jess would have his weekend off so we could get away from this place.

Early one morning, Lucy complained she was having trouble breathing. Her forehead was swollen. Jess and I checked her for rashes and asked the right questions, or so we thought. We didn't think to check inside her nostrils. Once again, the job site physician was needed. He examined her and discovered an object high inside her nostril. What was once a seed had sprouted into a coconut bloom causing one airway to close. It had grown into the sinus cavity in her forehead creating the swelling. He removed the coconut bloom, swabbed the area with antiseptic, and gave some medication to reduce the swelling before he left…shaking his head. I understood why no children were around this area. We were fortunate the physician was at the job site.

I wanted to be rid of this place, but the weather took a turn for the worse. A typhoon was wreaking havoc at the nearby village. Although it was miles away from our vista, the coconut trees were swaying and bending under the strong gales. Jess ran to the job site, returned with some of his laborers, and secured the shack with heavy ropes to nearby coconut trees. He feared we would be blown away...shack and all.

When the weather cleared, we packed our belongings into our open touring car, and, with Jess at the wheel; prepared for the long, winding, bumpy, treacherous drive home. Our troubles were not over. The long, narrow, muddy road was surrounded by tall overhanging trees, whose branches were broken by the strong winds of the typhoon. Several trees lay across the road and blocked any movement. We stopped often to pull limbs aside in order to continue. Before long, a large truck drew close behind us. We were moving as fast as road conditions allowed, but the native driver kept on honking his horn and waving us to one side. Jess pulled off the road onto a debris pile. As the tall cargo truck passed, it struck tree limbs to each side of us and covered us with leaves and broken limbs. Bobby and Lucy were wearing their mosquito net bags over their heads, but Jess, Emma and I were uncovered, as we had no roof overhead in the touring car. An angry red wasp, unhappy about being tossed about so rudely, hit my arm and stung me. After the initial shock and pain, I was thankful it had not stung Emma, whom I was carrying in my arms. We drove for over an hour before we found a small town with a drugstore. Jess spoke with the druggist who recommended camphorated oil and gave him a piece of ice to place on the wasp sting. My arm was already swollen and red. Jess drove for another four hours before we reached our home. I thanked God we were finally home.

※※

Wow! How did I ever survive a "vacation" without electricity or running water? Our clothes were laundered by boiling them in a pot on the wood stove, and hung inside the shack to dry so they would not be stolen. We survived! Junior had not missed us at all. He had Tota and she was all he wanted. On reflection, that "vacation" was a "walk in the park" compared to events during World War II.

Mary readied herself to attend Mass. *I must give thanks for all my blessings. I'm so grateful to be in the United States and to be an American.*

CHAPTER 65

The Depression Years

"You never miss the water till the well runs dry." This popular quote applied to more than just water. My one-month "vacation" in Botocan helped me to appreciate civilization. The running water, electricity, a real house with screens, a cook, maid, and neighbors who spoke the same language were cherished. Our small countryside house on the outskirts of San Juan, with all its amenities, was truly luxurious compared to Jess' shack in Botocan. *Welcome home!*

These experiences in Botocan were shared with my neighbor, Mrs. McKenny. She and her husband, Tom owned and operated a restaurant, *La Favorita*, in Manila. They hardly traveled, so she was amused by these "recently suffered" experiences in Botocan. She apologized for laughing when told the tale about Lucy growing a coconut bloom inside her nostril. I laughed with her, but at the time, it was distressing.

Outside news was nonexistent in Botocan. Having a daily newspaper and listening to the radio were two more luxuries we missed. Upon our return, we "caught up" with the latest news, and decided we were better off not knowing. More trouble was approaching. News of economic hard times in the United States drifted toward the Philippines like an unmanned raft bearing time-sensitive explosives. Leaders in Manila felt the problems in the United States would not impact the economy in the Philippines, after all, it was a distant land…a comfortable thought, but not true.

The Botocan Hydroelectric Plant was completed in June 1931…three months less than the two years allotted for the project. MERALCO officials were well pleased with Jess' speedy completion. He stayed to supervise the work crew during the clean-up process. A small celebration was held when they tore down his shack…lovingly called his "expansive living quarters." Once finished with the clean up, Jess reported to MERALCO headquarters and completed the paperwork so his work crew could be paid.

MERALCO offered Jess a job as manager for their hydroelectric plant at Santa Mesa in Altura. A generous raise, company benefits, plus the permanency of full-time employment with Manila Electric was included. His first major assignment was to replace all the transformers in this all-steel plant. Jess and his crew completed the job in less time than estimated and at a lower cost. His boss teased Jess about working so hard he might work himself out of a job.

MERALCO bosses were very pleased with Jess' work. He was given another raise plus fifty *pesos* per month rent allowance. Jess was anxious to share his news.

"Mary, we are going to find a better house to rent in the morning," Jess announced. "I want us to entertain my bosses, and this house is too small."

I agreed the house was small, even for our family. We had four small children and my mother to squeeze into a two-bedroom home. Two of the children's beds were in the living room. Entertaining his bosses in our small place was not possible.

We found a large home with four bedrooms, a large living/dining area divided by two large Grecian columns supporting a graceful archway, two large bathrooms with white tiled floors and large built-in bathtubs with tiled wainscoting, plus, a variety of fruit trees in the well-landscaped yard. The separate two-car garage had an efficiency one-bedroom apartment at its rear. The entire property was fenced with a massive black wrought-iron fence. The many murals throughout the house bothered me. Jess said it would be no problem to paint over those. The house was offered for rent at fifty *pesos* monthly. The rental allowance Jess was receiving would cover the cost.

The house was owned by Mrs. Ocampo, widow of the attorney for Parsons Hardware and Overland Sales Company. I visited her and was surprised to learn I knew Mrs. Ocampo. She was a former classmate of mine at Santa Isabel, the Sisters of Charity boarding school. Isabel Artacho Ocampo and I were glad to see each other once again. After chatting about our childhood memories, we shared recent events in our lives. She was delighted we would be in her former home and gave her blessing to having Jess paint over the wall murals. She had never liked them. Her husband thought they added a touch of class, but she felt they were garish.

Jess painted over the murals with two coats of ivory paint making the rooms appear more spacious than before. The paintings, of a ship in distress in a stormy sea, and "footless" ballerinas in long ballet skirts dancing across the walls waving long pink ribbons over their heads were transformed into clean, freshly painted walls.

The house at #50 Blumentritt was readied for us in July. We fixed the front and back yards so the children would have a safe place to play. The tall wrought iron fence would keep intruders out, as we were on a wide paved road with heavy traffic.

Jess had been with MERALCO for less than six months when the raft, carrying time-sensitive explosives called "The Depression," hit the Philippines. It struck with a vengeance. MERALCO and other large employers dismissed employees without five-year seniority.

"Mary, I will probably be laid off," Jess stated flatly.

"Don't worry, I have been saving money every month since you have been with them," I said. "We have enough to live on if they let you go. You will find other work…you always have."

Jess' boss called him. He had no recourse but to let Jess go, but Jess would be the first one hired if the economy improved. Jess understood and was thankful for the three months severance pay. It would be a lean Christmas.

After Jess was laid off, Mr. Russell called in early 1932.

"Mr. Hodges, you have been recommended to me as an honest, hard-working construction engineer," Mr. Russell stated. "The Naval Yard at Cavite needs a large concrete water tank built on site. Would you be interested?"

"Yes, I would," Jess replied, "I don't have the capital to finance a large job. Most military jobs don't pay until the job's completion."

"Well, let me make this proposition," Mr. Russell countered. "I'll provide the capital if you will do the labor. We can split the earnings. How about it?"

Jess agreed to meet Mr. Russell and work out the details. Jess, who always trusted other Americans, made a verbal agreement in good faith with Mr. Russell.

Work commenced immediately on the large concrete water tower and tank for Camp Nichols. Jess hired Mr. Fields, a former employee of I. Beck's American Bazaar, as his foreman.

Jess left home at four each morning.

Camp Nichols water tower, at the U.S. Naval Yard in Cavite, P.I., 1932.

Rather than waken our old cook to prepare breakfast and pack a lunch for Jess, I arose around three to fix what he needed, and returned to bed after he left. If I overslept, *Mami* would waken, dress, and prepare breakfast for the children.

It took over two months for Jess to complete the steel-reinforced concrete water tower and tank at Camp Nichols. Jess depleted our savings to pay for some tools and equipment. He met Mr. Russell at the job site and Russell said he would submit the bill for $10,000 to the U.S. Navy when they approved the project. Jess and his men worked swiftly to finish and get it ready for inspection.

The job was approved and the check was sent to Mr. Russell, who dealt with the Naval Operations Office directly. Jess left all arrangements up to him.

"Jess," Mr. Russell stated when he phoned, "I have the $10,000 check from the Navy made out to us. I'll bring it by your house so you can co-sign it."

Mr. Russell came as promised. Jess co-signed the check.

"Meet me at my hotel at four this afternoon. I'll cash the check at the bank and have the money for you," Mr. Russell said as he left.

Jess was at his hotel at four and waited for about an hour, but Mr. Russell never met him in the lobby as promised. Jess checked with the desk clerk to contact Mr. Russell, as he did not have his room number.

When the desk clerk returned, he dropped the following bombshell.

"I am sorry, sir, but Mr. Russell checked out before noon. He was returning to America. How may I help you?

Jess was stunned. He left without responding. When he entered our front door, I sensed something was terribly wrong.

"What's the matter?" I asked, as Jess was usually happy to be home.

"Mary, you will not believe what that low-down skunk did to me," Jess sputtered as he described Mr. Russell's deception.

I tried to calm Jess. He was furious…angry with Mr. Russell and himself.

Jess clenched his fists, paced, and spouted angry words. I had never seen him so furious. Our savings were depleted, he had no job, and we lacked money to pay for rent and food. The long arm of The Great Depression had reached across the ocean and wrapped its bony fingers around us…with Mr. Russell's help.

Jess ranted and spouted for over thirty minutes. I finally remembered he had received a letter from Texas. Perhaps the letter would chase his gloom away.

"Jess, here's a letter from Texas!" I said…mustering my cheeriest tone.

The expression on Jess' face changed immediately. He reached for the letter and read quietly. It was from his old friend, R. J. (Bud) Van Sickle. Bud, who was practicing medicine in Longview, Texas, gave an accounting of events in his life and the folks in Quinlan. He wrote about "making whoopee" in the various clubs in Longview. Jess laughed and read Bud's letter aloud to me. I was pleased to see Jess in a happier mood. Bud's letter was just the right medicine to chase the gloom away.

Jess had to stay busy. While waiting for job offers to come forward, he built playground equipment for our children. He made a double bench swing glider, painted it green with orange trim, and placed it in the front yard. It was attractive

DR. R. J. VAN SICKLE
PHYSICIAN AND SURGEON
203-204 CAMPBELL BUILDING
LONGVIEW, TEXAS

November 13, 1931

Mr. Jesse Hodges,
San Juan, Delmonte,
P.I.

My Dear Jesse;

    This no doubt will surprise you but never the less I am sure you have become accustomed to little surprises. I have thought of writing you for the past few years to learn what was going on in the far away Islands. Perhaps a short summary will tell you something of interest concerning some of the folk here.

    In 1917 I entered the war and served here in the U.S. and was in Europe a year. Since then I have been over a lot of the world but have never been out your way. I manage to finish medicine on my own accord which cost me about seven thousand dollars. No little task when I had to make it all myself. I finished at Baylor Medical College in Dallas. Of course I have had some work at Harvard, New York City College, and a few others.

    Up until four months ago I have been connected with various Hospitals but am practicing entirely for myself now and expect to the rest of my life. By the way what happens to be in store for an M.D. out your way? I was thirty two on the seventh of this month and still single for as paper marriage is concerned.

    Longview is the center of the greatest oil field in the world and if times were normal like they were a few years ago there would be a thousand millionaires in this little city. I have a good practice but a night time the various clubs in this village and elsewhere usually finds me making whoopee. My room mate and I are pretty well known for our famous parties for they happen every night nearly. Our common saying is, "Think nothing of it".

    Please let me hear from you at your convenience. The folk in Quinlan are the same as they were twenty years ago. Mother is in fair health. She is seventy four years old. Everett McKeen (Bob's boy) is married and is living in Chicago. he has made plenty good.

    Best of luck to you. As ever,

Your Friend,
Rayburn
R.J. Van Sickle, MD.
(Bud)

P.S. Your address may be spelled incorrectly. I can hardly cipher the letters. R.

and sturdy. The whole family piled in to give it a strength-tolerance test, and it passed with flying colors.

His next project was a teeter-totter, a seesaw that whirled around in a circle or a "seesaw-go-round." It was also painted green with orange trim. Neighbors and passers-by stopped to ask about the playground equipment. They wondered if Jess would build the same items for them.

Jess became creative. He built a four-seat Ferris wheel with a large crank in the center to manually turn the wheel, and tested it by using our older children, plus a neighbor's child as "customers." He wanted to use Emma, but I was afraid she would fall off. The Ferris wheel worked perfectly!

This project was followed by his masterpiece...a merry-go-round. It consisted of four benches attached to a circular hardwood base and rotated on a center spindle. The merry-go-round accommodated eight to twelve small children. It, too, was painted with the same Sherwin-Williams green and orange outdoor paint.

The playground equipment in our front yard created an interesting display. Many stopped to admire the equipment. Others thought it was for sale and stopped to inquire...so we took orders. Instead of another child, we gave birth to The Manila Swing Manufacturer Company.

My sister, Consueling, however, gave birth to another girl in May 1932. An affair with a neighbor, Mr. Segado (Chinese/Filipino), resulted in a pregnancy. Her husband, Juanito, was not aware of her infidelity, and believed Maria Teresa (Teresita) was his. Teresita was also called "Chini" because of her Asian features. I kept Consueling's secret.

CHAPTER 66

Manila Swing Manufacturer

In early 1933, The Great Depression engulfed Manila like a heavy fog and suffocated the economy with its oppression. No one escaped its heavy weight. The large home we had enjoyed for two years was no longer affordable. We relocated in Santa Mesa. Once more we stuffed our family, like so many Spanish olives crammed in a jar, into a small house in Sociego, a part of Santa Mesa. Jess was unemployed, so we took a deep breath, found a small showroom near the house in Santa Mesa, and moved all the playground equipment Jess made for the children from our front yard into the showroom. We were ready to announce the grand opening of The Manila Swing Manufacturer Company. *We must have been either desperate or crazy…or maybe both.*

The house in Sociego was tiny. We had only two bedrooms, one bathroom, a living room, and a back porch. Our servants were dismissed because there were no servants' quarters, and we had no money to pay their salaries. The showroom, nearby, had a small room in the rear. Jess prepared it for my mother's quarters and added one tiny bathroom. We felt like sardines.

The saving grace of living in Santa Mesa was having the mayor of Manila Tomás Earnshaw, a wealthy man who owned The Earnshaw Docks at Manila Bay, as our neighbor. His son was about the same age as Bobby, our eldest. They became fast friends and attended the same school…the American school, H. A. Bordner Elementary, where only American citizens and families of government employees were allowed.

The Manila Swing business grew slower than we hoped. We only took orders from customers who pre-paid one-third of the cost, with the balance due upon delivery.

We were in business for four months when the owners decided they needed the showroom space to create additional living quarters for their family. Once again, we searched for nearby showroom space.

Mr. and Mrs. Rivero, the Earnshaw's friends, learned of our dilemma and offered a showroom they had vacated. It was a larger showroom, but rent was the same. This place had a small apartment at the rear of the showroom, which was a perfect place for my mother. The children could stay with her while Jess and I worked to build up the business.

Business increased. We needed help. My sister Consueling, her husband, Juan Gonzalez, and their four children, decided they would combine business and pleasure during the children's school vacation. The two youngest, a toddler named Carlitos, and baby, Teresita, stayed behind with Juan's mother, Doña Petrona Bailon Vda. de Gonzalez. Consueling and her family stayed in the rear apartment with *Mami*, who helped take care of the children. They enjoyed the sights in Manila, and helped with customers in the showroom. My brother-in-law, Juan, helped Jess in building playground equipment and garden furniture. We became so busy, Jess had to buy a small used truck and hire a part-time driver to make deliveries to customers.

Jess decided to make children's rocking chairs, stools, step stools, and toys from lumber scraps instead of burning the larger scraps. I painted and decorated the toys and children's furniture with hand-painted Disney characters. These smaller items sold well as children's presents. After a month, more help was hired, as Juan, who was helping Jess, had to return to Bulan. It was time for the harvest on their plantations. Consueling and their children stayed for a longer visit, so I still had help in the showroom.

Señor Folch, a Spaniard with a large family, attended our church and desperately needed a job. Our parish priest asked us to hire him on a trial basis. He learned quickly and was a hard worker. Having good help allowed me to

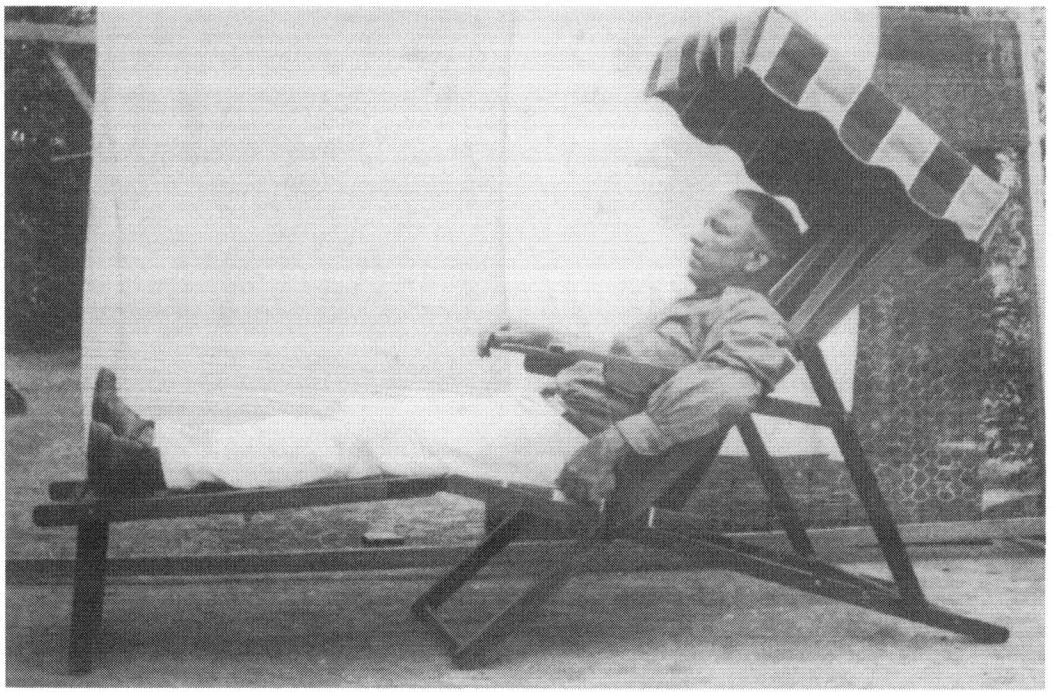

Jess takes a well-deserved rest in one of the many lounge chair designs produced by Manila Swing Manufacturer.

put together a small catalog of items we offered for sale at Manila Swing. Many pictures in the catalog included our children posed on the equipment as models.

In late October, Doña Petrona Bailon Vda. de Gonzalez brought her son from Bulan to Santiago, a Spanish hospital in Manila. Juan was suffering from an advanced case of bronchopneumonia. The doctors tried all they knew to save him during November, but he worsened. He died three weeks before Christmas. The family was devastated. Instead of a holiday celebration, we had a funeral. Consueling sobbed uncontrollably as she hugged us before gathering her six young children for the return trip to Bulan to live with her mother-in-law.

We worked with heavy hearts to meet the many orders placed for the Christmas season. We had no choice but to persist. We knew our business would slow down after the holidays, and needed to pay our bills.

Before Christmas, a customer, Mr. Kraut, admired the playground equipment and wanted to meet Jess. He needed a special gift for his sons. I called Jess from the workroom where he and *Señor* Folch were working.

"Mr. Hodges, it's a pleasure to meet you," Mr. Kraut said in his thick German accent. "Do you build other items?"

"Well, Mr. Kraut, we are experimenting with this business," Jess explained. "I was a contractor with MERALCO, but lost my position during The Depression. I am more accustomed to building houses and built the hydroelectric plant in Botocan recently. I think I can build anything you want."

Mr. Kraut was impressed. He and Jess discussed the projects Jess had worked on in San Juan and other areas.

"I am planning to build apartments," Mr. Kraut said. "Would you be interested?"

"I don't have enough capital," Jess replied flatly.

Mr. Kraut rubbed his chin, glanced at Jess, and changed the subject.

"Are you German, Mr. Hodges?" Mr. Kraut asked, and spoke German to Jess.

"No, and I did not understand what you said after you spoke my name," Jess said.

"Well, if you will consider working for me for a salary plus commission, I will provide the money for labor and materials," Mr. Kraut stated.

"I'll think about it and talk it over with my wife," Jess replied. "We will have to make changes in our furniture business if I work for you."

Mr. Kraut left after placing an order with me for his sons. He had a twinkle in his eyes as he left.

After Christmas, Jess and I discussed his offer and agreed it would be worth trying. We sold all the small children's furniture, toys, and most of the playground equipment during the holidays. Several pieces of garden furniture plus our samples remained in the showroom like forlorn puppies waiting for adoption. A decision was made to sell our samples and move the remainder to our house. We would take orders only on remaining items.

Jess worked for Mr. Kraut beginning in January 1934. He was kind to Jess and invited our family to his home to meet his twin boys, who were celebrating their seventh birthday. The twins would be leaving for Germany soon to attend a private school. Mrs. Kraut was concerned about this long separation. Conditions in Germany were deteriorating, but her husband insisted they be educated in Germany.

As Jess surveyed the land for the apartments, he asked Mr. Kraut what he wanted to do about a large, two-story building on the property.

"Well, I have it for sale…to be relocated," Mr. Kraut said. "No one wants to pay $1000 for it, plus the cost of having it removed. The highest bid I have received was $500. Jess, if you have a place to put it, you can have the building. All you will have to do is tear it down and clear off the area."

"Let me talk to Mr. Myers at San Juan Heights," Jess replied. "He may have a lot we can buy. We have wanted our own home for a long time."

Jess was excited when he told me his news. He visited Mr. Myers on the way home and learned Meyers recently opened a new section of San Juan Heights for development. The new street had not yet been named.

"Mary," he said, "we can name our new street if we take the first lot."

The long-awaited miracle was within reach. We were going to have a home…built just for us. My excitement caused the baby I was carrying in my womb to kick for the first time. *Thank you St. Expedito for answering this prayer.* San Expedito, the patron saint for the home and family, had interceded for us with Our Lord. We will name the new street *San Expedito*.

Mary smiled as she recalled their first new home. *Number 19 San Expedito was perfect with room for all. Jess had a large workshop for making items sold through The Manila Swing catalog. More children's furniture, children's bedroom suites, kiddie coops, and garden furniture were added. We were desperate in early 1933, but not crazy, although we were the only ones in Manila with this type of business. We won First Prize, a gold medal, at The Philippine Exposition, and continued to win other medals each year until we dissolved the business in 1939.*

CHAPTER 67

Oops! Another Girl!

The year 1934 was a prosperous one for us. Cole Porter's newest hit, *Anything Goes,* echoed across the Philippines with its resounding beat and distracted us from the growing menace in Europe. Adolph Hitler was elected as *Der Führer. Europe's problems won't affect us! They are far away!*

I hummed and swayed my ever-growing body to the strains of *Blue Moon* and *The Continental*. Our first new home on *San Expedito* was the answer to prayers. There were three large bedrooms, two baths, and a small apartment for my mother, a large living and dining room, an extra-large kitchen, expansive front and back porches, and separate servants' quarters for Santos and *Tota*. Jess had a salaried job plus commission, and our Manila Swing business was doing well with catalog sales. We won many awards for our designs. Another baby was on the way, and my mother was living under our roof again.

On May 22, 1934, at 7:15 p.m., we were surprised with another daughter! The pattern was broken. No more boy, girl, boy, girl sequencing in our family. Dr. Paz G. King, a Chinese female physician, at *Hospital de Español de Santiago,* delivered her during the worst typhoon to hit Luzon. We were preparing for a boy, and had to think of a name for this unexpected girl. My favorite soap opera on the radio was, *Mary Jane and Her Skeleton Family*. I liked the soap opera, so the baby was named Mary Jane. She was born on St. Rita's Day, so she was given Rita as her middle name, which may have been predictive since St. Rita is the patron saint of the Impossible.

We depleted our savings to pay for material to keep Manila Swing going and to finish our new home, but, once again, we had cause for celebration. The baptismal gown Emma had worn was readied. My sister Pilar and her husband, Tony Settember, would serve as godparents. They were delighted as they had only one son, Anthony. They wished for another child and wanted a girl, but that wish was not granted. My half-brother, Fr. Gamero conducted the rituals, and the family gathered at our home for a small celebration.

In early June, my sister Consueling came for a visit and brought Fanny, Pilachu, Teresita, and Carlitos with her. Her two oldest sons, Juaning and José

(Bull), stayed at the plantation with their grandmother, Doña Petrona. She was struggling to keep the plantation since the death of her son, Juan, and had been through this experience before when she was widowed. Consueling stayed with Lucing, Francisco and their family. She was disgusted with living on the plantation, and was determined to live in Manila.

The small house we had vacated in Sociego (Santa Mesa) was still vacant. Francisco took Consueling to see it, as she was receiving money from her mother-in-law, Doña Petrona, to pay for living expenses. She liked the area, they already knew the neighbors, and it was close to schools. Although it was small, it had more amenities than were offered in Bulan.

Pilachu was enrolled in boarding school and only came home on the weekends. Fanny, however, was unable to attend as she suffered from a "thyroid condition" which clouded her thinking and lowered her mental abilities. Carlitos, a toddler, and Teresita, the baby, were still in diapers.

To make ends meet, Counsueling offered a bedroom for rent via an ad in the church newsletter. Linda and Carmelo Lopez, newcomers to the Philippines from Puerto Rico, attended the same church and saw her ad. They seemed nice and offered to help with the children, if needed. Consueling was desperate, so she rented to them.

Fanny was sixteen years old and attractive. She had a sweet disposition, was friendly, but was not dependable due to her thyroid problem. Her condition was too advanced for doctors to treat.

Consueling returned to Bulan to see her oldest sons and visit her mother-in-law. She took Carlitos and Teresita with her, as the baby was still nursing. Pilachu would stay on weekends with Fanny. Since Pilachu should not miss school, Consueling asked, Linda and Carmelo, if they would check on Fanny while Pilachu was attending classes. They were more than happy to help. Consueling and the younger children would return from Bulan in two weeks.

When Consueling and the two youngest children returned, Consueling felt something was troubling Fanny. She was withdrawn and not her usual happy self.

"Mi hija," Consueling probed, "what is your problem? Why are you so sad?"

Fanny refused to talk. She remained withdrawn and sullen. She picked at her food and cried most of the time. She refused to sleep in her bed.

"Fanny," her mother ordered, "you must tell me why you are so sad. It breaks my heart to see you are not smiling and laughing. What has happened to make you change? Do you need to see a doctor?'

At the word "doctor," Fanny burst into tears and she began babbling so fast Consueling barely understood her between her heavy sobs. Her terrible secret spilled from her lips.

"*Señor* Lopez forced me in the shower," Fanny blurted while sobbing violently.

Consueling shook with rage and asked many questions. She listened and probed until she had all the lurid details. Carmelo Lopez raped her daughter. She hugged Fanny to quiet her and held her close until the sobbing stopped. She waited until Fanny was asleep in her arms before gently lowering her head to the cushion on the sofa. She covered her with a shawl, and prepared to confront *Señor* Lopez. Consueling would find out what happened.

Consueling waited until the younger children were asleep. Pilachu was doing her homework, and Fanny was still sleeping.

"Pilachu, I am going to talk to the Lopez's. Will you please listen for your younger brother and sister? I shouldn't be long," Consueling stated calmly as she left on her mission.

As she knocked on the door, she steeled herself for what she must do. *That animal has destroyed my daughter! He must pay!*

Linda Lopez answered her knock and invited her in. Carmelo, the villain, was nowhere in sight.

"Where is your husband?" Consueling inquired. "I need to speak with him."

"He is out playing cards with his friends," Linda replied. "He won't be home until late. Come in, please."

"I cannot come in or stay," Consueling said gritting her teeth. "Your husband has raped Fanny. She told me what happened."

Consueling's words spilled almost as fast as her tears, as she talked about her daughter being violated by Carmelo. Linda Lopez was aghast. Her eyes widened and her nostrils flared as she trembled before she spoke angrily.

"Your daughter is lying! She is crazy! She is mistaken! My husband would never harm anyone!" Mrs. Lopez shrieked. "Get out of here! Get out of here!"

Estephania Gonzalez y Gamero (Fanny) at her First Holy Communion

Linda Lopez approached Consueling and tried to push her out the door. Consueling fell backward in disbelief. Before she knew what was happening, she found herself in the hallway, with the door slammed in her face.

Consueling screamed through the door. Her angry words pierced the heavy wood like sharp bolo knives.

"You are the ones who will leave. You are the ones who will get out of here before I call the police!"

Consueling felt as if she had been beaten with a heavy stick. She ached from the inside out. She needed her husband, Juan, by her side...but he was with the angels.

Between being upset by these events and caring for my baby, Mary Jane, I forgot to register her birth certificate with the Local Civil Registrar. A letter I received from *Sr.* St. Claire Claver, M. I. C., the Assistant Mother Superior at the Chinese General Hospital, dated June 30, 1934, brought me to my senses. I needed to care for my immediate family. My youngest daughter did not have an official name, although she had already been christened.

About two months later, *Mami* noticed Fanny was behaving more nervously than usual. She insisted Consueling take Fanny to a doctor. Upon examination, the doctor discovered Fanny was pregnant. The news was devastating. He told my sister and mother the pregnancy would aggravate Fanny's condition. They tried medication at first but had to place Fanny in an institution for the mentally ill...under the care of a psychiatrist, at least until she gave birth to her child.

After the birth of her child, Fanny was given medication to calm her nerves and sent home with her infant. The resemblance to Carmelo Lopez was not to be denied. *Mami* told Consueling that the baby should be sent to Bulan to be raised by Doña Petrona. Consueling refused to discuss it, but *Mami* convinced her it would be the best solution for Fanny and her baby, Mari Carmen. Fanny's condition had worsened since giving birth. Consueling relented and talked with Doña Petrona, who agreed to care for the baby, thus solving one problem. She was thankful that Mr. and Mrs. Lopez left the Philippines. She could not bear to look at either one of them again.

Fanny's condition worsened. Once again she was confined in the psychiatric

Doña Luz Cucullu Vda. de Gamero *(Mami)*, 1934.

hospital and given medication. As she improved, she met a young man, Paulo Santos who was also a patient, and fell in love. Upon her release from the institution, Paulo visited Fanny at home. He was well liked by Consueling and *Mami*. Paulo proposed marriage to Fanny and received the family's approval. A small wedding was arranged and Fanny left to live with her husband.

Consueling found another apartment next door to Lola Lala. *Mami* was happy. She wanted all those troubles behind her and thought relocation would help Consueling.

In early 1936, Fanny and Paulo had their first child, a son. She would bring the baby boy to visit Consueling and our mother. Usually, Fanny behaved normally. During one of these visits, Fanny's behavior became violent. While nursing her baby, she slapped the baby's face hard several times. Her baby would scream and Fanny would offer her breast to resume nursing. *How strange!* I did not confront Fanny. I was afraid she would strike her baby again…or strike me. Paulo returned to take Fanny and their baby home. I told *Mami* and Consueling my concerns.

"I think Fanny is getting sick again," I stated. "She should not be slapping her poor baby."

The others had also seen Fanny strike the baby. They agreed and shook their heads. We felt so helpless.

Fanny stayed away for a while. After four months, she returned for another visit. We noticed how nervously she behaved, and discovered, after inquiring, Fanny was pregnant again. Her son was barely eight months old. She would be having another child in seven months.

Fanny was institutionalized for the third time. Their two children were placed under the care of Paulo's sister to allow Paulo to be by Fanny's side. He visited the psychiatric hospital daily. As her condition worsened, he stayed on the hospital grounds. He slept on a park bench and refused to leave, ignoring his own care. His body was discovered…lying across the bench. A tragic ending to one of two tragic lives.

Mary felt uneasy as she thought about Fanny and Paulo. She felt they had no chance to live a normal life. *Fanny had to be permanently institutionalized. When the Japanese took over the Philippines, those poor souls in institutions were treated poorly. Fanny died in 1942 from lack of food and medication. She died as she lived…tragically.*

CHAPTER 68

No Boys Allowed

In late 1936, the catalog sales for Manila Swing Manufacturer business grew. We were still having difficulties. The cost of materials to stockpile catalog items for customers ate into our profits. Jess built a workshop behind our new home and hired two carpenters, Eugenio and Paulino Reyes. Felix Ayala, a painter, was employed but later was fired, as his work was not satisfactory. Jess did the painting and I decorated. A driver was hired to transport lumber and materials, plus deliver the finished product to customers.

A new showroom in an upper-class neighborhood in Ermita on A. Mabini Street was rented. Our friends, the Adolfo Garcias, owned the building and lived in the apartment above the showroom. *Señor* Garcia reduced the rent as considerable repairs were needed. This showroom included a small bathroom and kitchen space at the rear, plus a small room for the children, if they needed to stay.

When the showroom was ready, our samples were put on display. My daily routine included taking Bobby, Lucy, and Junior to school on my way to work. Emma and Mary Jane stayed home with two maids. At 12:30 p.m., I collected the children from school, took them home, ate lunch, returned to work on items, and stayed until 6:30

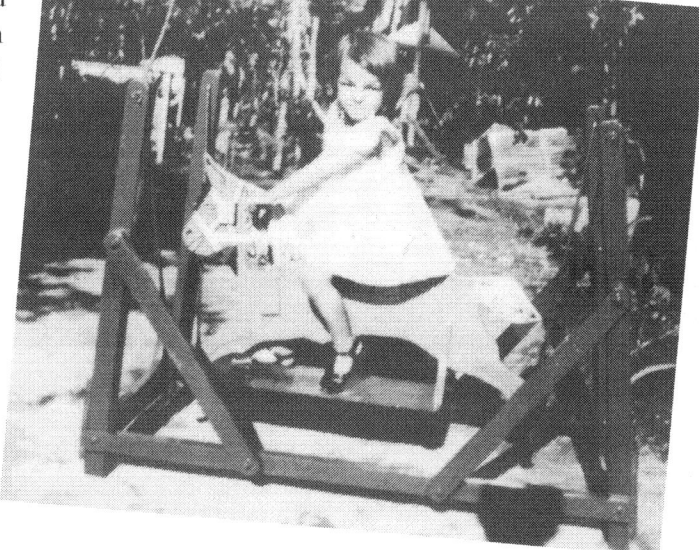

Mary Jane Hodges demonstrating the use of a "Rocking, Jumping, and Gliding Horse." Product of Manila Swing Mfg.

p.m. or later.

In order to prepare for the upcoming Christmas season, Jess hired two more carpenters, and I hired two single ladies, Adeling Ramos and her sister, Dorotea, to work in the showroom. The ladies offered to work for less if we would fix a room for them at the rear of the showroom. Jess enclosed a corner at the rear for their bedroom with access to the kitchenette and bathroom located in the opposite corner. By adding these employees, we were able to take more orders. Our business did extremely well from 1936 until May of 1938, but lawmakers were debating two new labor laws.

The new laws required employers to pay employees for days absent from work due to illness. It also required employers to provide hospitalization insurance. We could not stay in business if those laws passed. It would be impossible. As we debated our future, another child was stirring deep within my womb.

On July 2, 1937, the disappearance of aviatrix Amelia Earhart and navigator Fred Noonan over the Pacific Ocean

Marie Emma Hodges, "Shirley Temple of the Philippines," 1937.

filled the airwaves. Newspaper reports, the next day, speculated whether or not their plane had either crashed or landed on some remote island in the Philippine Sea. Updates on their disappearance were provided daily. Within a month, the topic no longer made headlines. Announcements of Japanese military action against China took its place on the radio. I paid special attention to the next announcement—a talent contest to select a "Shirley Temple of the Philippines." I jotted down details and began making plans.

Lucy and Emma were enrolled in dancing lessons and were doing very well. Emma had dimples just like the child star, Shirley Temple, and shoulder length hair that could be curled into ringlets! Shirley Temple dresses were sold at several stores on the Escolta. I would enter her in the contest...sponsored by Manila Swing Manufacturer. All she had to do was perform one of Shirley Temple's songs, do a little dance, and smile...to show off her dimples. *What a brilliant idea!* Contest forms were acquired and completed. Lucy had received a Shirley Temple doll for Christmas, which I borrowed, and took Emma to The Sun Studio to have her photo taken holding the doll.

Everything fell into place. Emma competed and won the contest. She was asked to sing some Shirley Temple songs on the local radio station, and was featured in *The Manila Tribune*. We had a celebrity in our midst. Everyone was delighted, with the exception of Lucy. Emma had managed to comb out some of the ringlets on her Shirley Temple doll and she felt it was ruined. It would never be the same. I tried to smooth things over and restore peace between the girls, but Lucy was still unhappy. I told her she could help me take care of our "real" baby due to arrive in three weeks.

On November 14, 1937, another baby girl bounced into our lives. We decided boys were not allowed. She appeared at 2:50 p.m. at the *Instituto Singian* at 277 General Solano in Manila with Dr. Alfredo Guerrero as the attending physician. I stayed four and one-half days in Room No. 6 and the entire hospital bill totaled fifty-two *pesos*. We first named our new daughter Mary Consuelo for my sister, Maria del Consuelo, but later, decided to name her Joyce Josephine. I liked the name "Joyce" because I enjoyed listening to a popular American singer who recorded the song, *"Trees"*, with lyrics taken from James Joyce's poem. Her middle name, Josephine, was a derivative of my father's patron saint, Joseph. I was so busy, I neglected to change her birth certificate listing her name as Mary Consuelo.

Overwhelmed with preparing for our Christmas season, arrangements for the baby's christening were not made within thirty days, but I did get her birth certificate filed by December 13. Her baptismal rituals were held March 19, 1938. The Reverend Patrick Kelly, an Irish priest, performed the rites. Her birth certificate was registered at Parroquia de Malate in Manila with V. J. Garcia, Registrar. Joyce's godparents were my eldest son, Robert Morris (Bobby) Hodges and Tarcila H. Villamill, a family friend, who lived at 1882 Aregon Street in Manila. Her birth certificate was not amended to carry her name as "Joyce Josephine" until October 18, 1940.

While regaining my strength following Joyce's birth, I returned to my regular schedule. Since Joyce was being nursed, she also served as the "model" for our kiddie coops, playpens, and baby beds. Customers were delighted to find a young working girl.

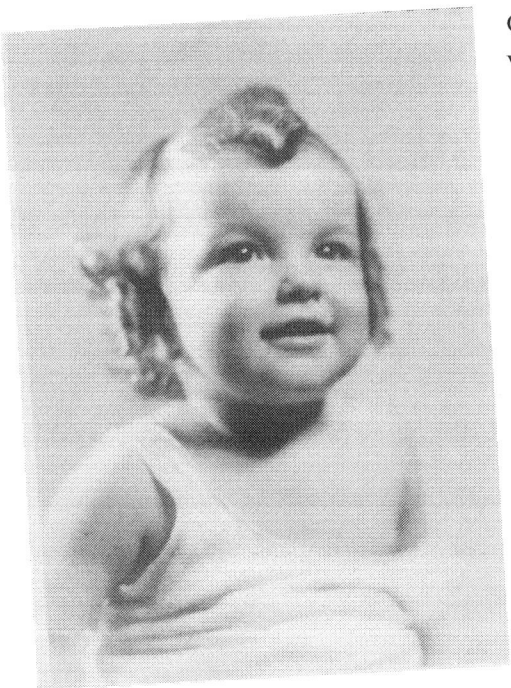

The 1937 Christmas sales outdid those of 1936. We jumped into 1938 with high expectations and were not disappointed. When Joyce was one year old, her maid, Ana, took care of her while I was busy with customers. Joyce learned to walk by holding Ana's hand to stroll on the sidewalks of A. Mabini. They took walks whenever our showroom was crowded or when Joyce became restless and needed some exercise.

A Chinese photographer owned the A. Mabini Photography Studio, in the same

Portrait of Joyce Josephine Hodges displayed in window of A. Mabini Photography by Zhou Sin.

block as our showroom. Joyce's curly locks, dimples, flawless peachy complexion, and bright sunny smile impressed him. His son was about Joyce's age. The two became acquainted and sometimes played together in our showroom.

Zhou Sin, the photographer, asked my permission to allow Joyce to sit for a portrait, which he would display in his storefront window. Ana took Joyce to the photography studio for the sitting. Two weeks later, Mr. Sin gave me several photos and a 16" by 20" portrait, which I took home. When Rosario visited, she wanted the portrait for her quarters in Antipolo. Mr. Sin displayed a 20" by 18" framed portrait of Joyce in his storefront window. When Ana and Joyce walked by the studio, Joyce would point at her portrait in his window and clap her hands. Customers often commented about her portrait in Mr. Sin's window next door.

In 1938 the labor laws requiring employers to pay employees for sick leave and provide hospitalization insurance passed. We decided to close the Manila Swing Manufacturer business. Our products were entered one last time in The Philippine Exposition and, for the fifth time, won the first prize. This gold medal would be our last.

In order to provide for the living expenses with six children, we decided to sell our home. Jess was doing small, odd jobs for Mr. Meyers, but the pay was not sufficient. Mr. Meyers helped find a buyer who paid our asking price. With the money, we bought an inexpensive lot from Mr. Meyers in San Juan Heights at 101 Blumentritt. The lot required much work, but Jess managed to level it and build a smaller house with materials he already had.

We kept only two maids, Dorotea, a high school graduate who tutored the children, and Adeling Ramos. We no longer hired a maid for each small child, as we had before. We were in our new home one-month when Dorotea decided she wanted to take a leave of absence to study dressmaking.

"Dorotea," I said, "I am in favor of your ambition as dressmaker, but I cannot hold your position for you because I need two maids to help with the children. If you decide to go, I will have to hire someone in your place."

"*Si, Señora,*" she replied. "I want to be a dressmaker, so I will go in two weeks."

Lola Lala visited after Dorotea left and noticed I needed help. She knew of two sisters who needed jobs as maids. She hired both for me at the same price I was paying for Dorotea's services. We had three maids for the price of two, but none were able to tutor the children. Jess and I took over those responsibilities.

Within two months, Dorotea returned and begged to be rehired. She was not happy.

"Dorotea," I stated, "We hired two maids for the price I paid you. My budget will not allow me to rehire you."

"Please, *Señora*," she begged. "I will work for you for the same price and sew clothing for your children."

I called my sister Lucing to see if she needed help. She was delighted to have more help and was able to pay their asking price. Since the new maids had worked only two months, they agreed to work for Lucing. The decision made Dorotea happy. I was pleased our tutor returned, plus we had a dressmaker for the children.

CHAPTER 69

The American Hatchery

Noises of war rumbled across Europe in 1938 and spilled across 1939 like the raging waterfalls at Antipolo. Once again the fabric of our lives was colored by news from Europe and Asia, caused by the actions of Japan, Italy, and Germany's leaders. This news paled in comparison to the death of Pope Pius XI. Cardinal Eugenio Pacelli was installed as Pope Pius XII. We listened to the radio; pushed aside the "bad stuff;" and, lifted our spirits with popular songs, like: *Flat Foot Floogie with a Floy Floy, September Song, Jeepers Creepers,* and *A Tisket, A Tasket,* being played between the "doom and gloom" of international newscasts.

We needed more "eggs in our basket" as Jess was still unemployed, and our debts grew faster than our income. An acquaintance with a poultry farm convinced me to raise chickens and sell eggs. Since our lot was large, we decided to follow her advice. We bought a small fifty capacity incubator and enough fertile eggs from her to experiment with this venture. *Our chicken ranch was on its way. We will keep the pullets for laying hens and fry the others!* We had much to learn.

Our home on 101 Blumentritt was across from the Dominican Church of San Juan. Fr. Angel paid a visit soon after Jess installed the chicken wire fence to keep the birds in our lot. Father Angel had advice on raising chickens.

"*Señora* Hodges," he said, "several parish priests have tried raising chickens in order to sell eggs, but found one cannot make money in the chicken business. We ate all the chickens, but still have two large incubators."

I showed him my small incubator and the second batch of fertile eggs.

"Fr. Angel," I said, "those chicks hatched from our first batch. The second batch will hatch soon. The American Hatchery is being born right before your eyes."

I pointed toward the young chicks scratching around the small pen Jess built to protect them. Thirty-nine chicks were picking through the feed troughs and chasing bugs, imaginary and real.

Fr. Angel was impressed by my indomitable spirit and sensed I was determined to succeed in my American Hatchery business.

"I will be happy to give you both incubators in our shed. One is a one hundred capacity incubator and the other one will hold two hundred," Fr. Angel stated.

"I appreciate your offer, Fr. Angel," I said. "I will discuss this with my husband and tell you what we decide. Thank you so much for your advice."

"Call me when you begin selling eggs," Fr. Angel replied. "Our Father Superior suffers from tuberculosis, and the doctor says he must have fresh eggs daily. We need at least three dozen."

When Jess returned from seeing about a job Mr. Meyers had for him, we discussed Fr. Angel's visit and his offer to give us the two incubators. Jess decided we should use the smaller incubator, as our lot was not large enough to handle many more chickens. We tackled the chicken business and tried to avoid financial failure for another year.

In March 1940, Jess was reading the newspaper and discovered the U.S. Navy was hiring contractors and laborers to build a defense plant at the Cavite Naval Base. The next morning, Jess hurried to submit his application as their foreman. We crossed our fingers, prayed, and waited.

Meanwhile, Jess continued with the small projects for Mr. Meyers. He also built several chicken runs to keep the chickens separated as they hatched. We began sorting pullets from fryers. Fr. Angel stopped by occasionally to show me how to manage my chicken ranch. He had raised hundreds.

"*Sra.* Hodges," Fr. Angel stated, "I wish you well, but I learned from experience money cannot be made from anything requiring feed. They will eat all your profit, and can also get sick and die."

I smiled and kept on putting the chicken feed into long troughs Jess had built. *I will make money. I must make money!*

The American Hatchery absorbed all our time and energy, but it was too small for the number of chickens we owned. We needed a larger place, and we needed money.

We would sell our home if we found a larger place to rent for our "chicken ranch." Money from the sale of our property could cover living expenses until Jess found a job. We might make money by selling eggs, live fryers or roosters. Cockfighting was practiced all over the islands. We would raise several different breeds.

A neighbor told me about Mr. Ansaldo, her friend in the poultry business. He had died recently, and relatives placed his home and chicken ranch for rent. She gave me his son's phone number, in case we were interested. Jess and I made arrangements to see the place the next day. The two-story house was small. It had only one large bedroom, a living room, a small bathroom, and a tiny kitchen with a large adjoining back porch. Included were two acres of land with plenty of fruit and shade trees, plus a small pond. The property was fenced and had a large corrugated tin building, which could house about four hundred chickens. It needed repairs, but we felt it was the right place for our chicken ranch. The rent was also reasonable.

We sold our home within two days of posting the "For Sale" sign in the front yard and had only one month to relocate to #43 J. Ruiz Street in San Juan. Jess worked to make the necessary changes. He divided the large back porch, making a dining room near the small kitchen, and created another bedroom from the remaining space. On the first floor, he fixed rooms for the incubators and a bedroom for Bobby. A room for Jesse Jr. was added. We launched our "chicken ranch" during June 1940.

When I think of all we did to get our "Chicken Ranch" going, I marvel it was done in a month's time. We arranged living quarters for our family, but the chickens were our first priority. We spent money on chickens because they provided income.

CHAPTER 70

Changes and Choices

The war in Europe and Asia devoured smaller countries like an ugly, angry beast attacking and destroying everything in its path. Germany invaded Norway and Denmark. Britain took steps to prepare for an invasion by Hitler and his Nazi troops. Chamberlain resigned and Winston Churchill filled his shoes as Prime Minister. We listened as his "blood, toil, tears, and sweat," speech echoed across the seas and chilled our bones. *Not another war! We've already had the war to end all wars!*

The strains of *When You Wish Upon A Star* filtered across the back porch/dining room as I prepared the evening meal. We no longer had servants. We barely had room for our family by filling the one large bedroom with small beds for the girls. We had no room for *Mami*, so she stayed with Consueling. I wanted to wish upon a star and make my dreams come true. *Maybe I should pray to St. Anthony so Jess can get a full-time job.*

The telephone rang and jarred me from my reverie. When I answered the phone, I felt this call was important. A husky American voice was asking for "Mr. Jesse Hodges." I hurried to call Jess. He was downstairs building more runs for the poultry.

"Hello," Jess answered as he held the receiver and tried to catch his breath. "This is Jesse Hodges."

"Sir, my name is W. B. Coombs, Director of Operations at the U.S. Naval Base at Cavite," the American said, "Your application for foreman to build our new defense plant at the United States Navy's Pacific Base at Cavite has been forwarded to me. I have several questions."

Jess talked on the phone for about twenty minutes while I listened quietly as I stirred the rice in the large pot and replaced the lid on the *camotes* simmering in their soft green leaves. *St. Anthony, please help Jess.*

When Jess put down the receiver, he glanced at me and smiled.

"Well, Mary, I'm working for the U.S. Navy. Mr. W. B. Coombs just called, and wants me as foreman on the new project at Cavite. I report to Cavite in July. Since it is about 137 kilometers from here, I will probably have to stay there during the week and come home on weekends until the job is finished."

I silently thanked St. Anthony for answering my prayers, but I had another problem. Jess was helping with the care and feeding of the chickens, plus delivering eggs to customers. I would have to enlist more help from the children. All were in school except for Joyce. Pilar had been begging me to let Joyce stay with her since I had so much to do with the poultry. Arrangements were made for Joyce to live with Pilar.

At the supper table, we held a family conference. Jess knew how to involve the children in family discussions and allowed them to have a voice in our decisions. It was decided. While their daddy was away at work, all would have to pitch in and help with household duties and the American Hatchery. The eggs were gathered twice daily and weighed, sorted, plus stored in a cool place. Mary Jane was in charge of delivering eggs to customers within walking distance in our area. Emma would tend to customers at our front gate. Jesse Jr. would clean and disinfect the roosts in the large barn and help grind the feed. Bobby would help with gathering and separating eggs for the incubators. He would also monitor the hatchlings. The different breeds must be kept separated. Rhode Island Reds, Plymouth Rocks, White Leghorns, and Cantonese breeding hens were in separate chicken houses. I would supervise, monitor chores, do paperwork, and be prepared for inspections. Anyone owning over twenty-five chickens in a poultry business must have a license, pay quarterly taxes, and be subject to monthly (unannounced) inspections by the Bureau of Animals and Poultry.

Jess found a small house to rent near his job site. He returned every two weeks for a weekend visit. On his way home, he would stop at the grocery store and buy fruit, candy, and a surprise for me. His visits were celebrated as if they were holidays. We were glad to have his help with the poultry, so we could take a break.

When the children were in school from 7:30 in the morning until 2:30 in the afternoon, I could not complete all the work required for the American Hatchery. I hired my nephew, Pacquito (Lucing's son), to help. The children rode public transportation to H. A. Bordner, the school for American children. A public school bus system did not exist in the Philippines. My hands were full with keeping the children fed, clothed, attending school and church, plus keeping the American Hatchery going without Jess' help.

By Mary Jane's sixth birthday in May 1940, I felt another baby stirring inside. The last time Jess' Uncle C. N. Hodges and his wife Linnie came to visit, Aunt Linnie asked if I would name our next son after C. N., as they were childless. He wanted a blood relative as his namesake. Jess and I talked it over after they left, but he was hesitant to do so.

"Jess, your uncle is wealthy," I said. "He owns many plantations, pawn shops, and other businesses in Iloilo plus other provinces in the Philippines. Think about all the property he owns in the United States. If we give him a namesake, he might be generous to our child."

Jess remained silent and shook his head.

"The man puts his money before anything else," Jess replied and left the room.

At 12:15 a.m. on November 23, 1940, Linnie May Hodges slipped quietly into our lives at The Singhian Clinic with Dr. Alfredo Guerrero attending. Jess agreed to name our seventh child after his Uncle C. N.'s wife, Linnie Higdon Hodges. When I sent Aunt Linnie the birth announcement naming our baby girl after her, she was pleased. She sent a lovely baptismal gown for Linnie plus one hundred *pesos* as a baptismal gift.

When Linnie was six months old, Aunt Linnie visited her namesake.

"I've come to get my baby and take her home with me," Aunt Linnie announced.

"Well, Aunt Linnie," I replied, "Jess is working at the naval yard at Cavite and is not here. You will need to speak with him."

She was serious. She mistakenly thought, since we named the baby after her, we would give her our child.

"When do you expect Jess?"

"He should be here tomorrow," I said. "He comes home every two weeks."

"I will be here tomorrow to talk to Jess," Aunt Linnie stated flatly, as if the decision had already been made.

When Jess returned the next day, I waited until the children had a chance to visit with him before breaking the news about his Aunt Linnie's visit and her wish to take our baby girl to Iloilo. We were discussing this issue when the bell at the front gate pealed. It was Aunt Linnie.

After greetings were exchanged, I prepared coffee and brought a tray of cookies to serve Jess and his aunt in the living room. They were deep into a lively discussion when I returned with the *merienda*.

"Jess," Aunt Linnie said, "C. N. and I want to adopt my namesake, Linnie. We cannot have children and you and Mary have a houseful. We are prepared to give her the best we can afford, and she will inherit all we have."

Jess shook his head negatively and smiled. He would have to be tactful.

"Aunt Linnie," Jess replied, "as much as we would like to at times, we cannot give our children away for adoption. You are welcome to visit your namesake anytime."

"I'm sorry you won't let us have her, Jess. It's breaking my heart to go home empty-handed," Aunt Linnie said as she prepared to return to Iloilo.

"Come to see us soon," Jess said, "and bring Uncle C. N. with you."

Mary smiled as she recalled the encounter. *Linnie was a sweet baby. It's no wonder she is such a caring person. She is a blessing and has a very strong faith in God along with a giving nature. Thank you, God, for providing me with so many blessings. While there have been sorrows and tragedies, there have been many joys.*

Angels vs. Devils

CHAPTER 71

The Approaching Menace

Rumors of war dominated the conversation. The men at the job site in Cavite laughed at Jess when he pushed to get the defense facilities built at a faster pace.

"Do you think the Japs would be so foolish as to start a war with the United States? No way!" A workman remarked.

Others asked Jess when he thought the Japs would attack.

"That's a good question. We need to finish and be prepared," Jess would reply.

They became upset with Jess and accused him of using those rumors to get the work done faster. They wanted to slow down the pace so the job would last longer.

The possibility of war with Japan had colored the news since late 1939. A letter written by his father, Robert W. Hodges, dated September 4, 1939, noted the following:

> I am dropping you a line to let you no I am up Sitting under my mulberry tree In my yard, to(o) I can't stand the Summer....
>
> It seame like the war are on In the East. Let them Fight. When Our President of U.S.A. call for all Americans, get Out off the P. I. So Japan can own the P. I. If you don't have money to passage to San Francisco, Call the U.S.A Will give all Free passage....
>
> Your Loving Father
> R. W. Hodges

Robert Wesley Hodges, Jess' father at the family home west of Quinlan, Texas.

This letter, and other letters from family members, cited the troubling news about war with Japan. In June of 1940, Jess noted the urgency. I could not have traveled until I had given birth and had time to recover. The "right time" to go to Texas passed by again. Jess was pulled off the job site at Cavite and had signed contracts to complete a project at the Baguio residence of the United States High Commissioner to the Philippines, Francis B. Sayre. In a letter signed by High Commissioner Sayre and dated April 1, 1941, as follows:

> Mr. Jesse A. Hodges
> Manila, P. I.
>
> Sir:
>   Under the provisions of paragraph 4 of the United States Civil Service Rule VIII, you are hereby temporarily appointed as construction foreman in this office at a salary of $200.00 per month, effective as of this date.
>
>   Francis B. Sayre
>   United States High Commissioner
>   To the Philippines Islands

Jess worked on all the changes itemized by E. D. Hester, Budget Officer for the Office of High Commissioner Sayre. He also made arrangements to work closely with the chief electrician at Camp John Hay in Baguio to test electrical materials as specified in his contract. By May 2, work on the Porte Cochere was almost completed. Jess also worked on the caretaker's house on the property. Additionally, he was to stay in Baguio to supervise building a new fence. The materials, ordered from Sears Roebuck, were scheduled to arrive on the S.S. President Tyler on May 9. The Quartermaster at Camp John Hay was assigned to transport those materials by June 1. Other instructions and specifications were detailed in a letter to Jess from Mr. Hester dated May 2, 1941.

Jess completed the work in Baguio within three months and returned to finish the defense project at the naval yard at Cavite. He could not understand why the High Commissioner's residence took priority over the job he started at the naval yard at Cavite.

"It's not for me to question which jobs have priority," Jess stated when questioned by me. "I just work for the U.S. Government and do what I am told."

The children and I were sad when he left Baguio because we stayed with him and enjoyed the mountains during vacation, until Mrs. Sayre intervened. The High Commissioner's wife enjoyed long afternoon rides in her chauffeured limousine. During her scenic tours, she peered through her lorgnette…"high society" glasses perched upon a long jeweled stick. Mary Jane and her friend, Jimmy, waved to her as she passed, but she never acknowledged them. Feeling ignored by "Her Majesty," they decided to fashion lorgnettes from thin wire attached to sticks and posed with them by the roadside, the next time she passed. She must not have appreciated their prank, as they were banished from Baguio for the rest of their vacation...and so were we.

On September 22, 1941, our son Bobby insisted on celebrating his seventeenth birthday by going with Jess to enlist at the Naval Recruiting Office in Cavite. He wanted to join the U.S. Navy so badly. His best friend, Jimmy Lupton, had already joined the year before. Bobby wanted to join at the same time, but he was only sixteen. He convinced the recruiting officer I would sign papers giving permission for him to join. My mother did not want me to sign his recruitment papers.

"Bobby is not yet eighteen. He is too young," *Mami* insisted.

"I have to let him join the U.S. Navy. He has wanted to enlist for more than a year," I replied as I signed the documents.

Bobby was so excited when he received his notice from Lt. Cmdr., U.S.N. (Ret) F. Baltzly, District Personnel Officer, dated October 1, 1941, which stated:

SIXTEENTH NAVAL DISTRICT

PHILIPPINE ISLANDS

COMMANDANT'S OFFICE, NAVY YARD, CAVITE, P. I.

October 1, 1941

TO WHOM IT MAY CONCERN:

Please allow the bearer to take passage on the Naval Ferry this date and tomorrow, October 2, 1941, for the purpose of enlisting in the Naval Reserve.

Robert M. Hodges
ROBERT MORRIS HODGES

F. Baltzly
Lt. Cmdr. U.S.N. (Ret)
Dist. Personnel Officer.

Nothing would keep our son from boarding the Naval Ferry on October 2. He returned daily to check the mail for news regarding his acceptance. Within three weeks he received a letter from Lt. Cmdr. Baltzly, Sixteenth Naval District, dated October 23, 1941.

My heart stuck in my throat as I read the notice Bobby handed me. Our son was officially in the U.S. Navy. He belonged to them.

Within three weeks, Bobby returned with a friend, Eddie, a lonely young sailor. Eddie missed his family and was so happy being with ours. He and Bobby visited on Friday nights. During shore leave, they changed into civilian clothes, and visited Bobby's friends. Uniformed men were not welcomed into private

> IN REPLY ADDRESS COMMANDANT, NAVY YARD, CAVITE, P. I., AND REFER TO
>
> **SIXTEENTH NAVAL DISTRICT**
> **PHILIPPINE ISLANDS**
> **COMMANDANT'S OFFICE, NAVY YARD, CAVITE, P. I.**
>
> No. ND16/P14-4/QR/FM   08/MT
>
> October 23, 1941
>
> Mr. Robert M. HODGES,
> 43 J. Ruiz,
> San Juan, Rizal, P. I.
>
> Dear Sir:
>
> You are hereby informed that your papers are all in order and you are eligible for enlistment as Apprentice Seaman, U.S. Naval Reserve.
>
> It is requested that you report to the District Personnel Office, Navy Yard, Cavite, P. I. at 0800, Monday, October 27, 1941, bringing with you duly authenticated evidence of United States citizenship.
>
> This letter may be used for a pass on Naval Ferries and through Navy Yard gates for this purpose.
>
> Yours very truly,
>
> F. Baltzly
> Lieutenant Commander U.S.N. (Retired),
> District Personnel Officer.

homes. On Sunday night, they donned their uniforms and took the last ferry to their receiving ship, a tanker called the *U.S.S. Genesee*.

The work at the defense plant at Cavite intensified and flowed into overtime in order to complete the ammunition dump, a large steel-reinforced concrete building. Jess returned only every three weeks. Work on the air raid shelter for employees had not begun. They thought they had plenty of time to prepare their defenses.

On Thanksgiving Day, Thursday, November 23, 1941, we celebrated Linnie's first birthday. Jess invited his bosses, Mr. Curavo and Mr. Neal as our guests at our Thanksgiving dinner. Mr. Neal sent his apologies. He stayed on base to keep the work going. Bobby invited his friend, Eddie. He was homesick for his mother's cooking.

"Eddie, when you are at our table, think about your mother and pretend she is with us," I suggested.

Robert Morris (Bobby) Hodges with cousins José Mari Gonzalez (Peping/Bull) and Juan Zenon Gonzalez (Juaning), November 1941.

We were listening to popular music on the radio while I put the finishing touches to our Thanksgiving meal. Lucy, Emma, and Mary Jane were helping in the kitchen when *Deep in the Heart of Texas* came rollicking across the room. Mary Jane was delighted and clapped in rhythmic response to the music while dancing around the dining table, as she placed the silverware for our meal. *Chattanooga Choo-Choo* followed and the girls danced around the kitchen to the syncopated beat of the Boogie Woogie. Suddenly, the announcer was spouting news of poison gas being used by Japanese forces invading China. Hundreds of unsuspecting Chinese were killed. I stepped quickly to the radio and turned it off. *We don't need to hear that…especially at Thanksgiving.*

I was thankful we had Bobby with us for our last Thanksgiving together. We had one last visit before World War II descended upon us bringing a reign of terror, death, and destruction.

Mary shivered as she felt a chill spread over her body. Images of the past claimed her emotions. The sadness never ends. The memories, emptiness, and longing linger in the background.

What happened to you, Bobby?

CHAPTER 72

Without Warning

On Friday, December 5, 1941, Bobby and Eddie returned for their usual weekend visit at our home. Consueling's son, José (Peping) Gonzalez, joined them for the weekend. Those two days passed quickly. At 11:00 p.m. on Sunday, December 7, they returned and asked me to wake them at two o'clock on Monday morning, December 8, to catch the three o'clock ferry. They had to report for Monday morning roll call.

"Bobby, tomorrow is the Day of the Immaculate Conception of The Virgin Mary. I must attend mass," I stated flatly. "I could not rest if I have to wake you at two, then wake the children at 5:30 a.m. so they can get ready for school. I still have all the work to do with the poultry. It would be best for you to leave now and catch the midnight ferry."

They understood and jumped into their uniforms while I called a taxi. After brief hugs, they left. *Those hugs were our last.*

Monday, December 8, 1941, was just another day of arising, waking the children, preparing breakfast, making sure they had their books, and getting them out the door by 6:30 a.m. to catch the public bus to school for morning classes. There was also the feeding of poultry before getting myself ready to go to church. My nephew Peping had spent the night to care for Linnie, our baby, while I attended Mass. Joyce was still with my sister Pilar. Jess was at Cavite, and Bobby on his ship. It was the lull before the storm.

Services at our church were at ten. As I left the church after 11:00 a.m., people were running in the streets and screaming. Something was terribly wrong.

"We are at war! We are at war! Japan has bombed Pearl Harbor!"

I was in shock. For several months, air raid drills and blackouts had been conducted monthly to prepare us for a possible attack. Civilians ignored the drills. Most thought Japan would not dare attack. Bombs bursting in the distance and people in panic in the streets validated the rumors.

My four children were stranded at H. A. Bordner School on Taft Avenue in Manila. Jess was at the naval yard in Cavite. Bobby was on a tanker in Manila Bay. Joyce was at my sister's home. My baby was at our home with my nephew! God save us!

I rushed to find the nearest phone to tell my nephew the horrible news and was told phone service was reserved only for the military. All streetcars and public buses stopped service. The only choices for transportation were horse rigs *(calesas)* or the *auto calesas* (modified jeep rigs). The usual rate for this transportation was ten *centavos* per passenger. As they passed the church where I waited for transportation, the jeep rigs were overloaded with eight to ten persons each. The fee had risen to one *peso*...ten times the usual amount per person.

I squeezed onto an *auto calesa* by sitting on a stranger's lap. It seemed like an eternity before reaching home around one in the afternoon. My nephew, Peping, met me at the front gate. Linnie was still asleep. He was greatly disturbed by the bombing in the distance and the panic in the streets.

"What is going on? Police sirens are going off, people are being arrested, the neighbors are out in their yards, but no one has answers. I tried to use the phone with no luck," Peping spouted.

"Peping, the Japanese have bombed Pearl Harbor. We are being attacked. There is no phone service or public transportation. I'm worried about the kids in school. How will they get home? Are Joyce and Pilar safe?" I trembled as I uttered those words.

We stepped inside our kitchen to check for news on the radio. Warnings were being issued about bombing, looting, and casualties. The disaster at Pearl Harbor filled the airwaves. Static chopped the announcer's words as bombs dropped on Luzon. December 8 was our "Day of Infamy."

The minutes dragged by while fear gripped my heart like a steel fist. My imagination raced as I paced along the path to our front gate. My fears turned to tears. I had to regain control of my emotions, so I prepared coffee for Peping and myself. We had not eaten lunch. Food was not a priority. *My children were out on the streets trying to find their way home. Where else did bombs fall? Did they fall at Cavite or on Bobby's ship? Has the school been bombed? What about Ermita ...Joyce is there with Pilar.*

Around three that afternoon, the children arrived...dragging their book sacks through the front gate. They were exhausted, hungry, and thirsty after walking about ten miles through chaos. Their arms ached from carrying their books. I spouted questions faster than they were able to answer.

Lucy recounted their daylong trek from H. A. Bordner American School to return to our home. They had arrived at school by public bus and, after leaving Mary Jane at her building; continued to the nearby high school. The normal routine was to wait outside until the bell sounded, stand in lines, and sing the school song. December 8, 1941, was not a normal day.

The American and Philippine flags at the main building at Bordner were at half-mast. Adults were rushing around searching for family members. Many were crying, and others were screaming out family names. Lucy knew something was terribly wrong, but had no idea what created the chaos. She, Jesse Jr., and Emma left Bordner High School to pick up Mary Jane at the Bordner Elementary building. They were on their own. There was no public transportation. Cars, vans, *calesas, carromatas,* and trucks rushed by loaded with people honking their horns as they fled Manila. Mass chaos surrounded them. Lucy and Jesse Jr. decided to follow the public bus route signs in order to find their way home. While following the bus route, mid-day explosions in the distance and planes flying low overhead filled them with terror. Bombs fell like rain in the distance. They were busy trying to dodge the crazy drivers who were racing across intersections, ignoring signal lights, and blowing their horns. Everyone was trying to escape.

Peping, concerned about his mother and family, left us to see if they were safe. I thanked him and prayed he would make it home safely. There was still no word from Jess, Pilar, or Bobby. *Angels in Heaven watch over them.*

We were taken by surprise. Only the Japanese families in the area appeared to have known. Our Japanese neighbors, who lived across the street and next to the Max Kessels, left two weeks earlier. They stored a trunk with the Kessels until they returned from their "vacation."

Remembering gave Mary chills and nightmares. She would not sleep well. *I did not sleep at all the night of December 8, 1941.*

CHAPTER 73

Waiting and Praying

A static-filled message crackled over the radio waves while breakfast was being prepared for the children, who were still sleeping. There would be no school, but we still had chores to do with the poultry. Warnings were issued for all citizens to stay off the streets. The area was under "blackout" conditions. No lights were allowed on at night. If lanterns or candles were used, windows must be covered with black fabric or shades. Violators would be arrested and fined. The newscast continued.

"Clark Field was destroyed when the Japanese dropped their bombs around 12:35 p.m. yesterday. All the planes were sitting on the tarmac, like so many sacrificial lambs. Within fifty minutes death, destruction, debris, damage, and demoralization swept across Clark Field while the invading enemy exited as stealthily as it had entered after delivering its fatal blow."

Still no phone service and no news from Jess, Bobby, or Pilar. I could not call my mother or any of my sisters. I had no way to find out about any family members. Tuesday, December 9, crawled by like a crippled centipede. The older children were quiet and still exhausted from their hazardous experience the day before. Linnie was oblivious to events around us. Tending to her and the poultry had a calming effect on me, as I did not want to frighten the others. I discouraged questions about their daddy, brother, and sister by giving anyone who asked a question a chore to do in the poultry barn. We still had work to do. Chicken coops must be cleaned; eggs must be gathered, sorted, and crated; and, the chickens must be fed. The children's questions subsided. The only answer I had was prayer.

As I lay down to rest with so many questions still unanswered, Mary Jane approached my bedside, lifted the mosquito net, and crawled in with me. She snuggled into her "spoon" position beside me as I put my arm across her body…my rosary still clutched in my hand. Her quiet breathing, as she fell asleep, helped me to relax.

Wednesday, December 10, the "Rising Sun" once again delivered their missiles of destruction across the Philippines. The Naval Yard at Cavite was hit hard, according to announcements on my small radio. I was able to catch bits and pieces of news between static bursts and dead air. We gathered around the dining room table to pray. No one was hungry, except Linnie, who smiled and babbled as she picked up food with her fingers and eyed each bit as if to identify its source.

The bell at the front gate rang. I looked out the window to see who was there and recognized Tony's car. He, Pilar, and Anthony were bringing Joyce. I rushed to open the large gate so their car could enter and park in the driveway. Tears, hugs, kisses, and words flowed for several minutes. Questions were asked about Jess and Bobby, but I had no answers. Pilar wanted to continue to keep Joyce, but I felt she should stay home until we had answers to our questions. Too many things were unknown and the family should be together. Jess would want it that way. They left after an hour. *Angels watch over you.*

On December 19, I received a letter from my son, Bobby. Enclosed was a Christmas card for his girlfriend, Sally. He wanted me to deliver it in person. The U.S. Navy receiving ship in Manila Bay had suffered a direct hit on December 9, and over five hundred sailors were killed. His friend Eddie was one of the unfortunate ones. He and Jimmy Lupton were assigned to the S.S. Genesee, an oil tanker, and were away from their receiving ship. I wept for Eddie and thanked God that Bobby and Jimmy were alive.

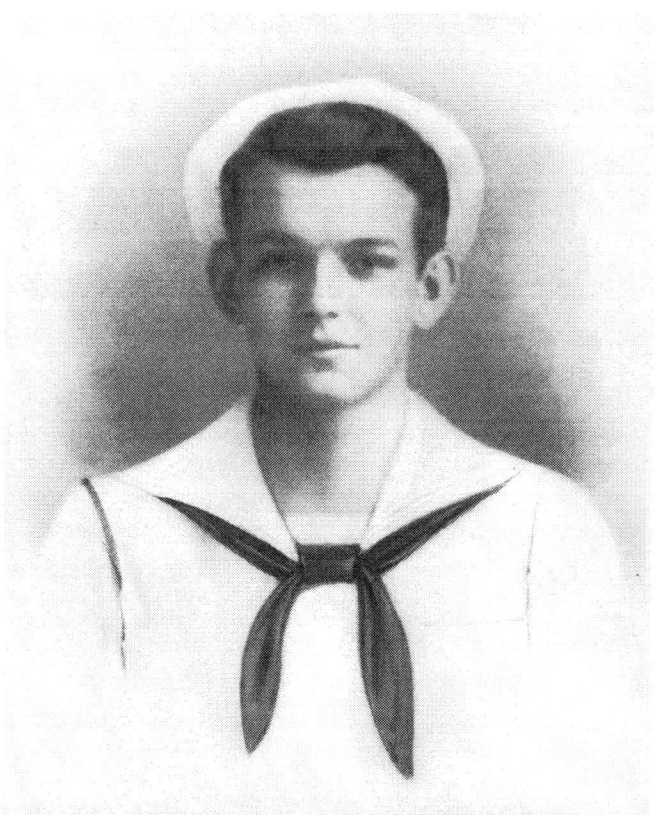

Robert Morris Hodges (Bobby) enlisted in the U.S. Navy in October 1941. A Christmas card received by his family on December 19 was the last contact with their son. Bobby was seventeen years of age.

We still had no news from Jess. The bombing targeted military facilities on a daily basis. Rumors were rampant about the impending Japanese occupation of Manila. The small defensive effort put forth by American and Filipino military forces was like a tiny mosquito trying to bite an elephant through its thick skin.

On December 22, Jess returned. His expression spoke volumes. He appeared exhausted, disheveled, and heartbroken. He was missing one of his work boots. The Japanese had invaded Luzon with a vengeance.

"Mary," he said in a shaky voice, "I stayed at Cavite to locate Bobby. His receiving ship was badly damaged by Jap bombs on the ninth. It was heartbreaking to stand outside and see pieces of mutilated bodies scattered everywhere. I kept asking questions and trying to find Bobby, but the officer on duty told me to leave…it was pointless to wait. They were removing the wounded before removing the dead. Until rosters were checked, there would be no information. We have to hope he made it."

His voice broke and he cried. I hugged him and told him, thanks be to God, our son was not on his receiving ship when it was bombed. I showed him the letter from Bobby. We held each other close without speaking.

Jess stayed a while. He had instructions to return to Cavite and transfer important papers and equipment to a designated office building in Santa Mesa. So much was destroyed at Cavite that naval officials needed a non-military site to regroup and plan their next strategy. The Japanese were obviously going to continue their onslaught against military targets.

Jess, his men, and many officers escaped being wounded by shrapnel when they hid inside the concrete-reinforced ammunition dump he and his men had built as part of the defense plant. It was a heavily fortified building, but also contained explosives. A direct hit would have killed all who were inside.

"The Jap planes flew low, Mary," Jess said, as he bowed his head. "The Navy did not have a decent antiaircraft gun on the place. Those old guns did not reach their targets. We were lucky the Japs didn't have good aim."

The ammunition dump was built beside a river. They peered through the four, small barred windows, and watched the bombs explode…sending water into the air. Waves of Jap bombers engaged in the carpet-bombing of Cavite, creating a continuous firestorm. After the last wave of planes, Jess and the officers surveyed the damage. River silt, water, debris, and damaged equipment surrounded the ammo dump. They had to step carefully to keep from slipping. A trio of reconnaissance planes dove toward them. In their rush to return to the ammo dump, Jess' boot stuck in the muddy ground. He lost his left boot in his haste to get inside. The abandoned boot was shredded by machine gun fire from Japanese planes as they strafed the area.

After several hours, Jess drove to Manila to secure the building for the naval operations center. He had to return to Cavite, after securing the building and transport workers, in the same manner he had driven home. The sound of planes overhead caused them to stop the car and jump into the nearest ditch or culvert to protect against shrapnel or machine-gun fire.

Mary's hands were trembling as she closed her notebook. Writing about this portion of her life was difficult as so many raw emotions and imbedded fears returned. Fear was a constant companion. She reached for her rosary. Prayer had a way of calming her nerves.

CHAPTER 74

The Long Vigil Begins

On December 23, 1941, more warnings were broadcast. The spirited patriotic music blaring from the radio did not change the news. Japanese forces were coming.

"Today, General Douglas MacArthur begins the withdrawal of troops from Manila to Bataan to prepare for the defense of the Philippines."

Long lines of army trucks loaded with American and Filipino soldiers streamed by our home, on the corner of J. Ruiz and Aurora Quezon Boulevard, as *Mami* and I watched from our front porch. Strains of *God Bless America* being sung by these men echoed as U.S. and Philippine army trucks lumbered by. They were crammed into vehicles headed for unknown destinations and destinies. Many sat with shoulders slumped…their eyes transfixed, as if trying to see what lay ahead.

"Those poor young men," *Mami* said as she trembled, "are going to the slaughterhouse."

Tears were streaming down our faces as we watched them go by. The children joined us after finishing their chores with the poultry. They huddled quietly near us. Our sadness spread over them like a heavy blanket. Fear crept inside our hearts and pushed the Christmas season aside. Fear would be our constant companion.

Jess arrived late in the company car. He had to wait for all the military traffic to pass before using the highway to drive to San Juan. Jess had made his usual stop at the Chinese grocery store, where we had a credit account, to pay our monthly bill before Christmas. He gave Mr. Chou his paycheck and received a few *pesos* in change. As he stacked items on the countertop to place on credit, Mr. Chou stopped him.

"*So solly, Misa Hodges, no can do cledit,*" Mr. Chou stated in his best English. "*Onree cash.*"

Jess understood. *Why would anyone allow purchasing on credit when the future was a big question mark?* He paid out his remaining cash, took his items, and left for home.

His thoughts turned to his day. When he left Cavite this afternoon, looting was rampant at all buildings vacated by military personnel on their way to Corregidor. Supplies at the naval base were stored in the Malinta Tunnel, where Jess had just completed some construction. *We need to stockpile soon for the near future.*

Manila and *Intramuros* were under constant attack by the Japanese. The Walled City, where I lived as a child, was in ruins. Most Catholic schools and institutions were destroyed. My sisters, who were nuns, barely escaped with their lives. They were able to relocate at the nearby Dominican convent and church in San Juan.

Our Christmas was spent quietly at church. We had neither Christmas lights nor decorations due to the mandatory blackout. The mood was tense and tenuous. We had no news from Bobby. The only gifts were fruits, nuts, and candy Jess had bought at the grocery store on his way home. He spent his last bit of cash to give our children a treat.

Scant bits and pieces of news from our small radio impacted our daily lives. The latest bulletin shot fear through us and brought us to our knees.

"Today, General MacArthur has declared Manila an 'open city.'" The strained voice of the announcer wavered as the news mingled with the static from our small radio on December 26. Our fate was sealed on the day after the "Christmas-that-never-was."

"An 'open city'? What does 'open city' mean, Jess?" I asked.

"It means the Japanese can come into Manila without having to fire a shot or dropping another bomb. It means we are stuck."

"What shall we do?" I asked with thoughts of impending doom racing through my head and the growing, gnawing fear clutching my heart.

"We'll do the best we can and hope it won't last long," Jess stated.

Commonwealth President Manuel L. Quezon advised MacArthur to declare Manila an "open city" to avoid its destruction. The government officials withdrew to Corregidor Island before proceeding to the United States.

Jesse left for the improvised naval center they had put together in Santa Mesa. Several items had to be destroyed and others brought home. He returned after about six hours with several cans of tomatoes, pork and beans, a sack of flour, and one hundred kilos of cracked wheat.

"Mary, we have work to do tonight," Jess said while bringing in the supplies. "We have to stockpile some food and emergency supplies tonight. We have no idea where the Japanese are or how soon they will arrive. Looters are everywhere, and we have to be ready for them. They will take anything that's not nailed down."

We spent the rest of the night gathering canned goods, nonperishable supplies, and medicine…anything we thought we might need in the near future…and stashed them away. Several cans of tomatoes were buried in the ground and others were placed in locked closets. The keys were placed on a long chain around my neck, and tucked inside my bra. *Would they be safe?*

Jess drove our car to my Dominican sister's convent to have them hide it inside their storage building. Surely the Japs and looters would not invade the convent and steal from the nuns!

On December 27, with Manila declared an "Open City" the Japanese bombed mercilessly, once again. They bombed when they did not need to lift a finger to claim Manila. Death, destruction, and despair took over. All MacArthur and the Filipino government officials had done to spare the city was for naught.

We knew no way to hide all our chickens. We also knew looters would be coming. What they did not get, the Japanese would confiscate. They had an army to feed. My heart was heavy as we took down the signs of our "American Hatchery." They would be ready to destroy anything American, including my family.

The eerie quiet of the night seemed more ominous than the loud blasts of bombs dropping across Manila on December 27. We knew the Japanese were coming. We knew we were trapped. We prayed and waited for the enemy.

The long vigil had begun, but we had no idea how long this Japanese occupation would last, or how we would be able to cope with all that lay ahead.

So much happened quickly. No one was prepared. No one had answers to our questions. Our lives were in the Hands of God and we had to trust in Him. Trust in God was all we had. We lived by faith and prayers.

CHAPTER 75

A New Year — A New Fear

New Year's Eve...we should have been celebrating, but not this year. The week following Christmas was one of dread, uneasiness, and quiet. No planes flew overhead. The radio was ominously silent, as if they were at a loss for words. Only a few strains of patriotic music were heard between the bursts of static. The only bright note was the moonlight bathing our surroundings from our vantage point atop the second landing of the concrete stairway leading to a screened-in front porch. *All is calm, all is bright*. These words depicted the moment. Suddenly, explosions ripped the silent night into shreds. Bright flames rose into the night sky. Something in Manila was being destroyed. *I wonder what is on fire? Where would they strike next?* Visibility was clear in every direction. My nephew, Peping, and Junior walked the perimeter of our property while Jess and I guarded the entry to our home...watching for looters or Japanese. We might be able to scare looters away, but not the Japanese...all of our defenders were gone.

"If the Japs want to bomb tonight, they could see without a problem. It's as bright as daylight out here," Jess spoke softly as I rested against his side.

"Well, it's after midnight. I think I'll go inside and try to rest a bit before morning," I said as I rose to open the screen door quietly, as the girls were asleep inside.

It was "blackout" dark inside with all the doors and windows closed and the wooden louvers shut tight. I lifted one louver gently to peek outside and realized the New Year arrived without our usual ritual...standing and toasting each other with wine or champagne. The fearful beginning of this New Year was an omen of things to come. I approached the bed and lay down to rest...fully clothed.

Around two in the morning, loud voices in the distance wakened me from my brief slumber. Loud, unintelligible voices pierced the early morning silence. They were chanting and roaring. As suddenly as they started, they stopped, only to begin anew. Once again, I tiptoed to the window, shifted one louver to peep out, only to see Jess asleep in his garden chair on the front porch. I slipped out the door and gently wakened Jess.

"Loud voices…over there," I whispered, pointing toward Quezon Boulevard.

We listened together as the voices and their intensity increased. *What was creating that noise?* Within the hour, we knew. Japanese troops were approaching on foot, and on bicycles as they spoke their guttural language with raised voices. At times they would break into a chant, which we did not understand.

"Peping…Junior…come inside, quickly! Hurry!" I called hoarsely.

We retreated inside our home and peered at this heart-breaking sight through the wooden louvers. The roar of big trucks and tanks added to the din created by the chanting voices. We never expected to see troops riding bicycles, but there they were…riding in formation on their black bikes. By dawn, Aurora Quezon Boulevard, the highway beside our property, was a mass of Japanese soldiers celebrating their victory of capturing Luzon. I trembled all over as my hopes vanished. We were under the rule of the Japanese army. There was no escaping.

Jess and I walked slowly into our bedroom. There was nothing left to do but take the time we had left to make some decisions about our lives and those of our children. I reached for my rosary as I slipped under the mosquito netting.

Chaos reigned for the next two weeks. Looters had a field day as they broke store windows and took what they wanted before the Japanese gained total control of Luzon. Banks and businesses closed. No money was in circulation as the

Japanese Occupation Currency

Japanese declared a moratorium on United States and Filipino currency. They printed their "Japanese Occupation Currency" which they "exchanged" for our American dollars or Philippine *pesos* at a rate of their choice.

Looters sold their stolen goods to acquire currency to buy Japanese occupation money. I bought six small cans of milk for fifty *centavos* each. The next day, the price rose to seventy-five *centavos* per can. The following day, each can cost one *peso*. Japanese soldiers roamed the streets and confiscated goods being sold on the streets and in stores. The Filipinos learned to keep their stolen goods hidden.

<hr />

Mary took a deep breath as she readied herself for bed. She was too tense to sleep. She looked through her photos instead and found the last family photo taken before Bobby left for the Navy in 1941. They looked so innocent. That innocence was lost with the Japanese occupation of the Philippines.

Mary Gamero Hodges and children at their home, 43 J. Ruiz, San Juan, P.I. in April 1941— *(left to right, back)* Lucy, Mary holding baby Linnie, Robert (Bobby), Jesse Jr.; *(front)* Joyce, Mary Jane, and Emma. The last family photo that included Bobby.

CHAPTER 76

Trapped

The Japanese forces swarmed over Luzon like a hungry colony of angry ants. There was no resistance. No one repelled these invaders as they took over Manila and all its surroundings. Manila and the U.S. Naval base at Cavite were under Japanese control. The Bataan Peninsula, where thousands of American and Filipino troops had retreated, was next. We hoped those troops could destroy the Japs and push them out of Luzon, but the Battle of Bataan would be a bitter struggle and a lost cause. There was no help. Officials of the commonwealth government of the Philippines had relocated to Australia. All we had was MacArthur's promise to return.

Within the next week, the Japanese captured all American citizens in Ermita and Makati, the residential areas of Manila, where many Americans resided. The University of Santo Tomas was confiscated to use as an internment camp for these prisoners of war. My uncle, Charles Swanson, and his daughter, Aurora Long, were among the first taken to Santo Tomas Internment Camp. American citizens were taken with no provisions made for their care. The Japanese were not concerned about their prisoners. They wanted all American citizens imprisoned and punished.

We wondered what was burning in Manila on New Year's Eve, and later learned the loud noises were of Japanese forces destroying *El Tiro al Blanco*, our Spanish club. They destroyed it to send a message to all citizens. They were in control.

One of the last places the Japanese searched for American citizens was in San Juan, where we lived. They captured most Americans living in Manila and were scouring the suburbs. Every time Japanese soldiers came to our gate, our fox terriers barked, which was my signal to meet them. While the younger children informed their daddy, my task was to keep the Japs away from the house where Jesse was hiding. Usually, they wanted several chickens, which they could see from the roadside. They pointed at the chickens and grunted. It sounded like guttural gibberish. They usually stopped a Filipino passing by, pushed him inside the gate, and pointed to the chickens. After he caught some hens for them, they would leave. Jess would have another reprieve...until next time. The chickens were a mixed blessing.

Japanese sentries were posted on the corner of every block. Everyone who approached a sentry, whether walking, riding a bicycle, or in a horse-drawn rig, must first, disembark, approach the sentry, bow low to him, and get his grunt of approval before rising from your bow and continuing your journey. If you had a package, the sentry would inspect it before allowing you to pass. If he liked what you had in the package, it became his.

Each time the small radio was turned on; more rules were being broadcast to the people. Sometimes, leaflets were dropped inside our mailbox by the front gate. Either way, we knew we had to comply.

> BY ORDER OF THE IMPERIAL JAPANESE MILITARY LAW, ALL FIREARMS (INCLUDING BB AND TOY GUNS) AND WEAPONS (SHARP KNIVES, BOLOS, SPEARS, ARROWS, ETC.), MUST BE SURRENDERED IMMEDIATELY. VIOLATORS WILL BE PUNISHED SEVERELY.

In the dark of night, while the children were asleep, Jess and I gathered his shotgun, Bobby and Junior's BB guns, toy guns, all large sharp knives, and buried them in the dirt floor of the large poultry house...covering them with chicken manure from the roosting area. The booty and its location was our secret. If the children were questioned, they would have no answers.

By mid-January, the Japanese distributed leaflets with more rules.

> ALL CITIZENS OF ALLIED COUNTRIES MUST REPORT TO THE OFFICE OF THE COMMANDANT AT SANTO TOMAS UNIVERSITY WITHIN THREE WEEKS TO BE INTERNED. BRING NECESSARY CLOTHING, PERSONAL ITEMS, AND TWO WEEKS SUPPLY OF FOOD. ALL WHO DO NOT COMPLY WILL BE SEVERELY PUNISHED.

Mary put down her pen, brushed a wisp of hair from her forehead, and put her elbows on the table. She cupped her face with her hands and trembled as she recalled reading the list of stringent rules distributed by the Japs. Goosebumps prickled across her skin. *We had to follow those rules or be punished or, perhaps, killed.* She collected her thoughts before picking up her pen once again. She must finish her story, no matter how it affected her. *Let's see, where was I? Oh, yes, the rules...those terrible rules making Jesse a prisoner.*

CHAPTER 77

Rules and Regulations

As each precious day of those allotted three weeks marched by, more Japanese soldiers marched down Aurora Quezon Boulevard and surrounded us. The Japs built an encampment just down the highway from us. Jesse stayed inside our home, afraid to step outside and be shot before he could surrender himself at Santo Tomas. We avoided all outside activity, as it might bring Japanese inside our property. We read over more regulations and set about to comply. The rule that gripped our hearts was the one that meant concentration camp for Jesse…and, perhaps, for the children.

Most Americans did not expect a long imprisonment. They were sure MacArthur's troops would swiftly rout the Japanese, and normalcy would be restored.

Their general, with his corncob pipe jutting stubbornly from the right side of his mouth, was in Australia regrouping American forces and would be back in no time. He would return soon…or so they believed.

> ALL RADIOS MUST BE BROUGHT TO THE MUNICIPAL BUILDING FOR INSPECTION AND REGISTRATION. ALL SHORT WAVE RADIOS MUST BE SURRENDERED OR RISK CONFISCATION AND SEVERE PUNISHMENT.

We only had one small radio. With radio in hand, I waited in line for several hours to have it inspected and registered. The only "news" we received by radio was information the Japanese wanted aired…mainly propaganda.

Another mandate spelled disaster for our family. We had no recourse.

> THE FINAL DATE FOR ALL AMERICAN AND ALLIED CITIZENS TO SURRENDER FOR ASSIGNMENT TO INTERNMENT CAMPS IS FEBRUARY 15, 1942. ALL OTHER CITIZENS ARE REQUIRED TO REGISTER THEIR CITIZENSHIP AND BE PROCESSED TO OBTAIN AN OFFICIAL REGISTRATION CARD. ANYONE FOUND WITHOUT A REGISTRATION CARD AFTER FEBRUARY 15 WILL BE PUNISHED SEVERELY.

My heart sank. I had to find a way to keep our children from being imprisoned in the concentration camps. Families of U.S. citizens were separated in the camps, with the men housed in a different camp or different area. I knew there was no way to spare Jesse, but I had to find a way to keep our children out of prison camp. Jess had never registered our children as American citizens with the U.S. Consulate. If my Spanish citizenship were reinstated, they could be considered Spanish citizens. My Spanish citizenship was allowed to lapse after I married Jess. Annual registration at the Spanish Consulate was a requirement of maintaining one's Spanish citizenship. I gathered my documentation and set forth on a seven-mile walk to the Spanish Consulate. Rumors of American children being sent to Japan kept me going. Prayers to St. Anthony were uttered with every step.

When I arrived at the Spanish Consulate, a family friend took me under his wing, and arranged to have my Spanish citizenship reinstated. I thanked him profusely for his kindness. Silent prayers of thanks to Saint Anthony for saving my lost citizenship guided my walk home. My children might now avoid prison camp. There were no guarantees.

On February 12, 1942, Jess and I gathered his personal items, and packed them in one small suitcase. Internees were allowed to bring only the minimum. I wedged a can of KLIM, a powdered milk concentrate, plus dried fruit, nuts, and two cans of sardines. He decided not to wait until the deadline of the fifteenth to keep from being sent to a prison camp farther from us. Our children already said their "goodbyes" before going to bed. They knew their Dad was leaving the next day. Valentine's Day was cancelled.

My brother-in-law, Tony Settember, arrived to take Jess to Santo Tomas. Tony, who registered as an Italian citizen, was free to travel about the city, as Italy was not an allied country. He arrived early, before the younger children had risen, so they would not witness this event. As they left, I uttered a prayer as I waved "goodbye." I was left with five children, whose ages ranged from fifteen to thirteen months. I prayed He would give me wisdom and guidance to care for them. I also prayed for Bobby, somewhere in Manila Bay near Corregidor, where Japanese were bombing incessantly. *Was he there? Was he safe?* Then it hit me...my birthday was in four days, and my life would be empty without Jess by my side. I retreated to my bedroom and sobbed all night long.

From the time the Japanese fully occupied Manila, Aurora Quezon Boulevard was filled with columns of Japanese troops marching by, raucously celebrating their victory. We were fingerprinted, registered, and given an identification card. We were required to carry the card at all times. A list of our names was attached to our front door. All whose names were listed must be present after curfew. Should we have more or fewer than listed, we faced severe punishment or death. We dared not leave our property during curfew. To do so meant certain death.

CHAPTER 78

Adapting to Change

On March 11, 1942, General MacArthur left Corregidor for Australia and General Jonathan Wainwright became the military commander in charge of the remaining U.S. and Filipino military effort in the Philippines. Our plight worsened. Jesse, and the internees in Santo Tomas Internment Camp, realized they would have to become responsible for their own health and welfare, as nothing was being done by the Japanese regarding the care of internees. During the first few weeks, several committees were formed and volunteers recruited. Jess, with his knowledge of construction, set about using scrap lumber to build makeshift cots, tables, chairs, and other useable items. There were more internees than space to house them. Women and children were separated from the men in one building. Classrooms were fashioned into sleeping/living quarters. Jess and about 1200 other men were housed in the Education Building. There were only thirteen toilets and twelve showers for over twelve hundred men. The paltry number of bathrooms was insufficient to provide for normal hygiene.

The internees took charge and put a plan in place to provide order to what they thought was their temporary imprisonment. A sanitation committee was formed with J. Hernden named as its head. Jess was named Carpentry Supervisor. They were assigned the task of preparing outdoor pits or *cubetas* for the men to use as toilets. The same committee was responsible for garbage disposal. Although the situation was chaotic, their attempts at organization helped to lessen the despair felt by internees. Shanties were constructed to house those internees who had no roof over their heads. Jess built one for himself in an attempt to shut out the madness surrounding him, but the Japanese insisted all prisoners must sleep in their assigned place in their assigned building…a space of about 16 square feet.

Once organization had taken place, the Japanese allowed families of internees to bring them food and medicinal items. The internment camp doors opened at 9:00 a.m., then closed by eleven. Everything brought in was inspected and everyone must be searched before entering the camp. The lines to enter formed before sunrise, so in order to deliver items to Jess before the gates closed, we arrived early.

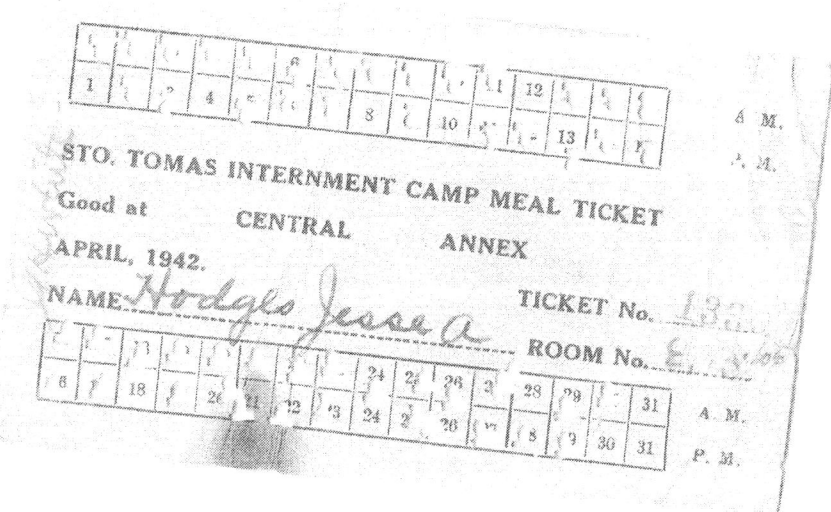

One of Jesse's meal tickets issued during his imprisonment at Santo Tomas (STIC).

Ground coffee beans and rice cakes, along with home-cooked chicken and rice with vegetables from our garden provided nutrition. Internees received only one-half cup of soupy, boiled rice daily as their rations. During the first year, they would allow us to see each other at a distance. The canvas bag of items I brought, after being inspected, was handed to Japanese officers in charge, who would hand the bag to Jess.

Jess had friends interned with him who had no family members, so they asked him if I would bring other things for them. They would pay Jess with "camp money" issued by the Japanese. Jess put this carefully worded request on a note and handed it to the Jap officer for censoring, before it was handed to me. His friends asked for ground coffee, boiled eggs, and cigarettes. I was so glad Jess was not a smoker. They used their money to purchase cigarettes instead of food and paid a dear price, for food was more important.

In addition to bringing the requested items for Jess and his friends, I also brought extra food items for Jess to give away or sell, like boiled eggs, fresh fruit from our fruit trees, plus Jesse's clean laundry. These loads were difficult to carry for a long distance. My nephew, Juaning Gonzalez, or his brother, Peping (Bull), would help some of the time. Once in a while, Emma or Mary Jane would help me. Their reward for carrying the canvas bag was a chance to catch a glimpse of their Dad. Occasionally, Mary Jane, Joyce, and Linnie would go. Mary Jane carried the package, and I carried Linnie. Joyce walked beside us holding on to my skirt or Mary Jane's. The internees were in line about fifty feet away from the table where packages were inspected. No conversations were allowed. We waved as we left. The walk home was always a quiet walk.

I needed a way to communicate with Jess privately, since we were not allowed to speak with each other. The sturdy brightly striped awning material I had bought to make garden umbrellas and covers for garden furniture when we owned and operated The Manila Swing Manufacturer Company, was used to make a carry-all canvas bag with wide straps. Within the seam of one strap, I created a secret pocket to hold a small, personal note or provide information to Jess. I felt it would help him keep his hopes alive and answer some questions

> *Darling, Jess, we are all well. Sending the following:*
> *600 cookies, maybe – 5.94*
> *20 baked Bibinkas – 2.75*
> *2 doz. Cupcakes – 1.87*
> *5 kilos sugar – 2.50*
> *Total – 13.06*

> *Sweetheart, the milk sells from 1.50 to 1.80 for the big cans and .70 to .90 for small cans. Yesterday, Sunday, I did not buy anything. I will get things this morning. I hope you enjoyed the kids yesterday. Linnie said, while coming out of the camp gate, "Good Daddy, give cookie, money, candy." She can talk nearly everything halfway. She is so sweet. I know you would be crazy about her if you were home. She is the toy of everyone here at home. I will try to bring the kids every other Sunday, if possible. By coming early, Officer Chittick's head is still cool, but if you arrive about 10, he has a hot head and allows no more babies in.*
> *Love and kisses.*

about our lives away from him. After the folded note was in the secret compartment, I stitched the opening together. Jess discovered the hand-stitched portion of the strap containing my note, and would send a reply the same way. We had a secret, but dangerous, way to communicate. Each time I delivered a package, I tried to remain calm and not draw attention to myself. I would be polite and smile graciously at the Japanese officers during the inspection of the canvas bag. I prayed quietly to myself the entire time, hoping none of them noticed our "secret seam" and the hidden note. It was a nerve-wracking experience each time. I made sure to bow correctly to the Japs and was attentive to their questions and grunts.

On one side of the note, I listed the contents of the package and pricing for each. He needed to charge friends who bought the items. On the other side I would write personal lines.

                                ~~~

Mary paused in the stillness of her kitchen. *It's a shame I was only able to save five of those notes Jess and I exchanged. They were my diamonds among the ashes of those fateful days.* She ran her fingers over the note she had just copied. *Jess had touched it, also.*

RULES GOVERNING THE SALE OR MANUFACTURE OF ARTICLES WITHIN THE CONFINES OF THIS CAMP.

1. Due to lack of seating facilities etc., no chairs, benches, desks, tables or other properties of this University can be used. Items of furniture owned by licensees must be used.

2. All articles of food must be covered at all times and items such as candy, cakes, pies, sandwiches, etc., must be individually wrapped in sanitary containers to avoid contamination from handling.

3. No raw meats or fish can be sold within the camp.

4. No fruits or vegetables can be sold inside any of the camp buildings. Such sellers must confine their activities outside. This will help eliminate, flies, ants and insects.

5. All cooked articles manufactured outside the camp must be subject to inspection by the Institute of Hygiene at the source of manufacture. This includes the outside premises and equipment.

6. A medical certificate must be secured by all sellers or makers of food products.

7. Samples of food products (not canned) must be submitted at least once a month for laboratory analysis and same can be requested any time if deemed necessary.

8. Each manufacturer within the camp will be allowed one selling agent and no more. Each maker and seller however, must secure a license. Said license must be carried on the person to whom it was issued. Such licenses are non-transferable.

9. Each license will cost ₱1.00 (One Peso) per month. This money will be turned over the Internees' Indigent Relief Fund.

10. Any license may be cancelled or suspended at any time through infractions of these rules, or if unsanitary conditions are found to prevail in the manufacture or sale of any article.

11. The Building and Ground Patrols have been instructed by the Executive Committee to enforce all orders issued for the compliance of the above rules.

    The issuance of a license to any person does not exempt that person from any work assignment in the camp and all persons receiving licenses are expected to continue their regular work details.

ISSUED BY ORDER OF THE COMMANDANT.

July 20th, 1942.

CHAPTER 79

More Challenges

On April 3, 1942, an official with the Imperial Army gloatingly announced their successful attack on our military forces on the Bataan Peninsula and their "glorious victory" with the capture of thousands of American and Philippine fighters. I stared at my small radio as more "glorious victories" by Japanese Imperial Military Forces intermingled with the static over the airwaves. My heart ached. I prayed for Bobby's safety. *Was he there? What was happening to him?* I reached for my rosary, sank to my knees, and prayed while tears streamed down my cheeks. Jesse Jr. entered the kitchen quietly and gently touched my shoulder.

"Mom, are you okay?" he asked.

I turned my head and noticed the concern on his face. I knew I had to pull myself together for my children.

"Let me have your hand," I said, as I rose from my kneeling position.

I whispered the reason for my prayers so we would not disturb the younger children who were still sleeping. As I explained about the loss of our last hope of being saved by our forces at Bataan, I could see his face turn pale. His head bowed. He knew we had not heard from Bobby. Junior loved his older brother and missed him terribly. He was old enough to understand. As the oldest male present, he was the man of the house.

By April 9, the American and Filipino military forces on Bataan had surrendered unconditionally. The next day was the beginning of the horrific and devastating trek later known as "The Bataan Death March." Thousands of Allied prisoners were sent on their way without food or water under the relentless heat of the burning sun. Malaria, dysentery, and quick thrusts of Japanese bayonets ended lives of many who gave their all, but in ways they could never have imagined.

The sad news of the fall of Bataan dashed many hopes. The radio announcer sounded elated as he spouted the news. Our daily doses of propaganda were served via the only news station allowed by the Imperial Forces. Our concern was for Bobby. The "not knowing feeling" gnawed away like huge, ugly rats gnawing at the bottom of sugar cane stalks. I knew if we did not find a way to set our emotions aside, we would fall like the tall sugar canes. I gathered the children around the dining table to pray. The younger children prayed aloud those simple prayers they had memorized, while the older ones held their hands in their laps and prayed silently. Prayer would be our solution to bring calmness to our lives.

Each day brought new challenges our way. Finding a way to provide food for my family weighed heavily on my mind. The canned goods and staples we had stored away were gradually being depleted. Jess scribbled meager news in his small notes hidden in the strap of his supply bag. Canned goods and cigarettes were rationed, but Japanese guards would confiscate the cigarettes. Jess didn't mind, because he did not smoke; however, other prisoners, who were suffering from nicotine deprivation, were enraged. Jess included two cans of meat products he thought the children needed more than he did. He wrote in his note that he met a Japanese officer, Lt. Kato, who had been educated in the United States. Lt. Kato told him I should visit the Red Cross food distribution center on Taft Avenue to get provisions.

The next day, I entered the Red Cross Center with trepidation, and asked for supplies for my children. I explained, although I was a Spanish citizen, I was responsible for the children of an American citizen who was interned in Santo Tomas, and the children were not interned because they were covered by my Spanish citizenship.

After completing the required paperwork, I was given several canned goods. These were taken home and hidden in various spots in case we had thieves or Japanese raids. I also had to make sure we had food, in case I became ill, had no money, or the food supply at the market was depleted.

Meat was scarce. We had no more chickens. The Japanese took most, and hungry natives stole the rest. All the beef was reserved for The Imperial Japanese Forces. Water buffalo *(carabao)* meat was sold for human consumption. We had not eaten fresh meat for several weeks. I bought water buffalo meat, cooked it until it was well done and served it for supper, but did not tell the children what they were eating. I was afraid they would spit out the expensive meat, but no one asked, for which I was thankful. Before bedtime, Junior broke out with an angry red rash all over his body. I smoothed baby oil on the rash, which allowed him to sleep. The next morning, his rash was worse, and his eyes filled with tears.

"Okay, we have to see Dr. Guerrero," I said in a firm voice.

Junior winced, as he was afraid of going to the doctor. He realized, however, he needed help to stop the terrible itching, which was accompanied by swelling in his hands and feet.

When Dr. Guerrero examined Junior, he shook his head.

"You have eaten *carabao* (water buffalo) meat, haven't you?"

Junior stared at me. He was stunned.

"Yes, I'm afraid so, Dr. Guerrero," I replied and glanced at Junior.

"Mom!" Junior spouted. "I thought it tasted funny."

Dr. Guerrero explained the *carabao* meat was "too hot," and many others were coming to him with the same symptoms. He advised me to not serve *carabao* meat to my family.

"Put baking soda in his bath water and have him bathe several times a day to stop the itching. You can also dust baby powder on the red areas. Medicine is scarce and I am not prescribing medications except for serious illnesses," Dr. Guerrero stated.

"Well," I told Junior as we walked towards San Juan, "our only other option is to buy horsemeat."

He shrugged his shoulders, stared at me, and was silent for several minutes. I mistook his silence for consent, so I stopped by the market to buy horsemeat.

"Mom," he said, "if it's okay with you, I'll skip the horsemeat."

The phone rang. Mary rose to answer its insistent ringing. What a surprise! Jesse Jr. was calling from Los Angeles.

"Junior, what a coincidence! I was just writing about the time you ate *carabao* meat and had a rash!"

He laughed. We talked for twenty minutes or so about other experiences we had shared. He called to say Lucija, his wife, was having more surgery on her leg. She had never been the same after enduring the ravages of World War II in Latvia.

"I will pray for her during my nightly prayers. Goodnight, son."

CHAPTER 80

The Final Blow

The morning headlines of *The Tribune*, on Friday, May 8, 1942, confirmed our fears. The report on the Japanese propaganda station was true. Within the hour, the voice of Lt. General Jonathan M. Wainwright was streaming through our radio. He ordered all American and Filipino military forces throughout the Philippines to surrender. Gloom descended upon our hearts like a heavy blanket on a hot day…suffocating our hopes for liberation.

Following the fall of Corregidor in May, the Japanese intensified searching residences in areas where Americans had resided in Manila and its outskirts. They offered monetary rewards to anyone who would report violations to Japanese authorities. Those who gave information would remain anonymous. In mid-June, Japanese soldiers entered the home of Johnny Harris, who lived across the street from my sister Pilar and her husband, Tony Settember. Mr. Harris, who claimed neutrality since he was from Switzerland, was arrested when the Japanese discovered a shortwave radio hidden in his bedroom wall. They knew where to search for the contraband. Perhaps a servant knew about this hidden radio and reported the violation in order to collect a reward.

Immediately after his arrest, the Japanese tied Harris to a nearby utility pole, stabbed him several times with their bayonets, and left him to die while neighbors peered from behind their curtains in shock. Everyone was terrified as the Japanese entered other neighboring homes. They searched the surrounding houses and took one man from each house for interrogation. My brother-in-law, Tony Settember, was among those taken.

My sister Pilar was sobbing incoherently when she called to tell me what happened. I was in shock. Our daughter Joyce who was only four years old, was staying with Pilar, Tony, and their son, Anthony.

"Where have they taken Tony? Are you all right? Are Joyce and Anthony okay?"

Questions spilled from my mouth as if racing to keep pace with my thoughts. Pilar continued sobbing.

"*O, Dios mio! Que podemos hacer?*" ("Oh, my God! What can we do?") Pilar sputtered.

"I am coming to see you. Control yourself…for the children's sake."

"No, stay there. You will be searched and poor Mr. Harris has been left to die on the utility pole in front of our house for everyone to see what happens to those who break their rules. It is horrible!" Pilar spoke hurriedly.

I was stunned by her response. To be searched and questioned as to why I was going into the house where Tony had just been taken away for interrogation might prove dangerous. They must not learn that Joyce was the daughter of an American.

"You must keep Joyce inside and away from the windows. The Japanese must not see her. I will call you in the morning."

The house was silent after I retuned the phone to its cradle. The silence reverberated in my ears, and mimicked the pounding in my heart. I had to collect myself so the other children would not notice my concern and agitation. *I must pray.*

Three days passed before Tony was released to return home. He and Pilar decided to relocate to Baguio. The Japanese troops were concentrated in Manila and its outskirts, and had not yet infested Baguio with daily searches and patrols. In Ermita, where they lived, Japanese soldiers entered homes daily and took what they wanted. Pilar hid her jewelry and Tony stashed cash in various spots, hoping the Japs would not find and confiscate their money and valuables. The move to Baguio was finalized. Tony needed the license for our poultry farm, so he would be allowed to drive to and from Baguio as a business owner. I had no car and the Japs had taken most of the chickens.

"*Nena*," Pilar announced, "We want to take Joyce with us to Baguio."

"No, Pilar," I stated flatly. "I promised Jess I would keep the family together in San Juan. As long as you were living in the area, it was okay for her to stay with you, but since you are moving to Baguio, she must remain with us."

"I am afraid you will not be able to feed all your children. How will you provide food, clothing, and medicine? You don't need to tell Jess. He is in prison camp."

"Stop, Pilar. God will help me provide," I spoke adamantly. "I will not break my promise to Jess. His last words before Tony took him to Santo Tomas were to keep the children together. I gave him my word."

Pilar's face was crestfallen. She had enjoyed having her around, and Joyce helped to keep Anthony entertained. Joyce also enjoyed the attention she received there.

"I will miss her, but I'll bring her to you before we go. I will also have Tony bring our ducks, geese and the goat. The ducks and geese are laying eggs, which should provide nutrition for the children."

Tony, Pilar, Anthony, and Joyce were a welcome, although amusing, sight as they drove into our driveway in their station wagon. The crates holding the geese and four ducks were in the rear, but Anthony was holding the goat, which had his head poked out of the car's window. We all laughed at this menagerie.

After unloading their vehicle and enjoying a brief visit, the Settembers needed to drive to Baguio. Several hours of daylight were required to drive the steep, winding mountain roads. Curfew, enforced by the Japanese, made driving at night prohibitive. Tony kept moving Pilar and Anthony toward their vehicle and Pilar kept returning for another hug, or something else she needed to tell me.

"Come on, Pilar. We have to go," insisted Tony as he waved to us. "I will come to see how you and the kids are doing, *Nena*."

We wondered if we would see each other again. I held the younger children closer to me as they left our driveway and headed for the mountains.

Mary lifted her teacup to her lips only to discover it was empty. She had been engrossed in her writing and did not recall finishing her tea. *I must hurry. Evening vespers at St. Williams will begin in thirty minutes.* Msgr. McCallum would be waiting. She reached for a tiny bell she kept on a shelf by the door and put it in her pocket. When the altar boy was absent, she was ready to help.

CHAPTER 81

Reality Descends

By July 1942, the reality of our situation enveloped me like the darkness imposed by the Japanese curfew. The usual celebrations we had enjoyed under American governance...Memorial Day, Flag Day, and Fourth of July, no longer existed. We had no holidays, period. There was no reason to celebrate. Reality kept me going. I had a husband imprisoned in Santo Tomas Internment Camp who needed supplies; a son in the U.S. Navy, who was God only knew where; and, six growing, hungry children to feed, clothe, and educate because the public schools were closed. Catholic schools had opened their doors once again, but I dared not send the children. I had promised Jess to keep them together.

Changes occurred daily. Our regular routines were disrupted. Speaking English in public was discouraged. Radio broadcasts were mostly propaganda and more rules and regulations. Missing from the musical selections were familiar tunes like, *God Bless America, Over the Rainbow, Three Little Fishes, When You Wish Upon A Star,* and, *You Are My Sunshine.* Only some Filipino popular tunes and Japanese language "lessons" were allowed.

We sometimes heard rumors, but dared not repeat them. Those who did were arrested and punished for passing on information favorable toward the American military effort. "Invisible" Fifth Columnists could be anywhere. These "invisible spies" might be neighbors or former acquaintances. They would report their own family members to the Japanese to get money or food. I reminded the children, if they had to speak while in church or while going with me to Santo Tomas, to use either Spanish or *Tagalog,* as it irritated Japanese soldiers when someone spoke English. We all learned to speak enough Japanese in order to greet the Japanese sentries posted at each corner with *"Ohayo"* or *"Konbangwa"* and thank them with *"Arregato"* once we were allowed to continue.

We were fingerprinted and registered to our restricted area called "City of Manila Neighborhood Association for San Juan." Our dated and numbered "Identification Card" bearing our left thumbprint along with our given name, maternal (maiden) name, surname, Neighborhood Association Number (8-4-4), occupation, age, sex, and a list of visible marks must be carried and presented

**CITY OF MANILA
NEIGHBORHOOD ASSOCIATION**
Identification Card

SAN JUAN   Date......March 1......, 194 4

Name......Mary......, ...Cucullu......, ...Gamero......
           (Given)   (Maternal)   (Surname)

Present address......43......, ...J. Ruiz......, ...San Juan......
                     (No.)   (Street)   (District)

N. A. No. 8-4-4   Occupation......Housekeeper...... Age...37... Sex...F...

Visible marks ....

(Left thumb mark)   Certified by: *Ceferino Alon*
                                    N. A. Leader

Mary Gamero
(Signature of holder)   D. A. President

3796—12

when stopped for inspection. Each Neighborhood Association was assigned a leader whose signature was affixed on each card along with our signature. Our assigned leader was Ceferino Alon, a Filipino who was a Japanese sympathizer. I claimed Spanish citizenship to keep my children with me, and used "Mary Cucullu Gamero" on the neighborhood card. "Mary Gamero Cucullu" was listed on my Alien Certificate of Registration (Spanish) with my married name not listed in order to avoid being questioned by the Japanese. Being caught without your card meant being arrested and severely punished. Annual renewal of registration was required and a fee was charged each time.

To keep from sinking into a deep depression, I kept the children and myself busy by assigning chores. Items we owned were collected to sell to friends and family members to have cash to buy food at the marketplace. Sometimes family members and friends gave me items they needed to sell, but feared being away from their homes or being questioned by the Japanese. I would sell their items and take a percentage as my commission. With this small business going on the side, when I was not busy preparing items for Jess to have in Santo Tomas, I was able to make enough commission to buy a little food. Keeping busy and praying helped me keep my sanity.

The children were assigned house and garden duties. Junior worked regularly in our small garden to grow vegetables. He planted *kamotes* (sweet potatoes). They never had a chance to produce yams, as I would snip the broad, shiny dark green leaves to cook with dried fish *(tinapa)* or an occasional fresh fish from our pond. He also planted leafy greens—*kangkong* (spinach) and *pechay* (bok choy)—from which I made a dish called *talilong*. This dish became a staple at our table and around our area. Peping helped him plant *kamoting kahoy* (cassava), *sitaw* (green beans), and *talong* (eggplant). We already had bamboo growing by the back fence. The tender shoots *(labong)* were edible when cooked in coconut milk. Peping acted as helper, advisor, and supervisor. He had the experience to make the garden a success.

Lucy was put in charge while I was away from the house either gathering or selling items. Emma and Mary Jane, along with Junior, cared for the turkey hen we had raised as a pet, plus the geese, four ducks, and the Billy goat, which Pilar and Tony had left with us. This helped to provide eggs to go with the vegetables. Linnie, the baby, was fed the turkey egg every day. There was no fresh milk for her…it was for the Japanese military. We had a few cans of powdered milk Jess and I had managed to hide. The brand name was Klim. *I still remember the radio commercial….Drink Klim….that's milk spelled backwards.*

We were fortunate to have several fruit trees around our house. Mango, guava, banana, papaya, *santol*, and *duhat* trees provided fresh fruit in season. We took the young shoots from the base of the banana trees that grew by the kitchen stairway, chopped them finely, and cooked them in coconut milk to make a filling dish. By adding rice, we could keep from starving.

Mary Jane was assigned to leave early each morning to stand in the ration lines. Sometimes, she returned empty-handed. Anything she was issued was utilized in some way. If it was not used, it was hidden and used later. I hid the rationed rice and other provisions. The rice and cracked wheat became infested with weevils….and later, mealworms. We had the added bonus of "mealworms" for protein. We ate anything to fill hungry tummies.

Mary pulled off her glasses, picked up her handkerchief, and wiped them gently. It all seemed like a horrible dream, but as she held her 1944 Identification Card in her hand, the emotions flowed. She shook off those feelings, rose from her chair, opened her cupboard, and glanced at the many canned goods and other foodstuffs. Her friends, and her son-in-law Carlton had teased her about storing so much food.

I will always have plenty of food in my house.

Mary smiled as she remembered Carlton's teasing manner. *He was a genteel man and always so helpful. He and Emma had reared a wonderful family.* Although Mary and her family had many difficulties, she always gave thanks for her many blessings during vespers. With God's help, she was able to endure many dark days.

CHAPTER 82

An Empty Christmas

Our first Christmas under the rule of the Imperial Japanese Forces was just a date on the calendar. The children and I missed Jess so much. Bobby's whereabouts and status was unknown. The only bright spot in December 1942 was an announcement that families of prisoners in Santo Tomas were allowed to bring a picnic lunch to share with their interned family on December 24. We prepared for the big event.

On December 23, the children and I gathered fruit and vegetables to prepare a Christmas dinner to share with Jess the next day. Junior found three papayas not yet stolen by thieves. Two were deformed...shaped like birds...complete with extensions that looked like wings. He also found one long stalk of bananas or *penca* on a tree near the back stairway of our house. The largest bananas, at the base of the stalk, resembled hands with fingers pointed toward the sky. Each "hand" was smaller as they tapered down and around the stalk on their way to the end where a heart-shaped bulb dangled like a decorative watch fob. The smallest bananas were used to make a pie, and the remainder placed in a sack to take to Jess. The heart-shaped portion was chopped and cooked in coconut milk spiced with curry powder.

Lucy and Emma gathered the young banana shoots, normally used as hog food. When prepared correctly, banana shoots were used in a salad. The young, tender trunks were chopped into small pieces, sprinkled with salt, squeezed firmly to remove the sticky sap, washed well, placed in a bowl, and sprinkled with oil and white vinegar. Sadly, we did not have dried fish to add protein.

The children prepared Christmas cards for Jess. They were warned to keep them simple and cheerful. We needed to lift his spirits, as his days were much drearier than ours. Each one was reviewed to make sure nothing was included to draw the attention of Japanese censors. Everything we brought would be inspected, and our bodies would be searched.

We gathered the items to take for our "picnic" with Jess and traveled the six miles to Santo Tomas. Junior and Lucy carried the food baskets. I carried Linnie, while Emma held Joyce's hand. Mary Jane followed carrying the bananas.

We walked quietly. We dared not speak English because that drew attention to us. We knew not to look at the Jap sentry's face, as we bowed and waited for permission to pass. We had seen others get their faces slapped hard...so hard they would be knocked down for staring at the sentry's face. Inspection of our baskets and sack of bananas was completed in silence. We hoped the sentry would not confiscate anything. We barely had enough for us. I always prayed silently at each stop.

After about two and one-half hours, we arrived at the entrance gate to Santo Tomas. A long line had already formed to enter the camp. After each person was searched, every identification card reviewed, and all parcels checked for contraband, we were allowed to enter Santo Tomas. The children knew they must not talk or complain. To speak without being addressed would deny our entry to see Jess. I cautioned them to not cry in front of Jess. They were to take turns giving him hugs and kisses and not raise their voices to attract the attention of the Japanese guards.

At last we were seated together in the visitation area and prepared to share our picnic with Jess. He took one of the oddly shaped papayas in his hands for closer inspection. Several internee friends, who had no family members present, noticed the papayas, and stopped at our table. They stared in amazement. None had ever seen oddities like those papayas before. They wondered if the papayas were protesting the Japanese occupation. As we continued our visit, tears welled in their eyes, as they watched Jess and the children enjoying each other. Their families were safe in America.

Linnie was in Jess' lap the whole time...staring at him as if she were trying to figure out who he was and why the other children were making a fuss over him. Jess held onto her and squeezed her gently as if each squeeze might be his last.

We were required to leave at three. I was thankful for the time we shared together. Just before three, Jess took my hand and pulled me toward him.

"Mary, rumors are being whispered around camp that the American Red Cross sent packages, but the Japs aren't telling American families or letting anyone in here have them. Ernest Stanley saw some boxes stamped with a red cross in the commandant's office when he was called in there to interpret for them. He said the Japs were going through them and pulling out all the cigarettes and other stuff they wanted. If I do get a package, I will send it to you through the Spanish Embassy," Jess whispered in my ear and squeezed my hand.

I nodded. We each said our goodbyes, shared more hugs and kisses, lifted the empty baskets, took Linnie off Jess' lap, and exited the front gate. *Will we see him again?*

Our return to our restricted area was quiet. The older children helped taking turns carrying Linnie. They sensed I was exhausted, both physically and emotionally. Junior was tight-lipped the entire time. Joyce asked questions about the prison camp and I tried to answer them so the children would not sense my concern. Once again, we had to go through the process of bowing and scraping before each sentry on the corner of each block.

Once home, we gathered around the table to give prayers of thanks for the time we shared with their daddy. Perhaps we would be allowed to see him again soon. There was no visit from Santa Claus, no Christmas tree with presents underneath, no gift baskets with candies, fruits, and nuts... *nada*. The only sign of Christmas was a manger scene I placed by my bedside. Normally, it would be in a central location in our living room, but it would be safer by my bedside...in case thieves broke into our house. The small figurines would fit under the bedding if thieves or Japanese soldiers surprised us. Those hand-carved pieces of ivory were precious in more ways than one. The visit with Jess was our priceless Christmas gift. We wished for one other...a message that Bobby was safe. Perhaps we would have good news soon.

Mary removed her heavy glasses, rubbed her eyes, and peered out the glass portion of her kitchen door. Her Japanese persimmon tree was beginning to bear fruit. *I was grateful to be so close to my church and family after Jess' death, but was unaware a Japanese persimmon was growing next to the kitchen door.* Mary had nursed a strong distaste for anything "Japanese" for many years. She refused to buy products "Made in Japan." She learned to curb her distaste, but a trace, too painful to erase, lingered. *Will I ever be able to forgive? Will I ever find peace?*

CHAPTER 83

Learning to Cope

We managed to survive one year under the Japanese occupation. We learned much the first year, but had much more to learn in 1943. We had no idea what was happening other than whatever happened before our eyes…that was our reality. Our restricted area was our world. Sometime we heard rumors, but nothing was verified, and we certainly could not repeat any "outside news." Our only news was "spoon-fed" Japanese propaganda aired on the radio and what was allowed in the local newspapers.

Ceferino Alon, the Japanese-appointed leader of our restricted area, stopped by for surprise inspections of each house in his assigned area accompanied by two Japanese soldiers holding rifles with fixed bayonets. A detailed list of all of the persons residing in the house posted by the front door, as required, was checked. These inspections took place anytime…day or night. Everyone listed must be present after curfew. If an "extra" person were found during curfew, Japanese punishment would be severe…torture followed by a slow death in public for all. Fear ruled our actions.

During each weekly visit to Santo Tomas, changes were taking place. The prison camp became overcrowded as prisoners were brought from outlying camps and provinces. Over 5,000 internees were now imprisoned in Santo Tomas. The internee committees were struggling to provide for the mass influx of new prisoners. The meager rations were stretched. More shanties were built, and additional outdoor toilets were needed. Jess and his construction crew were kept busy…expending precious energy they needed just to maintain a functioning body. Finally, with more prisoners going hungry, becoming ill, and more than the Jap guards could tolerate, the camp commandant announced that eight hundred male internees would be transferred to *Los Baños,* another prison camp about 37 miles away. Jess' heart sank. He prayed he would not be chosen.

The year prior, I had been allowed to bring Jesse's dirty clothes home and do his laundry weekly. We were allowed to have brief conversations the following week when I returned his laundry along with various bits of food. Changes were put into place.

Laundry for internees was stopped. A Japanese guard discovered a note hidden in the cuff of one of the internee's trousers. The information on the note could only have come from news delivered via an "outside" source…a short wave radio. The internee was questioned, tied to a lamppost in the courtyard, severely beaten, stabbed with a bayonet, and left to die. His remains were left for all internees to view as a warning. I thanked God they had not found the notes I had been slipping in to Jess. My notes were mainly love notes to Jess to keep his spirits lifted. Sometimes I would list the cost of the items in the food bag, in case he wanted to sell items to fellow internees.

New and stricter rules were enforced. All visitors were required to form two lines outside the camp's main gate. Talking was forbidden. All bags and packages were inspected in the presence of the person who delivered it. Visitors remained behind the inspection tables in the receiving shed while the guard delivered the bag or package to the designated internee, who stood in line with other internees about fifty feet away. We were not allowed to wave or signal to them. We only watched and smiled as they stood at attention and stepped forward to receive their bag or package from the guard when their name was called. With my myopic eyesight, I hardly ever saw Jess' face…only his body shape. The only way I knew he was present to receive his package was when I brought one of the children. We had a prearranged signal. If their daddy were in line, they would reach for my hand and squeeze it. Their touch would make my smile turn into a clownish grin. The internee was required to exit the area when they received their items. I always waited for Jess' extra empty bag, and my precious hidden note. At that point, we were also required to leave…without talking.

About three weeks before Mother's Day, I was waiting in line for my turn to enter the main gate of the camp when my friend Chata Berlanga saw me from across the street. She started across the street to join me. She chatted as she approached, and I put my finger to my lips as a signal to be quiet. She did not understand and kept talking. A Japanese sentry noticed her. He intercepted her, as she crossed the street, slapped her hard, causing her to fall down. I felt helpless. I remained quiet. I prayed for her as she slowly rose and walked in the opposite direction. I made the Sign of The Cross…hoping the sentry would not come toward me.

Samples of the notes hidden in the seams of Jess' supply bag while he was interned in Santo Tomas.

After the usual ritual of inspection, the guard handed the exchange bag to me. It contained something. Jess sometimes returned it with one or two items he made. This time, he had made a pair of *bakyas* (wooden clogs with inner tubing straps nailed to the wooden soles) to use as "shower shoes" or wear for gardening. It was a distraction to have the guard look at the "gift" rather than check the empty bag closely. The precious cargo…his handwritten note, was more important to me than any gift. I could hardly wait until I reached home to rip open the seam and retrieve his note.

Jess signed his full name as if it were a business letter…his usual habit. I hid the note between our wedding photo and its protective mat. If Ceferino Alon and his guards or Japanese soldiers inspected, they would not find it or the others…hidden with our American flag.

On May 9, 1943, the Japanese loaded 800 male internees on trains to send to prison camp at the University of the Philippines College of Agriculture in *Los Baños*. Jess breathed a sign of relief for he was left behind. Perhaps he would be allowed to see his family on Father's Day. He prayed this wish would be granted.

We kept to our daily routines of gardening and picking fruit before it ripened. If we allowed the fruit to ripen on the tree, it would be stolen during the night.

Mary Jane was sent regularly to stand in the ration lines to secure items given away each week. Sometimes it would be a bottle of vinegar or a piece of fabric. Anything given was accepted graciously. I sent Mary Jane because Lucy and Emma were blossoming into womanhood and would be a temptation for Japanese soldiers. Many young girls in the area had been raped by Japanese soldiers…others disappeared. Mary Jane, who was nine years old, was old enough to follow directions, but not attract attention. I hoped the Japanese soldiers would not bother her. Junior was never sent to stand in line because, at fourteen, he was getting taller…almost a man, and his Caucasian features were obvious. We did our best to keep him out of sight.

Residents of our restricted area were allowed to stand in line at the nearby slaughterhouse to collect animal parts not used by the Japanese for their troops. Mary Jane, with bucket in hand, would leave for the slaughterhouse by seven in the morning and stand in line for several hours for her turn to get some of the remains from the weekly slaughter and return with what she was given. Sometimes, it would be the tongue, brains, tail, entrails, or blood. All of it was much-needed protein. We knew tongue, brains, and oxtails were delicacies in many parts of Asia. We learned entrails and congealed blood were edible, as well. The intestines were cut into segments and the excrement was flushed out. Each of the entrails was turned inside out to remove its inner lining. After cutting the intestines into bit-sized pieces, they were cooked with sweet potato leaves or banana shoots. We ate to satisfy our hunger. A wartime dish named *dine guan,* made of sliced congealed blood sauteed with onions, became a delicacy for us and the natives. Sautéed chicken blood and entrails were served over boiled rice. There was much to learn…we learned to survive.

Two weeks before Father's Day, we were informed that some internees would be allowed to have their families to come in for a visit on Father's Day.

                              SANITATION & HEALTH DIVISION
                              SANTO TOMAS INTERNMENT CAMP
                                   July 9th, 1943

Memorandum to:-
Mr. J. A. Hodges,
Supervisor,
Carpentry Section

    To assist and further strengthen this organization as a whole, I have appointed Mr. A. W. Schell Assistant head of this Department, effective Monday, next July 12th.

    With this staff addition it is hoped to relieve me from undue office ties, and allow greater freedom for my personal contact with Camp needs; in addition Mr. Schell will periodically pay you a visit and endeavour to solve any difficulties you may encounter and co-ordinate work generally.

    Mr. R. Anton has been entrusted with the position of Chief Inspector vacated by Mr. Schell, and no doubt he will also visit you, but with a different objective, in either case I know that I can rely upon your whole-hearted cooperation.

    I am also taking this opportunity to thank you and your co-workers for the excellent work that is being performed under extremely difficult conditions, and look forward to the future success of this Department with your continued collaboration.

    Thanking you,

                                 Yours very truly,

                                 J. HEARNDEN,   HEAD
                                 SANITATION & HEALTH DVISION

cc to:
Mr. R. W. Crosby

Jess, as chairman of construction, was selected to have this family visit. His prayers were answered. We were elated! The children had not been near their daddy since Christmas Day. We made plans for the special event.

Those two weeks crawled by like an inchworm measuring a yardstick. Once again, I cautioned the children about talking and following the rules, which had changed. Only the youngest, Linnie, Joyce, and Mary Jane would be allowed permission to hug and kiss their daddy after they had been searched. The rest of us had to stand behind a line five feet away. Lucy, Emma, Junior and I watched as Mary Jane carried Linnie to Jess. Joyce followed, holding onto Mary Jane's skirt. It was frightening for them to be at Santo Tomas. We were only allowed to stay for fifteen minutes before everyone was ordered out. It was not much, but better than nothing.

Japanese propaganda was plastered on every wall in all public areas in Manila. During June, members of The Preparatory Commission for Philippine Independence (designed by the Japanese military) were busy developing a new constitution for a Free Philippines since the Japanese had "rid the islands of American oppression." The new constitution was finalized on July 10 and ratified by the Japanese puppet government two months later. This constitution was devoid of a bill of rights and was comprised of twelve articles borrowed from the 1935 constitution. It met the approval of the Japanese Imperial government. All of these actions were taken in an attempt to pacify the Filipinos and gain their trust. The second Republic of the Philippines was in essence a puppet regime under Japanese rule.

Our lives fell into a pattern of searching for items to sell in order to buy food sold at the market and to pay the rent on the house. Most of the time we barely made ends meet. I scraped together food to put in Jess' canvas bag until the end of August, when the Japanese, with no explanation, stopped allowing anyone to bring packages to internees. Conditions in Santo Tomas were worse. Conditions worsened everywhere. The Japanese were more irritable and demanding. Food supplies diminished. The internees were given only a half-cup of watery rice daily, if they presented their meal ticket for the camp assistant to punch. No extra punches or servings were allowed. How would Jess survive?

My goodness, I'm tired. I did not realize recalling those difficult days would be so hard on me.

Mary scurried to put her notes away and get a quick bite to eat before getting ready to go to vespers. She must light a candle for Jesse and Bobby tonight. They were always on her mind. She wished she had a penny for every minute she thought about them…she would have a fortune.

CHAPTER 84

Something's Up

Usually, the only planes overhead were those bearing the insignia of The Rising Sun…a single round red full-moon circle near the end of each of wing. We had become accustomed to the drone of Japanese planes overhead and hardly paid attention. On September 20, 1943, however, changes were in the air. Angry sounds from overhead spilled over our restricted area. Machine gun fire filled our ears and the grinding and turning of the airplane engines whined and echoed above the trees. Strafing action sent bullets through the tree limbs shattering branches and sending pieces of bark all around us. It was a dogfight! My children were standing at the rear of the house watching this aerial show as if they had bought tickets!

"Run for the shelter!" I screamed as I grabbed Linnie and shoved Joyce in the direction of the henhouse where Jess, Peping, Juaning, and Junior had dug an air raid shelter on the opposite side near all the banana trees. I put the two youngest ones inside, stepped out and screamed again. The rest scurried along and jumped inside the shelter.

"Yuk," Mary Jane said as she slipped in the slimy drainage trench in the middle of the shelter floor. A swarm of angry mosquitoes buzzed around us… protesting our intrusion into their peaceful abode. Jess designed the shelter so moisture would collect at its bottom in a narrow trench, leaving the rest of the shelter dank, but not dripping wet. Each side had parallel earthen benches so those seated faced each other, knees almost touching. There was room for all of us to sit, including Peping. He and I sat nearest the narrow doorway. The wooden roof of the shelter was covered with old mattresses and tin to help keep out the shrapnel. The shelter would be useless if we suffered a direct hit, but, hopefully, would prevent wounds or death by shrapnel.

We waited until it was quiet outside. The stillness was deafening. I gradually peeked out. It was quiet again. I allowed the children to resume their chores. *I wonder how much time we will have before we have to hide in the shelter again?*

With that thought in mind, I prepared a bag of necessary items I could grab for the next event. We had experienced a "preview of coming distractions." This first dogfight was a warning. We must be better prepared for others.

The next day, I visited my mother, who was living with my widowed sister, Consueling. The Japanese had barricaded several main roads so horse rigs and vehicles must stop for inspection. I kept my head down and kept walking, stopping only to do the usual bowing to each corner sentry. When I arrived at Consueling's home, *Mami* was very concerned. She had no news from her sister, Herminia, or Herminia's four sons, who lived together in their large apartment building in The Walled City *(Intramuros)*. She knew something was wrong.

"*Mami*, let me rest, then I will walk to *Intramuros* to check on *Tia* Herminia and my cousins."

She prayed quietly with her rosary in her hand, while I stretched out on the couch to rest. Consueling prepared *merienda*. What formerly would have been a sumptuous "coffee break" was reduced to a sip of an innocuous hot beverage and, perhaps, a cracker.

Following the brief rest and meager *merienda*, I began my trek. After over two hours of walking steadily, I arrived at the large arched gate of *Intramuros*. Japanese sentries were at the gate and no one was allowed through, I tried to explain I had come to see my family, but the sentries just grunted and indicated with their arm movements to go. I heard women screaming and loud gunfire through the thick walls. I left as fast as my legs would take me.

When I reached Consueling's home, her son, Peping, was describing the tragedies in The Walled City. He knew *Mami* was worried about Herminia and her sons, so he had gone earlier to investigate. Peping had returned from his investigation and was reporting the disastrous results, when I arrived. Their expressions of horror and sadness told me the news was bad. *Mami* was rocking…her hands covering her face. Her rosary, intertwined in her fingers, was swinging slowly back and forth like the pendulum on a grandfather clock. She was clearly in shock. Consueling was unable to raise from the couch…disbelief on her face. I rushed to her side and embraced her.

"What has happened?"

"*Tita Nena*, Luis Jr., José, Angel, and Alfredo are all dead," Peping uttered through clenched teeth.

"What!" I exclaimed.

"Just as I arrived near the gate of *Intramuros* this morning, my friend, Leandro, caught my arm and stopped me from going closer," Peping began.

He described his conversations with his friend, Leandro. He had difficulty controlling his emotions.

> "Peping, stay away from *Intramuros*. The Japanese have taken over. They are sending the women out and killing all the able-bodied men."
>
> "What do you mean? Why are they killing them?"
>
> "They made them dig a trench, then the Japs had them line up beside it and either shot them or used their bayonets to shove them into the trench. They poured gasoline over them and set them on fire! It was terrible!"

"*O, Dios mio!* That cannot be! I must find them."

"No, Peping, they are already gone. They are with God. You cannot help them. You will only be caught yourself. You must go."

"As I turned to leave, *Tia* Herminia came through the gate screaming. She looked back in time to see three of her sons blasted with machine guns. She collapsed in my arms and I brought her here. She is resting in *Mami's* bedroom," Peping spoke softly.

Peping's news was devastating. I was numb. *They are fanatics! How can they be that cruel! We had no defense against their madness.*

As I collected myself, I knew I must return to our restricted area to make curfew, but hated leaving my mother, aunt, and sister with this sadness. I wanted to stay and console *Tia* Herminia, but if inspectors arrived in my absence, my children would be punished severely. The thought sent a chill through me.

"I must go, *Mami*. The children are alone and I have to return before curfew," I said, while giving her and Consueling a quick peck on their cheeks.

"I'll walk with you," Peping stated firmly.

I was glad to have him with me. His muscular presence would dissuade an attack by robbers. We moved along briskly and quietly. Nothing eased the ache in our hearts. *Life is like a fluttering butterfly. One minute, you are flitting from one blossom to the next, enjoying the nectar each has to offer, and suddenly...you are crumpled on the ground...never to fly again.*

The cruel hand of fate reached out once again. On November 14, 1943, a fierce typhoon struck Manila and dumped over twenty-seven inches of rain. It was terrible! The flooding and raging current washed away our garden while the strong winds destroyed many of our fruit trees. A large portion of our food supply was ruined. We were kept busy finding containers to catch the rain leaking through the many holes in our roof caused by flying pieces of shrapnel. Mopping up water that blew across the dining area was useless. We were soaked and had nothing to eat except one-half a banana each, as we could not cook outside in the fire pit. We had no electrical power and no news...not even propaganda. We were trying to survive. I did manage to give Joyce a hug for her birthday. Love was the only present we had to give each other.

We retired early and hoped the flooding waters would recede before morning. My thoughts flew to Jess and conditions at Santo Tomas. *Was he safe? Was he alive? Was he in a dry place?* A wave of depression swept over me and I fought back tears. I reached for my rosary by my bedside. *My faith will sustain me.*

The next morning, after having nightmares about Jess drowning in the floodwaters, I divided the four remaining bananas among the children for their breakfast as we had neither gas nor electricity for several months, but had been cooking with twigs and fallen tree branches outside in a fire pit. Water was still rushing around the house, so I could not cook outside as we usually did. As they gathered around the table, I told Mary Jane to hurry and dress after she finished her piece of banana. I would take her with me. I wanted to see what conditions were around Santo Tomas. She could help carry the package for Jess, in case visitors were allowed. I prayed the front gate to the prison camp would still be open.

We waded in water around our ankles most of the time, but at Santa Mesa, the water rose to Mary Jane's waist. I held the package with one hand while clasping her hand with the other to keep her from being swept away by the current. Several ahead of us were screaming about snakes being in the water. We walked slower...looking for snakes as we waded. By the time we reached the front gate of Santo Tomas, it was closed and we were soaked.

We needed to rest. Mary Jane and I stopped at Lucing's home in Santa Mesa. After patting ourselves with dry towels, Lucing gave us water and a thin slice of *papaya*. The short visit gave us a chance to rest before returning home through the flooding.

When we reached the gasoline station at the foot of the San Juan Bridge, the bodies of four Filipinos had been pulled from the raging waters and were draped across the railing at the foot of the bridge. The swiftly moving waters of the San Juan River had claimed more victims. Their *calesa* (horse drawn rig) was also salvaged from the muddy receding waters. The horse had disappeared.

"God has protected us once again," I told Mary Jane.

Her big brown eyes opened wide with astonishment at the shock of seeing those corpses. She was quiet the rest of the way to 43 J. Ruiz.

The ringing of the telephone brought Mary out of her fog of depression. *Who is calling at this hour?* When she answered, her granddaughter, Missy, spoke. She recently returned from Spain.

"*Ola, abuelita, como estas?* I have just returned from my studies in *España* and wanted to see you. May we come for a visit?" Missy laughed as she spoke.

Missy and Mary Jane arrived twenty minutes later. Mary opened the kitchen door to let them in and gave Missy a "Welcome Home" hug. She enjoyed the cards and letters Missy had written from Spain, but she was glad to have her in Texas. Terrorist activities in Spain filled the daily news.

They recounted their adventures in Spain, as Mary Jane had flown to Madrid to help Missy prepare for her return to Texas.

"I called our relatives in Madrid, the one who is a vice-president of *El Banco de España,* and he and his wife met us at our hotel. They showed us an excellent place to enjoy *tapas y copas,*" Mary Jane chattered. "The next day we visited *El Prado* to see Dali's works. *Guernica* was quite amazing."

"We decided to fly to Barcelona and celebrate Mom's birthday in The Manila Hotel," Missy added. "We enjoyed *mimosas* with our breakfast in bed. Later, we visited *Plaza España,* a miniature version of Spain, where each province is represented by its crafts and cuisine."

"Since we were close to Italy, we decided to shop for a wedding gown for Chip's fiancée Carmen in Rome," Mary Jane added. "Although there were hundreds, we returned without one. Wish Carmen had been with us."

After recounting their adventures in Rome, The Isle of Capri, Florence, and their return to Barcelona (because Missy wanted the unusual throw rug she had seen previously), they laughed as they told of experiences in Malaga and Marbella.

"We had a delightful time on those beaches and ate plenty of seafood. We hated to go, but we had return tickets," Missy said. "When we arrived at the airport, we discovered Spain was having a 'labor strike' and no flights were leaving. We were stuck in the airport, but found ways to amuse ourselves. We were playing gin rummy when my alarm clock buzzed in my carryon bag. The Spanish soldiers on duty at the airport rushed to us with their guns pointed. I was embarrassed and explained I had forgotten to turn off my alarm clock. They checked my bag and found the alarm still buzzing. We were all relieved. Two of them sat down with us to learn how to play gin rummy."

Mary rubbed tears from her eyes due to all of their laughter. She stifled a yawn and glanced at her watch. She had been up since six this morning, and it was time for the evening news. Mary Jane sensed her mother was tired. They gave her "goodnight" hugs, and left.

What a day this has been! I think I will go straight to bed.

Mary walked to her bedroom, with Booger following at her heels. They both needed a good night's rest.

CHAPTER 85

Peril All Around

As 1943 stretched toward yet another year under Japanese rule, I tried to ignore the upcoming holiday season. Conditions had worsened. The Japanese halted all visits to Santo Tomas Internment Camp. No food or packages were allowed. We could only exchange messages via mailed postcards or letters with internees. The Japanese censored these letters or postcards. I chose my words wisely.

Inspections and searches of homes and individuals increased. Money was scarce. Most of our items of value had been sold to family friends and relatives. Any money I could spare was mailed to Jess to buy food and supplies. I prayed the Japs would not confiscate the meager amount I sent so Jess could have something. The remainder was used for rent, fees, utilities (water only), and food. I had to find a way to make more money; otherwise, we would all be tossed from our living quarters and surely die.

Whenever I had a serious problem, I always visited my half-sister, Maming, a nun at *El Collegio de La Consolacion*. After giving the children instructions, I left for her convent. Maming had guided the Gamero family for many years. She kept the family together after my father died and sacrificed her own wishes to take care of us. She would help me.

Since money was scarce and the limited transportation was expensive, I walked the five miles to her convent. Upon my arrival, we embraced and held each other before speaking. She insisted I sit and rest while she prepared refreshments for us to enjoy during the visit. She was the Sister Superior at the convent and was allowed to have guests. I was relieved to have time to collect my thoughts before asking for her help.

"I already know why you are here, *Nena*," Maming stated firmly. "You need money to feed your family. I was worried this might happen."

"We were managing fairly well until the typhoon struck in November," I explained. "It destroyed many of our fruit trees and washed away our garden. We still have banana and bamboo shoots to eat."

"Are you still selling items?" Maming queried.

"Yes, but most of the valuable items have been sold. I have been selling items for my friends and neighbors, and they pay me a commission," I offered.

"You must continue, but you will need to expand your business," Maming stated.

"What do you mean?" I asked.

"I mean you can become an agent to sell furniture or appliances from the sellers' homes," Maming explained.

"How will I carry heavy items? What about furniture?" I sputtered.

"As an agent, you will either bring or send customers to those homes to see the items for sale. Since the prices would probably be discounted, the buyers would be responsible for the removal of those items after you make the sale and collect your commission."

I was stunned. She obviously had spent much time thinking about this plan.

"How did you think of this business, Maming?" I inquired.

"It's what I had to do after our father died and after that German husband of Salud's threw us out."

Maming had spoken from experience. She had been through this process before. I still had questions to ask.

"How will I begin? Where will I find customers? Will you help me?"

"Yes, *Nena*, I have already talked with members of our family and they are talking with their friends and neighbors. With their help, I have made a list," Maming spoke as she drew a small ledger from the pocket in the skirt of her habit.

I was amazed as I thumbed through the listing of names, addresses, plus items to sell with pricing set by the owners. She and my sisters had already organized a network of Spanish customers for me to contact. I was in business once again, thanks to Maming and my family. I gave her a hug, kissed her cheeks, and wiped a tear away.

"You must go. Some of those addresses are on your way home," Maming stated. "Be careful. God go with you. Give the children kisses from me."

I thought about her words on the way to my first stop…Mrs. Amechazurra's. Lucing had known her husband and told me her sad story. Mrs. Louise Amechazurra had suffered many difficulties. An English lady, she met Don Amechazurra at Frank and Lucing's table at *El Circulo Social,* a favorite dance club. According to Lucing, it was love at first sight. They married eight months later and had three children before the Japanese invasion destroyed their lives.

Although she had changed her first name from "Louise" to "Luisa" when she married, Mrs. Amechazurra, an Englishwoman, was taken to an internment camp in January 1942. The children, ages four, three, and ten months, were left in the care of her Spanish husband. Mr. Amechazurra tried desperately to convince the Japanese officials he needed his wife at home to care for their children, since their baby had not yet been weaned from his mother's breast milk. Each day, Don Amechazurra took the two older children to his mother's home, left them in her care, and carried the ten-month-old baby in his arms to show the Japanese how desperately this baby needed its mother. The Filipinos in the area noticed his frequent trips to the Japanese Central Office and suspected him of being a Japanese sympathizer. *Perhaps he was giving the Japanese information about their guerilla activities.* They did not bother to ask questions for fear Mr. Amechazurra was a Japanese sympathizer and would report their activities.

One morning, after he had left the two older children at his mother's and was walking towards town and the Japanese headquarters, the natives attacked him. He was killed…beaten to death. The baby's neck was broken in the fall. Their bodies were left near the door of the only Catholic church in town.

The local priest made the horrible discovery. Don Amechazurra and his family were his parishioners. He called upon his assistants to transfer the bodies inside the church before contacting the local authorities. The Spanish Consulate was also contacted and advised of the dual tragedies. After attending to those official matters, the priest delivered the sad news of the loss of her son and grandchild to *Sra.* Amechazurra and the two remaining children, who were now without a father, mother, or baby sister.

Spanish Consulate authorities kept pressuring the Japanese officials to release Luisa Amechazurra from prison camp. They insisted this poor woman was no threat. She was released from the prison camp to take care of her two remaining children. Sadly, she was placed under house arrest and required to wear a red armband. She was thankful to receive visitors from the Spanish community.

Mrs. Amechazurra was in dire need of money to buy food, clothing, and other items for her two remaining children. She had talked with Lucing who promised to help. Lucing gave her name to our older sister, Maming.

I knocked at the Amechazurra's front door and waited nervously to meet this poor lady who had already suffered greatly. I prayed quietly to be of help to her.

A young, fair-haired lady opened the door quite timidly and invited me inside. A red armband encircled her left arm. She was a marked woman…marked by the Japanese. After a brief exchange of information, she apologized to me for not being able to offer tea or refreshment. She stated her needs.

"I have collected items I must sell. Here is a list of the items. I followed the written instructions of the Sister Superior that your sister, Lucing, brought to me."

```
1 Tea Set: French porcelain
    (white and black with gold rims)        ₱300
1 Wall Mirror: 6" 2-½'                      ₱250
1 Silver Tea Service: Tray, Sugar, Cream,
    and Tea/Coffee Pot                      ₱250
1 Bedroom Suite: Bed, Arm Chair,
    High Back Chair, 2 Night Tables,
    1 Dressing Table with Chair         Best Offer
```

"Please tell me at least two days prior to bringing anyone to see these items. I will need to prepare the children for a visit from strangers."

"Thank you, Mrs. Amechazurra. I will have someone for you by next week." It was getting late…time to scurry home. It was more dangerous to walk alone. Several bodies had been found in the streets. According to my neighbor, Max Kessel, robbers would attack anyone walking alone, kill them, and steal everything…including their clothes. I reached inside my pocket for my rosary and prayed while increasing my stride. *Dear God, watch over my children, Jess, and Bobby. Thy will be done.*

❦

What would I have done without my faith? I depended on prayer to see me through those difficult days…and I still do.

Mary rose stiffly from her kitchen table where she had been writing. She shrugged her shoulders and approached the refrigerator. She was getting hungry. *I should never be hungry again. I think I'll have pan con chocolate. Hot chocolate and a slice of pound cake should satisfy me before church. Let me see…what did I do with the cocoa?*

CHAPTER 86

Survival Tactics

Malnutrition, poor sanitation conditions, lack of preventive health care, and the absence of medication took its toll. Three weeks before Christmas, Junior became seriously ill. His bones ached severely. He was restless. His temperature rose rapidly. I kept him isolated in his room and ordered the rest of the family to stay away from him. By the third day, his temperature dropped and his skin turned yellow. I suspected he had yellow fever, but now I was sure. I knew in three or four more days he would become violently ill with body temperatures rising even higher than before, as the virus invaded his liver and other vital organs. We had no medicine or a doctor. I prayed he would not go into a coma. I offered boiled water and prayers.

Lucy and Emma took charge while I stayed with Junior in his room. Mary Jane continued her ration line assignments. They prayed for their brother every day as they took over his chores and completed theirs.

The week before Christmas, Junior's fever broke. He was able to eat a few bites of mashed mango and wash it down with some coconut water. He did not leave his bed. He was weak. I felt a wave of relief. He did not drift into a coma. The thought of losing a son...either Junior or Bobby...was heartbreaking.

When he felt better, Junior limped about the house, as much as he was able. I felt the aching in my bones. I touched my face and realized my temperature was rising. I knew I had to isolate myself and prepare for the worst. Lucy, Junior, Emma, and Mary Jane were called to my bedroom door.

"You four have the responsibility of keeping the family going. Mary Jane will have to go every day to stand in the ration lines to see what she can bring home for us. When your cousin, Peping, comes on Friday, tell him to stay outside because I have yellow fever. He needs to see if he can sell the items in my shopping bag and buy food for you at the market. He must tell *Mami*. She must not try to come here to take care of me. Lucy, I will need you to put water and fruit at my bedroom door. Do not come inside unless I tell you. Remember your prayers."

Lucy and Emma were speechless. Mary Jane stared without blinking. Junior stood with his head bowed. He knew full well what I was about to experience.

Christmas 1943, I drifted in and out of consciousness. Occasionally, I heard the children tiptoeing near my bedroom door and whispering to each other. I knew they were worried about me. The fever had ravaged my body. It was painful to try to turn over in the bed. Lifting a glass of water to my lips was difficult, but I knew fluids were necessary to flush the fever from my body. The sickly yellow tinge crept all over me, and I felt as if I were on fire from my rising temperature. Merciful sleep was the only medicine I had, along with my prayers. I feared I would slip into a coma and never waken. *What would happen to my children? God help me. Angels watch over me.*

When I was able to struggle out of bed and walk out of my bedroom, it was 1944. The old year had slipped away, taking the yellow fever with it, and the new one waited quietly…resting upon the shoulders of angels.

In my weakened condition, I tottered to the dining table and summoned the children. They stared at me…waiting for a sign I was better.

"Thank you for your prayers. I'll be okay," I said weakly.

Linnie, who was three years old in November, stepped gingerly toward me.

"Mama sick?" She asked as she held out her arms.

"Mama's better, but I cannot lift you, yet."

Lucy lifted her and placed her in my lap, where she nestled her head against my breast and became quiet. The others remained quiet as well.

By mid-January 1944, my strength was returning gradually. I resumed my business as a sales agent. I would need Peping's help. He and I devised a plan. He would come to our place at ten each morning. I used the rest of the day to conduct my sales and return one hour before curfew. He would meet me at the corner of N. Domingo and J. Ruiz to return to his home before curfew.

Peping, the children's protector four days each week, also guarded our fruit trees, still recovering from the devastating typhoon, and vegetable garden, that he and Junior had replanted. Crimes against residents increased. Hungry natives tried desperate ways to find food. Animals of all kinds, including dogs and cats, were stolen and eaten. Rats became an edible commodity. Robbers did not wait until dark to steal fruit from our trees or vegetables from the garden. We needed every bit of food we raised in order to survive.

Our plan worked. I began my sales business in earnest. I contacted persons on the list Maming had given me and gathered pricing information. Armed with the pricing, I walked to marketplaces or Spanish businesses and began negotiations. I became discouraged as money became scarcer and not many people were interested in buying furniture or silver tea sets. There was a demand for Philippine currency…code name…"thread." The value or amount of the currency, for example, five *pesos* was the "thread count" or "five count thread." Customers were willing to pay one hundred Japanese *pesos* (funny money or "Mickey Mouse" money) for one Philippine *peso*. Rumors were flying about American invasions in the Pacific, and the "funny money" would be worthless. Well, I needed the "funny money" to buy food for my children. I begged my family to give me their Philippine *pesos* to exchange for Japanese occupation money. I would divide the "funny money" profits with them.

Dealing in Philippine money exchanges was dangerous. The Japanese had confiscated a large amount of "thread" at the onset of the war. No one was allowed to have Philippine or U.S. currency in their possession. Several "thread" dealers were caught with currency sewn into their skirts or pants. They were arrested and tortured in public to make them reveal their sources. The small amount of "thread" I carried was rolled into "curlers" and hidden in my hair. After being told several horror stories, I stopped dealing in "thread," although it was profitable. I was thankful I was never caught.

≈≈

The rain was pelting against the glass in her kitchen door. Mary glanced through the raindrops to check the sky. Angry dark clouds were swirling high above her neighbor's roof, while the weathervane perched atop was spinning wildly. *I'd better check the weather report. There might be a tornado warning!* She stepped into the living room. Booger was curled up on the couch waiting. Her dog did not like thunderstorms and usually stayed in her lap…shivering each time a loud clap of thunder shook the windows. *It reminds me of typhoon season in Manila. I'm glad to be inside.*

"It's okay, Booger. It's okay," Mary murmured gently as she reached for her rosary, while Booger crawled into the safe haven of her lap.

CHAPTER 87

Terror, Tempers, and Torture

February 1944 dragged through our lives like soldiers returning from battle. The oppression of the Japanese authorities suffocated the tiny spark of hope we tried to keep alive. The constant struggle of making enough money to buy food while keeping the children focused on completing their chores, attending church services, and dealing with many unknowns took its toll. Depression fell over me like a heavy yoke…another burden I must overcome. My weakened condition plus the stressful situations all around us left me drained.

What was happening to Jess? Where was Bobby? Were they alive? When will we get relief? How will we survive? My cross was too heavy. My God, please help us!

All of these thoughts and many more plagued my emotions. I was short-tempered with the children and would sometimes take my frustrations out on them. When my emotional dam would burst, they would stare…frightened, as if seeing a stranger. They became withdrawn and silent around me, which only made me feel worse. All except Linnie who continued to hold her arms out to me. She was my innocent, unaware angel.

During one of my mother's visits, I screamed at Lucy. I berated her when the floors had not been cleaned before my mother's arrival. My dam burst.

"Keeping the house clean is your responsibility! Why were the floors not cleaned?"

"It was Mary Jane's turn to push the coconut husks over the floors to clean them. She left early to stand in a ration line today," Lucy explained with fear in her eyes.

"Why didn't you get Emma to take care of the floors?" I demanded.

"Emma was doing the laundry and I was washing the vegetables for our next meal," Lucy said calmly.

Her calm demeanor made me angrier. *Was this insolence?* I was moving toward Lucy with my upraised hand when *Mami's* stern voice stopped me.

"Nena, deja lo. No importa." (Baby girl…let it go. It's not important.)

Her sharp words returned me to my senses. I was making a mountain out of a molehill. I left the room to collect myself, and, as I did, *Mami* comforted Lucy.

"Your mother is not herself. She has many responsibilities weighing heavily on her mind. You must be strong. God will give you strength."

Lucy nodded her head and sat beside her grandmother, who comforted her. Lucy felt safe in *Mami's* arms. She needed a protector.

Hunger tends to diminish one's reasoning powers. Fear of death or torture becomes less ominous. The need for food overwhelms all the other needs of a human being. Only one thing matters…to have something to eat, no matter what.

During the first year of the Japanese occupation, a military encampment was built near our restricted area. We became accustomed to its presence in our midst, much as we had become used to seeing sentries at every major intersection. Everyone knew the Japanese had plentiful supplies of food in their encampments. Native workers at these encampments bragged about the amounts of food they took from the place as "garbage." While much of the food was garbage, some of it was in unopened canned goods. Smaller unopened cans were hidden inside larger, soiled opened cans. Most of the "garbage" was taken home for their families and friends; however, some managed to sell their "stolen" canned goods at the marketplace.

These natives were observed at the marketplace by a fifth columnist, a Japanese sympathizer, who knew he would be rewarded by providing information. When the workers returned to the encampment, they were arrested and tortured in public.

This torture took place on Aurora Quezon Boulevard alongside of our place in San Juan. Five young Filipino men were stripped of their clothing, "skewered" with a grid of bamboo poles (three vertical and three horizontal), and made to march by the roadside. A horizontal pole was placed across the groin; a second one across the small of their back (which pushed their bloated stomach forward); and the third at the front of their throat, extending across the shoulders. The vertical poles created the "grid" to which the horizontal poles were lashed with rope. Victims were made to march until they fell. As each fell, they were tied behind a Jap army truck and dragged along the highway until dead. Their remains, with bamboo grids still in place, were left by the roadside as a warning to others.

We faced these atrocities regularly until they became commonplace. In certain cases, they were friends or relatives. When the Japanese occupied the Philippines in 1941, our local veterinarian, Dr. Buencamino, asked his trusted chauffeur to help him hide his guns and knives, as all weapons were being confiscated by the Japanese. The chauffeur dug a pit at the base of the concrete steps. Dr. Buencamino placed his weapons in a metal case, which was placed inside a wooden crate. The contraband was buried. A large concrete slab was placed over the area, making the slab a part of the landing for the steps.

In 1944, Dr. Buencamino had hardly any business. Most of the cats, dogs and other animals he treated became food for the hungry. He would have an occasional *caretela* or carthorse to treat, and even those were becoming scarce as horsemeat was also being consumed along with water buffaloes. His vehicles had been confiscated during the early years of the Japanese Occupation. He no longer needed his chauffeur.

Offers of food and/or special privileges were made by the Japs to anyone who would provide information or report infractions of rules. The chauffeur, desperate to provide food for his family, reported the weapons buried by his former employer.

Dr. Buencamino was arrested. A rope was tied around his neck, and he was dragged behind an army truck all around the central business district for the public to see. The Imperial Japanese Military's rules must be followed. At the sight of our friend being dragged through the streets, leaving blood and pieces of flesh in its wake, I thought about the weapons Jess and I had buried in the chicken house. I was glad only he and I knew about their location. I prayed Jess would not be tortured to the point of revealing those secrets. I prayed Jess was still alive. My prayers continued all the way home from the central business district. I would not sell anymore today.

The following week, Peping arrived for our usual exchange of duties. He was troubled.

"Peping, what's wrong? Tell me."

"*Tita Nena*," he stammered, "I have sad news."

I steeled myself for his news. *Is Jess dead? Does he have news about Bobby? Is my mother dead? Is it about someone else in my family?* My heart was racing.

"*Tio* Gambe was arrested by the Japanese last week and was tortured."

José Gambe, my cousin, was the caretaker of one of the lighthouses in Manila Bay.

"What did José do? Why was he tortured? Is he dead?" I spoke in a low voice as the children were within earshot.

"He is still alive but not well. He was accused of having information about enemy (American) troops near his lighthouse. He was taken to Japanese headquarters and interrogated. They stripped him, hung him by his thumbs, burned his legs with their cigarettes, and kept asking him to tell them what he was doing with American soldiers at his lighthouse. He kept denying those accusations, as they kept repeating the same questions. When he asked for water, they urinated on him. They kept him for two days before they released him, although he was a Spanish citizen."

None of this information could be repeated. It was dangerous to have information and even worse to repeat it. The walls had ears. We all were at the mercy of the Japanese or the invisible Fifth Columnists. No one was exempt.

Fear was a constant companion. Evidence of tortured souls surrounded us. The Japanese made certain their messages were delivered. They knew many of the people attended church and set up their "stocks" in front of churches where their victims' were bolted into those racks and their heads were sawed off in public for all to see their blood spilled, and hear their screams echo through the sanctuary. Others were stripped of their clothing and tied to trees or utility poles while the Japs allowed their attack dogs to do their damage. Different forms of water torture were also on display…many too gory to describe.

Mary rubbed the back of her neck to work out the stiffness. Arthritis had settled in her spine and was painful. *Nothing like the pain my poor cousin, José, must have felt when those Japs tortured him.* She learned later José had seen several Americans who were separated from their group. He hid them in the lighthouse, helping them escape after the Japanese patrol left. How strong he was. He knew he would be tortured. *I must light a candle for him at church tonight.*

CHAPTER 88

An Eggshell Existence

The lack of food was very serious by June 1944. We had experienced considerable weight loss, edema, and muscle weakness. Many around us were dealing with paresthesia and beriberi. Anything edible was eaten...from insects to weeds. Water was boiled before drinking because the Japs made a habit of tossing bodies of their tortured victims into the rivers...our local water supply. Sewage from their nearby encampment spilled over the adjoining property for local rains to wash their excrement into nearby rivers. Sanitation did not matter to the Japanese. They had other interests.

"Comfort Women," who had been recruited by the Japanese under false pretenses, roamed the streets like zombies searching for their lost souls. Many young Filipino and Asian girls were enticed into prostitution for the Japanese military with promises of money, jobs, and/or a continuing supply of food. These "women" were at the disposal of all Japanese soldiers. When meeting a Japanese soldier in public, she opened her kimono, revealed her naked body, and engaged in sexual activity. The "comfort woman" pulled the kimono's sides over his arms as a "discreet" screen. They moved from one encounter to another giving "comfort" to Jap soldiers. My only recourse was to turn my head and walk away. I later learned, if they became pregnant, their abdomens were slashed open and they were left to bleed to death. Many were given sterilization shots to prevent pregnancy. If they tried to escape, they were found, tortured, and killed.

With a scarcity of food, our drinking water compromised, and rampant sex and crime on the streets, it was impossible to sell anything to make money. We had to survive on what was around us.

Junior and Mary Jane had been observing a fresh mound of dirt growing each day beside the fishpond in our back yard. They wondered what might be building the mound, and provided daily reports at the dinner table.

"Mom, I'm going to see if I can trap whatever is building that mysterious mound. Maybe it will be something we can eat for my birthday!" Junior exclaimed.

A trap was devised and the plan set into place later that evening. He wakened early to check the trap. He and Mary Jane ran to the pond. A large, angry iguana was trapped...his heavy, meaty tail lashing back and forth. They were afraid to get close.

Peping arrived and helped them drag their catch toward the house. He was amused at the antics of two scrawny kids helping him pull the heavy trap with all their might. The iguana made hissing sounds, and they jumped. Its tail flipped from side-to-side, and the loose flap of skin under its neck waved like a distress flag. Junior was proud of his trophy.

"Well, I see you have captured your birthday dinner!" I teased.

Peping grabbed the trap and lifted it gingerly, as the iguana was still lashing back and forth. He placed the trap under the guava tree by the front steps for viewing.

Everyone gathered around the trapped iguana. Questions popped like popcorn in a hot skillet.

"Are we going to eat it?" Emma asked...hoping the answer would be in the negative.

"Sure, we will eat it," I answered. "Iguanas are clean. They eat tiny fish and water plants. This one is huge. It's over two feet long...plenty of meat for all of us. Let's go inside while Peping and Junior prepare the iguana for cooking."

Junior was pleased as I served his "catch." Bits of the iguana were boiled in coconut milk with chopped banana shoots. The others were not sure about this exotic concoction. They all watched me as I took the first few bites.

"Tastes like chicken," I announced as I chewed the small bits of meat.

It had an odd aftertaste, but I said nothing. It was food.

Hunger pushes reason out of one's mind. This was our meal,...Junior's birthday dinner. We would eat it or be hungrier. The children followed my example.

The next day Junior, who had eaten several servings, vomited several times. *Perhaps he had overeaten. His body was no longer accustomed to large amounts of food, especially meat.* I became concerned when the vomiting did not stop. While I was with Junior downstairs, I heard similar sounds coming from upstairs. Emma and Mary Jane were vomiting.

Peping arrived the next morning, bringing *Mami* for a visit. When I told her what was happening, she was horrified.

"If the bile from the iguana spills over its meat, it can be poisonous!"

Peping ducked his head. The bile duct had burst when he pulled out the iguana's entrails. He thought he had washed it all off.

"I'm sorry, *Tita Nena*," he stated. "I thought I had washed the meat well, but the bile must have tainted the meat. Vomiting should get rid of the poison."

I made sure everyone had plenty of boiled water to drink. I also put a slice of *calamancit* (lemon/lime) in the water to help them get the awful taste from their mouths.

Since the only way I had of communicating with Jess was by writing letters or postcards mailed through the postal service, I prepared one of the three remaining postcards and decided to mail to Jess the next week. The iguana incident was not mentioned. Jess, if alive, did not need to hear his children had ingested tainted iguana meat. He had other worries. I remembered his whispered words about being able to get Red Cross packages through the Spanish Embassy. If I received a reply, he would be still alive. I worded the postcard carefully.

June 27, 1944

Jess — We are all well. You may send things to us through Embassy — glad you are well. Children are doing o.k.

Mary G. Hodges

Mr. Jesse Allen Hodges
Philippine Internment
   Camp No. I
(Santo Tomas)
Manila

After signing my name, Mary G. Hodges, I slipped it under my pillow before retiring for the night. I hoped it would give me peace of mind. I had no peace in my heart.

Two weeks later, I prepared a birthday card for the children to sign. I mailed it to Jess for his birthday…the last day of July. I needed to keep sending mail to him. My nerves were shattered. A note from Jess would provide a glimmer of hope for us all.

In early August, three Japanese soldiers knocked at our door before breakfast. Two were holding rifles with fixed bayonets. The one in the middle, an officer, held his hand on the curved saber hanging by his left side. My heart beat rapidly. He scanned our posted list of registered occupants before speaking. I felt myself trembling and tried to steel myself.

"Mrs. Hodges, your husband is dead and we need you to claim his body."

I was speechless and stared at his mouth…not believing his words. *This cannot be! This cannot be!*

"You must come with us immediately."

I stumbled into the living room and rushed to the girls' bedroom. They were still asleep. I reached Lucy's bed, touched her shoulder, and whispered my instructions.

"I have to go. I'll return when I can. You can fix breakfast for everyone when they waken."

I grabbed my small purse and left before she started asking questions. The reason for my absence was not to be divulged…not yet.

I was taken to military headquarters where lengthy interrogations began. Each time I would ask about Jess, they would ask a different question. They asked if I knew of subversive activity against the Japanese in our area. Had I been in contact with guerillas? Had I helped anyone to do subversive activity? The questions seemed endless, with no respite and no information about Jess.

I prayed silently between responding to questions. If, by chance, I uttered a prayer aloud, they would slap my face. By the end of the day, I was confined in a room with several other women...all were terrified, as I was.

The next day brought more questions. Was I a Spanish citizen or an American sympathizer? Most of the questions were inane. It became difficult to focus. When I asked to have the question repeated, I was slapped again and my glasses were knocked from my face. When I tried to retrieve my glasses, they were kicked into a corner. I lost control. I put my hands over my eyes and sobbed. They left me alone for another night. No food or water was provided...just the anticipation of more questions.

After two days, they released me. I was relieved, but the question of Jess' condition had not been answered. I did not dare raise the subject. I would go home to check on the children and pray for Jess. As I returned to San Juan, I passed by three poor souls who had been tied to utility poles and left to die. *Praise God, I am still alive. I pray my children are safe. I prayed for the families of those poor souls I had just passed.*

I was home with my children...laughing, crying, and lying about what happened. I did not want them to worry. I explained the bruises on my face were caused by a fall when I tripped over a rock in the road (Lie # 1). I told them I was okay and their daddy was fine (Lie #2...I had no idea how he was.). I stopped chattering when I noticed Peping's face. He appeared distraught.

"Peping, is something wrong?" I asked.

"I'll discuss it with you later," Peping said as he averted his eyes.

His news was not for the children's ears. I waited until they were outside doing their chores before I confronted him.

"Tell me what happened," I demanded.

"You knew *Tita* Charing was sick before those Japs took you away," Peping stated.

"Yes, how is she?" I prompted.

"She died yesterday," he stated. "She had no medicine to help her fight the pneumonia. She was weak from lack of food."

I rested on the overstuffed sofa. My mind was racing with all the questions I needed to ask, but the words would not come. I felt numb and overwhelmed by all the recent events. My sister, Rosario (Charing) was dead. *God give me strength.*

"I must go to see Maming at her convent," I whispered. "Tell the children I will return before curfew."

At the *Colegio de la Consolacion,* Maming and I shared strong hugs when I entered. Two other sisters, Lucing and Consueling were waiting for my arrival before preparing Charing's body for burial in the family mausoleum. We had no money for a funeral. I joined them in dressing Charing in one of Maming's habits. Charing was never a nun, but she had dedicated her life, at her father's request, to care for her brother, Rev. Gamero, and his work at The Cathedral of Our Lady of Peace at Antipolo. We had buried him in late 1940, after his bout with pneumonia. Charing was with him until the end. She had fulfilled her father's request in an admirable way and served her brother until his death. *Thank God he did not live to see the horrors of war destroy his parish and church in Antipolo.*

By the end of August, I had received a reply from Jess. *He was alive! Those Japs tricked me to try and get information. I gave none.*

Jess wrote he was sending a package to us via the Spanish Embassy and he was well. *Was he "well," or was he trying to lift my spirits? Were we playing the same game?*

I gathered the children and announced their daddy had sent presents. I watched the excitement build before I stated it was a package being held at the Spanish Embassy. I would go the next day to retrieve it.

"Maybe this will be an early Christmas," I said as cheerily as I could.

"Come on, finish your chores. It's nearly bedtime."

The next day, when Peping arrived, I left for the Spanish Embassy. Before I was allowed to get the package, I had to provide necessary identification and sign the proper forms. I was handed a large package wrapped in brown paper and adorned with Red Cross symbols on each side.

The children were waiting at the gate, except for Linnie, who was taking a nap. When I entered carrying the large package, they grew excited. I handed it to Peping, who placed it on the dining table. The children rushed to their places...each chattering to the other.

"Wait, have we forgotten our prayers?" I inquired.

They clasped their hands and bowed their heads in preparation. We gave thanks for the package sent from The Red Cross and for Jess. All heads raised and all eyes gazed at the one large box in anticipation. They were ready for their "early Christmas." I had no idea what the box contained. Opening the box, I saw several small packages inside.

"Okay, enjoy your gifts," I announced.

Junior undid the string around his, unfolded the brown paper, and opened the box. Inside was a pair of brown gloves. He slipped one on, and shrugged his shoulders before he spoke.

"I guess I can use these to work in the garden."

He tried to hide his disappointment. He knew I was trying my best to be cheerful and did not want to spoil the mood for others.

Lucy opened her package neatly. Her box contained a scarf. She folded it, returned it to its box, and smiled. Emma and Mary Jane were tearing theirs open. Emma, who was merging into her teenage years, laughed as she pulled a Shirley Temple paper doll out of her box. The doll was a part of a "book" with pages of paper "clothing" to be cut out on the dotted lines. The variety of "clothing" delighted Emma.

"How did they find out I was 'Shirley Temple of the Philippines'?"

"They must have heard about your singing on the radio," I teased.

Mary Jane hugged a Jane Withers doll and gave it a kiss. She was quite happy to have a new doll, although none of us had any idea who Jane Withers was. We only knew about Japanese propaganda.

Joyce also hugged her cute baby doll. She was excited.

"Look, look! I have a baby!"

Linnie, who had been wakened from her nap, had already returned to sleep in my arms. Since we were all tired, we each slipped quietly to our rooms to prepare for another day…another day of not knowing. At least we had today. We had shared one happy moment…and Jess was alive.

Sadly, I had to sell Mary Jane's doll in October to buy food. It was hard, but I think she understood. Mary glanced at the kitchen clock and realized she only had thirty minutes to prepare for vespers. She fixed food for Booger, to keep the dog occupied while she slipped out the kitchen door.

CHAPTER 89

Danger and Despair

Tension and fear permeated our lives, as the Japanese were stricter and more invasive with their inspections. If three or more persons were together in a public area during the day, Japanese soldiers would isolate them and interrogate each. If individual answers did not coincide, they would be taken and tortured. Public gatherings were out of the question.

Japanese propaganda about their conquests was promoted on their radio broadcasts, the local newspapers, and on large posters hung prominently along the major avenues of Manila. They were attempting to convince the public that the Japanese were winning the war. One poster on Taft Avenue boasted of their occupation of Australia. We had no way of knowing what was fact and what was fiction.

I tried to ignore the propaganda and put my faith in God. The children and I practiced our habit of nightly prayers. We found peace and consolation in those rituals.

On September 14, 1944, before I recited my rosary, I took my last postcard out of my nightstand drawer and wrote to Jess. Perhaps I would get another reply.

```
                  Sept. 14, 1944

Dear Jess:

        We are all well and getting
along o.k. Received the bundle thru Embassy.
Hoping you are well. Love from all.

                              Mary G. Hodges
```

I tucked the postcard under my pillow, reached for my rosary and recited my prayers. My thoughts were on Jess the whole time. I hoped God would forgive me.

The next day, I began my usual morning ritual of boiling cracked wheat in pre-boiled water for the children's breakfast. The cracked wheat was infested with mealworms. Those mealworms were a gift of protein. The children learned to eat what was placed in front of them. Hunger makes one learn to eat anything.

After Peping arrived, I grabbed my shopping bag and left for the market. I was careful in selling the goods I carried, making sure to show items only one person at a time. A gathering of three or more was not allowed. I wished to avoid questioning by the Japanese. I protected my customers. After a long day of walking and standing, I decided to ride one of the *carreteras* (horse rig) home. It was getting late and I did not want to risk being attacked, robbed, and/or killed. A *calesa* was at the corner. The ride to San Juan cost one hundred *pesos*. I paid the driver and took the nearest seat. The rig was the safest and quickest option.

At the next corner, the driver stopped, as usual, to allow riders to step down from the rig, bow before the sentry, pass inspection, and remount the rig. Two soldiers were standing beside the sentry on duty, and they decided to ride the rig. Their camp was near our restricted area. They did not have to pay as all Japanese military were given free passage on all types of transportation. I was uncomfortable with them facing me in the opposite seat. They stared at me...making me more uncomfortable. I diverted my eyes and stared at my swollen feet.

"America?" One of them grunted at me.

"No, no...*Spaniska*," I replied using the term the Japanese called the Spanish.

The other soldier grunted at his partner. He appeared to be Korean, as he had a full beard and did not understand the Japanese term *Spaniska*. His partner tried to explain the term. He grunted his response before leaving me alone.

After making all the usual stops to bow to each of the sentries (while the Jap soldiers remained on board arguing), the rig arrived at Punaglabang, the area of their encampment, and the soldiers left. I breathed a sigh of relief after bowing to the sentry and resuming my trip. I was anxious for the rig to stop at the next corner of Santo Domingo and J. Ruiz, where Peping would be waiting. I stepped from the rig, bowed, waited for his "grunt of approval" before glancing around. Peping was not there. I became nervous. I was late. He had already left for his home to make curfew. I hurried to 43 J. Ruiz and hoped my children were safe. Thank God, all was well. They had already eaten their bowl of soupy rice and were at the table waiting for my return for the ritual of our nightly prayers.

"I'm glad you saved this food for me, but I've already eaten," I lied as I took the bowl of soupy rice they saved for me and divided it among them.

They scraped every bit from their bowls. I kept smiling and chatting about my day while asking questions about theirs. Linnie crawled down from her chair and pulled herself into my lap. Hugging her made me forget my hunger. I felt contentment, but it was the lull before the storm.

On September 21, 1944, the Americans initiated air raids of Manila Bay. The early morning raids roused everyone. The children swarmed around my bed chattering like a flock of scared birds.

"Run!" I shouted.

I grabbed my bag of emergency supplies and crawled down the rickety back stairs. We swatted mosquitoes as we entered the dark, damp space and took our usual places on the "benches" Jess had carved from the earthen pit. We hoped no snakes were inside as before. We waited and listened. After the roar of plane engines, strafing, or bombing subsided, I eased out of the shelter to check conditions before allowing the others to emerge. We had been spared once again.

Someone knocked at the door. Mary rose from her writing and peeked out the window. A new car was parked in her driveway. She tiptoed and peered through the tiny peephole. She saw only the top of a man's hat.

"Who is it?" Mary called.

"It's Father McCallum. May I come in?"

Mary undid the chain and welcomed her priest into the living room.

"Come in. All I could see was the top of your hat," Mary said.

They chatted about his new car, before he explained the reason for his visit.

"The newspaper is sending a photographer to take a picture of the statue in front of our church for the Lenten season," Father McCallum stated. "I wanted you in the photo, Mary. Will you come?"

"Of course I will," Mary replied. "I'll come right away."

Mary Gamero Hodges and Msgr. McCallum adimiring the statue in front of St. Williams Catholic Church in Greenville, Texas.

CHAPTER 90

Dealing With Despair

The American air raid of Manila Bay and other Japanese military installations heralded the beginning of surprise attacks by the United States military in their quest to liberate the Philippines. Where we had some semblance of routine in our daily lives before September 21, 1944, we now had suspense. We must be ready at all times...day or night...for these unexpected raids. We had survived the Japanese occupation of the Philippines. We hoped to survive our liberation. Our destiny was in the hands of God.

The children were eating their usual bowl of boiled cracked wheat (mealworms and all) when the bell at the front gate rang. *Oh, no! I hope it is not another inspection by the Japs.* The children froze in their seats as I investigated. A young Spanish woman was waiting and sobbing. I glanced up and down J. Ruiz. *Was she part of a group trying to entrap us?*

"*Buenos dias,*" I said in Spanish. "*Que quieres aqui?*"

"*Yo soy Gloria Sanchez. Me puedes ayudar?*" (I am Gloria Sanchez. Can you help me?)

She spoke rapidly. She had passed by every day and noticed we had several fruit trees. She had no money, but she needed food, as she had not eaten in three days. She was due to deliver her first child soon. As she broke into deep sobs, I relented, opened the small door in the gate and asked her in. Something about her tore at my heartstrings. I sensed she was desperate.

Once inside our dining room, I had her take my seat at the table while the children all watched silently with inquiring eyes at this stranger in their midst. I picked up a wooden bowl and handed it to Lucy.

"Would each of you please share at least one spoonful of your breakfast with this lady?" I asked. "She has not eaten for three days."

The bowl was passed around the table and each one shared a part of their breakfast with this stranger. Lucy handed the bowl to me and I placed it in front of *Señora* Sanchez. She thanked them all in Spanish and ate every bit of the cracked wheat...the mealworms did not phase her. After she put down the bowl, she thanked us all again.

"I am thankful for your help. The Japanese killed my husband when they took our house. They took houses all around their encampment because more of their troops are coming in from the provinces and their camps are full."

I listened quietly. *Should I believe her story? Perhaps she was a Fifth Columnist and was trying to get information to sell to the Japs.* We waited for her to finish.

"I have no place to go," Gloria moaned. "What shall I do?"

She sobbed harder. I tried calming her as I told the children to begin their chores.

"My sister lives next door to a midwife in Santa Mesa," I stated. "I can take you with me as I go to sell my items today, if you think you can walk there. You can rest in our living room until my nephew comes to supervise the children."

Peping arrived, and I explained the situation to him. I was taking her to a midwife who lived next to his mother. Gloria and I left for Santa Mesa. We took our time, as she was not able to walk fast. I hoped and prayed she would not give birth on the way.

We arrived at Consueling's house. I explained Gloria's situation to my sister and she summoned the midwife. After I spoke with the midwife, she agreed to let Gloria stay at her place. She could remain after her baby was born and help with the housework. Gloria agreed. She had no other choice.

When Peping arrived the next week to stay with the children, he told me Gloria had given birth to a tiny baby boy. There was a problem. Gloria was not able to nurse her baby, but fate stepped in. This midwife had taken in a young Filipina, who had been raped and impregnated by Japanese soldiers. She had given birth the same day. She had plenty of breast milk and agreed to nurse Gloria's baby. *God works in strange ways.*

On my next selling trip to Santa Mesa, I stopped to see Consueling, after selling my items at the market. Gloria saw me walk into my sister's house and rushed over with her baby boy…swaddled in a torn bed sheet. *She has no clothes for her baby.* She put her son in my arms and thanked me again for my help. Her next words took me by surprise.

"Will you be my son's godmother?" Gloria asked. "You have been so generous, and I wish to honor you in this manner."

I agreed to make the arrangements with the priest at our church and tell her when they were completed. I made a mental note to get Bobby's christening gown and his baby clothes. *I would bring those to her on my next trip to Santa Mesa.*

I wasted no time in making all the arrangements for the coming week, as the bombings were occurring more often. The future was unknown. I brought Gloria the baby clothes and Bobby's christening gown. She was elated.

"What name shall be given to this child?" Father Gomez asked.

"Robert Luis Sanchez," Gloria replied. "I want my baby to have the first name of Mrs. Hodges' first son."

I smiled and nodded. Bobby would have been pleased.

One month later, the Angel of Death took Robert Sanchez away. The young

Filipina who had been nursing him had placed her bastard son in an orphanage and returned to the provinces, where there were fewer Japanese. There was no milk for young Robert, and Gloria was unable to feed him.

 I stopped by my sister's home before helping Gloria dress her poor son. Bobby's christening gown became his burial robe. We took the baby to the pauper's cemetery and buried the child at the foot of his father's grave. This tiny angel would meet his father in heaven.

◈

Mary put her pen down. Her heart felt heavy, just as it was on the fateful day they buried tiny Robert. *We cannot reason why events happen. Sometimes it is difficult to see God's plan, but we must never question it or lose hope.*

CHAPTER 91

Misery Everywhere

By October 1944, misery swept through the countryside like a horde of locusts. The hollowed faces of the people told the story. Additional Japanese troops were funneled into better homes surrounding their military encampment. With no warning, the Japanese ousted many of our neighbors and took over their homes. Five of our neighbors' homes were occupied by Japanese troops. I thanked God our place was an old farmhouse in disrepair, with an adjoining henhouse. I prayed they would not like it.

On October 3, it rained hard, or as Jess would say "rained cats and dogs." Our roof, riddled by shrapnel, was like a sieve. We had just finished strategically placing pots, pans, and other containers to catch the rainwater, as we had done many times before. We were shocked when four Japanese soldiers, led by an officer, opened our living room door and stepped inside. We waited, as was the protocol, until we were given instructions or were asked questions. We watched as they inspected each room. One flipped the light switch with no result. We had not been able to afford electricity or gas…for over two years. A half-full glass of water with a lighted wick suspended in floating coconut oil was our only lighting.

The rain dripping into containers scattered about on the floor, the dining table and chairs, plus the rickety stairs at the back door, caused them to shake their heads. Their parting remarks made me happy.

"Oh, no. No good," The officer muttered.

I breathed a sigh of relief. They did not want our place. I was glad. Then, the large chicken house drew their interest. They wanted a closer inspection. They moved outside and entered the chicken house. After checking the building, they decided it could be used to store drums of gasoline. The "enemy" would never bomb a chicken house. *Dear Lord, our air raid shelter is right next to the chicken house!* They left to make arrangements to transfer the gasoline.

I was beside myself. I alternated between worrying and praying the rest of the day. *I could not go to sell goods today. I must remove all the weapons Jess and I had buried in the chicken house. What if the Japanese tried to clean out the chicken droppings or level the dirt floor? What if they found those weapons?*

After the children were asleep, I slipped downstairs. I wakened Junior gently, and told him what we had to do. I made him promise not to tell anyone. As I prayed silently, we moved quietly to find the "buried contraband." Jess' shotgun, the bolo knives, BB guns, and toy pistols…all metal objects we had buried at the onset of this war were rusty and useless. Under the cover of darkness, Junior and I tossed the "rusty remains" into our small fishpond.

Our task completed, we returned quietly to bed. *Thank God we did not have a late night inspection by the Japanese. Angels were watching over us.*

The next day, Mary Cuzner, Emma and Mary Jane's piano teacher, appeared at our front gate. She was distressed.

"Mary, the Japs took our home yesterday…furniture and all."

"I am sorry," I responded. "Please come in."

"No, I do not have time. I just wanted to bring this sheet music I managed to save for your girls. I must return to my mother. We have been given a room at the convent where your sister is the Sister Superior," Mary stated. "I must go as Mother has taken ill with this terrible blow. She was already consumed with worry about my father."

I thanked her and told her I would pray for her and her mother. The girls would miss her as they enjoyed taking free piano lessons from her. She taught them out of the goodness of her heart. Her father, Harold Cuzner, was also a prisoner in Santo Tomas.

We waited anxiously for the arrival of the drums of gasoline, but, thankfully, none were brought to our chicken house for storage, yet. Perhaps they had found a better place for their gasoline storage. I prayed to God this would be true.

Peping arrived with terrible news. The Japanese had occupied Cullion Island, the government leper colony, and released all of the lepers to roam the streets of Manila. They wanted Cullion Island as a vantage point in the defense of Manila against American forces. Most of the lepers were begging for food on the streets. It was heartbreaking.

More and more of the elderly and young native children resorted to begging on the streets. When I went to do my selling at the market place, I passed young children on the sidewalk scantily clad or naked, their legs and stomachs swollen from beriberi. Some of the poor children were already dead…lying on the sidewalks. Old men squatted against utility poles, holding an empty piece of coconut shell in their outstretched hands…begging for money. Several of these poor souls were already dead…slumped like a puppet with no strings…their coconut shells filled with Japanese paper money, usually one-*centavo* pieces. The authorities left them for a couple of days hoping their relatives would claim their bodies, but no one did. Burials were expensive. Filipino authorities wrapped the corpses in *sawali* mats and disposed of them…either in a pyre or a river. We became accustomed to seeing corpses in the area and braced ourselves for the unknown. We were numb…desensitized to death around us. *The Lord giveth and The Lord taketh away.*

Mary pulled off her heavy glasses and rubbed her eyes. *Dear God, please help me finish my writing project. The more I remember and write, the more difficult it becomes. It is like living through those terrible times again.*

The ringing of the phone jarred Mary's concentration. She ambled over to answer it. It was Linnie.

"Hi, it's me," Linnie said. "I'm going to buy groceries and called to see what you needed."

Mary had to collect her thoughts before giving her reply.

"Well, I need sugar, instant coffee and cocoa," Mary replied.

"I'll be there shortly," Linnie replied.

Mary was thankful Linnie would be coming to see her. Linnie was the child who never had a childhood. She had survived being a "war baby" and became one of the sweetest persons. God had blessed her with this child and those blessings multiplied. Linnie was always ready to help. She had a positive outlook on life. When conditions appeared negative, Linnie was always supportive. Her smile and Christian lifestyle reached many.

CHAPTER 92

Risks and Realities

By early October 1944, many of those facing starvation and disease attacked Japanese soldiers in public hoping the Japs would kill them and end their misery. Japanese authorities decided to provide a block system of rationing stations in the city and its surrounds. They learned that deprivation and starvation led to rioting by Filipinos. Since the Filipinos outnumbered the Japanese, they chose to ration food to calm the people.

One person per household was allowed to stand in line to receive rations. A copy of the certified list of registered occupants for their specific address must be presented to receive rations. Distribution of those rations began early each morning and continued until thirty minutes before curfew or until all the rations for the day were depleted. I was taking items to sell at three different marketplaces in order to earn a decent commission and could not lose one day in a ration line. Mary Jane was already assigned to get what parts she could when animals were butchered at the Japs' slaughterhouse. She was also the only one old enough to stand in line for rations and, hopefully, not be raped by Japanese. Mary Jane would have to take on the extra duty. We needed those weekly rations. She walked with our neighbor, Max Kessel, or one of his family members.

Mary Jane might bring something home from her day of standing in line or bring nothing at all. Rations would vary from one tin of canned fish and one-half cup of uncooked rice; or, a gallon jug of vinegar diluted with water; or, two yards of brightly colored outing; or, a half-pound of dried beans. The certified list Mary Jane presented would receive an "official dated stamp" on the back each time rations were issued. We were thankful for anything. If the rationed item were something we could not use, I would try to sell it.

During the second week of October, Lucy, Mary Jane and I walked to my sister, Lucing's, home. Lucy and Emma needed new blouses, as their bodies were developing. I had some fabric and felt Lucing could make blouses for them. We were able to get a ride on a jitney, a type of transportation contraption with two long benches so riders faced each other in the back of a truck. The makeshift cover for the passengers was a wooden frame covered with either a fitted canvas covering or *sawali* tacked to the frame. There was room for only one more passenger after we boarded. At the next stop, a very inebriated Jap officer staggered on board. He plopped onto the bench beside Mary Jane, who was sitting next to me, and he faced Lucy. He looked at her and wobbled as his one-sided smile grew wider exposing his widely spaced front teeth. He began pointing at Lucy and babbling something to her in his slurred speech. Suddenly, he leaned toward her and put his hand on her leg.

"No, no," I spoke quickly as I shook my head side to side and pointed to Lucy, *"Spaniska, Spaniska."*

He wobbled back and forth in his seat, gave me a bleary-eyed look, grunted, and kept his hand on Lucy's leg. She was terrified and looked as if she could burst into tears.

I reached across and pushed his hand off her leg and repeated my earlier statement about being Spanish. He looked rather surprised and started to react when I pushed hard against Mary Jane causing the drunken Jap to fall off as the jitney came to a stop. I yelled at the driver in *Tagalog* to hurry and drive away while holding onto Mary Jane, who was terrified. Lucy's face turned very pale. The driver chastised me for my actions. He was afraid we would all be killed, and we could have been, for the Jap was wearing two side arms. We got off at the next stop and walked the rest of the way to Lucing's home. My heart was beating wildly…Lucy still looked ashen. Mary Jane kept looking behind us…hoping the drunken fool wasn't around. We hurried to Lucing's.

Early on October 20, the bell at our gate kept ringing. I scurried to see who was creating such a clatter. Mrs. Harris, our neighbor, burst into sobs as I approached the gate. As I opened the gate to let her in, she began talking between sobs.

"Mary, I need your help. The Japanese are going to execute my husband!"

I gave her a hug. She was trembling and continued sobbing.

"Come in while I get dressed. I'll put the coffee on." (Our "coffee" was made from unidentifiable wild beans roasted over our outside fire pit. It was not the "real thing" but would suffice.)

The children were still asleep. I roused Lucy and asked her to prepare coffee, while I dressed. Lucy made sure Mrs. Harris had her coffee and brought me a cup, as well.

"I'm going with Mrs. Harris to help her with a problem. We will go to The Philippine Red Cross to see Lt. Kato," I told Lucy as we left. "Peping will be here soon."

Upon our arrival at The Philippine Red Cross, I asked to speak to Lt. Kato, the Japanese officer who had befriended Jess and me earlier. Perhaps he could write a note to the camp commandant on Mrs. Harris' behalf. We waited for about thirty minutes before we were ushered into his office. He came from behind his desk as we entered.

"Good Morning, Mrs. Hodges. What brings you here so early?' Kato asked.

"Mrs. Harris has received word her husband is to be executed. Would you please write a request to the camp commandant to allow her to see him? I will go with her to Santo Tomas," I stated.

Mrs. Harris, trembling beside me, was terrified of being near Japanese. Lt. Kato stared at Mrs. Harris, rose from his chair, and paced back and forth behind his desk.

"Her request would be denied. She will not be allowed to see her husband," Kato said. "I do not know why he is being punished, but since he has been sentenced, he is guilty and must suffer the consequences. Take this note to the camp commandant. I doubt anything from me will change his decision."

He scribbled Japanese characters on a sheet of paper...top to bottom...right to left, as he spoke. When he finished, he folded it, and handed it to me, as Mrs. Harris covered her face with her hands and moaned softly.

"Thank you, Mr. Kato. At least we will have tried," I replied as I took the note and guided Mrs. Harris out the door.

I hailed a *calesa*, because Mrs. Harris was, understandably, in an emotional state. After boarding and paying our fare, we sat quietly listening to the "click clack" of the horse's hooves on the paved streets, and watched the driver guide his ragged rig skillfully through the busy streets. Upon our arrival at Santo Tomas, I took her arm and guided her to the sentry at the front gate. I repeated the words "camp commandant" several times and showed him the note addressed to the commandant, so he could understand. Finally, we were allowed to enter and followed another Jap soldier to the Education Building. We entered an outer office on the first floor, where an unkempt Jap officer, possibly an aide to the commandant, sat behind a small desk and grunted to us as we walked in. I approached his desk and held out the note Lt. Kato had given me as he stood. After giving it a cursory glance, he grunted, and disappeared into an inner office. We stood and waited about ten minutes for his return, before being "grunted and motioned" into the commandant's office. The stern-faced lieutenant colonel remained seated as we stood in front of his cluttered desk. He was holding Mr. Kato's note. He did not speak. He turned the note over as he put it down on his desk, and wrote his set of characters on the back. It all looked like so much chicken scratching in the sand. When he finished, he returned it to me and dismissed us with a wave of his hand.

Since neither of us could read the note or its response, we returned as quickly as possible to Lt. Kato's office. He was busy, but took five minutes to see us. I handed him the note. His face turned dark as he read it. He was frowning as he spoke.

"Note is trouble. Has question: *'Are you Japanese or American? Mr. Harris caught with note of American military action. Could only come from guerilla*,'" Kato stated, as he threw the note away. Our meeting was over...our efforts—futile.

Mrs. Harris crumbled before my eyes. *Her only son was tortured to death for passing short wave news in camp during the first year...now her husband would be executed.* I put my arm around her and helped her out of the building onto the sidewalk along Taft Avenue. Nothing more could be done. I guided her gingerly around two old men sitting on the sidewalk begging for money with their outstretched coconut shell halves. Once proud men were now beggars. When we reached the corner, I flagged a passing *calesa* for the trip back to San Juan. Mrs. Harris could no longer walk.

In mid-October, I was awakened in the night by sounds of distant thunder. I crawled out from under the tattered mosquito netting and peeked through the wooden louvers. An eerie glow filled the southeastern sky. *Bombing was in progress…locations unknown.* The faint rumblings of explosions were constant. The bombing was not loud enough to waken the kids. They had learned to ignore distant noises. I returned to bed and reached for my rosary.

The next morning, Peping arrived with a big grin on his face.

"Did you see the sky last night, *Tita Nena?*"

"Yes, I did," I replied. "The rumbling noise brought me to my feet and I peeked through the louvers. What was going on?"

"The Americans bombed the Jap ships in the Gulf of Leyte last night!" Peping said excitedly. "MacArthur and his troops will be here soon."

"*Quieta te!* The rumors might frighten the kids," I whispered hoarsely, as I walked outside to our fire pit to begin breakfast.

"It's not a rumor," Peping stated, as he followed behind me. "MacArthur said he was returning. He is on his way. He is keeping his promise."

I shook my head in disbelief, threw some small sticks into the fire pit, lit the paper under the kindling, and put the water on to boil for our morning *lugao* (soupy rice). *Will MacArthur return?* I did not want to raise my hopes and have them dashed again. The small spark of hope inside me grew like the little spark that ignited the flame in our fire pit. I whispered a silent prayer as I stirred the watery rice. *God, deliver us from evil.*

With November fast approaching, I searched for items to sell as Christmas gifts. Filipinos who collaborated with the Japanese had become wealthy and would need gift items for their children. Most of the department stores still in business had meager supplies. Most of their merchandise was made in Japan. I asked Mary Jane to give me her Jane Withers doll. I could sell the new doll, since it was an American product, at a good price and buy food. She was sad to lose her new doll, but knew we needed food.

When I showed the doll to one of my friends, Marita Salanga, she thought the doll would be perfect for her daughter. She despised the Japanese and was delighted to have an American-made doll for her daughter. She had some used baby toys her children had outgrown and asked me to sell them. The Salangas lived over their small grocery store about two blocks away from our area. I could count on them to have some money to buy from me. During my selling trips, I was always glad to see their little grocery store, because it meant I was almost home. I would never forget their kindess.

Toys were collected by my sisters and taken to my oldest sister, Maming, at the convent, and I would put as many as I could carry into my shopping bag to sell them at the marketplace. A few of the toys would be gifts for my children. I kept an airplane for Joyce, a truck for Linnie, a small ceramic baby doll for Lucy,

Lucy Hodges wearing a gown given to Mary Gamero Hodges by Mary Cuzner. Photo taken at Sun Studio, May 1945.

and a well-worn doll for Mary Jane...with a slightly soiled cloth body, plus face, arms and legs made from cardboard. One hundred *pesos* were tucked away for Junior and Emma to buy their own gifts. A black and gold lace evening gown was a special surprise for Lucy. Mary Cuzner managed to salvage this lovely gown and one other when the Japs confiscated her home. Lucy would be delighted.

On November 14, I was trying to make it home from my day of selling to sing *Happy Birthday* to Joyce on her seventh birthday. Curfew was approaching fast. The sun was already setting. As I left the marketplace, a small boy, about eight years old...his legs swollen with beriberi...hobbled toward me. He was holding some Chinese slippers (*chinellas*) to sell. I averted my eyes and kept walking, but he persisted and kept on following me...calling to me as he hobbled.

"Please, *señora*, please buy these...cheap. Only five *pesos*. I am hungry."

"I'll pay you for one pair in front of the police station just ahead," I stated and kept walking.

He trailed behind me like a puppy. When I reached the police station, which had a small light in front, I gave him his five *pesos* and took the red pair of *chinellas* as a birthday gift for Joyce...the blue ones looked dingy. The boy went back toward the marketplace with his money clutched in his hand. I put my purse snugly under my left arm, grabbed my shopping bag (containing sale items plus three coconuts), and stuck my right hand in my pocket to reach for my rosary. With dusk creeping in like a heavy cloud of black smoke, I walked as fast as I could and prayed.

I was hurrying ahead when screams pierced the air. Someone was attacking the young boy. To go back and help him would be dangerous. I hurried to reach the armed sentry at the corner. After the usual bow and inspection, he allowed me to pass. As I continued toward J. Ruiz, I heard the sentry grunting at someone else at his corner post. My nephew, Peping, who usually waited at the next corner, was not there. I was in front of the Salanga's grocery store when I felt someone tugging at my purse. I screamed, grabbed my purse with my right hand, and dropped the shopping bag. Coconuts, *chinellas*, and other items spilled from the bag onto the street.

"*Magnanakaw! Magnanakaw!*" (Thief! Thief!)

Mr. Salanga rushed from their apartment above the store. The thief ran in the opposite direction...toward J. Ruiz when he heard Salanga's voice yelling. I began picking up my shopping bag and the fallen coconuts. One had cracked and the coconut water was dripping through the narrow opening. *That could have been my head!* Mr. Salanga helped me gather the rest of the spilled contents of my bag and guided me inside his home in the dusky darkness. Marita met me halfway down the stairs and gave me a hug. I gave thanks to God for Mr. Salanga's help.

"Mary, I'll put your bag in our living room and bring it to you tomorrow. When you feel able, I will walk you home," Mr. Salanga stated. "The thief may be waiting for you, since he ran toward J. Ruiz."

"I must go now. The children are alone and I have to be there before curfew. We have only fifteen minutes," I spoke haltingly as my heart was racing from my narrow escape.

I picked up the *chinellas* for Joyce. The other items could wait until tomorrow. Marita gave me another hug before we left. We walked silently and scanned the shadowed portions of the street. Mr. Salanga left me safely at my front gate.

"God be with you, Mr. Salanga," I said. "Thank you for saving my life."

✎

Mary checked her watch. She had written for over two hours and was tired. *I'll be able to rest and relax at vespers. I always find peace when I am in church. I must light a candle for Mr. Salanga. His quick action saved me and Joyce's red chinellas (Chinese slippers).* She covered her writing materials and prepared to leave for St. Williams. The short walk from her house to her church was a welcome respite.

CHAPTER 93

Living on the Edge

During November, bombing raids by the United States intensified. Rationing was discontinued. It was not wise to stray far from the air raid shelter. The children were instructed to watch and be wary of unusual activity in our area. They must obey Peping, and stay inside the shelter until Peping gave the "All Clear." Mary Jane was the only one allowed to leave to go to the slaughterhouse.

Air raids, aerial dogfights, and "ack ack" (antiaircraft fire) became common. Sometimes the children were so interested in the overhead show, they disregarded their instructions about the dangers from shrapnel. They were excited when the Japanese used colored "ack ack" in their attempts to shoot down American bombers and fighter planes.

I was in the middle of my shrapnel sermon when a fighter plane flew low towards the house. As we jumped into our shelter, the plane strafed the back stairway of the house leading to our kitchen, and shattered some of the steps plus some nearby banana trees. The raid continued for several hours. As silence enveloped the evening, we emerged from our mosquito-infested, damp shelter and heard screams coming from our neighbor's home. One of their family members did not make it to their shelter in time. Shrapnel had pierced her throat. She bled to death in her daughter's arms.

Three days before Linnie's fourth birthday on November 23, 1944, we noticed increasing movement of Japanese troops away from Manila. On the night of November 19, columns of Japanese soldiers marched on Aurora Quezon Boulevard beside our quarters. They stopped to rest by the roadside. The older children were still awake. I called for silence. They tiptoed into the darkened living room and listened to the guttural sounds spewing across our yard...about fifty feet away from us. There was no laughter. I peeked through the louvered window. The Japs were urinating on our fence. Others were stretched on the ground...knees bent. Eventually they regrouped and marched toward the mountains and away from Manila.

Early the next morning, the drone of a large plane flying low overhead caught my attention. I stepped out the back door. A large American plane soared above our front gate. The Japanese antiaircraft shells popped all around it. While I was yelling at the kids to get in the shelter, the plane was hit and exploded. The force of the explosion shook the house and knocked me down. Junior and the older girls rushed to me.

"Mom, I saw something big and black land near our front gate!" Junior yelled. "It might be a bomb!"

"Everyone to the shelter…hurry!" I shouted. "Be careful!"

We huddled inside the shelter for about twenty minutes before loud voices near our front gate aroused our curiosity. A large, cylindrical black object had fallen just inside our fenced yard. Neighbors were trying to decide what the object was and were talking excitedly about it.

Junior and I eased toward the object near our front gate. We saw neighbors tearing camouflage-designed material and tucking pieces inside their clothing. They were tearing off pieces of a parachute! The American airman slumped on J. Ruiz appeared to be dead…his hair and skin burned badly. The neighbors had already checked and had placed a large part of his parachute over his body. Nothing more could be done for the poor soul. If anyone tried to move his body, they faced torture or severe punishment.

Junior ran forward, forgetting the unknown black object nearby. He wanted a piece of the parachute. He tore off a large piece of the green/gray-splotched material and held it for me to see before he handed it to me. I stuffed it inside my pocket and talked with the others about the large black metal object lying inside our gate. Junior inched toward it.

"Don't get close," I warned. "It might be a bomb."

Junior ran to get a long fishing pole. When he returned, he pushed it gingerly against it. The object rolled over easily. He approached, leaned forward, and touched "the bomb" with his hand. Black soot covered his fingertips.

"It's not heavy, Mom. Might be some kind of copper tank," Junior concluded as he wiped the soot on his shorts.

He picked up his "souvenir" and hid it inside the chicken house before the Japs arrived. He ran around the yard searching for more of the plane's debris.

Sadly, the pilots of the B-24 were blasted from their plane by the explosion. Their mutilated bodies were found near our area. Japanese soldiers were standing guard beside the bodies. One Jap had their "dog tags" dangling from his hand. They were considered "trophies." Their bodies lay crumpled beside the concrete support beam of one of the city's water supply pipes. *I must tell our priest.* The three blocks to our church on Blumentrit Street were filled with curious natives. Fr. Sanchez was distressed by the sad news. The Spanish priest gathered his assistants, and was able to convince the Jap guards to allow him to perform a Christian burial for those two poor souls and the one on J. Ruiz. They were buried in the spot while the Japs stood guard. The crumpled one on J. Ruiz, probably the bombardier, was buried with them. God rest their souls.

I devised a signal to warn the children about air raids. I tied a whistle to a length of string and hung it around my neck. The sound of the whistle meant they were to go immediately to the shelter. I wore it all the time…even when bathing. I also cut sturdy guava limbs into three-inch segments, tied lengths of sturdy string around each and had each one to wear these "stick necklaces" while in the shelter. By placing the sticks lengthwise, across their teeth, their mouths remained slightly open during heavy bombing, and reduced the impact of the explosion's vibration against their eardrums. The sticks also eased the strain of holding one's mouth open for a long time. They could be removed between explosions for a "quick" swallow to moisten parched throats. Swallowing with sticks in place was quite difficult. We learned these "tricks" the hard way during the early bombings. *Experience was the best teacher.* Once, after Linnie held her mouth open for a long time, she was unable to close it when the stick was removed. Her jaw had locked. Massaging her jaws relaxed the muscles and she was okay, again. Necessity was the mother of invention.

The day after Linnie's birthday, Mary Jane and I were walking past the Japanese encampment on our way to sell, when I noticed several young American prisoners. My heart sank. They were stripped of their clothes and made to stand in the hot sun. We kept on walking by, as I feared we would be punished if we did not keep moving.

The marketplace was bare. Only seven vendors with their fruit or coconut stalls, remained. There were fewer shoppers. I felt it would be pointless to stay. Mary Jane and I left for San Juan and our family. We were tired and hungry. Our cupboard remained bare.

Early the next morning, I decided to return the other sale items in my possession. I also wanted to see my mother and give her a hug for Christmas. I stayed longer than I intended. It was well past curfew when I returned. I opened the door to find the kids waiting in the living room for my return. Lucy was visibly pale and shaking. The rest stared at her silently.

"What has happened?" I whispered, after seeing their faces in the dimly lit room.

"We had a visitor about thirty minutes before curfew," Lucy said.

"Who was it? What did they want? Are all of you okay?" I rattled.

"Lt. Kato was here. He asked for you."

"What did he want?" I asked.

"He felt sad about not being able to help you and Mrs. Harris the other day. He brought rice and sugar," Lucy announced.

"What did you do? How long did he stay?"

"He said he was leaving the Philippines. I think he was sad," Lucy stated.

I sank into the nearest chair, as my knees were feeling weak. We were losing the only Japanese officer who had been helpful to us.

"He asked me who played the piano. I called Mary Jane in to play for him," Lucy stated. "She played *Indian Drums* and other pieces. I was so glad she did not play *God Bless America.*"

Lucy shivered again as she recalled the events. I made the Sign of The Cross and thanked God my children were spared. I was also thankful the visitor was Lt. Kato. If another Japanese officer had come, we would have been in violation of curfew, since I was not present…as listed on our door. We would have been punished severely.

The phone rang. Mary eased her tired frame from her chair and answered. It was Lucy. She and Buddy were coming to mow her yard.

"I was writing about December 1944 and the visit Lt. Kato made while I was away from the house. I still shake when I remember. I'm glad you're coming over. I need to take a break from my writing, and the lawn does need to be mowed," Mary said.

She cleaned off the table. *Buddy will want a snack when he finishes the yard.* Mary worked fast. They would arrive in ten minutes. She searched her cupboard for those Girl Scout cookies. *I have at least two more boxes.*

CHAPTER 94

No Silent Nights

December 1944 brought a special gift in the form of a rumor. *American troops had landed on Philippine soil!* We kept listening. The only sounds during the night were those of the movement of more Japanese troops toward the mountains and bombing in the distance. The Japanese were building a jungle front line from the Sierra Madre Mountains in Antipolo through Rizal to Appari Cagayan. Occasional air raids buzzed through our days and nights. We learned the word *kamikaze*…suicide planes. The Japanese would fight until death. Sometimes the commotion was directly overhead, and other times at a distance. Through it all, we prayed and spent much time running in and out of our air raid shelter. We were on constant alert. There were no silent nights.

On December 8, the third anniversary of the horrendous attack on Pearl Harbor and Manila, "Puppet President" José P. Laurel (and his cabinet) were ordered, by General Tomoyuki Yamashita, to transfer the seat of government to Baguio. Yamashita would continue to pull the strings of Japanese control over the Philippines from his mountain fortress.

Air raids were more frequent. According to rumors, MacArthur had control of Leyte. None of these rumors were confirmed and the Japanese propaganda kept extolling the exploits of the Imperial Japanese military. The only signs we had to help us believe the Americans were coming were the increasing air raids on Manila. *Those American planes must be nearby for so many to come so often.* Once more, hope for our liberation was more than a spark. We kept fanning that spark into little flames through prayers, pleading that we would survive the return of the Americans. I prayed Jess would be spared. Rumors about our son, Bobby, came through from time to time, but nothing was confirmed. I was told he had survived "The Death March" in Bataan, but was taken from the military concentration camp at Bilibid Prison to Palao. *God help him*.

The night sky once again glowed from the aftermath of air raids, this time to our southwest on December 15. Peping arrived early the next day with news of the American takeover of Mindoro. Since Yamashita relocated the largest contingent of Japanese troops to the Sierra Madre Mountains east of Baguio, there was hardly any resistance.

"Where did you get your information?" I asked.

"Ah, *Tita Nena*, you might be in danger…if you knew my sources," Peping responded seriously.

"Don't tell me," I replied. "If you say it is true, I believe you."

Two days later another typhoon was brewing to our southeast. Two days passed before the flooding and heavy rains diminished. This typhoon was not as destructive as the one in November. We took pans and buckets to remove floodwater from our air raid shelter. Junior and Peping made sure no snakes were hiding inside the shelter before we devised a bucket and pan brigade to remove the water before the next air raid.

I tried to sell items at the market place and along my walks in the business district. It became more difficult, as the rumors of the American troops landing at Leyte and Mindoro were spreading like wildfire across Manila. Many prepared for the American invasion by packing their food supplies in bags to carry on their backs or atop their heads. I stopped by *La Consolacion* convent to see my sister, Maming. She was delighted to see me. It had been a long time since my last visit.

"*Nena*, I'm glad to see you," Maming cried as she gave me a hug.

We chatted about family events before I told her I would be returning the items I had not sold to her. If owners still wanted them, they would be at the convent.

"I want to make sure these are returned before something happens," I stated. "I cannot find buyers anymore as most people have no money and others are using the money they have to buy food and supplies for the American invasion."

Maming was silent, but nodded her head. She pointed in the direction of a long hallway. At the far end of the hallway were several Japanese soldiers. I gasped hoping they had not overheard my conversation about the American invasion.

"The Japanese are inside the fortified sections of our school and convent," Maming said in a low voice. "Our lives have become more complicated."

I nodded my head, gathered my shopping bag, and left in the opposite direction without encountering Japanese soldiers. Once again, angels were there. I hurried to return to my children in San Juan.

Christmas was one day away. On Christmas Eve, we attended Mass early, as usual, in order to return before our curfew. Not many parishioners were at our church. *I wonder where they are?* I realized some had already evacuated the area. Many of the Filipinos had relatives in the provinces, and they were getting out of harm's way. The children and I had nowhere to go or the means to go there if we had a refuge. I prayed fervently for the safety of my family.

Once home, the children prepared for bed after our nightly prayers. They had long since stopped thinking of Christmas and all it had once meant in the way of gifts and Santa Claus. When the house became quiet, I lit a coconut oil glass "lamp," found the gifts I had hidden, and placed them around my manger scene. With rosary in hand, I curled up on the side of my bed and fell asleep.

After our boiled cracked wheat soup for breakfast, I called the children into my bedroom. I gave Lucy the tiny porcelain doll, and her soft smile was all the thanks I needed. I gave Junior and Emma one hundred Japanese *pesos* each. While it would not buy much, perhaps they would enjoy buying a trinket. (The Japanese money would be worthless when the Americans regained control of the islands.) Linnie was clapping her hands together as I was distributing the gifts. I handed her the toy truck. Joyce was puzzled with her small airplane, but after a while, she was holding it in the air and flying it around her head. The old doll with the cloth body, printed cardboard head and limbs was handed to Mary Jane. I knew she missed her Jane Withers doll, but she said nothing, except "Thank you" before leaving the room to find her "quiet place."

The next day, Junior took his hundred *pesos* to Mr. Salanga's store and bought six ten-inch breadsticks. When he returned, he gave one breadstick to each of his sisters and kept one for himself.

"Junior, those breadsticks cost twenty *pesos* each," I stated. "Why did you buy them?"

"Well, Mom," Junior responded, "it was my money and I wanted my sisters to enjoy the bread with me, besides, I got six for the price of five."

I hugged him and thanked him for being so generous with his gift. I had another Christmas blessing. My son gave me another reason to give thanks.

I spent the next week making sure each child had an emergency bag ready in case we had to evacuate the premises. I thought we might go to my sister's convent, but the Japanese had infiltrated those quarters. The Japanese also barricaded themselves in many of the fortified buildings in The Walled City. The only other place we had was our chicken house. The next day, Junior, Peping and I relocated Linnie and Joyce's bunk beds into the chicken house to be closer to the air raid shelter. Mary Jane shared the downstairs bedroom with Junior. They were in charge of getting the two youngest ones, with their emergency bags, to the shelter at the sound of my whistle. Lucy, Emma, and I managed on our own. A plan was in place. Whether or not it would work was another issue. We must be ready, as only God knew what 1945 would bring.

My goodness, how did I manage to keep my sanity? Mary stirred around the kitchen and put the kettle on to prepare hot chocolate. *I need a treat to lift my spirits!* While the water was heating, someone knocked at the kitchen door. Emma arrived with an armload of groceries. *Oh, I hope she remembered to buy those goodies on sale at Mary of Puddin' Hill.*

Mary ambled to the door, smiling, and let her inside. Emma helped put the groceries away. Tucked away in a separate sack were those goodies from Mary of Puddin' Hill.

"Let's have *merienda*. You can tell me about your day," Mary said, as she reached for a cup for Emma. *How lucky I am to have family nearby.*

CHAPTER 95

The Beginning of the End

New Year's Eve, 1945, was relatively quiet. It was just another day to us. The most important activity for the evening was to attend Mass and get to our quarters before curfew. On our way to church, I noticed the almost empty streets. Attendance in church was also low. I hoped and prayed the services would not be disrupted by an air raid. We settled into our pews quietly and recited the litany. The priest announced the service would be brief. He must have been concerned about the occurrence of an air raid. *God be with us.*

New Year's Day began with bombs bursting all around us. I think we broke our record for getting to our air raid shelter. Japanese antiaircraft fire filled the sky overhead with pastel-colored ack-ack. The kids were entertained by the different colored puffy antiaircraft bursts dotting the sky as if painted by a nervous watercolor artist. I would not allow them to remain, as they might be wounded or killed by shrapnel.

The bombs were bursting closer to our area. The impact as they struck their targets caused our bodies to vibrate. We huddled in the damp shelter with guava sticks in place and clamped our hands over our ears. The bombs struck closer than before. Dirt from the sides of the shelter crumbled around us and dust fell on our heads from the makeshift roof over the shelter. I reached for my rosary...hoping my actions would calm the children.

After about four hours, the bombing stopped. The stillness wrapped around us like a blanket. The rhythm of our own breathing, as we sucked and expelled air around the guava sticks in our mouths, was the only sound. I removed my guava stick and Linnie's and watched the rest of them gingerly remove theirs. Everyone was stretching their cheeks by opening their mouths wide, holding them wide open, and then closing them gently. Our jaws ached from keeping the guava sticks clenched between our teeth. Junior and I left the shelter and scouted the area. Seeing no major damage this time, I returned to tell the others to eat fruit before going to rest...our routine between air raids. We all remembered to use the bathroom.

The next week, I returned items given to me by family and friends to sell.

Those items must be returned before a bomb hit our place and destroyed everything...including us. I dreaded leaving the children, but knew conditions would probably worsen.

We endured daily air raids. Most of them were in the direction of Manila, but several were close enough to us to keep us terrified. The strain of being under attack was affecting all of us. We were sleep-deprived, tired, hungry and thirsty.

In mid-January, we were exhausted. We relocated our beds into either the chicken shack or downstairs. If a typhoon hit Luzon, we would have to move all of our bedding and "camp out" upstairs, as floodwaters would rise just under the second story.

We were experiencing a continuing series of air raids and all of us were trembling from the strain of being crammed in the damp shelter with no food, little water, or sleep. Mary Jane and Junior decided they were going to their beds downstairs. Junior led the way out of the shelter and Mary Jane followed. I chastised them as they were leaving.

"You may not be able to return before the next raid begins," I stated.

"We can hurry, if we have to," Junior interjected. "I'll bring fruit and another bottle of boiled water."

About fifteen minutes later, another air raid filled the skies with planes and bursting antiaircraft shells. I stuck my head out of the shelter and blew my whistle, which was competing with the sounds of bursting ack-ack. Within seconds, they rushed in...gasping for breath. An important lesson was learned...the hard way.

On the last day of January, after Peping arrived to stay with the kids, I left early to help my mother. She was relocating to Consueling's new lodging in Legarda. My sister's house in Santa Mesa was completely destroyed. *Mami* had just settled into her new bedroom, when more antiaircraft bursts erupted. Explosions peppered the sky. People were running in the streets and screaming. My nephew, Juaning, came rushing in...breathless after running all the way from the Walled City.

"*Tita Nena*," he yelled, "you'd better go as fast as you can to San Juan and your kids. The Japs are exploding drums of gasoline! They are retreating! "Canoes" are on their way!" ("Canoes" was a code word for "Americans".)

"Juaning, I can't believe they are coming?" I said. "Are you sure?"

"Yes, *Tita*," he babbled. "I was told they are near the *Malacañang* Palace already!"

I gathered my bags, kissed my mother and sister, and headed for the door. As I reached the door, I held my breath to hold back the tears. *I might never see them again*.

There were no *caretelas* or *caramattas* in sight...no transportation of any kind. I prayed fast...keeping my feet in step with my words. I became worried. *There were no sentries at the corners of each block...their usual posts*. I prayed aloud.

Upon my arrival, I gathered the kids around me and told them the Americans were already near the *Malacañang* Palace. They were excited and jumped up and down yelling, "God Bless America!" I had to quiet them immediately. If

Japs were within earshot, we would all be killed. They calmed down, but the excitement was still shining in their eyes…like kids having their first bite of candy.

I instructed everyone to have their emergency packs ready and to sleep in the chicken house, except for Mary Jane and Junior, who slept downstairs. I did not sleep at all during the night. Manila was burning. I stared in horror at the horizon. The wide wall of flames raged furiously against the blackout of curfew. Angry flames, like long, burning tongues, licked the darkness from the night sky. I kept my rosary in my hand the entire night, and prayed for all the lost souls and my family.

The tramping of many feet marching on Aurora Quezon Boulevard beside our place began around nine the next morning. In the distance, a raised flag caught my attention. I thought my eyes were playing tricks on me from lack of sleep. Fear gripped me. Was it really an American flag or were the Japanese playing a cruel trick on the people to lure them from their shelters and kill them? I did not dare take a chance. I blew my whistle to alert the kids. We just had time to hurry inside and get our guava sticks in place before the explosions began. Incendiary bombs exploded in the area. They just missed our old shack. Flames licked at the trees about fifty feet away from us. One bomb hit Mr. Uy's house located on the corner. Linnie cried. I pulled her to me to quiet her. We had to be quiet. If Japs were in the area, they might toss a grenade into our shelter. Bits and pieces of concrete, burning wood, and other debris were landing all around our shelter. Shrapnel was piercing the roof on our shelter. The jagged shards tore through the tin roof, dense mattresses and struck the layers of wooden roof. I hoped the mattresses and tin piled on top would keep shrapnel from coming through.

Once again, silence reigned. We debated whether or not it would be safe to leave the shelter, when Peping called from outside.

"Are you okay, *Tita Nena?*"

He was dripping wet and had a waterproof bag tied to his broad shoulders. I was surprised to see him and hugged him as I exited the shelter. He was soaked.

"My goodness…what happened to you?" I cried.

"I was worried about you since you were alone," Peping stated. "I decided to check on you and bring rice, but the Japs destroyed the San Juan Bridge last night, so I had to swim across the river. If I had crawled over on the water pipes, I would have become an easy target for anyone."

"You put yourself in danger of being killed," I protested.

"No," Peping said, "The Japs are near Ermita…burning the houses. I did not see many Japanese vehicles in the area."

God put us through those experiences for a reason. What was the reason? When will I have the answer? She pondered those mysteries as she put away her writing tools for the night.

CHAPTER 96

Digging In

From February 2 through the 11, the bombing, trench mortar, and antiaircraft shelling was incessant. We stayed in the air raid shelter most of the time…day and night. We only left long enough to "take care of business," which meant finding the nearest bush or tree. With the upstairs bathroom blown to smithereens, and the downstairs bathroom about fifty yards away, we had no other choice. I rationed the small supply of boiled water we had, along with dried fish, fruit, and the remaining canned goods. We did not dare leave the shelter long enough to try to cook on our outside fire pit. The mosquitoes in our shelter were the only ones having a good meal.

Beginning February 4, the Japanese were in hand-to-hand combat in the streets. American troops had encircled Manila. As the Japs retreated, they mined streets, bridges, and set up barricades covered with barbed wire along the way. Entire neighborhoods were set on fire in an attempt to dissuade American troops. Residents were killed as they attempted to flee the ring of fire. Members of the Japanese Navy, whose ships had been destroyed, were holed up in government buildings…prepared to fight until death. Their ships were sunk and they were bent on destroying Manila and anyone in their gun sights. Once again the night sky burned brightly with the flames of destruction. Very few escaped the wrath of the Japanese.

A sudden burst of sniper fire and another air raid caused us all to shrink deeper into our shelter. As usual, we waited for the commotion to subside before venturing outside.

We listened each day to all the sounds as we crouched inside our shelter. Peping stayed with us since the day he swam across the San Juan River to check on us. We were no longer concerned about having our names checked against the certified list on the door. Mr. Ceferino Alon was nowhere around, and the Japs were leaving.

The sound of tanks grinding along in the distance filtered into our shelter. Curiosity got the best of Peping, so he decided to investigate the source of the grinding noise coming from the direction of the San Juan River two miles away. He was absent about an hour, but it seemed much longer.

"*Tita*, the noise is the sound of American tanks and trucks building a pontoon bridge across the river. Since the Japs destroyed the bridge, the Americans are preparing a temporary crossing!" Peping explained breathlessly.

We stayed within the confines of our shelter for another night. Exhaustion and sleep deprivation caused the younger ones to sleep where they sat, sometimes leaning against each other. The older ones made sure their guava sticks were in place whenever bombing resumed. The sound of the explosions did not rouse Linnie or Joyce. Mother Nature had taken over and sprinkled sleep dust into their eyes. We had grit, dust, and mosquito bites all over us. It was useless to try to keep the dust wiped off or the mosquitoes shooed away. Those layers of dust might help discourage the mosquitoes.

Early the next morning, we strained our ears to try and filter sounds floating around in the deafening quiet. Mary Jane cocked her head to one side.

"Mama, something coming," she whispered. "It sounds like those tanks we heard yesterday…coming this way."

She eased her head out of the shelter. Peping grabbed her, back inside but not before she got a good look.

"The tanks are on our highway!" Mary Jane announced.

As the older kids scrambled to see, I ordered them to stay inside the shelter.

"Be quiet," I said. "They might think we are Japs and shoot in this direction."

We listened…trying to glean information from sounds. The rumbling of tanks stopped. It was so quiet for such a long time; all we could hear was the buzzing of the mosquitoes looking for their next meal. Peping decided to take action.

"I'm going outside to see what is happening, *Tita*," Peping said. "Stay inside the shelter and remain quiet until I return."

We waited for over fifteen minutes, but Peping did not return. Junior eased toward the opening of the shelter and peeped outside.

"Mom, I'll go see why Peping has not returned," Junior stated flatly.

"Be careful. Those could be Japanese tanks out there," I said.

Once again, we waited for around fifteen minutes, but all was quiet. We prayed silently. Suddenly, a shadow crossed at the opening to our shelter.

"*Gringos!*" We heard Peping yell.

An American soldier stuck his head just inside the opening of the shelter briefly.

"Hi," the soldier said.

"Wait, wait," I said, "it might be a Japanese trick."

After waiting all those years, I was still not convinced the Americans had returned. I still heard gunfire in the distance and was reluctant to exit the shelter.

We started to emerge from the shelter…our limbs stiff from sitting…and broke into tears at the sight of the young American soldier covered with grime. His bright blue eyes sparkled from under his heavy helmet. Soot covered his face.

Mary Jane was the first to rush out and hug him. She was laughing, crying, and chattering. The rest of us followed. We could not contain our joy. We had waited a long time for liberation. We were dirty, hungry, sleepy, tired, and happy to be alive. The soldier raised his hand and gave instructions.

"Folks, it's not over. It will be okay for a while, but stay close to your shelter as the Japs are still shooting and so are we."

Peping and Junior stood beside the soldier. They were grinning from ear to ear.

"Why didn't you return?" I asked. "We were worried about you."

Peping explained they were stopped by American soldiers at bayonet point and warned not to move. When Junior explained our family was waiting for them in the family air raid shelter, they let them go and the young GI followed

"I'm glad I checked to see who was in this shelter," the soldier stated. "We had orders to throw a grenade into every hole or shelter in San Juan because a Jap encampment was nearby. That's what I've been doing. I decided to check this one."

"Thank God you did," I replied. *I never did get his name.*

Mortar shells exploded in the distance. We jumped in the shelter to see what night would bring. Yes, American troops were in our area, but the Japs were not giving up the fight. Manila, Ermita, the Walled City, and Santo Tomas were being shelled incessantly throughout the night. We felt better to have the Americans around us, but the war was not over. Not by a long shot or any other kind.

After the shelling died down, we were all aching to leave the shelter and "take care of business." The only sound we heard was that of tanks, troops, and trucks rolling down Aurora Quezon Boulevard next to our property.

Mary Jane dashed upstairs to get a box of cigars she knew her daddy had kept to give his guests on special occasions. The arrival of American troops was a special occasion! With no regard for her safety, she ran to the highway, hugged the first soldier she saw and started talking about her daddy.

The soldier thought she was calling him "Daddy" and retorted.

"Whoa, I'm not your Daddy."

Mary Jane shook her head from side-to-side.

"No, I'm trying to tell you about my daddy being a prisoner in Santo Tomas."

She did not wait for his reply and kept handing out cigars to American soldiers resting by their tanks on Aurora Quezon Boulevard. When she returned with the empty box, she told me what she had done.

I managed to prepare a pot of boiled soupy rice to sustain us. I mixed a small amount of KLIM (powdered milk) with a large amount of boiled water from our water bottle to have nourishment, in case we had to stay in the shelter for several more days. We had already been in the shelter ten days and nights and were praying our confinement in the shelter was over. But it wasn't

The routine of listening, watching, waiting, and swatting mosquitoes resumed. Sniper fire popped throughout the night like firecrackers on the Fourth of July. The Japanese were committed to remaining in control of the Philippines. The massacre in Manila and surrounding areas raged throughout the night and into the next day.

Meanwhile, internees at Santo Tomas were hoping against hope that all the bombing, strafing, and battle sounds in the distance, would soon result in their liberation. An earlier strafing in December created a stir when goggles were dropped in a patio area bearing a message of hope. With little or no rations, internees knew they could not survive much longer. The evening of February 3, 1945, followed the same pattern as previous days. Internees on the second and third floors of the Education Building prepared to retire before nine to conserve energy. The first floor of the building housed the office of the commandant and other Japanese offices. Sixty or so Japanese security guards shared the second floor quarters with internees. Robert Robb, Harold Suarez (former owner of Manila's famous Arcade Café), Slim Brown, and Jess were standing near the balcony just before 9:00 p.m., when they heard the commotion.

"That's shooting down at the front gate!" Jess yelled.

Slim Brown looked over the ledge of the balcony and noticed the flares sweeping their building from left to right.

"Hey, there's an American flag down there!"

Jess cleared his throat as surges of emotion swept over him.

"I'd been thinking I'd never live to see this day," Jess said as his throat filled again.

The internees moved toward the door of Room 216 only to be blocked by five Japs in combat gear...rifles fitted with bayonets pointed straight at them. They were motioned to go back into their room and were made to take their beds, mattresses, and chairs into the corridor and place them against the rear windows and stairwell at the north end of the building. The forty-three internees from Rooms 215, 216, and 217 were crammed into a room that should accommodate only twenty. They were required to sit on the floor. The rumblings of tanks moving toward their building, machine gun fire, and exploding grenades filled their ears. Suddenly, it hit them...they were hostages of those nasty Nips! About two hundred more internees were stuck on the third floor.

An American's voice could be heard giving orders outside their building.

"Vacate those shacks around this building right now! You are in danger!"

Jess could hear tanks being positioned at each end of the building and at the central entrance in the middle. Lt. Col. Toshio Hayashi, in command of the Jap guards was in full combat gear...a pair of binoculars dangling from his neck. Hayashi looked rather cowardly crawling around on his hands and knees avoiding the windows.

The same voice from outside instructed all internees to take cover or lay on the floor. Jess huddled shoulder to shoulder with the others and ducked his head. A barrage of mortar fire blasted the first floor. The wooden floor shook and seemed to come up and hit the internees in the face. Dust was falling everywhere. An ominous silence followed the shelling.

Around 11:00 p.m., the American officer's voice called for the Japs to surrender. Hayashi and his men did not budge. The call to surrender was repeated, but again, with no response from Hayashi. The shelling was repeated, and the floors shook once again. No one dared move.

Three hours passed with no change. Around 2:00 a.m., some of the Jap guards who were sitting around the walls began to doze. Johnny Elam, Charlie Core, and Slim Brown took this opportunity to crawl toward the balcony. They remembered the twenty foot rope placed there as a fire escape after the first

American bombing raid on Manila. They made it almost all the way down but were too weak to hold on. They were hurt when they fell, but they were free.

The bright Sunday morning sun glared into the second floor windows. The internees lay there and listened. The voice of Ernest Stanley, an American missionary held at Santo Tomas who acted as Japanese interpreter, called out a message to the Japs. Lt. Col. Hayashi grunted some orders to four of his guards, who went down the stairwell to meet Stanley.

Stanley, accompanied by an American officer carrying a white flag, was escorted into the second floor corridor to talk with Hayashi. After some back and forth conversation, Stanley and the American officer left the building.

Around two that afternoon, a large pot of beef stew was brought in by some of the camp cooks and left in the corridor. Hayashi grunted and made eating motions. The internees grabbed their tin cups, cans, and spoons from their rooms and lined up to get their first meal in almost two days. Women and children were first, but before they could finish getting their portion, the Japs pushed them aside and ladled stew into their mess kits…there were sixty-seven of them. By the time the rest of the internees got to the pot of stew, it was two-thirds depleted.

Some internees choked on the first few bites because they were not accustomed to eating meat…they were used to mush. Following the "meal," the Japs allowed everyone to take turns going to the toilets, accompanied by guards. By the time everyone was finished, the Japs made all internees lay on the floor again. Since night was approaching, some fell asleep from either exhaustion or being full. Our stomachs could only tolerate about one-half cup of food at a time.

Early the next morning, the Japs lined up in the corridor in full battle gear. Their guns sported fixed bayonets, and their mess kits dangling from their knapsacks. With Lt. Col. Hayashi in the lead, they marched out of the Education Building where they were met by an American military escort and marched out of Santo Tomas. Hayashi had negotiated the deal that no more internees would be harmed if he and his men were allowed to rejoin their troops in Manila.

As ex-hostages shuffled out of the building, an American officer barked some orders.

"Clear the building immediately. Do not return to get any belongings as the building may be booby-trapped. I'm sending some GIs in to secure the building."

Jess and the other internees did not understand what he meant by "GIs," as he had never heard that term used before. He was just glad to be alive and out of there. *Many angels had watched over him and were still watching.*

Mary recalled reading the article in *Collier's* magazine several years later. She and Jess had talked a little about his being held hostage, but his internment held too many painful memories. He would usually change the subject. Lt. Col. Hayashi and his men were escorted to an area of Manila of his choosing, where they rejoined Japanese troops. The next day, they encountered American and guerilla fighters. Most of them, including Hayashi, were killed. Others were taken as prisoners.

CHAPTER 97

Liberation at Last

Just when we thought our troubles were over, the unexpected happened. Early on February 13, 1945, we had visitors. Someone was knocking at our front door. Lucy, Junior and I, the only ones up, were sitting around the dining table. I rose from my chair to answer…accompanied by Junior. I looked before opening the door and saw two American MPs (Military Police). I greeted them and invited them inside, but they did not budge. The taller one spoke quietly.

"Mrs. Hodges, I'm afraid we bring sad news. I'm so sorry. Your husband was struck by shrapnel during the liberation of the prison camp and was killed. We have come to help you make arrangements."

"*O, Dios mio…Dios mio!*

My heart sank. I felt weak and sank backward onto the nearby sofa. Lucy heard my cries and rushed in from the dining room.

"What's wrong, Mama, what's wrong?" Lucy demanded.

Junior, who had accompanied me, clenched his jaw and returned to the dining room. *How can this be? He lived through this war only to die before coming home! It's not fair!*

I reached into my pocket for my rosary, rose to my feet, and gave Lucy instructions.

"Take care of everyone and pray. I must go to Santo Tomas. I will return when I can."

The MPs escorted me out our front gate and we began our trek. The pontoon bridges at the San Juan River were being repaired from the recent shelling and were blocked with military vehicles. One of the soldiers apologized.

"Mrs. Hodges, I'm sorry you had to walk this far under these conditions. Our jeep is parked on the other side of the river. We can ride from there."

They helped me walk across the large water pipes in order to cross the river. I was praying so we did not speak. Once across, I put my rosary in my pocket, and they helped me climb rebar and parts of the destroyed bridge to reach street level. Once again on level ground, I reached for my rosary and prayed during the remaining five-mile drive to Camp Santo Tomas.

When we entered the main office, one MP asked me to have a seat while the other located the officer in charge. When he entered, he appeared tired. His uniform was soiled and rumpled, as if he had worn it for days. His face was gaunt.

"Mrs. Hodges is here to see her husband's body before he is buried," the taller MP advised the officer in charge.

The officer appeared confused. He checked over one roster before picking up another.

"What's your husband's name, ma'am?"

"Jesse A. Hodges," I replied hoarsely and clutched my rosary tighter.

"In which building was he housed?"

"The last time we communicated, over a year and a half ago, he was in the Education Building. He also built a small shanty to use as a workshop." I rose from the chair and approached his desk.

"The internees in the Education Building were liberated about a week ago. The Japs took all of them hostage when we first broke down the gate to Santo Tomas. Several were killed. We still don't have a complete listing of all internees."

My head was swimming as I tried to take in all this information. *Was Jess alive? Was he dead? Where is he?*

"We have a Mr. Harnes and a Mr. Hughes who were killed, but we don't have a Mr. Hodges."

I leaned against the officer's information desk so I wouldn't fall, as I felt dizzy. I stared at him without speaking.

"Mrs. Hodges, there has been a mistake. Let's see if we can find your husband. Civilians are not yet allowed on the grounds with the internees, but since you were brought here by military escort under difficult conditions, I will make an exception."

My military escort led the way and I followed. I had no idea what I would find. I held onto my rosary and kept praying.

As we approached one group of shirtless internees who were chatting in a group, I scoured their gaunt faces. They were emaciated. Their bony skeletons were covered with wrinkled, splotched skin. *Dear, God, where is Jess? Will I recognize him?*

I kept moving behind my escorts and praying. As we approached the Education Building, a voice behind me caused me to stop.

"Hey, what are you doing here?"

It was Jess! He was alive! He walked toward me with much effort, his homemade *bahkyas* sliding up and down on his bare skinny feet. I was in shock, but managed to meet him halfway. I was speechless as I hugged him hard. Jess broke the silence.

"Hey! I think you just cracked my ribs! I'm surprised to see you! The guys in charge said civilians weren't allowed in camp until they were sure all the fighting was over," Jess said as he held me.

"Well, two MPs appeared at our house early this morning and said you had been killed. I was brought here to see your body before they buried you!" I said while crying and laughing. "When we arrived, I found out two others were killed by shrapnel, but I still knew nothing about you."

"Yes," Jess stated, "those two men were sitting against the wall of the Education Building after the Japs had held us hostage. I was sitting next to Mr. Hughes. We were told to get away from the walls, but there was so much noise, they probably missed the warning. Shrapnel sheared off the head of Mr. Hughes and the other man's torso was destroyed. I saw his head fall off as I got away from there as fast as I could. There was so much commotion and confusion, I'm not surprised they reported me dead because I stayed in hiding until all the shelling stopped...then I must have fallen asleep from exhaustion."

Jess cried and quivered, as he talked. I tried to hold him closer, but he winced.

"I think you did crack several of my ribs!" Jess said as he held his side. "I want to go with you, but we can't be released until the Japs give up. They are still checking us all out also, to make sure we can survive after we go home."

"It's okay, Jess. Stop talking about it," I whispered gently. "We need to forget all the terrible stuff."

My escorts stepped toward us, met Jess, and suggested we needed to go as they were escorting me home. Jess and I hugged gently, said our goodbyes, and I begrudgingly left him behind. *The children...I can't wait to tell them the good news!*

I was chattering like a monkey all the way to San Juan. The two escorts smiled and nodded. The pontoon bridge had been repaired and we were able to conclude the return trip without any walking. As we entered the front gate at our house, I rang the bell to alert the children to our return. The large smile on my face relieved their worries...all was well. They pelted me with questions, but I waited until the two escorts left my side before I told them about my day. We gathered around the dining room table to give thanks.

Whew! I'm weak again. I must go to church early tonight and give thanks once again. God has cared for my family and me. Mary picked up her notebook, stacked several photos in the box, and prepared a snack to have before leaving for St. Williams.

RING OPEN WIDE THE GOLDEN GATES AND LET THE VICTORS IN.

THE LIBERATION BULLETIN OF PHILIPPINE INTERNMENT CAMP NO: I. AT SANTO TOMAS UNIVERSITY MANILA, PHILIPPINES.

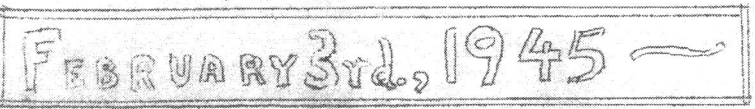

FEBRUARY 3rd, 1945

copyright 1945
Peter C. Richards
all rights reserved

WITH THE FORCES
ITS
Chesterfield

They satisfy

SAN MIGUEL BREWERY

Mobiloil
Mobilgas
STANDARD VACUUM OIL CO.

And so to Freedom with
ASIA LIFE INSURANCE COMPANY

P. R. Danner,
Philippine Manager.

Steel for every purpose
everywhere

UNITED STATES STEEL
EXPORT CO.

After 37 long months we celebrate our first day of freedom to-day with the final departure of the Japanese from the City of Manila, and await with bounding hearts our own, our friends, our allies.

CHRONOLOGY OF EVENTS

1942
- Jan. 4. 1st. group arrives at Santo Tomas for internment.
- 17. Holy Ghost Home for Children starts.
- 31. Central Kitchen opens.
- Feb. 15. Three men shot for escaping.
- 21. 113 China refugees arrive from Sulphur Springs.
- Mar. 8. 12 Navy Nurses arrive.
- Apr. 8. The Earthquake.
- 15. Last Wheat bread.
- June 17. 43 Consular repatriates depart.
- July 1. Japanese take over from Philippine Red Cross the financing of the Camp at 40 centavos per person per day.
- 2. 72 Army Nurses arrive.
- 27. 2nd. Executive Committee take over.
- Aug. 24. Santa Catalina Hospital starts.
- Sep. 12. 113 Internees leave for Shanghai.
- Oct. 31. 11 of High Commissioner's staff arrive.
- Dec. 17. South African Relief Supplies arrive.
- 19. Cebu Internees arrive.
- 23. 1st. Movie.

1943
- Jan. 6. Canadian Relief Supplies arrive.
- 12. 28 men taken out to Military Camps.
- 16. Tacloban Internees arrive.
- Mar. 10. Bacolod Internees arrive.
- May. 14. 1st. Los Baños Transfer.
- 17. Re-internment of aged, sick and children previously living outside Camp.
- June 21. Iloilo Internees arrive.
- Sep. 26. 124 Repatriates depart.
- Nov. 15. The Flood.
- Dec. 10. 2nd. Los Baños Transfer, including 1st. group of women.
- 15. American Relief Supplies arrive.

1944
- Jan. 2. Davao Internees arrive.
- Feb. 1. Military Administration takes over Camp. Filipino Doctors and Nurses, also market vendors barred. Daily cereal ration 400 grams per person per day.
- 7. Package Line closed.
- 10. Holy Ghost Children's Home Closed.
- 18. 2nd. Executive Committee abolished and 3-man Internee Committee appointed by Japanese.

1944

- **Feb. 20.** Military take over Bodega and all food supplies therein.
- **21.** Sulphur Springs Camp closed. American mail arrives.
- **22.** Local newspaper prohibited.
- **Mar. 1.** Three U. S. Army Doctors arrive.
- **Apr. 7.** 3rd. Los Baños Transfer.
- **May. 12.** Last Ricebread.
- **June 6.** Central Kitchen starts cooking in outside kitchen permanently with wood.
- **July 1.** Last Stage Show.
- **7.** Religious group brought in to Gymnasium incommunicado for transfer to Los Baños. Similar groups from all over the Islands follow during the month.
- **20.** Internees photographed in groups of 5, with numbers on their chests.
- **Aug. 1.** All money, except 50 Jap. pesos, to be turned in for deposit with Bank of Taiwan.
- **30.** Remedios Hospital Convalescent Home closed.
- **Sep. 1.** Old Men's Home at Hospicio de San José closed.
- **13.** Daily cereal ration 300 gms. per capita.
- **15.** Daily cereal ration 250 gms. per capita.
- **20.** Daily cereal ration 300 gms. per capita.
- **21.** THE AIR RAID.
- **23.** Produce for Vegetable Market so reduced that market at last closes.
- **Oct. 9.** Whole front campus taken over by the Japanese Military for storage of their supplies including arms and ammunition.
- **14.** Chairman of Internee Agents banished to Los Baños.
- **Nov. 17.** Net daily cereal 255 gms. per capita.
- **Dec. 5.** Last Los Baños Transfer.
- **12.** Net daily cereal ration 210 gms. per cap.
- **20.** Net daily cereal 187 gms. per capita.
- **23.** Chairman of Internee Committee and 3 others arrested and subsequently taken out of Camp by Military Police.
- **25.** 3785 happy Internees saw, read, recited or heard verbatim reports of the LEAFLET:—

  "The Commander in Chief, the Officers and the men of the American Forces of Liberation in the Pacific wish their gallant allies, the People of the Philippines, all the blessings of Christmas and the realisation of their fervent hopes for the New Year
  Christmas 1944"

- **Dec. 26.** Complete Census of the three camps, Manila, Los Baños, Baguio, ordered to be assembled, copied and delivered in 48 hours.

GENERAL ELECTRIC COMPANY (P.I.) INC.

THE INTERNATIONAL HARVESTER COMPANY OF PHILIPPINES.

PHILIPPINE REFINING COMPANY INC.

GOODRICH INTERNATIONAL RUBBER COMPANY

PEACE — — FREEDOM

Speed — Accuracy
Economy
with BURROUGHS
Quality Equipment
and dependable
Worldwide Service

"LEST YOU FORGET"
    Santo Tomas
    MEMORABILIA
  and WHO'S WHO
Complete Story
Roster, Sketches
A book to keep.
    Leave your address
    with FRED. STEVENS
    Box 1447 -- Manila

SAFE **PENNZOIL** LUBRICATION

H.G. LYMAN   REP.

"MIZPAH"

WESTERN EQUIPMENT
& SUPPLY CO.
(WEANDSCO)
Bill Chittick

Electrical Supplies
--Installations--

That Final Step to
Security & Contentment
YOUR ANNUITY
with the
MANUFACTURERS' LIFE

Ask NED HALL, Manager,
NOW for latest details

PHILIPPINE
MANUFACTURING
COMPANY.

Purico.
Star Margarine.

1945
Jan. 6. Japanese staff, ordered to leave, spend all night packing and burning papers.
    7. Committee members held as hostages all day pending planned departure of the Commandant's staff.
    9. Commandant issues statement that owing to change of plan he and his staff are not leaving. He expresses concern over food situation.
   10. Leaflet:- "....The Battle of the Philippines is in it's final phase...."
   11. We all saw the Stars on their wings!
   14. War Prisoners' Bureau moves from Far Eastern University into Ed. Building.
   17. One man escapes from Gym.
   31. Chairman of Camp Medical Staff jailed by Japanese for refusal to exclude the words "malnutrition" and "starvation" from Death Certificates.

Average daily per capita calories issued by Japanese Army to Camp:- 723.7 during January.

Feb.3rd. 10 U.S. Planes parade to Santo Tomas, drop goggles and message of good tidings into East Patio.
About 6.00 P.M. continuous machine-gun fire can be heard to the North. Fires break out all around, especially to the North.
9.00 P.M. THE TANK ARRIVES.
Feb.4th. Third Anniversary of the Inauguration of Santo Tomas Internment Camp..plus one month....37 long months.

The Camp Industries on the 4th. Floor of the Main Building produced for general sanitation purposes the following articles:-

Coconut Oil	1,589.2 kilos
Caustic Soda	1,385.7 kilos
Soap	7,632.0 kilos
Calcium Hypochlorite	2,253.0 kilos
Alcohol	82.45 litres

Deaths up to January 31st. 1944 (25 mo.)	185
From Feb. 1st. 1944 to Sept. 30th (8 mo.)	54
from Oct.1st. to Dec. 31st.(3.mo)	43
in January 1945 (one month)	32

THE DUNLOP RUBBER COMPANY LTD.

ELIZALDE & CIA.
Philippines Agents

MARSMAN & COMPANY INC.
Industrial & Management
Engineers
Commercial & Manufacturing
Enterprises
Mining
Appraisals

Head Office: Manila.

MARSMAN TRADING
CORPORATION

Suppliers - Indenters
Manufacturers'
Representatives.

Branches
throughout
the Philippines

GREETINGS
to our FORCES
of Liberation.

CARDINAL INSURANCE COMPANY
Manila

Fire   Marine

We follow the Flag

AMERICAN HARDWARE
& PLUMBING CO.
Manila

Wholesale - Retail
Building Estimates

Radiograms   Radioletters

GLOBE WIRELESS LTD.

Radio Communication
to and from
America   Hawaii
and ships at sea.

Prompt Friendly Service

The total area of the Camp itself, including Santa Catalina and part of Calle Gov. Forbes, but excluding Seminary and other University property not available to Internees:- 195,345 square meters (approx. 50 acres).

Total Garden Areas:- 30,126 sq. meters.
Shanty Area "A"   17,620 "   "
   "   "   "B"   8,605 "   "
   "   "   "C"   17,490 "   "
   "   "   "D"   9,769 "   "

Length of each outside wall:- 465 meters.

Number of Shanties:- 683
Number living in Shanties:- 1108

As a result of the number living in Shanties the space available for sleeping quarters in buildings ascends to 38 sq. feet per person.

A school of approximately 700 children and young people, from Primary to College Grades, operated with permission but no help from the Japanese and staffed by qualified teachers or by experts in technical fields, was conducted in spite of grave lack of classroom space and shortage of textbooks and stationery.

A similar number of persons attended special adult classes until prohibited early in 1944.

Sanitary Facilities available to male and female Internees.

	Showers	Washbasins	W.C.	Urinals
Male	38	32	47	19
Female	33	24	53	

Number of Persons per Unit

	Showers	Washbasins	W.C.	Urinals
Male	32	64	44	108
Female	50	70	31	

Two bathtubs in entire Camp;
one allotted to Childrens' Hospital;
one for women's hair washing.

No water on 3rd. Floors of Buildings 50% of time.

AMERICAN CHAMBER OF COMMERCE
INFORMATION SERVICE
on Escolta.

REGISTER YOUR NEW ADDRESS
as soon as you have one
so that your friends can find you

The Daily average per capita value of the Food, supplied since February 1944 by the Japanese Army to the Santo Tomas Camp, compared with recognised Standard Requirements:-

	Protein Grams	Carbo-hydrate Grams	Fat Gms	Calories
Required by avg. man, light labor	70	455-510	75-100	3,000-3,500
Required lying quietly in bed.	at the rate of			2,400
Supplied by Jap. Army to Internees (All labor in Camp)				
1944 February	36.6	295	13.8	1,452
March	39	349	11.7	1,660
April	35	289	9.8	1,380
May	38.7	306	13.8	1,503
June	39	355	17.8	1,736
July	28.5	257	19.8	1,321
August	29	285	11.5	1,360
September	27.8	252	12.6	1,229
October	24	203	12.4	1020
November	25.5	194	13.4	999
December	19.8	185	9	898
Average 1944	31.2	270	13.2	1,323

Meat, Milk and Eggs were totally absent, while up to September inclusive a gross daily average of one ounce of fresh fish per person was provided; also an average of two small bananas per person per month, and no citrus fruit at all. Green vegetables were almost all supplied by the Camp Garden.

During 1944 the Camp Garden supplied the Camp with 247,765 lbs. (approx. 124 tons) of Produce. 117 tons were green vegetables, of which the largest crop was Talinum, 75 tons.

Average loss of weight among adults (19 years and over) during internment:-

	Av. Loss upto 15th Aug. 1944	Av. Loss since 15th Aug. 1944	Total Avg. Loss at 20th Jan. 1945
Men	27 lbs	24 lbs	51 lbs
Women	16 lbs	16 lbs	32 lbs
Total Avg.	22 1/2 lbs	20 lbs	42 1/2 lbs

ATLANTIC GULF & PACIFIC COMPANY.

ENGINEERS, CONTRACTORS, MANUFACTURERS.

MANILA TRADING & SUPPLY CO.

Exclusive Dealers of

F O R D Products.

GREETINGS and BEST WISHES
to our
LIBERATING FORCES

Thanks for Everything

HAMILTON-BROWN
Quality—Apparel
Escolta   Manila

KLIM

Price Jan. 20th. 1945
US$125 per lb.
and worth it!

GETZ BROS. & CO.
Manila.

FRED. WILSON & CO. INC.
Manila.

Machinery & Supplies

CENSUS STATISTICS OF THE THREE CAMPS	Manila Camp 1	Los Baños Camp 2	Baguio Camp 3	Total
Americans	2870	1509	394	4763
British, misc.	745	329	63	1137
" Australian	100	33	--	133
" Canadian	61	56	9	126
Netherlands	50	89	--	139
Polish	25	22	--	47
Norwegian	10	10	--	20
Italian	--	16	--	16
French	7	1	--	8
Spanish	2	--	--	2
Egyptian	2	--	--	2
German	1	--	--	1
Swiss	1	--	--	1
Slovak	1	--	--	1
Nicaraguan	--	1	--	1
Chinese	--	--	1	1
Mexican	--	--	1	1
Totals	3785	2146	468	6399

PRICES OF COMMODITIES IN CAMP
on December 31st, 1944

Sugar, per kilo equivalent of US$	105.00
Rice, per kilo	60.00
Corned beef, per 12oz. can	40.00
Evaporated milk, per 14oz. can	20.00
Margarine, per lb.	90.00
Vegetable lard, per lb.	90.00
Unrefined coconut oil, per quart	70.00
Smoking tobacco, per 1/4 kilo	40.00
Cigarettes, per pack of 30	18.00
Charcoal, per kilo	10.00

INTERNEE COMMITTEE

C. C. Grinnell, Chairman.
L. Earl Carroll.   S. L. Lloyd.

INTERNEE AGENTS

Clyde A. De Witt, Chairman.
H. B. Pond.   T. J. Harrington.

LIBBY'S 100 FOODS

Libby McNeill & Libby

THE NATIONAL CITY BANK OF NEW YORK

GENERAL MOTORS

wishes all internees

all good fortune in picking up their lives where they dropped them in 1942.

THREE YEARS CAN'T STOP US!

FIRESTONE TIRE & RUBBER CO. (P.I.) INC.

SWIFT'S PREMIUM HAMS & BACON

Swift & Company

UNITED ARTISTS CORPORATION.

A. SORIANO & CIA.

PLAN OF CAMP AT SANTO TOMAS, MANILA

Extra copies may be obtained (subject to Military or other regulations)
by mailing ₱1.00, Philippine currency, or 50 cents, U. S., to the
publisher at No.6 TM-011, San Miguel, Manila, Philippines.
    Published and edited by Peter C. Richards.
      Reproduced on the GESTETNER Duplicator,
        which, without breakdown, worked every
          day throughout it's internment.

CHAPTER 98

A Happy Birthday

On February 15, we were told civilians were finally being allowed on the grounds of Santo Tomas Internment Camp. Lucy, Emma, Junior, and Mary Jane could go with me right away, but I was afraid to take the younger children because they could not walk the long distance easily. Street battles were still raging in Manila. My nephew, Peping, would take care of Joyce and Linnie. They were so sad to be left behind.

The streets were still littered with debris. We picked our way through large chunks of concrete, twisted rebar, and broken lumber for about six miles from San Juan to Santo Tomas. We had to walk carefully across the large water pipes to get across the San Juan River as the pontoon bridge was being used for vehicular traffic only, and we could not afford the price of transportation.

Jess was anticipating our visit and was waiting near the front gate with an American soldier. The kids overwhelmed Jess with their hugs and kisses, as they had not seen him in two years. He staggered backward in his weakened condition as they swarmed around him. He had lost over sixty pounds during his thirty-seven month confinement in Santo Tomas and was in poor condition. Once everyone had a chance to greet Jess, we turned to the American soldier standing nearby.

"Mary," Jess said, "I want you to meet my nephew, Howard. He is my brother, Jim's, oldest son. Howard scanned the internee rosters searching for my name. When he walked up to my cot, I was quite surprised and glad to meet him!"

We all greeted Howard warmly. Howard smiled as we pelted him with questions about Texas. He was amazed that we spoke English so well.

"I had no idea what y'all looked like or if y'all spoke English," Howard drawled. "All I ever saw were baby pictures of y'all and maybe some of y'all as li'l kids."

"Well, Howard," I replied, "the last photo we have of you was one when you were about eleven or twelve. You've changed."

"Aunt Linnie is the one who has really changed," Howard noted.

"Aunt Linnie? Where did you see her?" I countered.

"I was so surprised to see you a couple of days ago, I forgot to tell you that Linnie and her sister, Era Boman, were brought to Santo Tomas around the end of June 1943. C. N. escaped to the mountains with some of his native employees. I had no way of letting you know," Jess stated.

We chatted about the many ways Jess helped the two sisters before Howard and Jess took us to see Jess' Aunt Linnie and her sister, Era Boman. Although I had never met Era, I had been around Aunt Linnie several times. I was shocked to see how emaciated they were. Aunt Linnie and her sister, Era, were just skin and bones. The last time I had seen Aunt Linnie she carried her two hundred pounds on her large frame well. She looked like a skeleton with skin hanging in folds off her large frame. Linnie and Era were happy to see us. They hugged and kissed us all.

"Mary, I thought of you often," Aunt Linnie stated. "How did you manage to take care of yourself and all your children? What did you do?"

I gave a brief description of how we kept a garden and had our fruit trees to help provide food. I also told them about my business of selling items from family members and friends for commission.

"Enough about me," I continued. "How did you get captured and brought here?"

"It's a long story," Era began. "I'll hit the highlights if we can find a place to sit."

Jess led us to a group of benches where we settled in to hear Era's account of their experiences. She was shaking as she began.

"C. N. sent me a cable in January 1941 saying he needed help to take care of Linnie. His increasing businesses and Linnie's ill health had him overwhelmed. I arrived in Manila in February 1941 to take care of Linnie in Iloilo. After taking Linnie to Baguio for health spa treatments for her arthritis, I took charge of the office work. I told C. N. I would stay until Linnie was well enough to travel to Texas. I began looking for passage to Texas before November and discovered no ships were leaving for the United States. During Thanksgiving, the American colonel in charge of Panay's defense warned us about the possibility of war with Japan. He suggested we find a place to hide. Makeshift air raid shelters were built at the home and office. This was a temporary move toward survival. After some discussion, C. N. decided the best place to hide was at his ranch near Passi. Detailed plans were put into place. In addition to personal needs, food, and medicines, we packed C. N.'s important business papers and valuables…both personal and those from pawnshops. The first bombing of Iloilo by Japanese was on December 18, 1941. Panic took over Iloilo, so we left for the ranch as quickly as we could with several loads of paperwork and valuables. We had to travel on dirt roads, by boat, and on several sleds pulled by *carabaos* to get to the ranch. After Linnie was settled in, I helped with the chores and selling of cattle to Col. Neil Britton from Enid, Oklahoma, who was in charge of looking for beef for the USAFFE. He turned out to be very helpful. To make a long story short, we were not bothered until April 1942, when we heard about Japs in nearby Jarro. We found a secluded place to dig a long pit and buried all the papers and valuables before the Japs arrived. They surprised us on June 21. C. N. was not at the ranch, so Linnie and I were captured and taken to their headquarters at Dao, where we were kept for several days. From there we were put on a train to Iloilo, where we were deposited at the Iloilo Central Ward School, their prison camp. We were there about a year before we were brought to Santo Tomas. Thank God, Jess found us and was able to help us."

We were amazed and wanted to know more, especially if they had heard from Uncle C. N., but Jess was tiring and wanted me to see Mr. Myers, his friend from the San Juan Heights project. We hugged Aunt Linnie and Era and wished them well. Jess led us to Mr. Myers room, where he was resting.

"Mary, it's good to see you," Mr. Myers rose from his cot with considerable effort as he greeted us. "Jess worried so much about you and the kids. I always assured Jess you would take care of the family. I told him I had lots of faith in you."

Thanks to Mr. Myers, Jess kept his chin up and hoped all would be okay with us. His friendship had been a comfort to Jess during those difficult days in prison camp.

Era Higdon Bowman *(left)* and her sister Linnie Higdon Hodges, spouse of Charles Newton (C. N.) Hodges (Jesse's uncle). Photo taken in 1941 at their home in Iloilo, P.I., prior to WWII. Both sisters were interned in Santo Tomas during the Japanese Occupation. A third sister, Mrs. O. C. Howell (Emma Higdon) was a resident of Commerce, Texas.

The day passed swiftly. We still had much to say and many questions to ask, but I needed to return and give Peping time to get home before dark. Snipers were very active at night. As we took turns with goodbye hugs and kisses, Jess pulled off one of his bakyas he had made. He turned over this wooden shoe, twisted its heel, and revealed a secret compartment he had hollowed out in the wood. He had several Philippine *pesos* and a few American dollars hidden inside its cavity.

"A couple of hours before the cavalry burst into Santo Tomas, I took twenty dollars and bought a can of Spam one of the fellows had hidden in his bunk," Jess said. "That can of Spam kept several of us alive. Just before we were taken hostage in the Education Building, Aunt Linnie, her sister, Era, Mr. Myers, Mr. Cuzner, Mr. Pate, and I finished the whole can. Those bites of Spam and a few bites of the beef stew the camp cooks brought in were all we had to survive the three day siege."

Jess gave me the Philippine *pesos* to take with me to buy food. It felt rather strange to hold Philippine currency in my hand. Not long ago, I was terrified I might be caught with this "thread" in my possession. What a rare feeling to be free of fear!

On our way home, we stopped by Lucing's house to see *Mami* and give her the news about Jess. We dared not stay over fifteen minutes, as we had several miles to walk, and snipers emerged from their hiding places like mosquitoes at night to attack their unwary victims. We had come a long way and did not want to lose our lives when the end of the war was close at hand.

On February 17, two days before my fortieth birthday, I received a surprise. Jess rang the bell at the front gate accompanied by his nephew, Howard Hodges, who had transported Jess home in a jeep.

"Hey, everyone, I'm home!" Jess yelled…his voice cracked with emotion.

He was waving a small rectangular slip of paper in the air over his head and had a large smile on his gaunt face. We all ran to see Jess and Howard.

After everyone had a chance to hug and kiss Jess and greet Howard, Jess held a slip of paper in front of his chest for all to see.

#10 RELEASE FROM INTERNMENT

Date: February 17, 1945

The bearer, J. A. Hodges whose signature appears below has been permanently cleared and is eligible for release from internment and can return to his/her home.

[Signature: J. A. Hodges]
Signature of Bearer

[Signature]
E. M. Grimm
Colonel, TC
Commanding

February 19, 1945, was a truly happy birthday for me! Jess was my gift. If Bobby had also been there, my birthday would have been completely happy.

CHAPTER 99

Misery Revisited

Bombing, shelling, burning, and street fighting raged in Manila and *Intramuros* (The Walled City). We were on constant alert for snipers and grenade attacks in our area although we had American soldiers nearby. Their presence, while comforting, was also cause for concern. Japanese raiding parties were moving around in the dark of night and wreaking havoc on American military units. We were still not out of danger, so I kept my whistle around my neck.

Peping arrived with a copy of the February 20 issue of *Free Philippines*, a free newspaper published three times weekly since our liberation. Most of the articles were written by experienced Filipino reporters and was an attempt by the United States and the Philippines to bring the "real" news, not propaganda, to the public. Jess and I were finishing our morning coffee, so Peping joined us at the dining table. Jess asked me to read the articles aloud as his eyes had weakened and his old eyeglasses were no longer effective. I picked this article to read first because Felipe was related to our veterinarian, Dr. Victor Buencamino, who was killed by the Japs.

REFUGEES SALVAGE HOPE, LITTLE ELSE, FROM RUINS
By Felipe Buencamino, III

Out of the smouldering ruins, off the pontoon bridge spanning the Pasig River leading to liberated north Manila, limped and crawled hundreds and hundreds of disheveled, unkempt, bewildered men, women and children carrying little bundles of food and clothing, and bringing eyewitness accounts of Japanese bestiality, reminiscent of the infamous rape of Nanking.

Walking with advanced patrols through the ash-covered streets of Paco and Malate down Taft Avenue and Remedios rotonda, I saw soul-searing sights that reminded me of the last phases of the death-march from Bataan to Capaz. Only here were not defeated soldiers but non-combatants, old men and children, helpless women that for ten tortuous days were cornered with desperate Japanese marines.

Free Philippines newspaper
containing the article reprinted below.

The first man I saw amid the fire-levelled district of Paco was former Senator Elpidio Quirino. He was not the same man I had seen so many times in the past, banging the gavel in the rostrum of the Senate. Senator Quirino had aged in ten days and his face had a lost expression. His wife and two daughters, Norma and Fe, had been killed by the Japanese. His son, Tommy, was injured and is at present in a field hospital.

As the Japanese retreated from Paco, they threw grenades at big residences, set fire to all houses and buildings. I saw the mansion of Chief Justice Jose Yulo completely razed to the ground. The residence of Minister Quintin Paredes of the department of justice of the defunct puppet republic was also swallowed by the flames.

Paco railroad station, Hale Shoe Factory, Rosenthal Building, Insular Saw Mill, Philippine Refinery, Manila Gas Co., Manila Cordage, Esco Shoe are now mere heaps of debris. I saw endless lines of small nipa shacks—homes of at least four thousand laborers—reduced to ashes. Paco church is partly standing, its side badly battered by Japanese mortars, its silver dome making a weird contrast with the cinder-strewn sections around it.

All Herran and General Luna, parts of Vermont, Wright and Remedios are burnt. Standing at the ruins of Paco Catholic school, I could see all the way up to Philippine Women's University and beyond. Practically nothing but crooked steel electric posts, tangled wires, ash-covered streets, piles and piles of mortar and stone stand on the way.

Philippine Columbian, Central School, the residences of Dr. Antonio Sison, Director of the Philippine General Hospital, Mr. Jesus Bayot, Mrs. Baltazar and Manuel Roxas, former speaker of the house of representatives, are now nothing but charred remains. All along Vermont and Taft Avenue, in the ditches and cinders of houses were numerous corpses of Japanese riddled by bullets, with faces turned upward to the sky.

Amid the ruins, the piles of corpses, the dangling wires, broken posts, burning houses, around jeeps and cars and trucks, trudged in endless files men, women and children rendered homeless by Yamashita's so-called defense of Manila. Aware of the care given by American troops to civilian homes, the Japanese marines converted private homes and public buildings into little fortresses. When a building was no longer tenable, the Japanese poured gasoline on it and razed it to the ground.

What touched me more than the sight of ruined public buildings and the ashen remains of the houses of personal friends, was the plight of wounded civilians being carried in push carts red with blood, women pale in dust-covered stretchers, gaunt children weeping, men on crutches, old persons with bandages around their heads, blinded women, boys begging for water.

Each person I interviewed told the same story—Japanese brutality, rape, burning of houses, machine gunning of those trying to escape from the flames, regardless of age or sex, mass-murder of males, grenading of bolted buildings and residences.

I met Mrs. Pura Villanueva-Kalaw, widow of the late Don Teodoro

Bombed remains of the Santa Domingo Church in *Intramuros* near Santo Tomas.

Kalaw, sitting on the ground, beside a cart containing all that was left of her belongings. She said that the historic papers of the Katipunan and the original documents of Philippine Masonry were lost in her burning home. She said however that the diploma of Jose Rizal and the original writings of Apolinario Mabini, brains of the Philippine revolution, were saved from the flames.

I saw Vincente Francisco, well-known criminal lawyer, walking with his wife who was weeping. The attorney's house was burnt and his son Manuel and daughters Gloria and Remedios were lost in the fire.

I saw Susan Magalona Ledesma sitting on a boulder, her face covered with dust, drinking out of a tin can. I met the family of Mr. Jesus Bayot running out of the flames that enveloped their home. I helped Cecelia Lichauco, to an ambulance. Her leg was bleeding due to wounds inflicted by a Japanese machine-gunner. I saw beautiful Conchita Sunico, popular Manila socialite, tramping through the ruins of Paco, blood flowing from her injured feet. I saw Dr. Antonio Vasquez, personal physician of President Quezon and his son Dr. Luis Vasquez helping the wounded, giving first-aid treatment to the injured amid intermittent sniper fire.

I met Mrs. Alejandro Roces, Sr., and daughter Bebeng looking for shelter, asking acquaintances for the other members of their family. I saw Renato Arevalo and his aunt vainly searching for his mother, an aunt and sister Clara. I saw the family of Judge José Abreu sitting under the shade of bushes, happy that they were able to escape from death, sad that they had lost everything. I talked to Dr. Gomez who recounted how the Japanese threw grenades inside the civilians' dugouts and his gaunt face revealed the thirst and hunger he had endured for days.

In mud-covered undershirt and with bandaged hands, Dr. Aristeo Ubaldo and his son-in-law Dr. Lozano told how they escaped from death in the hands of the Japanese. They said that with three hundred others, the Japanese locked them in the apartment building of Dr. Paz Mendoza Guazon. Before burning the building, the Japanese threw grenades inside. Many died. "We don't know how we escaped," said the doctor.

Eyewitnesses told me that hundreds of men were locked in St. Paul's Institution. First candles were thrown by the Japanese, and then grenades. Daniel Vasquez said, "Only a miracle saved my life."

The daughter of Miguel Cuaderno, between sobs said that her father, who was President of the Philippine Bank of Commerce, was killed by the Japanese.

All the civilians I interviewed were happy the Americans had liberated them. Almost all asked me to write about what the Japanese have done, that the world may know.

I was trembling when I finished reading the article. I knew many of the people mentioned and was saddened about the devastation of homes and families. The Roxas family were our friends. I put the paper down as I could tell it was affecting all of us.

Jess tried to put on a brave face, but his depression, plus his weakened condition, affected his emotions day and night. By the third night of his return to us, we retired to our bedroom, and I asked him if he would be more comfortable in a bed by himself, since each of us had become accustomed to sleeping alone for over three years.

"No, Mary, that is not the problem," Jess stated. "I've had something I needed to tell you, but I did not want to spoil your birthday celebration."

I perched tensely on the edge of the bed after closing the bedroom door, as the children were asleep. I did not want "sad news" to spill from our bedroom and cause concern. I waited for Jess to speak.

"Mary, Mr. Pate was transferred to Santo Tomas from Bilibid Prison when the military prisoners were taken to Bilibid from Corregidor," Jess stated. "All the civilian prisoners were brought to Santo Tomas."

What does Mr. Pate's transfer to Santo Tomas from Bilibid have to do with sad news? I was puzzled and failed to see the connection. The frown on my face made him plunge into the rest of his explanation.

"Mr. Pate told me he had met Bobby in Bilibid Prison," Jess said. "He said Bobby was in fair condition and had high spirits, even after the long Death March from Bataan, however, Bobby was shipped to Palao, where the Japs used prisoners to build a new air strip."

"Bobby is alive? He is in Palao?" I shrieked and clapped my hands to my face as I jumped to my feet. "Why didn't you tell me sooner?"

"Wait, Mary," Jess interjected, "let me finish."

I waited. There was more to his story. I stared at Jess as he lifted his right hand to his cheek to brush away a tear.

"Three of the prisoners from Palao were brought to Santo Tomas after we were released from the hostage situation in the Education Building. I spoke with them."

I felt fear gripping my heart. I did not utter a word but listened intently to Jess.

"Those boys said Bobby was with them when the Americans stormed the gates of their compound. They told me what happened," Jess stated. "The Japs ordered all of them into a tunnel at gunpoint. Minutes before the Americans burst into their camp, the Japs threw live grenades at them while they were dodging and running like crazy to get away. The American soldiers found the three of them under the bodies of several of the other prisoners. They said Bobby must not have made it."

The dam of bravado burst. Tears were flowing freely down our faces. We spent a long time quietly holding each other. We still had no verification Bobby had been killed in Palao, but the odds for his survival were diminished. I refused to believe our son was dead. I must keep on searching and hoping for a miracle.

"Jess," I whispered, "we must not tell the children. They would be heartbroken, like us. We must not lose hope. He might still be alive."

Jess agreed. Nothing good would come from destroying their hope for Bobby's safe return to our family.

The next morning, I busied myself with preparing breakfast on the outside fire pit. We still had no gas or electricity as the battles in Manila and *Intramuros* were still raging. The shelling and fires from bombing continued every night from February 22 through February 28. We would pray for those souls still under fire and try to enjoy the blessings of having Jess with us. We also prayed for Bobby.

CHAPTER 100

GI Joes

February dragged itself into March, and the street fighting, mortar and machine gun fire kept on in Ermita, The Walled City, and Manila. There was occasional sniper fire in our area, so we kept a careful watch…day and night. The curfew, imposed by General MacArthur, was an attempt to keep everyone off the streets for their safety. American patrols in the area made us feel safer, but we were still cautious. The children wanted to play outside and climb the fruit trees after they returned from their half-day at *Colegio de la Consolacion,* but it was still not safe. We were in a "holding" pattern.

Jess was getting more rest but was still depressed. During the last week of February, Jess decided to go to Santo Tomas to avail himself of the free medical services provided to all internees. During his checkup, they discovered Jess had lost more weight after his release from prison camp due to his severe depression affecting his appetite. Jess was hospitalized and intravenous fluids were provided to build his energy level and raise his spirits. He knew he needed medical help. We had no money to buy food—much less pay doctor bills.

While Jess was hospitalized, Emma and Mary Jane visited the nearby First Cavalry encampment. The first person they met was a young GI working on a truck. As they approached him, he spoke.

"Howdy! What are you gals doin' here?"

He had a thick Texas drawl, a big grin, and a pleasant manner about him.

"Oh, we just wanted candy," Mary Jane said honestly.

Several soldiers who had come by the house offered them Butterfinger or Baby Ruth candy bars. The first ones they tried made them sick because they were not accustomed to eating rich, sweet foods, but the candy was so tempting, the kids were willing to take another chance, and try it again.

"Sure, I've got candy here. Come and get some," he replied.

After accepting the candy and chatting with the soldier, he talked about himself. He put down his tools, wiped his hands on his fatigues, and smiled.

"My name's Buddy Collins, and I'm from Texas," he said in a booming voice.

American GIs following the liberation of Manila.

"I am Mary Jane Hodges and this is my sister, Emma," Mary Jane replied. "Our daddy is also from Texas."

Each of the girls was nibbling on the candy bar they were given. They did not gobble them down as they had their first candy bars. They learned their lesson well.

"So your dad's from Texas! How about that!" Buddy crowed.

They had a long chat before the girls decided it was time to get home. As they were leaving, Buddy asked a question.

"Say, you girls have any more at home like you…'cept older?"

They nodded their heads as they began walking. He popped another question.

"Well, I'll tell you what, you girls run home and bring her here, and I'll give you more candy," Buddy boomed. "Say, where do you live?"

"Forty-three J. Ruiz in San Juan…right on Aurora Quezon Boulevard."

Mary smiled as she put her writing materials away for another day.

The wheels were set into motion for Fate to step in and change the lives of Cornelius "Buddy" Collins and our daughter, Lucy. Their story would fill the pages of yet another book. Many of the GIs were welcomed into our home in March, April, and May of 1945. Let me think. I remember Raymond Russell from Oklahoma; Marvin D. French from Kansas (the guys called him 'Frenchy'); Ben Mosher; Dennis Goforth; Tony Davenport from Florence, Alabama; 'Kaintuck' (What was his name?); and, Hubert Poskey from Texas. Poskey helped us complete the reams of paperwork required to obtain passage to America. He and Frenchy took us to the collection center at Santo Tomas to ride the "ducks" to Manila Bay so we could board our ship, the S.S. Uruguay. Manila Bay was mined and full of debris. Large ships dared not enter, but the "ducks" could skim over the top of the water and deliver us to our ship. I must light extra candles for them at vespers tonight. If not for them and many others who helped to liberate us, we might not be in America…we might not be alive.

CHAPTER 101

The Battles Continue

The Battle of Manila started on February 3 and stretched through the third of March like a long, poisonous snake leaving death everywhere it struck. During this same period of time, battles were ongoing in *Intramuros*, where my aunt, Herminia and her family lived, and Baguio, where my sister, Pilar, and her family fled to escape the Japanese. Pilar and Tony had no idea Baguio would become the center of the Japanese/Filipino puppet government. General Yamashita's forces built fortified bunkers to protect himself and his officers. They were entrenched and ready to do battle. We prayed for family members who lived in or near those areas.

The Japanese Navy occupied Ermita, the former American section of Manila. Most of their ships had been destroyed at sea or in Manila Bay. They were bitter and would fight until death. They vowed to destroy all of the homes in Ermita, located near the sea. They killed all of the male residents, drove the women and children from their homes, and burned all of their houses.

On February 26, Corregidor was taken from the Japs. The sky was ablaze from the fires in Manila, *Intramuros*, Ermita, and Corregidor. We prayed for our troops as they mopped up the pockets of Japanese resistance in San Juan. Another week would crawl by before the major battles on Luzon subsided. The Japanese were fanatics.

I went to see Jess several times in the camp infirmary, but the doctors at Santo Tomas were not ready to release him, until he improved considerably. He still suffered from depression. The doctors said when Jess felt stronger and was in control of his emotions, he would be released. In mid-March, Jess' nephew, Howard Hodges, brought Jess home. His return was like a double-edged sword. *Would he be home to stay?*

While the kids were happy to have him home, they tiptoed around him as if he were made of very fragile glass. Their behavior concerned Jess, so I spoke to them and encouraged them to act normally. Linnie, still not sure who this "stranger" was in their midst, finally crawled into his lap all on her own after the first week. Her actions and childlike trust helped Jess tremendously.

C47 dropping supplies to American troops on Corregidor Island.

In March, we had news of my sister, Pilar, and her husband, Tony Settember. Following their liberation in Baguio, they were brought to Santo Tomas for physical examinations, clothing, and assistance. They had lost all their belongings. They survived a terrible experience in their air raid shelter near the foot of the mountains in Baguio.

Pilar, Tony, and José (my sister Lucing's son, nicknamed *Pépe*/Peping), were all inside the L-shaped shelter with other area residents. Pilar was very worried about their son. Anthony had not been seen for over a year. José, Lucing's son who was staying with the Settembers, was seated on the opposite end of the shelter while Pilar, Tony, and others were seated on the upper level toward the rear. The shelter suffered a direct hit from mortar fire causing that portion to crumble, burying all sixteen persons including José (*Pépe*/Peping). Pilar and Tony, along with the rest of the occupants of the upper level were buried waist-deep in debris.

The next day, their screams caught the attention of American troops as the area was being combed for Jap snipers. Tony was yelling in English, colored by his thick Italian accent, hoping the Americans would come to their rescue. The GIs pulled away enough of the rubble from the opening and around their bodies. When enough debris was removed, they pulled them from the remaining debris, causing those being rescued to lose their shoes. After they were rescued, they realized how close they had been to being buried alive, like those poor souls at the other end. Pilar was inconsolable when she was told the others had suffered a direct hit. They prayed for the dead before leaving the site.

Three couples, including Tony and Pilar, were the only ones rescued. They were given water to drink from the soldier's canteens, and were told to move down the mountainside and away from the fighting, as the battle was still raging. They began their trek without shoes…the cuts on their legs bleeding as they stepped. When they reached the streets of Baguio, panic was rampant. The people were running in all directions to get away from another wave of carpet-bombing. As they ran toward the hospital, it received a direct hit, killing many of the occupants. They changed direction and ran toward my aunt's house. Before they arrived there, they discovered the bodies of our aunt, Rita (Adriensen) Swanson, Arturo (her son), and his wife in the street…their home demolished.

They found Arturo's two dazed, young children wandering in the street, crying, and took them along. Before long, they arrived at a friend's house, and rested for a short while before leaving the children with them. It would have been impossible to walk long distances with those children, especially with no shoes. Their feet and legs ached and bled with each step.

Before long, they met more American troops moving up the mountain. Tony talked to the officer in charge, who arranged their transport to the nearest liberated internment camp to check in as directed.

Over a year earlier, Anthony had slipped away from Baguio when he heard about American invasions. When MacArthur landed in the Lingayen Gulf, he joined the First Cavalry and became a part of the liberation of Manila…working on the grave detail. After Manila was liberated, Anthony saw one of his father's friends and was told that his parents were taken to a camp in Northern Luzon, but his father was killed. He borrowed a jeep and drove to the camp. As he drove through the camp's gate, he was surprised to see his father, as he had been informed earlier, that his father had been killed. Their reunion was a mixture of joy and sadness. Anthony was excited to learn that both his parents had survived, but sad to hear his cousin, José Luis, was killed when their air raid shelter had suffered a direct hit. Had he stayed in Baguio, he would have been sitting in that shelter beside his cousin José Luis.

∽∾

Mary was thankful she had not allowed Joyce to go with her sister Pilar to Baguio. Joyce might not have survived. *I am so glad I listened to Jess and kept the children together.*

Mary stared wistfully at her hand and touched the ring Mary Jane had asked her jeweler at Drake's Jewelers to design from their yellow gold wedding bands and their children's birthstones. Her children had presented her with this treasure for Mother's Day, a year after Jess died. She touched each of the nine birthstones representing her nine children. They were nestled between the rings she and Jess had given each other on their wedding day. *Her children were still together in this ring.*

(L-R) Anthony D. (Tony) Settember Jr. and his father, A.D. (Tony) Settember. Ontario, California, 1945.

CHAPTER 102

Making Decisions

By early April 1945, although street fighting was still occurring in outlying areas, we felt safer, as most of Luzon had been secured by American troops. We went only to secure areas. We visited my mother and sisters in Santa Mesa. We attended church services together as "the Gamero family" and prayed for those family members who had not survived this terrible war. Special candles were lit for the souls of Lucing's son, José Luis; Consueling's daughter Fanny; our sister-Rosario (Charing); all four of Hermiñia's sons; and, Bobby. We gave thanks for the rescue of Jess, Tony, and Pilar. Lucing still could not bring herself to speak to Tony and Pilar about the loss of her son.

Following the family service, we met at Lucing's home for a light lunch, and felt almost "normal" again. As we listened to strains of *Rum and Coca-Cola* streaming from Lucing's small radio in her kitchen, Lucy, Carmen *(Nena)*, Lucing's only daughter, and Pilachu, Consueling's daughter, were sharing some of the new "boogie woogie" steps they had learned from some of the American soldiers. Suddenly, the song was interrupted by the announcement of President Franklin D. Roosevelt's death. The loss of one of "The Big Three" on April 12, 1945, raised concerns.

The discussion around the dining table, where the adults gathered, turned to the future of the Philippines. The Settembers, still housed at Santo Tomas, made plans to go to America and settle in Southern California. Before the war started, Tony was employed by International Harvester. He had been in touch with his former bosses and was offered a position in the rebuilding of the company in the Philippines. Tony felt his family would be safer in America, as the Philippines might not have a stable government under the banner of independence.

"I guess you guys will be going to Texas, right?" Tony asked Jess.

"We won't be going to Texas," Jess said quietly.

The room became very quiet and everyone stared at Jess. No one believed those words.

"Not going to Texas? What do you mean, Jess?" Tony gasped.

No one stirred. The room was so quiet, that a spider crawling up the wall would have created a disturbance. *What is he thinking? Why should we stay here?*

"While I was in the infirmary at Santo Tomas, I was given paperwork about being repatriated to America," Jess began haltingly. "My friend Mr. Pate visited me. We had a long talk about either staying in the Philippines or going to Texas. He asked me to stay here with him and assured me there would be plenty of work in the construction business rebuilding all of the homes that were destroyed. He made me an offer, so I signed the paperwork to stay in Manila. At least, here, I have a job offer. I might have land in Texas, but I'm not sure. I know I don't have a job offer in Texas."

They were so disappointed in his response. They just knew we would all be going to the United States. Tony and Pilar did not believe their ears.

"But, the Philippines will be getting their independence before long," Tony blurted. "Do you want your family to go through that experience?"

Jess' face turned red. He was beginning to shake. His emotions were getting out of control again. He excused himself, and left the room.

The kids were visibly upset. Pilar asked if they could take Joyce with them. Joyce began chattering about going to California with her *Tita* Pilachu and Uncle Tony.

"All of you stop worrying and pray," I ordered. "Ask God to decide what is best for our family, and we will find the right answer. No, Pilar, Joyce is staying with us."

The discussion was ended. The room became quiet. Lucing went to the kitchen to prepare a small *merienda* to enjoy as a family before everyone had to leave. I prattled about several unimportant matters just to have more time with Pilar, who was disappointed to leave Joyce behind. *I might never see Pilar again since she will be leaving for America, in mid-May while we remain.*

After Pilar and her family left, I returned to Lucing's bedroom where Jess had retreated to escape questions. He was sitting on the edge of the bed…staring into space. I joined him, put my right arm around his shoulder, and gave him a squeeze. We needed to go home and rest. We would talk about this matter later.

Jess' depression worsened with each passing day. He was so weak. His stomach had shrunk so much; he ate only small bits of bland food, otherwise, he became nauseated. He was warned before leaving Santo Tomas about the dangers of overeating after a long period of food deprivation. Several of his friends in camp died as a result of gorging food. He quivered or shook at loud noises or when the children let out a shriek. His nerves were shattered. He needed professional help.

I visited my sister Maming at *Colegio de la Consolacion* the next day. She had provided help and advice before, and I hoped she would again. After describing our situation and Jess' depression, Maming decided I should have the children come to her convent during the day. The nuns just reopened their school the week before to help bring stability to the chaos surrounding them. The children would attend half a day and would not be charged.

"It's a good plan, Maming," I stated. "I will go and talk with Jess about your idea. Jess will be able to rest better during the day without the children making noise."

When Jess and I discussed Maming's suggestion, he was in agreement, but he wanted Junior to stay with him. He was still thinking about the small amount of time he had spent with Bobby. While Jess was away on job sites, his days with Bobby were lost. He wanted to spend more time with Junior. He had already missed over three years. Junior was almost seventeen and would probably join a branch of the military before long. *I signed for Bobby when he was only seventeen.*

So, Lucy, Emma, Mary Jane, and Joyce attended school for half a day at *Colegio de la Consolacion* under Maming's watchful eye as the Mother Superior. Junior stayed home with Jess, and Linnie tagged along with me. This allowed Jess time to rest and relax. Junior adored his father and never complained when asked to do a difficult chore.

I was having a hard time scraping together enough money to feed Jess and the family. The Japanese occupation money was worthless. Only Philippine and American currency was being used and I had little of either one. Food products were expensive. One tomato cost one *peso*. One egg was twenty-five *centavos*. I only had two cans of beans left. The canned tomatoes we had buried had rusted and ruined. I still had one can of powdered milk (Klim) left. Mary Jane would go daily to the nearby artesian well to get drinking water, as the Japs had fouled the city water supply. I would mix the powdered milk with boiled water, so Jess and Linnie would have more nutrition. I was so relieved to receive a notice from Santo Tomas stating rations for families of internees were ready for distribution.

The following day, Jess and I pushed a small garden cart to Santo Tomas to collect our rations. Different kinds of canned goods, (including Cudahy's canned beef), sugar, flour, salt, rice, dried beans, and powdered eggs, were offered. We were amazed. We could now have a "real" meal. The officer in charge reminded everyone to eat small portions. Several internees had already died from overeating.

We walked to Santo Tomas three times a week to get our rations. Jess felt better because he was able to do something to provide for his family. He was careful to eat small portions regularly to improve his physical strength. The exercise of walking the six miles each way, with plenty of "rest stops" in between, also energized him.

On May 22, we were so busy, I forgot all about Mary Jane's birthday. Lucy reminded me when the girls returned from *Colegio de la Consolacion*. I rushed around through the rations to put together a small celebration and surprise her for dinner. I managed to put together a fairly decent meal. Since there was not enough time to make a birthday cake, I fixed a small stack of pancakes, pushed a single slightly used birthday candle in the center and marched in singing the birthday song. She seemed pleased, made her silent wish, blew out the candle, and shared the pancakes with the others.

"What was your wish?" Emma asked.

"I can't tell because it won't come true," Mary Jane replied.

The kids enjoyed the rations and the wide variety of food, but they were still unhappy their father had decided the family should stay in the Philippines. They all wanted to go to Texas. Jess and I had several discussions after the kids were asleep each night.

"Mary, I hope I've made the right decision to stay here and work," Jess said late one evening, as we watched the bright moonlight filter through the trees. "My health is not improving. I hope I will be able to work and support our family."

"Jess, you did what you thought was right," I said. "We will be okay, you will see."

I was supportive as his emotions were near the breaking point. It bothered him when the kids spoke wistfully about going to Texas, or complained about staying here.

"We would have to start with nothing in Texas," Jess stated flatly. "My nephew Howard waited until he thought I was in control of myself before he told me about my dad's farm. He said after my dad died in February 1941, Della and my half-brothers took over the farm. Since Della had not heard from us, she felt all the land and the home place belonged to her and her kids. Howard said that Jim, and I inherited part of my dad's farm, but it may no longer be there for us, since my stepmother, Della, remarried during the war. Della planned to divide the land among her children. She felt they had earned that right. We might go there and have nothing…not even a job."

"Let's sell what we own here, Jess, to have money," I suggested. "We can find ways to make money, if you want to go to Texas."

"Well, Mary, your mother would have to stay in the Philippines," Jess said. "You have been close to her, and she has lived with us for many years."

I thought about Jess' words. It would be difficult to leave my mother. My heart wrenched.

My sister, Lucing, and *Mami* visited after church the next Sunday. We talked about Jess' decision to stay in the Philippines, as we shared a light *merienda*. Jess discussed our children's unhappiness with staying. He wondered if he had made the right choice, and was having second thoughts about repatriation.

"Well, Mary is close to her family," Jess said. "*Mami*, you have lived with us a long time, but you are not an American citizen. We cannot take you with us to America."

The hairs bristled on the nape of *Mami's* neck. Her fiery Spanish temper was about to be unleashed. *She would not allow Jess to lay the blame for staying in Manila at her feet.* I waited for the explosion.

"Jess, do not make the same mistake my husband made after the Spanish-American War," *Mami* retorted. "Spain offered repatriation for all Spanish citizens, but Don José did not want to leave his position at the bank or the students at his boarding school. What happened? He died. Our children never had the chance to see Spain. So, if you get the chance, take your family where they belong. They will be better off than being here in the Philippines. It may be difficult for Americans when independence is granted. When you are established, you can send for me."

In early June, as we were at Santo Tomas to get our share of rations for the second week, an announcement was broadcast over the camp loudspeaker system.

All Americans who had signed their repatriation papers indicating they would stay in the Philippines will be given an opportunity to change their decision if they wish to leave. Please come by the main office to register your intent.

Jess and I stared at each other as they repeated the announcement. We did not say a word. We located the camp office, pushed our cart beside the front door, entered, received instructions on the paperwork, and signed the papers. My head was swimming.

"You will be leaving July 24 on the last ship for repatriates. You'll need to return to finish your paperwork and get immunized. Bring birth certificates for all of the children when you bring them for their immunizations, which will begin next Monday."

We were so excited when we left the camp office; we almost forgot our cart with our rations. We were anxious to tell the kids our news! *We're going to the United States! We are going to Texas!* As we hurried home with our cartload of rations, Jess appeared to be more at peace.

"Mary, I want to tell the kids. I feel I owe them this surprise."

I agreed. We talked about the many things we needed to take care of in preparation for leaving the Philippines on July 24. I felt overwhelmed at the prospect of leaving my mother and sisters. My past and present were in Manila...my future was in Texas. I knew nothing about Texas. *Would it be like the cowboy movies we had seen before the war?* I did not ask Jess. He had enough on his mind. I did not add my concerns to his already troubled mind.

CHAPTER 103

Making Plans

Jess acted like a kid in a candy store. He did not wait until we were inside the house to break the news. We were going to Texas! I'll never forget the expressions on our children's faces. The older ones were stunned. Lucy, Junior, and Emma stared at Jess with glazed disbelief in their eyes. Mary Jane and Joyce started dancing like Indians doing a Rain Dance. Linnie laughed at their antics and clapped her hands. Lucy was the first to speak.

"May we please tell our friends in the neighborhood?"

"Sure, you, Emma, Junior, and Mary Jane may go, after we get this food upstairs," Jess stated.

Joyce was still dancing and grabbed Linnie's hands to start a game of "Ring Around the Rosy." They played while the others emptied the pushcart of all the ration items. When they finished emptying the cart, they ran to tell the Kessels, Quintos, and Hughes families their news.

Upon their return, Jess called everyone together and explained how life would be in the United States. He had brought paper and pencils for Lucy, Junior, Emma, and Mary Jane for his assignment.

"In Texas, we will not have servants in our home like we have had here before the war. We will have no laundry woman to do your clothes. Everyone will have to pitch in and do the household chores. If we live on a farm, you will also have to do farm chores and gardening. Do you understand?"

Heads bobbed around the table in agreement. Everyone had listened intently and all were still smiling. I don't think they truly understood the extent of work on a farm. They just wanted to go to Texas, and waited for his next pronouncement.

"I want Lucy, Junior, Emma, and Mary Jane to each take writing paper and pencils and write down your answer to this question," Jess announced. "Why do you want to live in the United States?"

Linnie was busy dipping a cookie in her glass of freshly made KLIM milk while Joyce propped her elbows on the table...her chin in her hands, waiting for her snack to be delivered. I was in the kitchen preparing a little *merienda* to have as they began their writing project. I switched on the small radio so we could listen to music while we had our snack. Jess made sure each of the older kids had their writing materials.

"I'll take your written answers when you have finished," Jess stated as he followed Linnie's example by dipping his cookie in his coffee, laced with KLIM and plenty of sugar.

Strains of *Sentimental Journey* drifted from the kitchen into the dining area where they were writing. *It was wonderful having electricity again and hearing something other than Japanese propaganda or native music. The lyrics of this song were particularly haunting.* As each one finished, their completed composition was handed to Jess. He read silently as he sipped his coffee and munched on cookies. After he finished, he handed them to me. When all were through, Jess and I agreed their answers were quite similar.

"We are Americans. We want to live in Texas where our dad was born. We want to live with other Americans. We want an American education."

As I cleared the table from our *merienda* and "writing exercise," Jess shared his concerns about going to Texas. We did not have enough money. What we had was used to keep us alive after we were liberated, as the Japanese currency was worthless. How were we going to raise money?

"Jess, we can sell our furniture, the piano, your tools, the poultry equipment, and anything else people will buy."

"We don't have much time to get it all done," Jess stated flatly.

"Don't worry, Jess," I said, "my prayers will be answered."

Emma and Lucy were busy dancing around the living room to the strains of *Accentuate the Positive*. Their "boogie woogie" looked pretty wild to Jess and me. It was hard to get used to the new music and see the way the young people danced. In all my days of dancing, we had never danced that way. *Where did they get the energy? Who created that crazy "boogie woogie?"*

The next day we took inventory. The older kids and I made large signs to post on our fence along Aurora Quezon Boulevard to advertise the sale. Many people who lost all their belongings would welcome buying discounted used items…or so we thought. We posted prices on all the larger items and prepared for the shoppers.

Jess rubbed his hand longingly over the smooth mahogany dining table and chairs he had so lovingly made. He had hoped to take his prize project to Texas one day, but as repatriates, we were allowed to take only clothing, photos, and small mementos. I knew what Jess was thinking.

"*El hombre propone y Dios dispone,*" I stated. "My mother always said, 'Man proposes and God disposes.'"

Jess grimaced and muttered quietly under his breath. He ran his fingers across the smooth, shiny mahogany table as if to give it one last loving caress.

~~~

Mary pulled out photos she had kept of the pieces of furniture Jess had made. He was a creative individual and enjoyed every piece he built. Those were his "other" babies. *Too bad they would be left behind. We would have to start all over again in Texas.*

CHAPTER 104

Paperwork and Prayers

Jess and I were still going three times weekly to Santo Tomas to get our rations. The entire family went with us two of those times to undergo physical examinations and take their immunizations. We still had reams of paperwork to complete before being issued our papers of embarkation for July 24. We were also busy with bargain hunters coming by to see our sale items and dickering about pricing.

In early June, I was given the rest of the required paperwork at the Office of Repatriation. I separated the forms into stacks...eight stacks—one for each of us. It was going to be difficult to complete those forms and turn them in within three weeks for processing. I could not understand some of the questions, or why they had to be asked in the first place. While I was poring over the forms and trying to understand what information was needed, several of the soldiers, who had become regular visitors, stopped by the dining room, and saw me at the dining table with this sea of paperwork scattered before me. They were there to see Lucy and Emma, but stopped to greet me before enjoying the girls' company. Hubert Poskey saw the piles of paperwork and shook his head from side to side. He and Tony Davenport knew we were trying to prepare for repatriation. They enjoyed being with us and enjoyed calling me "Mama."

"Wow, Mama," Poskey said, "you look like you could use some help with those piles of forms."

"I sure do," I replied. "I don't understand half of what I am reading. I must not make mistakes. I have to get everything right."

Poskey joined me at the table, while Tony left to chat with Lucy. Poskey grabbed a stack of forms and began scanning each page. Jess entered and pulled up a chair.

"Let me have a pencil and I'll start by asking you two some of the questions," Poskey stated. "I'll write your answers on one form in the right places. Most of answers will be identical on each of the forms. Let's do the ones that will require individual answers first, then we can complete the general questions."

The question/answer session continued for two hours before Poskey had to return to his unit. Much had been accomplished, but there was still much to do.

Hubert Poskey, a native Texan, assisted Mary and Jess Hodges with the mountains of forms required to emigrate to the United States. Photo at right taken in 1945; inset from his obituary in 2009.

"I'll return tomorrow night, Mama," Poskey stated, "and I'll help you finish the rest."

Jess and I were so relieved and so thankful. I gathered the completed forms, stacked them on an empty chair, and gathered the remainder to finish later. I still had to collect the required documents before repatriation authorities at Santo Tomas would accept the paperwork.

The next morning, Mary Jane knocked on our bedroom door. She was carrying a piece of folded paper in her hand.

"I wanted to show you the birthday card I made for Junior."

Today was June 9. My mind was so full of paperwork and forms. All I had on my mind was preparing for our voyage to America. I took the folded paper from her, praised her creation, and thanked her for being so thoughtful. I was shocked to have, once again, overlooked one of their birthdays.

"I'm glad you made this card for your brother," I responded. "We will fix a very special birthday dinner."

We celebrated Junior's birthday much in the same way we had celebrated Mary Jane's. The birthday cake was, once again, a stack of pancakes. As he made his birthday wish and blew out the remainder of the birthday candle we had used on Mary Jane's stack of pancakes, Jess led the singing of the birthday song.

"Well, what did you wish?" Mary Jane inquired.

"My wish has already been granted," Junior stated. "We are going to Texas!"

"That was also my wish on my birthday," Mary Jane added.

The next day I took most of our Philippine *pesos* to exchange to American dollars. The exchange rate was one dollar for two *pesos*. While I was away, Jess was offered one thousand *pesos* for his tools we had priced at $750. Jess accepted this lower offer. The Filipino customer did not have the money with him. He would go to his bank in his home province to get a loan. He promised to return in three days with the money. When I returned, Jess told me about the deal he had made. I was so disappointed, as the amount was $250 under our asking price.

"Jess, those tools are worth more than two thousand dollars," I stated. "We needed to get our asking price of $750 for them. Tools are scarce because the Japs confiscated cars and anything made of steel for their war effort."

Jess was quiet. He sensed I was upset. I left the room... tight-lipped. The damage was done. A miracle was needed.

On June 13, 1945, we celebrated the Feast of St. Anthony, patron saint of miracles and lost causes or items. We were rich in many ways, because we had survived the horrors of World War II thus far, but we were poor when it came to material wealth. We needed to have enough money for a small nest egg for expenses in Texas. I prayed to St. Anthony from the depths of my heart to help us in our endeavor. I begged for a miracle to undo the deal Jess had made for his tools, and asked St. Anthony to send us a buyer who would pay our asking price. Jess and the Filipino customer had no written agreement. We had about a month to accomplish this task.

When I returned from church services, Jess met me at the gate with a big grin on his face. He hugged me before speaking.

"Mary, your St. Anthony bought my tools for the amount we were asking," Jess teased. "Since the other fellow didn't show with the money this morning, as he said, I sold the tools to a Spanish man... an acquaintance of mine."

"St. Anthony bought your tools?" I asked. "Jess, stop teasing me."

"No, it was St. Anthony... Mr. Angel Anthony Marino," Jess stated. "I built a house for him years ago. He and his brother, Don José Marino still own the chocolate factory and they plan on rebuilding when possible."

My prayers were answered. St. Anthony had worked another miracle. After sharing a snack for lunch, I left to cash "St. Anthony's" check. I asked for five hundred in U.S. dollars and the remainder in *pesos*. I left the bank, took one hundred and fifty *pesos* to our church (for St. Anthony), and splurged for a *calesa* ride home. I found a seat beside an elderly

The San Augustin Church, completed in 1599, is the oldest in the Philippines. The ceiling was hewn from stone and the edifice still stands after being restored by the United States.

lady, who looked familiar. I stared at her, and suddenly realized I had known her since I was eleven. Her family name escaped me. She and her sister, Antonia, lived in the same rooming house on Muralla Street in *Intramuros* where my family had also lived. They were teachers and operated a private kindergarten in The Walled City. I reintroduced myself, as she did not recognize me. Too much time had elapsed.

"*Sra. Fernanada, come estas? Yo soy Maria Gamero,*" I explained.

She was surprised and happy to see me. We chatted about my family before I asked about her sister, "Tonia." She told me Antonia had been killed during the devastation of *Intramuros*. She was living by herself at the *Hospicio de San José*, a home for the poor and elderly. Her home was destroyed. Her sons were tortured and killed. She cried as she described the atrocities in *Intramuros*. Visions of the same atrocities befalling Herminia's sons raced through my mind as she spoke. I felt so sorry for her as she was alone. I gave her twenty *pesos* as I prepared to leave the *calesa*. She thanked me profusely, but I stopped her.

"You can thank, St. Anthony. Without his intercession, I would not have any money to share," I stated as I left the *calesa* at the J. Ruiz stop.

I hurried home and handed Jess the bank envelope containing the five hundred dollars. He stuck the money into his pants pocket.

"Jess, maybe you should find a safer place to keep our nest egg," I stated.

He hid the nest egg behind the framed diorama of St. Anthony I had hanging on the wall beside our bed. St. Anthony would guard our nest egg.

"Where's the rest of the money?" Jess asked as I prepared a light *merienda* for us.

"I gave the church one hundred fifty *pesos* as an offering to St. Anthony, and I plan to take three hundred fifty *pesos* to my mother later this afternoon," I stated.

Jess stared at me quietly. He knew I was still uneasy about leaving my mother behind in the Philippines. He knew we might never see her again.

When we finished our *merienda*, I left Lucy and Emma in charge with preparations for our dinner while I visited my mother and sisters. The girls were expecting Hubert Poskey and Tony Davenport to come by. Poskey was trying to finish the paperwork with Jess answering any questions he might have.

When I arrived at Consueling's home, I was surprised to find mother's sister, *Tia* Herminia, my cousin, Pilar, and another sister, Lucing, there as well. Herminia had been staying at *El Hospicio de San José* since their home in *Intramuros* was destroyed. I told them about seeing *Sra*. Fernanda on the *calesa* ride, and that she, too, was living at the *Hospicio*. Herminia promised to visit her. We enjoyed our visit, but I still had much to do. I promised to come by to see everyone again before we left for the United States. I gave *Mami* the money and told her I wished it were much more. She was grateful and hugged me tightly as I prepared to leave.

Upon my return, several customers were sorting through the remaining items we had for sale. I was pleased and silently thanked St. Anthony for, once again, coming to our rescue. We would need part of the money from these sales to pay our bills and the rent for our home. We owed about one year's rent on the place. The owner felt sorry for us and had not kicked us out onto the streets. We would leave a bonus for him by paying rent for a full year.

≈≈

The ringing phone startled Mary. She was concentrating so hard on her writing that she lost track of the time. She eased herself out of her chair, stepped carefully around Booger, who had curled up by her feet, and walked toward the phone. Emma was calling to see if she wanted to go shopping tomorrow. Mary was delighted to accept. She chatted briefly with Emma before she noticed the time.

"I have to go," Mary stated. "It's time for vespers. I can't be late."

Mary powdered her nose, refreshed her lipstick, and grabbed her purse. She fixed a snack for Booger so the tiny Chihuahua would not want to follow her out the kitchen door. *I must not be late. I need to give my thanks to St. Anthony once again.*

CHAPTER 105

Preparing to Sail

The American authorities urged repatriates to pack only needed items. The limit was one bag, box, or trunk per person. Our problem was not having too much clothing, but barely having anything to wear. Being under the rule of the Japanese for over three years without a viable source of income negated any clothing purchases, if we could have found anything to buy. Any money we had was spent for food or rent. All of the children had outgrown their clothes...outer and undergarments. Junior, who was thirteen when Pearl Harbor and Manila were bombed in 1941, was now seventeen. He had no long trousers to wear. All he wore were shorts fashioned from former long pants. Most were Bobby's old clothes. His waist had remained basically the same size due to starvation. There were no ready-made garments, as most of the stores were destroyed along with their merchandise. Jess' long pants were not long enough for Junior and the waist was large, even for Jess in his emaciated condition.

We were informed, while getting rations at Santo Tomas, that clothing for Americans was provided via the Red Cross Center at camp. I gathered the children for a trip to Santo Tomas. When we arrived, I approached one of the female attendants at the Red Cross Center to inquire about getting clothing for our children. My first mistake was asking the wrong person. She was the Wicked Witch of the Red Cross.

"This clothing is only for the internees," the Wicked Witch snapped.

"But, I was told by the official at the repatriation office the clothing was for American citizens," I countered. "My children are American citizens...you can check with the Office of Repatriation."

My second mistake was in challenging her authority. All she heard was my thick Spanish accent. She bristled like a Halloween black cat, gave us all a haughty look, and told me to leave and take my "orphans" with me. I was in no mood to argue with her. She was in charge. To challenge her might cause us more problems, although I knew she was wrong. We would find a way to get some clothing without having to deal with her.

I still had fabric at home. We needed to have clothes made for our trip to

Texas. I decided to ask my sister, Lucing on our way home to San Juan. She offered to help, as I knew she would. She was an excellent dressmaker. She gave me a few pieces of José Luis' old clothes and underwear for Junior to use. She cried as she handed me several items of his clothing. *She would never forgive Pilar and Tony for taking her son to Baguio.*

Many young soldiers visited our home regularly before we sold most of our furniture and other household goods. Our home was now a shambles, so all of the young people would gather at our neighbor's home. The Kessels lived across J. Ruiz Street, opposite our front gate. Lucy and Emma would go there to enjoy the young men's company along with many of the other young people in our neighborhood. If they weren't at the Kessels, they would go with the fellows to the USO headquarters and dance. I felt they would be safe, but Jess wasn't too sure. He was very protective.

Tony Davenport and Marvin French were regular visitors. They knew we would be leaving for Texas on July 24, and offered to help transport us to Santo Tomas on our day of departure. We appreciated their offer and made plans accordingly.

Jess built wooden boxes for each of us to use as "luggage," except Lucy and Emma, who packed in a steamer trunk Jess had used when he returned to Texas in 1917 to visit his father. Most of our clothes were "hand-me-down" apparel for the girls and used clothing from Lucing's deceased son. All of the clothing was lightweight, as we lived in a temperate climate. Cold weather existed only in the mountains, and even then, was mild. No one had coats or sweaters. Jess reasoned heavy clothing would not be needed, as we would be arriving during the summer season in the United States. He recalled Texas summers were hot.

We still had to make arrangements for the remaining unsold items. Peping offered to stay in the house and continue selling until our lease expired. His cousin Gimay would take the remainder to sell in her father's store in Bulan. They would take a commission and give the rest of the money to my mother.

Our packed "luggage" had to be delivered to Santo Tomas two days prior to our sailing on July 24. Tony Davenport arrived in an army truck to transport our luggage to Santo Tomas for inspection. After inspection, the "luggage" was sealed and taken from us. We went with Tony since more immunizations were needed. The remaining immunizations would be completed on board our ship. We also reviewed last minute details regarding our paperwork to ensure all was in order for the voyage.

The next day, I made my last visit to see my mother. When I first arrived at my sister's home, where *Mami* was staying, our visit was quite the usual. As I prepared to leave to return to San Juan, my mother gave me a strong hug.

"We will meet again in Heaven," *Mami* said as her lips quivered.

"*Mami*, when I have my citizenship, I will send for you," I promised.

Those two days flew by as we said our goodbyes to friends, family, and neighbors. Many of the American soldiers we had met returned one last time to wish us well on our trip to Texas. While much of the street fighting had ceased on Luzon, battles still continued on many of the surrounding islands. The war was not yet over and we knew our trip across the ocean would be hazardous. Fear did not deter the children's spirits. They were going to Texas!

Marvin French arrived as promised early on July 24 to take us to Santo Tomas for our departure. We found my widowed sister, Consueling, waiting for us. She had brought *Mami* to give us all one last farewell. We chatted for about thirty minutes before visitors were asked to leave.

"*Nena,* if I can find an American soldier to marry, I might surprise you with a visit!" Consueling teased.

We hugged, kissed, and made empty promises. I felt I would never see them again. It was a bittersweet departure. I was sad to leave my mother and sisters behind, but happy to start a new life in Texas.

Around four in the afternoon, several "ducks" (DUKWs) arrived to transport the repatriates to the port of embarkation at Manila Bay. The bay was closed to the S.S. Uruguay, as well as other ships, because it was dangerous. Debris from U.S. and enemy ships created a hazard. Manila Bay was also heavily mined. The "ducks" traveled on land and water and were used mainly to transport troops and/or supplies to and from ships in areas where ships were unable to dock. They transitioned from street travel to skimming the top of the ocean just like a duck. It was quite an experience being tossed about on the undulating waves as we crouched on the floor of the DUKW and held onto each other.

Some felt nauseated as we approached the S.S. Uruguay. The ship loomed like a giant crouched in a frothy sea with waves lapping her sides. As we arrived, the ship's horn bellowed a surprise "welcome" and scared several as they emitted screams. Our eardrums, conditioned by months of bombing, vibrated once again. The younger ones automatically reached for their guava stick. *Where were those sticks?*

A floating pier or barge was in place beside the ship so each DUKW could be secured to allow passengers to step from the amphibious craft and climb a long stairway stretched diagonally from the ship's main deck to the floating pier. The pier was rocking as waves lapped all around. We waited until everyone else had left the Duck before we attempted to leave. Once on the floating pier, we held onto the younger children while the older ones led the way up the wobbly stairway. We held on tightly to the wet ropes and stepped on each riser. When we reached the main deck, we were ushered into a large meeting room. While waiting our turn to be called, waiters offered refreshments. It was hot, loud, and chaotic. Names were being shouted across the room. Other repatriates around us were talking with raised voices. There was much excitement and confusion, but we did not complain. We were on our way to Texas. Nothing else mattered.

Mary and her family met and overcame many challenges, but the biggest challenge was yet to come. They had taken the first "baby" steps on their way to Texas…the "giant" steps were waiting.

Mary was not aware Cornelius "Bud" Collins was aboard the S.S. Uruguay and had seen them arrive. Fate had stepped in once more to bring changes to Lucy's life.

Mary recalled Consueling's last statement about marrying an American soldier and surprising her with a visit. *Poor Consueling! One year after our arrival in Texas, Consueling contracted typhoid fever and suffered a painful death.* She would see Consueling in Heaven with the rest of the Gamero family angels.

CHAPTER 106

Learning the Ropes

"The Hodges Family?" The officer called, and we gathered together like a mother hen with a bunch of chicks searching for food. "Welcome aboard the S.S. Uruguay. Your family has been assigned to stateroom thirty-five on the forward top deck on the starboard side, the right side when you are moving toward the ship's bow. Please follow your cabin steward, Tom."

We marched behind Tom in silence and looked at the different areas of our ship as we climbed toward our deck. *Forward? Starboard? Bow? We had a new language to learn.* When we arrived at our stateroom, we stepped over the raised threshold to find three other people inside: two *meztisos* (Filipino/Americans) and one American lady. Tom was surprised to see the stateroom already occupied. He excused himself and noted he would return shortly.

While Tom was away, I glanced around the stateroom. It consisted of a small living area containing a sofa bed, a larger bedroom area containing two sets of bunk beds parallel to each other against the inside walls (on either side of the only porthole), and a small bathroom with the basic essentials, separating the living and sleeping quarters. Clearly, eleven persons occupying this stateroom would be problematic. We waited for Tom.

Upon Tom's return, he ushered the two *meztisos* out the door, relocated the American lady into a stateroom across from ours, and, once again, vanished…taking the two *meztisos* with him. We made use of the facilities while he was away, as it had been a while since we had access to a toilet. I let Linnie go first and stumbled over the raised threshold as I followed. I was not accustomed to stepping "over" when entering any room. Moving around on this ship would be different. When I flushed the toilet, the loud suctioning noise of the flush scared both of us. As we stepped over the raised threshold and exited the tiny bathroom, I warned the others. Everyone had a good laugh at my expense.

Tom returned shortly to say he was having problems finding another stateroom for us. Jess told him we would rather keep the family together and would be fine in this stateroom. Tom showed us the information sheet provided for each room. He showed us where the life jackets were stowed and demonstrated their proper wear on Junior. He showed us the lifeboat drill information posted on the inside of our stateroom door and noted Lucy, Junior, and Emma were assigned to lifeboat Number Three; Mary Jane, Joyce, Linnie, and I would go to lifeboat Number Two; and, Jess would go "topside" with the men. There would be no exceptions. The practice lifeboat drill would be within the hour. My heart sank. *Our family would be separated!* He cautioned us to remember to step over the raised metal threshold at each door opening on the ship. Everyone glanced at me and smiled, knowingly.

Tom showed us a schematic of the ship and described how to get to the main dining room where our meals would be served. We were assigned "First Sitting" with breakfast from 7:30 to 8:15 a.m. and supper from 4:30 to 5:15 p.m. Standard times were printed on our meal tickets for our convenience. Tom explained that "time" on the ship was measured differently than on land. The hours marched military style from 0100 to 2400 hours, with twenty-four hundred being midnight. Meal announcements would be by four dulcet-toned chimes…a different sound than the bells. We counted the number of bells being chimed to determine the time.

Tom demonstrated the opening and closing of the one porthole in the room and cautioned us to never throw objects out the porthole. We were also instructed to keep the porthole closed at night. He would come by to lock the porthole of every stateroom under his watch each night, and everyone must be inside the assigned room. The ship would travel in blackout conditions every night, as we were in enemy waters. A lifeboat drill would be held before sailing away from Manila Bay. A sinking feeling filled the pit of my stomach as this realization sunk into my brain. *We were still not out of danger.* I reached into my pocket, clutched my rosary, and prayed silently…moving from one bead to another.

Our heads were reeling with all of the information and instructions we were just given. Tom sensed, by our expressions and shaking heads, we were confused. He assured us we would become accustomed to the ship's routine.

"If you have questions, be sure to push the button for your call light," Tom stated. "I will be nearby."

"What about our luggage?" Jess inquired.

"It will be brought to your room, probably while you are at dinner," Tom replied. "I'll point out the dining room on this ship's diagram. Each of you must show your pink meal ticket. You get only one and you must show it at each meal."

He handed the pink meal tickets to me before he left. He pulled the life jackets from the top of the small closet so they would be accessible to us.

"You might want to go ahead and get these on since there are eight of you," Tom reminded us. "Everyone is to report to their assigned lifeboat stations wearing their life jackets. This practice drill is required before we sail."

Jess and I created an inspection line making sure all life jackets were being worn properly. Linnie and Joyce could hardly move even though they had the smallest life jackets. They were not prepared for the little ones. Just as we finished donning our own life jackets, Tom knocked on our door.

"Need help?" Tom inquired as he pulled on his life jacket.

"No, I think we have the situation under control," Jess announced.

"Are there smaller life jackets for the little ones?" I inquired.

"I'll see what I can do, Mrs. Hodges, but those may be the smallest we have," Tom replied and disappeared down the passageway.

The signal for the lifeboat drill blared over the loudspeaker system. It was quite loud and scared me. Having our family separated made me nervous. *What if we have to abandon ship? Dear God, please be with us.*

The drill was a chaotic experience. Several people were laughing and pushing each other. Others were quiet and wore a haunted expression on their faces. We arrived at our lifeboat stations and were given instructions as to what we must do should we experience a true emergency. *I had my rosary in my hand and prayed for the safety of my family.*

We were instructed to return to our cabins and stow the life jackets in the same place we had found them. Most of the passengers complied. Others waited on deck to watch the crew at work. We stowed our life jackets after our lifeboat drill, and took turns washing our hands before dinner while I made sleeping assignments. Junior and Mary Jane would share the sofa bed in the small entry room; Lucy and Emma would each have a top bunk of their own on the two sets of bunk beds; Jess and Linnie would share one of the lower bunk beds; and, Joyce and I would share the other. Everyone took turns peeking out of our porthole while waiting for the dinner chimes. Joyce and Linnie were not tall enough, so Junior and Jess lifted them so they could have a peek.

When the dulcet tones of the dinner chimes floated over the loudspeakers, we marched from our stateroom with Junior and Mary Jane leading the way, one behind the other down the narrow passageway. We were pleased to find the large, luxurious (to us) dining room ringed by white-jacketed waiters wearing large smiles. I showed our eight meal tickets to the headwaiter. He motioned for one of the waiters to come forward. Our meal tickets were returned to me as he spoke.

"The Hodges family will be at table nine. Enjoy your dinner."

We were ushered to our large round table, seated, and graced with a large white napkin placed across our laps with a flourish. We were provided with a choice of beverages and two entrees.

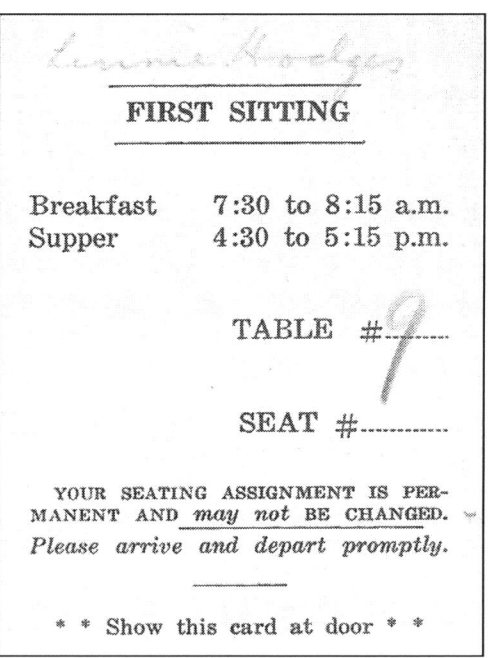

Linnie Hodges' meal ticket showing the dining table assignment on the S.S. Uruguay during the family's passage from the Philippines to the United States in 1945

A basket of piping hot bread was passed around the table. Pats of butter were stacked in a chilled bowl. We felt like royalty!

When our plated food arrived, the savory aromas wafted around our heads as each one received the entrée of their choice. The noisy chatter of the dining room melted away to a low murmur as all enjoyed the meal. After eating less than half, most of the kids stopped eating. Jess was disappointed they had not eaten more.

"What's the matter?" Jess asked. "Aren't you kids hungry?"

"Jess, their stomachs have shrunk so much they can only eat a small amount at a time," I explained. "If they stuff their small stomachs, they will get sick. We don't want to think about them being sick in that small stateroom with only one bathroom."

Jess was quiet and tried his best to eat the whole portion he was served to set an example for the kids. Before long, he felt miserable. As he left the table. I shook my head from side-to-side. Junior rose to follow his daddy, but I had him return to his seat.

"Your daddy needs peace and quiet," I explained.

"Why?" Junior asked.

"I think he's overeaten. He has to 'feed the fish'," I said.

My message got through to the older kids. The younger ones were still busy eating small bites of their dessert. After we left the dining room we looked for Jess, but he was not on deck. Several others were topside "feeding the fish." We did not see Jess. He had returned to our cabin and was miserable. The children and I stayed on deck to give Jess some peace and quiet while we watched the ship slip away from Manila Bay. *Goodbye, Mami. Goodbye, sisters. Goodbye, Philippines.*

We returned to our stateroom just before sundown. Jess was sitting quietly on his lower bunk holding his head in his hands...a wet face towel pressed to his face. Tom knocked on our door and Junior opened the door for him.

"Do you need anything?" Tom asked.

"No, I think we will be okay," I answered. "Jess just ate more than he should."

Tom gave us a knowing look as he locked the porthole.

"Sorry to lock your porthole," Tom stated. "We can't take chances on being seen by the Japs."

We took turns either taking showers in the tiny shower stall or sponging ourselves with a "bird bath." Jess did neither. He was still sick. Linnie was sleepy, so she crawled into the lower bunk and faced the wall. Jess waited until she was asleep before resting beside her with his back against hers. We were squeezed together like sardines. We hardly slept. It was stifling inside our stateroom. We were accustomed to sleeping with open windows and covered by mosquito nets. Sleeping on a lower bunk bed with a child created more heat. Our clothes were damp with perspiration causing our clothes to stick to our skin. Jess and I did not sleep at all.

In the cover of darkness, the S.S. Uruguay made its way slowly southeast through the southern ship channel, avoiding the heavily mined area between it and its northern twin, then due south before changing to a southeasterly course through Balayan Bay...slipping between Batangas and Mindoro into the Sibuyan Sea. We continued southeast through the San Bernadino Strait before setting our course due east toward Guam.

    Tom arrived early the next morning with a pail of fresh water for our use. Seawater was used for the ship's showers, toilets, and lavatories. The fresh water in the pail was used for brushing teeth or drinking. He opened the porthole after he put the small pail of water in the bathroom. He and Jess chatted briefly making small talk. Tom told us someone would be in to clean the room while we were at breakfast. We were all anxious to leave the small room and walk to the dining room. The fresh sea air was a welcome relief after being stifled in our cabin all night in the dark.

CHAPTER 107

Sailing…Sailing

We stepped from our cabin into the narrow passageway at 7:30 a.m. to report for breakfast in the dining room. Once again we were greeted by the headwaiter and ushered to table nine. The waiters were dressed casually in short sleeved white uniforms. They bustled about our table making sure we had our choice of bacon, sausage, eggs, biscuits, butter, jellies, fresh fruit, or cereal. The kids' eyes opened wide when the basket of sweet rolls and muffins was placed on the table. They knew they would like to eat the portions served, but they also recalled their daddy's experience of "feeding the fish." They chose wisely and ate only until they were full…which did not take long.

Following our breakfast, we returned to our cabin to take care of "business." I did not want the children to use the public facilities on the ship. We had come this far. I did not want them catching any diseases. Tom was waiting in the passageway near our door with the ship's daily newspaper, *Golden Gate*.

"Here's the ship's newsletter for you to read," Tom announced as he handed Jess a copy. "The *Golden Gate* is printed daily and provides information about events regarding the war and on the ship, like movies, plus announcements."

"Say, I have a favor to ask," Jess stated.

"Sure, I'll help if I can," Tom responded.

"If we promise to keep our cabin dark at night and not open the passageway door, may we please keep the porthole open? Jess pleaded. "We were miserable last night."

"Let me think about your request and check with my supervisor," Tom replied. "I'll tell you this evening."

Tom sauntered down the passageway handing out the *Golden Gate* to others along the way. We all hoped and prayed he would return with permission to keep our porthole open day and night.

Jess rested on the small sofa bed while Junior read the *Golden Gate* to him. Lucy, Emma, and Mary Jane waited their turn for the bathroom occupied by Joyce and Linnie. The younger ones had priority in these matters.

I glanced out the open porthole and saw only blue skies and equally blue seas, undulating as the forward progress of our ship sliced through...disturbing its calm surface. Manila and the Philippines were no longer visible. Junior read the date, July 25. I realized this day was Pilar and Tony's wedding anniversary. I hoped they had experienced a safe trip to California, as they had left for the United States in early May. I was wondering how they were celebrating their anniversary. Previously, our whole family would gather at their home for a celebration. They were alone in a new place, and so were we.

My thoughts wandered to my mother and other sisters. Today was only the second day of being away from them, but I knew *Mami* would be sad, because I was feeling the same way. *Mami* would be moving into the *Hospicio de San José* today to live with her sister, Herminia. My poor *Tia* Herminia, who lost her four sons when the Japanese destroyed *Intramuros*, had no choice but to live in the *Hospicio*, a home for the poor and elderly. *Mami*, who would have lived with us had we stayed, decided she would stay with Herminia and not be a burden to her remaining daughters. Pilar and I had left the Philippines, Consueling was returning to Bulan, and Lucing had her hands full in finding a home and feeding her children.

I dismissed my sad thoughts, unpacked, and straightened the few pieces of clothing we brought. I needed to find a laundry room. I took pencil and paper and made a list of questions. Jess and I stayed in the cabin with Joyce and Linnie while the others went topside or visited the ship's library to check on the movies mentioned in the *Golden Gate*. They found the meeting room where movies were shown.

While walking around the deck, Lucy was surprised when a booming voice greeted her. It was Bud Collins, the GI she had met when the First Cavalry bivouacked near our home in San Juan. He had "bent" the rules and stepped over the rope dividing the civilians from military personnel on the ship. They chatted for a while before Bud was reminded to return to his area of the ship.

We became accustomed to the daily routine onboard. The ship was moving along a direct route away from the Philippines, but we were still in enemy waters. Tom stopped by to bring us the good news.

"I talked with my supervisor about keeping your porthole open at night. Since you have so many in this stateroom and will supervise the use of the porthole, he felt it would be okay," Tom said. "I'll still be coming by to check, as I am ultimately responsible."

Jess thanked him. I breathed a sigh of relief and thought of another question.

"Will we need mosquito nets with the porthole open?" I inquired.

Tom had to stifle a grin at my question, so he could answer with a straight face.

"No, Ma'am, I don't think mosquitoes can fly that far. If there are any on board, it's because we brought them with us, but I don't believe you will be bothered."

After he answered, I chastised myself for asking such a silly question. He will probably have a good laugh each time he retells that story to his companions.

On July 28 Tom brought an amended listing of the lifeboats and their stations. The original list of July 24 was rescinded. We were to prepare for another lifeboat drill to practice the new assignments. Tom noted the drill would probably occur right after lunchtime.

"Remember, since everyone is having lunch topside on their own, your family needs to return to your stateroom when they are finished," Tom stated.

"Thanks, Tom, and we all want to thank you again for allowing us to keep our porthole open at night. It has helped to have fresh air in this small cabin, and, by the way, the mosquitoes did not bother us, either," Jess said with a twinkle in his eyes as he grinned at me.

I read the revised lifeboat assignment sheet and was glad they had grouped most of us in lifeboat #1. All members of the family were listed except Jess, who was to report topside again, only this time, by himself. They misspelled Emma's name. She was listed as "Eunice." She was not happy. I told her we would tell Tom. Once again, we donned our life jackets and listened for the signal for the lifeboat drill. As before, the drill was a combination of noise and laughter. Many of the passengers were not taking the drill seriously. The officer in charge took note of their attitudes and brought everyone back to reality by reminding us we were still in enemy waters. It was important for everyone to remain quiet in case instructions were given.

When we returned to our cabin to put away our life jackets, Tom was there, so I showed him the error with Emma's name. He was sure all errors would be corrected and would bring us a revised copy.

Lucy, Emma and Mary Jane decided to visit the recreation room to find a game or puzzle to break the monotony of the day. Mary Jane was delighted to find a piano in the room and asked the Red Cross attendant in charge if she might be allowed to play.

Lifeboat assignments for the S.S. Uruguay.

```
                                SS URUGUAY
                      Office of the Transport Commander

                                                        30 July, 1945
MEMORANDUM)
           :
        TO )    All concerned

        1. Memorandum, dated 28 July, 1945, Office of the Transport Commander
SS URUGUAY, To: All Concerned, is rescinded and the following substituted.
The following life boat stations are in effect:

           BOAT NUMBER 1                              BOAT NUMBER 2
    A DECK FORWARD  STARBOARD SIDE              A DECK FORWARD PORT SIDE
           MAJOR KEEGAN                              MAJOR GARDEN

FRIEDMAN, Patria----------Room 37        BILIK, Justine------------Room 23
    "     Erlinda                        BRESLIN, Pacita-----------     29
    "     Frederick                          "     Mary
    "     Stanton                            "     Ann
                                         DUCKLE, Katherine---------     20
HARTUNG, Marion-----------     25        FOWLER, Marjorie----------     23
                                         KEESEY, DeFrose-----------     44
HODGES, Mary G.-----------     35        KING, Dorothy-------------     25
    "     Lucy                           LIZARRAGA, Marie----------     20
    "     Emma                           MARTIN, Theresa-----------     27
    "     Mary                           ROYAL, Dennis-------------     27
    "     Joyce                          SWEENEY, Alice------------     10
    "     Linnie                         WATERS, Elise X-----------     46
                                             "     George
MAHONEY, Anne-------------     25            "     Mary L.
                                             "     Charles Jr.
LECHE, Angelita-----------     39            "     Douglas
    "     Edward
    "     George
    "     Mary
    "     Felicidad

LEVY, Rosalind------------     25

           BOAT NUMBER 7                              BOAT NUMBER 8
    BOAT DECK FORWARD STARBOARD SIDE           BOAT DECK FORWARD  PORT SIDE
           CAPTAIN TOOMEY                            MAJOR SALZER

BURTON, Annie Laurie------Room 23        ALHEIT, Eleanor-----------Room 23
CHASE, Barbara------------     23        BERG, Fanny---------------     29
ESTEVA, Jeanette----------     37            "     Evelyn
    "     Maria T.                           "     Elise
    "     Guadalupe                          "     Elaine
    "     Rosario                        CLARKE, Virginia----------     27
    "     Alberto                            "     Susanne
GEDDES, Dorothy-----------     23        CLINTON, Harriet----------     23
McILVAINE, Sixta----------     33        FREDERICKSON, Ruby--------     23
    "     Marian                         HARVEY, Margaret----------     27
    "     Sally Ann                          "     Florence
MILLER, Alice-------------     31        PASATIEMPO, Remidios------     44
    "     Liselette                          "     Sylvestre--------     51
    "     Marcel                         THOMAS, Tamara------------     29
REITER, Ramona P.---------     39            "     Barbara
    "     Elma                               "     Shirley
    "     Rosie
```

365

"You go right ahead," The lady said. "I'm sure we'll enjoy it."

She and Emma took turns playing and also played duets. Several of the passengers their age gathered around requesting songs. After about forty minutes, the Red Cross lady asked Mary Jane if she would like to play for the wounded service men in the infirmary, which she did. If she had a request for a song she did not know, she would ask them sing or hum it. She enjoyed playing the piano for them, and I think they were glad to have the diversion.

On July 30, Tom brought another memo regarding the lifeboat assignments. The list of July 28 was rescinded. The new list had Emma's name spelled correctly, but Junior's name was missing. Junior would report with Jess topside, gather with the enlisted men, and be assigned to any available lifeboats. In a way, I was okay with this change. Jess and Junior would help each other. We experienced another lifeboat drill before our evening meal. The officer in charge complimented the passengers on remembering their instructions.

I remembered the next day would be Jess' birthday! He would be fifty-six! After three years of missing his birthday celebration, we should make it festive for the whole family. I stepped into the passageway. Tom would help.

"Tom, I need a favor," I said.

"I'll be happy to help, if I can," Tom replied.

"Tomorrow is Jess' birthday," I said quietly. "We want to surprise him with a celebration. It's been over three years since we celebrated together!"

Tom smiled and said he knew what to do. He would speak with the chief steward. There would be a cake for supper tomorrow night. I smiled and thanked him. *No stack of quickly made pancakes with a used candle to celebrate Jess' birthday. He deserved a "real" birthday cake.*

I returned and reminded the children quietly. We were going to surprise their daddy on his birthday. The older ones slipped out to visit the library to make birthday cards. Linnie and Joyce were not told, as we did not want to accidentally ruin the surprise.

The next evening we helped the waiters sing the birthday song. The surprise got the best of Jess as tears filled his eyes. It was a wonderful birthday…his first to celebrate with our family in three years. His "real" birthday cake was ringed with candles, one for each of us to blow out and "make a wish," before the cake was placed before Jess, so he could make his wish and extinguish the last candle.

"What did you wish, Daddy?" Junior asked.

"Well, my wish has already come true," Jess said as he flashed a big smile. "But, I think all of you know what it is."

Mary took time to glance over the tattered and yellowed copies of the *Golden Gate* she had saved all these years. She was so glad she had those mementos. They helped her prepare a more accurate account of their lives in the Philippines and their trip aboard the S.S. Uruguay. *My goodness, we enjoyed all the delicious food on the ship after starving for over three years. We went from one extreme to the other.*

CHAPTER 108

Water Everywhere

We were into our second week aboard the S.S. Uruguay and the older kids had learned their way around the two upper decks assigned to civilians. Military personnel were on the lower decks, and the members of the staff were housed below decks. Lucy, Emma, Junior, and Mary Jane knew how to find the library, dining room, meeting rooms, and the nursery. Lucy would usually slip away and meet Bud Collins on deck while Mary Jane would take Joyce and Linnie to the nursery where S/Sgt. Emmett Wahlstrom was in charge of about sixty kids. Wahlstrom, of Minneapolis, and T/5 Sam Little of Celvo, Missouri, were assigned to serve the kids luncheon sandwiches, milk, and ice cream. These men did all the serving and cleaning, and PFC Robert Strangfield showed the kids an afternoon movie from two until three o'clock. They also took care of the mid-afternoon snacks after the movie was shown. American Red Cross representatives on board provided assistance in the nursery, located on A deck aft (in the once upon a time peacetime ship's bar) for the convenience of civilian passengers.

On the morning of August 2, we were wakened by an announcement on the loudspeaker. Everyone was to put on their life jackets and keep them on until further notice. We all followed instructions but were puzzled about the reason for this announcement. On our way to enjoy our breakfast, our ship's course changed from its usual forward movement to a different one…zigzag. We noticed the serious demeanor of the crew and the solemn attitude of the waiters in the dining room.

After our breakfast, the older kids wanted to go topside for fresh air. On deck, rumors of a nearby American ship being torpedoed were spread to all who would listen. The older kids rushed to tell us. *We were still in enemy waters! There was a reason for the lifejackets.*

"Sorry about having to keep the life jackets on," Tom said. "You can remove them when sleeping, but keep them by your side."

"Tom," Jess said, "Why is the ship moving side to side?"

"Well, the zigzag course is an evasive measure to avoid Japanese subs that might be in the area," Tom said. "We should be out of enemy water within the next ten days."

I was concerned... *ten days! What had happened? We must be in serious danger.* I reached for my rosary and prayed.

Tom stopped in later and gave us a copy of the *Golden Gate*. The older kids enjoyed reading the latest issue to see which movies were being featured, and if they would be allowed to view them. They had not seen movies in over three years. What a treat this was for them. Civilian adult movies were shown in the Officer's Dining Hall and the enlisted men viewed movies selected for their viewing in their Mess Hall. The enlisted men were assigned to one of two showings based on the decks they occupied. The August 3 issue of the *Golden Gate* listed *Bar 20* with William Boyd beginning at 2045 (8:45 p.m.). The older kids wanted to see a "cowboy" movie since we were going to Texas. I told them they would see the "real thing" in Texas.

The newsletter also carried the news about the latest American military efforts and successes. We were reminded about being in enemy waters and all passengers must continue wearing life jackets daily. Wearing those life jackets daily solved one problem... we did not have to worry about the clothes we wore... they would be covered.

While we were having breakfast, Commander Spaulding's voice over the loudspeaker was announcing the ship's crossing of the International Date Line sometime during the day. It was Sunday, August 5.

"We hope you like Sundays, because tomorrow will also be Sunday, August 5," Commander Spaulding stated.

Crossing the International Date Line was a unique experience on our ship. We laughed the next day when Junior asked if we would be going to church services again. I gave everyone a choice. The older children decided to stay in the cabin and read the two different issues of the *Golden Gate* dated "Sunday, August 5, 1945." Jess listened intently as they took turns reading those issues aloud. Several items of interest included news of the conclusion of the Potsdam Conference in Europe. None of us knew about the war in Europe. All the "news" we had was Japanese propaganda programmed into us daily. It was time for us to learn what happened elsewhere in the world while we were under the Japanese rule. Those years were devoid of the truth and world events. We had so much to learn. The children were behind in their education, as they had not attended school during the Japanese Occupation. I hoped they would learn quickly.

On August 6, an announcement over the loudspeaker gave a lengthy account about an atom bomb dropped on Hiroshima by the "Enola Gay." The August 8 issue of the *Golden Gate* touted an article describing an eyewitness account of the bombing.

```
Guam released last night the first eyewitness
account of the atomic bombing. Col. Tibbets,
pilot, and Capt. Parsons, safety man in charge of
the delicate job stated that the bomb exploded
in a white flash and the heat was actually felt
in the plane, which was lifted by the blast.
The smoke billowed up to 40,000 feet, at which
```

> altitude it was still hanging four hours later when recon planes took photo results of the demonstration.
>
> Still later observation reported 60% of the city of 300,000, an area of 4.1 sq. miles, destroyed. Five major industrial plants and seven charred bridges across the Hiroshima canal showed in the photo.
>
> The demonstration was planned over a year ago, but perfection of the weapon slowed the bombing. The bomb is considered the best kept secret of the war.
>
> Honolulu reported this morning that a fighter plane could carry the bomb though no more details on its size were given.

The "buzz" around the dining room was all about the atom bomb. We hoped the war with Japan would end before long. We were still in enemy waters. We were still "running dark" in the ocean at night...on a zigzag course. We were so tired of wearing our life jackets. They were beginning to irritate the skin around our necks. The younger kids not only had chapped necks, their chins were also chafed.

We left the dining room to return to our quarters. Heavy clouds loomed overhead. I told everyone to hurry. A sudden cloudburst doused us all...water was everywhere. We patted ourselves and our life jackets with towels to get them partially dry.

Mary recalled those days with life jackets adding heat and discomfort to everyone. The heavy canvas stuffed with kapok, a type of cotton grown on trees in Asian countries, chafed our skin. *We did not fully understand the reason for those safety precautions until we arrived in San Francisco and read the headlines of the August 15, 1945 issue of* The San Francisco News *and recalled Commander Spaulding's earlier comments.*

CRUISER SUNK; CARRIED ATOM BOMB CARGO
880 Lost On Indianapolis as Two Blasts Rip Her Bow
Only 316 Out of 1196 in Crew Saved; Men Washed Into Sea Go Mad, Perish

The Indianapolis, just days before, had unloaded uranium and atomic bomb parts at Tinian and was bound from Guam to Leyte. The cruiser was sunk just after midnight on July 30. Two torpedoes struck her bow, hitting her communications area and she sank within fifteen minutes according to eyewitnesses. No call for help could be issued as the communications center received a direct hit. A report of the sinking, was in simple code on a standard frequency, and was sent by the Japanese. American military personnel, responsible for monitoring that channel, intercepted the report. They took no action, as the report was considered a Japanese ploy. Of the 1196 men on board, only 316 survived. An American reconnaissance plane spotted the survivors three days later.

As we approached The Golden Gate Bridge in San Francisco on August 13, 1945, Commander Albert P. Spaulding, Captain of the S.S. Uruguay, told us, in his farewell speech:

> WE WERE FORTUNATE. WHILE SAILING TOWARD GUAM TO PICK UP MEDICAL SUPPLIES, WE NARROWLY MISSED BEING HIT BY A TORPEDO. THE TORPEDO HAD COME ACROSS OUR SHIP'S BOW. AN AMERICAN SHIP, THE INDIANAPOLIS, BOUND IN THE OPPOSITE DIRECTION FROM GUAM TO LEYTE, WAS SUNK AND 880 LIVES WERE LOST.

I thanked God for bringing us safely across 6,858 miles of perilous waters... not counting all the "zigs and zags."

Wednesday, August 15, 1945

CRUISER SUNK;
880 LOST ON INDIANAPOLIS AS TWO BLASTS RIP HER BOW

Only 316 Out of 1196 in Crew Saved; Men Washed Into Sea Go Mad, Perish

By United Press

GUAM, Aug. 15.—Two tremendous explosions ripped the bow of the heavy cruiser Indianapolis, bound from Guam to Leyte with a cargo of atomic bomb parts, only 15 minutes before she sank July 30, leaving 880 officers and men killed or missing, survivors said today.

Only 316 of the ship's complement of 1196 escaped drowning or death from burns, thirst and exposure, Hawaii, in the record time of 74½ hours. It was disclosed in Guam. The previous record was made in 1923

CHAPTER 109

Aloha

Excitement filled the air as we arrived in port at Honolulu on the morning of Thursday, August 9. We were told the day before to have our papers in order for inspection by U.S. Immigration Service personnel. No one would be allowed to disembark. Immigration officials would come on board for the inspection. A schedule of inspection was provided on August 8 and everyone must comply. We were to bring everyone in our family, along with the completed forms and documentation to the dining room and listen for our names called by the officials at the times specified on the schedule. We no longer had to wear our life jackets!

We waited quietly at table nine, our assigned dining table, and kept our fingers crossed. After getting everyone's attention, one of the officials made an announcement.

"All repatriates, whose paperwork is not in order, will be required to leave the S.S. Uruguay for a return trip to Manila."

We hoped our paperwork would be approved, as we had no desire to make the return trip to Manila. Texas was our destination.

While we waited, one of the immigration officers got everyone's attention and asked if anyone in the room could speak Spanish. I was surprised at the question and raised my hand.

"Would you mind coming forward, please?" The official asked as he waved me forward to the bank of tables they used for processing passengers. "We need your help."

I approached the table where other officials were talking with repatriates. A distraught, young Filipina sat wringing her hands. She had been crying. Officials had questioned her, but she did not understand English. Customs officials thought, perhaps, she might speak Spanish. That's why they decided to ask for volunteers in the room who could speak Spanish. When I spoke to her in Spanish, she did not understand me either. I asked her, in *Tagalog* (the main dialect of Luzon), if she spoke *Tagalog*. A smile broke across her face and she answered immediately. She had lost her paperwork, along with the address and phone

number of her brother, who lived in San Francisco. I explained her story to the immigration officer. He shook his head.

"Please tell her she will have to leave the ship here until we find a way to contact her brother. If he is not located within two days, she will have to return to Manila."

I gave her the sad news. She put her hands over her face and wept as I translated his message. The officer called a Red Cross worker over and asked her to escort the Filipina to her cabin to get her belongings in order.

We did not have to wait long after she left before our names were called. All of our paperwork was in order, thanks to Hubert Poskey and several other GIs who graciously helped us.

We returned to our cabin to put the paperwork away before going topside to gaze at the nearby port and listen to sounds of lilting Hawaiian music riding across the lapping waves. A small welcoming committee of natives wearing brightly colored shirts and sarongs gathered on the pier to entertain us and welcome our ship. Petals of brightly colored flowers were tossed into the water. We watched them dance across the rippling waves…swaying to the rhythmic strumming of ukuleles.

It took most of the day for immigration officials to check everyone's paperwork. We all felt sad for those who had to leave the ship at this point. Although it would have been a treat to leave the ship for a short visit, we were happy we would be staying on board. We had no desire to return to Manila, especially by ship.

After the immigration officials left our ship, the S.S. Uruguay weighed anchor and set a course for San Francisco. No zigzag this time! We were ready for San Francisco to open her Golden Gate to us. We would arrive in about three days.

Everyone was in a happy mood at the supper table. We had fresh mangoes and pineapples included with our meal. We tried not to overeat. We had made it this far and hoped to never "feed the fish" like Jess.

I still miss those delicious mangoes, papayas, âtés, duhat, guavas, and fresh pineapples. They made me homesick for my mother and sisters. The fruit in Texas is not as tasty!

Mary gently folded the fragile mementos from the Philippines. She laughed to herself as she recalled bringing all of the "junk" (as Jess called her mementos). She had still made the right decision in bringing them to America for they helped to tell her story.

CHAPTER 110

Gratitude and Goodbye

The atmosphere aboard ship changed over the next two days. The crew seemed to smile more and move with a "quickness" to their step. Everyone was friendlier. Repatriates, who had not socialized, made an effort to converse with us. The waiters teased the kids and played pranks on them…all in fun. There was more laughter and happy faces. We were heading for San Francisco…the United States of America!

On Saturday, August 11, Tom brought us two copies of the *Golden Gate*. These were "Souvenir Editions," and he felt sure we would like to have an extra one to keep. We were excited as we read the article citing Captain Albert Spaulding's comments.

> Capt. Albert P. Spaulding, Master of the Ship, commented that this group, composed of those returning for discharge plus civilians, was the first of its type aboard this ship, and expressed pleasure on the part of the ship's officers and himself on their excellent conduct. "It was as good if not better," he said, "as that of the most disciplined of crack ETO divisions…I hope some can take a trip with us in peacetime, in the meantime, my best wishes to you all."

Following Capt. Spaulding's words was a paragraph from Col. Odell, who expressed these touching thoughts.

> Col. Irving Odell, Troop Commander, hoped that this voyage was setting a new precedent for us in the war—the last voyage under war conditions and one "back to normal existence and a lasting peace." In complimenting the troops on excellent

CAPTAIN'S DINNER
ON BOARD THE
T. E. S. URUGUAY

Albert P. Spaulding, Commander
Captain, USMS

⚓

STAFF

Chief Officer	WILLIAM O. CRAMER
	Commander, USMS
Chief Engineer	WILLIAM N. MATCHES
	Lieut. Commander, USMS
Chief Purser	NICHOLAS R. SENA
	Lieut. Commande[r]
Chief Steward	JOSEPH
	Lieut. Commande[r]

Colonel IRVING ODELL, USA
Transport Commander
Captain JAMES D. McKENZIE, USA
Asst. Transport Commander
Major H. H. LIVINGSTON, USA
Transport Surgeon
1st. Lieut. JAMES T. KEATING, USA
Asst. Transport Surgeon
Major MAXWELL B. COURAGE, USA
Transport Chaplain
Captain TIMOTHY E. ANGLAND, USA
Commissary Officer
1st. Lieut. SIDNEY ROSENTHAL, U[SA]
Special Services Officer
Lieut. LAWRENCE R. FLORY, US[ ]
Gunnery Officer
Lieut. (jg) CARL J. HEISSER,
Communications Officer
Lieut. (jg) HOWARD A. PR[ICE]
Asst. Gunnery Officer
Lieut. (jg) GEORGE L. SC[ ]
Asst. Gunnery Officer

AT SEA - AUG[UST]

Menu from the Captain's Dinner aboard the S.S. Uruguay.

MENU

Chow Chow   Anchovy Canape   Assorted Olives
Florida Fruit Cocktail

⚓

English Brown Barley Soup

⚓

Ham Jambalaya & Rice, Spanish Style

⚓

Broiled T-Bone Steak, Maitre d'Hotel
Roast Stuffed Chicken, Giblet Sauce

⚓

Spinach á l'Anglaise   Buttered Wax Beans
Baked Idaho or Mashed Potatoes

⚓

Assorted Cold Cuts   Tuna Fish Salad - Mayonnaise

⚓

Assorted Cheese & Crackers
French Apple Cake
Fresh Fruit   Ice Cream & Cookies
Coffee

MARTIN ELORRIAGA
Chef de Cuisine

---

behavior and in giving his best wishes, the Colonel added the wish that all would turn to the "even greater tasks of peace with the same energy and wisdom that defeated the enemy."

The rest of the news in the *Golden Gate* was dedicated to expressing appreciation to members of the crew, entertainers, Red Cross volunteers, and all who provided special services. A brief mention was made about Japan's terms in their first attempt to surrender. All countries participating in the Potsdam Conference rejected their offer. Japan was in no condition to dictate their terms after the second bomb was dropped on Nagasaki.

On August 12, we had a specially prepared "Captain's Dinner" with a printed souvenir menu. All of the ship's officers under the command of Capt. Spaulding were listed beside their designated position. All of those under the command of Colonel Irving Odell, Transport Commander, were also listed along with their assignment. The menu, created by Martin Elorriage, Chef de Cuisine, was quite different.

I had no idea what kind of food Jambalaya was or how it would be prepared Spanish Style. I decided to ask our waiter. He responded by asking questions.

"Have you had Cajun food before, ma'am?" He inquired.

"What does "Cajun" mean?" I asked.

"Well, do you like spicy food, ma'am?" He asked.

"It's been a long time since I've eaten any highly spiced food," I responded.

"Perhaps you should try the Roast Stuffed Chicken."

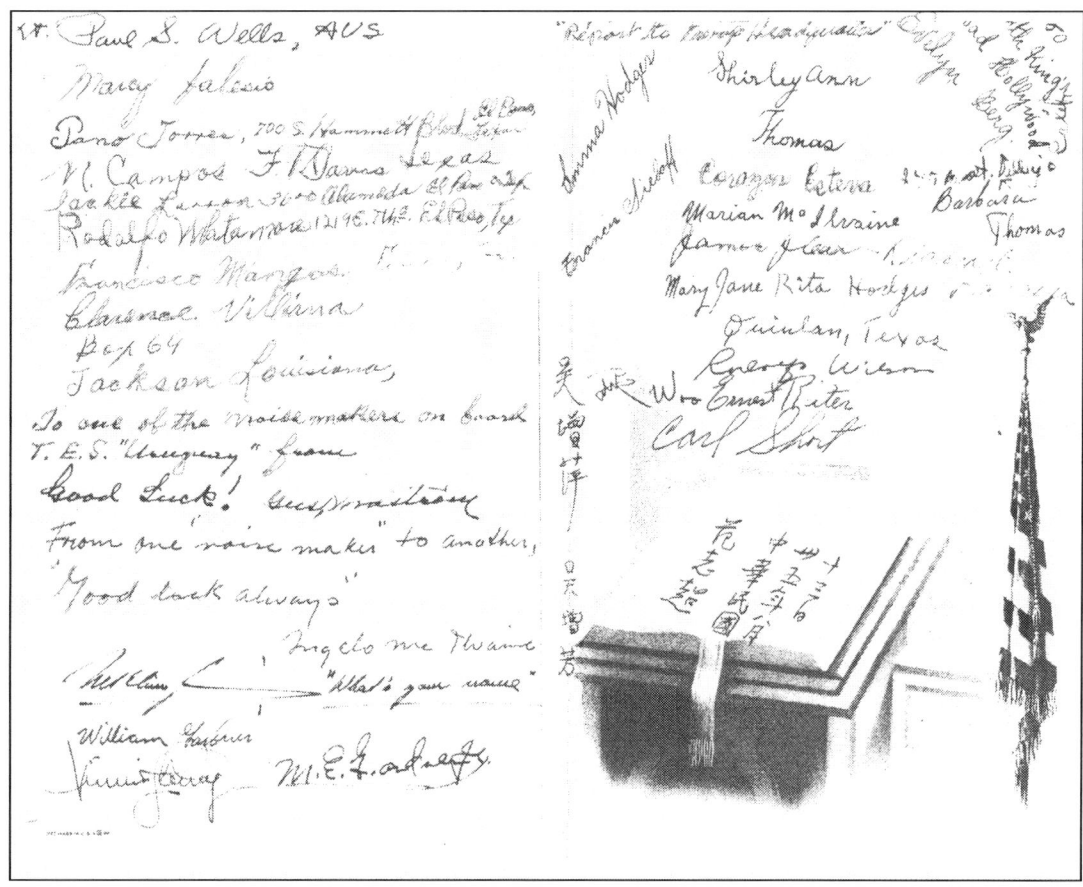

A copy of the signed menu sent by Jerry Yrissary to the author during her research for this book. She and her sister Emma had signed his copy.

Junior decided to try the Ham Jambalaya. After taking a bite, he grabbed his water glass and pushed his plate away. Our waiter saw his reaction and brought him the chicken. Junior had never eaten Cajun food before. It was quite spicy.

It was time to say goodbye to all of our friends on the S.S. Uruguay. Two young repatriates, German (Jerry) Yrissary and his brother, Mario, stopped by our table to have Emma and Mary Jane sign their souvenir menus. They had become acquainted on board during their visits to the recreation room. We thanked all of the waiters who had taken care of us during our voyage. I was sorry we had no money or gifts to give them…just our heartfelt thanks. We had so many people to thank; we should not have waited until the day before our arrival at San Francisco. Jess had saved several dollars to give to Tom before we were to leave the ship. Tom was a kind man and so helpful to us.

We had one more night on the S.S. Uruguay before its scheduled arrival in San Francisco. We were packed and ready to leave the S.S. Uruguay early the next morning. Our new lives in America were about to begin.

Mary thought about the last night aboard the S.S. Uruguay. She did not sleep. *Many questions raced through my mind on August 12, 1945, like heavy traffic on a crowded highway. These questions bumped into each other and multiplied. We had taken a big chance by leaving the Philippines to start over in Texas. It felt a bit like diving off a high diving board without being able to see any water below. What a true leap of faith!*

CHAPTER 111

Goodbye, S.S. Uruguay Hello, San Francisco

As our ship approached the famous Golden Gate Bridge on Monday, August 13, 1945, many of the passengers on deck were leaning over the rail. Two large tugs had come alongside to guide our ship into port. Jess decided we should stay in our cabin, as the decks were crowded. He was concerned one or more of the kids might get lost or pushed in all of the excitement. We took turns staring out of our porthole. A live band, aboard a welcoming launch, played patriotic music as they approached our ship. The launch was festooned with red, white, and blue bunting. Young ladies, dressed in fur coats, were singing and waving small American flags. We had only seen ladies wearing fur coats in the movies before World War II.

Occasionally, a piece or two of soldiers' uniforms flashed by our porthole…on their way to the bay. I guess those soldiers being discharged tossed them as a symbol of their return to civilian life. I wished for a pole with a hook on the end to snag a piece or two for Junior.

Our ship seemed to list to one side as it approached the Golden Gate Bridge. We envisioned the bridge being "golden" and were disappointed to see it was a dull brown. The sight of moving toward the longest suspension bridge in the world (as noted in our ship's newsletter *Golden Gate*) was a thrill. While the bridge appeared to be long from where we were standing, it did not seem tall. Jess was concerned our ship would not be able to go under the bridge.

I stepped out of the cabin hoping to find Tom, but the passageway was empty. I wanted to ask him why our ship was leaning to one side. It was difficult to walk without holding to the handrails on either side. It was exciting, but also frightening.

As we docked, we listened to announcements being made over the ship's loudspeaker. We were to disembark by decks, with the repatriates being allowed off the ship first. When our deck was called, we waited until our passageway was empty before leaving the cabin. Jess wanted to make sure we all stayed together as we left the S.S. Uruguay.

At last, we were on American soil. It felt odd…not because it was American soil, but because the pavement beneath us was solid. It was not moving! Our "sea legs" had to become accustomed to land once more. I tried to stop for just a minute to say a silent prayer of thanks for our safe journey to America, but chaos was all around.

As we stepped away from the ship, we held the younger children's hands. Confusion reigned. Several repatriates were yelling at others who had come to meet them; the GIs, still on board, were shouting at folks on the pier; the loudspeaker was blaring instructions; and, vehicles on the bridge and its surrounds were honking their horns. Adding to this was the blast of the ship's horn. It was noisy and confusing.

It was also cold. Our tropical clothing offered no protection against the chilly San Francisco weather. We wore some knit long-sleeved tops The American Red Cross had given us, and Mary Jane wore her WAC (Women's Army Corps) boots, also provided by The Red Cross, and the only shoes she had. I understood why those young women were wearing fur coats, and wished we had some as well.

We were supposed to go by The American Red Cross area at the pier after leaving the ship, but missed it in all the confusion. Large buses were waiting beside the pier. Many of the repatriates were walking to them…so we followed.

Upon reaching the buses, I showed our papers to an officer standing nearby who assigned us to the third bus. The other two were already filled. We boarded the bus, found seating, and prepared for transit to our hotel. During the brief trip, we huddled together for warmth. We had no idea San Francisco would be so chilly in August…much colder than we had ever felt before.

Shortly, our bus stopped at The Granada Hotel at 1000 Sutter Street…not far from the pier. We were the last ones off the bus. Again, Jess was cautious. We waited inside the crowded, but warm, lobby of the hotel and listened for our names.

When "Hodges" was announced, I learned they had reserved four rooms for us. Jess told them we only needed three rooms. Lucy and Emma shared one room; Junior and Mary Jane, the second room; and, Jess and I kept Joyce and Linnie with us in the third room. The hotel manager thanked us for releasing one room, as hotel rooms were scarce.

Once we were checked in and took our "luggage" to our rooms, we discovered the hotel did not have a restaurant. What would we do for food in a foreign city, with a small amount of money and no transportation? We would have to find a place nearby to buy food and bring it to our hotel room.

Since it was so chilly, we left the older children in charge and Jess and I walked to a small grocery store on the corner near the hotel. We picked out about five pounds of grapes, five apples, a wedge of cheese, some milk, and a box of crackers. Jess and I laughed as we returned to the hotel. We had come from the S.S. Uruguay, where sumptuous meals were served, to a small corner grocery store for our first meal in San Francisco.

The kids were disappointed with the food choices for their supper. They already missed being at table nine on the S.S. Uruguay.

"We should be thankful we are in the United States," I stated. "At least we have food to eat and a chance to start over in Texas. Do you want to go back to Manila?"

I had said the magic words. They became quiet and ate grapes, cheese and crackers, and saved the apples for breakfast. We retired early, as we were tired from the excitement, the many changes, and the uncertainty we faced. Tomorrow would be a better day, we hoped.

Wow! Their first day in San Francisco was an eye-opening experience. Mary leafed through the pile of forms and paperwork she had saved. *I can't believe we had to sort through so much in a short period of time. No wonder our paperwork was missed and created a big problem for me later when I was applying for citizenship.*

CHAPTER 112

V-J Day

Tuesday, August 14, 1945, we crawled out of bed and wished we were still on the S.S. Uruguay. After spending our first night in the United States in San Francisco at The Granada Hotel, we were exhausted. Although we had comfortable, large beds (rather than bunk beds), and a warm room, we had not rested well as we were not accustomed to the big city's sounds. Police, ambulance, and other sirens wailed through the night as if they were trying to outdo the honking car horns and clanging bells of the trolleys. This din-filled night was in stark contrast to the quietness of the S.S. Uruguay and being rocked to sleep with the swish of splashing water. The older children were on the fourth floor, away from the street sounds, and were able to rest. We had too many new sounds, sights, and aromas to learn in San Francisco.

Our family gathered in our room on the first floor to share the apples, slices of the remaining cheese, and crackers. We were almost out of milk, so we entrusted Lucy, Emma, and Junior to walk to the corner store to purchase some, plus some breakfast rolls or doughnuts. Upon their return, the milk was poured and the doughnuts divided. Suddenly, Emma squealed.

"Ooooooh! Something's wrong with this milk. It tastes sour!" She said as she ran to our bathroom to wash out her mouth.

The other kids had the same reaction. I was puzzled and looked at the carton.

"It's buttermilk! Jess, what is buttermilk?" I asked, as I smelled the open carton.

Jess laughed as he looked at our faces. The kids who had tasted the milk looked like they were in pain.

"That's what you'll have to drink in Texas," Jess replied. "It's what's left after you take the sweet cream off the whole milk to make butter, then let it clabber."

We decided we had a lot to learn. We had eaten and tasted a lot of strange foods in order to keep from starving, but buttermilk tasted awful…the worst we had ever put in our mouths. Needless to say, another trip was made to the small grocery store to buy "better milk" instead of "buttermilk."

The whole family enjoyed bathing in "real" water for a change. We only had seawater for bathing on the ship. Sometimes it would splash in our mouths and we would have to get a swallow of "real" water to wash out the salty taste. They older girls noticed a difference in their hair after they shampooed with "real" water. The fresh water Tom brought us daily was only for drinking or brushing our teeth. Now we had "real" water flowing from the faucets.

We needed to locate the American Red Cross offices to make all our final travel arrangements for Texas. I also had to find the public welfare department and the Immigration Center in San Francisco to complete more paperwork before leaving for Texas. Jess and I decided we should buy more snacks to have for our lunch and some "better milk" before trying to find the Red Cross offices.

We returned to our room by 10:30 a.m., where we had left Lucy, Emma, and Junior in charge. After eating a light snack, we prepared to leave on our various errands. We promised to return by 2:00 p.m. so they could stroll around our hotel area to see sights of San Francisco, ride the trolley, or go "window shopping," Jess and I had agreed they could go as long as they did not wander far from the hotel and get lost. First, we needed to find the Red Cross office to work on our travel plans to Texas and see if they had any coats or sweaters. We were cold!

We took a taxi to the pier area to find the Red Cross offices, and discovered, to our dismay, that the Red Cross officials were only present during a ship's embarkation or disembarkation. A police officer at the gate told us we would have to go to the City Hall of San Francisco and speak to officials at the Office of Public Welfare. We were so disillusioned. We returned to the hotel to make calls and finalize plans. We had wasted our time, money, and half a day.

After we returned, Lucy, Emma, and Junior left to explore the area around our hotel. We gave them money to ride the trolley, so they could see more sights. After they left, we ate a snack before Jess visited the front desk to get information on the location of the public welfare offices, and the immigration center. It took him longer than I expected to get phone numbers and addresses for those places. He returned about three in the afternoon with slips of paper, maps, and candy. *Jess always enjoyed surprising the kids.*

While the kids were busy with their candy, he and I made lists. Jess tried to make calls to the various agencies around three-thirty. The phone lines became busy. We could not make calls. *What was happening?*

Horns were honking and people screaming in the hallway and outside. The chaotic sounds intensified. Jess decided to walk to the Front Desk and find out what was happening. He got as far as the hallway when someone shouted at him.

"It's over! The war is over! The Japs have surrendered!"

Jess hurried into our room to tell me the news. While this was long-awaited and welcome news, we had another fear. *Our kids are out in the streets! We had no way to reach them. Where were they? Would they get lost?*

Thankfully, we did not have to wait long for their return. Around four-thirty, they burst into our room all excited. They had been riding the trolley from in front of the hotel to the end of the line and back. They had no idea why people were hugging, screaming, and shouting in the streets. They were frightened when cars blew their horns repeatedly. They couldn't even window shop as businesses locked their doors, pulled down shades, and lowered awnings to cover the plate glass windows, as Sutter Street became chaotic.

Jess told them the news about the Japs surrendering. They became more excited and wanted to join the celebration, but Jess insisted they stay inside. Jess was always cautious…a good trait to have on this particular day and the next.

◈

San Francisco suffered the deadliest riot in the city's history beginning on August 14, 1945, and continuing through most of the next day and night. *Most of the rioting was on Market Street…about three blocks from us.* What started as a celebration, rampaged through the night, and turned into a disaster by the next night. *We heard explosions, glass breaking, and multiple sirens all day Wednesday and most of the night. Fires and fireworks were visible from our hotel windows. We felt we had jumped from the Japanese "frying pan" into the American "fire." We stayed inside the hotel through the next day. We only had three apples and one sleeve of crackers left to celebrate Lucy's nineteenth birthday on the fifteenth, and no milk of any kind. We did not dare get outside of our hotel.* The rioters refused to leave Market Street until military and civilian police forced them to leave just before midnight on the fifteenth. *We did not sleep at all.*

CHAPTER 113

Final Destination

On August 16, the city of San Francisco and its residents were dazed by the rioting and public celebrations of V-J Day. The Japanese had accepted unconditional surrender, and General MacArthur was named as head of the occupation forces in Japan. Dropping of the first atomic bombs on Hiroshima on August 6 and on Nagasaki on August 9 set the stage. *We were sailing through enemy waters on those dates. Angels were truly watching over us.* World War II was finally over. Most of the fighting had stopped, but the scars would always remain.

Our rooms were reserved until the seventeenth, as we thought we would already be on our way to Texas, however, since all the government offices were closed on the fifteenth and sixteenth, we had to wait until the seventeenth to arrange for our transportation to Texas. Our hotel stay had to be extended until August 20, as the weekend was approaching.

Jess and I left the older kids in charge while we returned to the small grocery store on the corner. We had long since finished all the snacks. We bought four pints of milk plus more fruit. Emma, Junior, and Mary Jane wanted to window shop and Mary Jane wanted to ride the trolley, as she had not yet had that experience. They promised to be careful and not be gone long. Lucy would stay with Joyce and Linnie. A plan was in place. They left for their adventure with Jess cautioning them to be careful.

After having coffee and a doughnut, Jess called the Red Cross Center to arrange for our transportation and an extension of our hotel stay. They promised to call the hotel to extend our stay, but told us to visit the San Francisco Public Welfare Department for transportation arrangements. We took a taxi and our paperwork to the Public Welfare Department, and explained our situation. We needed assistance for transportation to Texas. After checking our paperwork, they made the necessary travel arrangements and provided us with a copy of a letter they were sending to the Texas Department of Public Welfare, informing them of their assistance and our needs.

We returned to The Granada Hotel to give our kids the news, but they had some news of their own. Emma, Junior, and Mary Jane had ridden the trolley and got off in front of a large department store, The Emporium, on Market Street. The girls decided to go inside and look around the "many wonders of their new world." Junior wanted to stay outside, but the girls talked him in to coming inside for a little while. The first thing they found was an escalator. They had never seen one before and didn't even know what it was called until the "accident" occurred. Mary Jane, wearing her only pair of shoes, the WAC boots, decided to try out the moving stairway, except she stepped up on the "Down" escalator and the moving steps closed on the toe of one boot and the dangling shoelaces. She twisted her ankle, causing her to fall while the moving step continued to chew the front part of the boot, and the alarm sounded. She was terrified. A nearby clerk saw what happened and came to her rescue. Her boot was damaged, but still wearable. Emma was silent and just stared at her. Junior laughed and told her she was going to "catch it." Jess and I were speechless. He just sat and shook his head while I chastised Mary Jane for her "accident" that damaged her boots. We did not have time for this foolishness. We had to finish our plans to go to Texas.

Our tickets were valid for transport from August 17 through August 20. Jess checked at the Front Desk to see if they had received the call from the Red Cross to extend our hotel stay until August 20. The call had not yet been received, but the hotel manager assured Jess he would tell him when confirmation was received. We would not be tossed out of the hotel, thank goodness. Jess also asked how to make bus reservations for our family to Oakland, as we were supposed to board our train to Dallas in Oakland.

Mary and Jesse Hodges after arriving in the United States, August 1945

Santa Fe ticket packet for travel from California to Texas.

"Let me get the *concierge* to help you with those." The manager stated and escorted Jess to the *concierge's* desk. Jess pulled out the remaining dollars he had and hoped there was enough to pay for our tickets, as the Red Cross had not covered the cost of the one-way bus trip to Oakland. He had already set aside enough money to pay for our hotel rooms…two dollars per day for each room. He paid for one week's stay for three rooms while the *concierge* arranged for bus tickets. When the *concierge* finished his conversation with the Greyhound ticket agent, he wrote down the amount Jess owed and told him the tickets, held in his name, would be waiting at the bus station on Monday morning. Jess handed him eight dollars for the tickets and thanked him for his help.

We spent the weekend doing laundry by hand, visiting the small grocery store on Saturday to buy more snacks, and packing for our trip to Texas. We had to leave by 9:30 a.m. on Monday, August 20. Our bus would leave for Oakland at 10:15 a.m., and our train for Dallas at 2:00 p.m., from the Santa Fe Passenger Terminal in Oakland.

To this day, I wonder how we made all those connections, but we did. I knew angels watched when we boarded The Pullman Company sleeping cars with our First Class tickets. We were pleased with our berths and were happy to discover our meals in the dining car were included in the price of our tickets. We were hungry.

Those snacks were the only food we had eaten for the last week. We had not eaten a hot meal since we left the S.S. Uruguay.

Riding, eating, and sleeping on a train was a new experience for us. The meals in the dining car were more than adequate, but did not meet the standard we enjoyed on the S.S. Uruguay. The Santa Fe's food was much better than eating grocery store snacks. We enjoyed the scenery as the Santa Fe chased the wind across the desert, but we were having trouble dealing with the heat. We changed from being chilled the entire time we were in San Francisco, to being "cooked" by the dry heat of the desert. These were the days before air-conditioned trains. There were stops, but we always stayed on the train to keep Jess from worrying about someone being left behind. At night, the heat subsided. The gentle rocking and swaying of our sleeping cars, the "click clack" of the metal wheels on the silver rails, and the occasional sound of the train's whistle echoing across the land reassured us. We were getting closer to Texas.

We spent three days and two nights on the train on our way to Dallas. We were traveling through West Texas during lunchtime on August 22 and were surprised to see stretches of sand and tumbleweeds. It was similar to the desert we had just crossed. The kids hoped to find cowboys and Indians like those in *The Lone Ranger* but none appeared. As we neared Fort Worth, civilization reappeared. We passed horses, cows, and goats, but no cowboys. When we arrived in Dallas around noon, we were confronted with another challenge.

There were no scheduled connections from Dallas to Greenville, Texas, until the next week. The ticket agent in San Francisco had booked us on a train leaving for Paris, Texas, the next day at 10:00 in the morning. Jess was visibly upset.

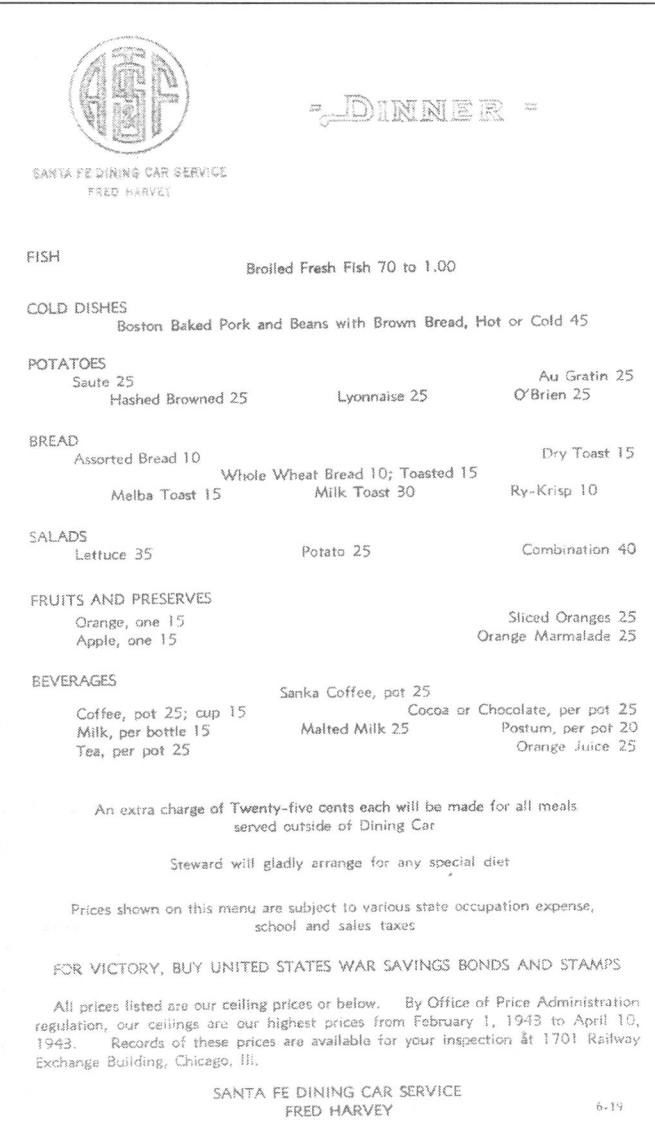

Santa Fe dining car menu.

"We're traveling to Greenville, Texas. It's not that far."

"Yes, sir," the ticket agent agreed, "but the only way y'all can get there from here is to take the mornin' train to Paris. It has a 5:30 afternoon connection to Greenville."

"What are we going to do tonight?" Jess asked.

"Reservations were made for you at The Morris Hotel just across the street."

"What about our luggage?" Jess asked.

"Your luggage is checked through all the way to Greenville."

Jess shook his head from side to side as he returned. He explained our situation, so we took our hand luggage and crossed the street to The Morris Hotel.

Our plans had been made for us. We had to be patient and hope we would reach our final destination before long. Three rooms were reserved for us at The Morris Hotel. We decided on the same arrangements for sleeping we had used in San Francisco. After leaving our hand luggage in our rooms, we ate snacks at the hotel's tiny café. We were tired and ready to return to our rooms to shower and rest. Lucy and Emma decided to rinse out their lingerie and hang them in their bathroom to dry. The next morning, we visited the hotel's small café, ate a small breakfast, returned to our rooms to "take care of business," and met in the lobby to check out by 9:30 a.m. After gathering in the lobby, we returned to the train station to board our train for Paris.

We had been traveling about thirty minutes and the Texas heat was intensifying, so Lucy checked her hand luggage for her small folding fan. Something else was missing. She realized she and Emma had left their lingerie hanging in the hotel's bathroom in Dallas. She quietly told me about their loss. I shook my head in disbelief.

We arrived at Paris around 1:00 p.m., snacked, took care of "business," and waited in the passenger terminal for the train to Greenville. It was very hot in the waiting room. We visited the water fountains for cool water repeatedly. We noticed one of the fountains was marked "Whites Only." We had never seen signs like those before. Drinking so much water caused us to also see the bathrooms were similarly marked. Jess explained it was due to segregation. We knew nothing about segregation and were too tired to learn. We did not ask questions and just followed instructions.

At 5:20 p.m. we boarded the passenger train for Greenville. Once again, the stifling August heat surrounded us as if we were fertile eggs inside an incubator. We were ready to "hatch" any minute. The children sat by the windows, watched the passing scenery, and felt the hot outside air sweep across their faces. We were thankful to be riding the train during the "cooling down" period of the day.

It was after seven in the evening when we arrived at the Katy Depot on Lee Street in Greenville. As we left the train, we noticed a large sign spanning the length of Lee Street. In its center, it stated: GREENVILLE WELCOME. On the left side were the words: THE BLACKEST LAND, and on the right…THE WHITEST PEOPLE. Mary Jane, the inquisitive one, needed an explanation. Jess told her the soil in this area was black land, which made it excellent for farming crops like corn, cotton, grain, and so on. By the time he began his explanation about, "THE

WHITEST PEOPLE," no one was listening. Exhaustion and hunger had taken control. We needed food and plenty of rest.

The Greyhound bus terminal was near the Katy Depot, so we checked on taking a bus to Quinlan, our final destination. The last bus to Quinlan had departed earlier. Another one was scheduled for 6:30 the next morning...another snag in our plans. After arranging for bus tickets for the next morning, we were told rooms were available at The Greenville Hotel next door. It was the best choice for accommodations close to the train station. Two rooms were available at the hotel. Our luggage remained at the bus station to be loaded on the morning bus to Quinlan. The same clothes we had on would be worn again the next day. We bought snacks for our supper, and retired early. We were to be at the bus station by six the next morning.

It was early the next morning when I realized other items had been left at The Morris Hotel. Before we left the Philippines, Harold Cuzner, Professor of Forestry at *Los Baños*, gave Jess a white pith helmet as protection against the hot Texas sun. He had given me a lovely, hand-carved cane shaped like a snake with green beads for eyes and a long yellow bead for its tongue. We were so disappointed to have carried those gifts all this way only to lose them just before arriving at our destination.

After checking out of The Greenville Hotel, we hurried to the Greyhound Bus Station, bought cookies and milk for breakfast, plus chewing gum, as we would not be able to brush our teeth. Large signs were posted on the wall. "COLORED" was posted at the rear of the waiting room, and "WHITES ONLY" at the front. Most of the "Whites Only" seats were occupied, so four of us sat in the nearly empty "Colored" section to munch our breakfast. It made no difference...the seats were alike.

Greenville's welcome sign hanging over the west end of Lee Street. The Greenville Hotel is shown on the left.

An announcement over the loudspeaker called for all passengers leaving on the 6:30 a.m. bus for Quinlan, Terrell, and Kaufman to board. Again, we waited until everyone else was on before boarding. The seats at the front of the bus were taken. Jess wanted us to stay together, so I led everyone to the long empty seat at the back, which was perfect. Lucy took the aisle seat beside a middle-aged man, slumped in the seat next to the window...his head against the glass and his eyes closed. Emma was in the opposite aisle seat. The man stirred as she sat down, looked at her, and stared at the rest of us at the rear as we were quite noisy arranging ourselves so the little ones could see out of the windows. He looked at her, and stared at us again.

"Whar y'all live?"

"We don't have a place," Lucy replied truthfully.

"Whar y'all frum?"

Lucy explained we were from the Philippines and were moving to Texas, her daddy's home state.

"No wunner y'all dunno whar y'all live. Y'all dunno whar tuh set. Back uh the bus is jes fer coloreds," He shook his head in disbelief as he spoke.

Lucy had no idea what he meant by "coloreds," so she just turned her head toward the aisle, and closed her eyes. She was tired of travel, transfers, hotels, and Texas heat.

About 7:15 a.m., we arrived in Quinlan. The sleepy little town consisted of one main street with several stores, two service stations, and a post office. Only one store was open at that time of day. The Griffis Drugstore, in the center of town, was also the regular bus stop. Mrs. Mary Lee Griffis, the owner, emerged from the drugstore to meet us. The bus driver unloaded our "luggage" and placed the boxes and steamer trunk on the sidewalk. He stepped inside the drugstore to check for passengers, and, finding none, left for his next stop...Terrell, Texas. We were at our final destination, and our future was in God's hands.

The small town was nearly empty. We had not made arrangements for any of Jess' family to meet us, as he wanted to surprise his stepmother, Della Hodges. We waited around The Griffis Drugstore discussing what our next steps should be. Jess decided to ask Mrs. Griffis about some of his former acquaintances.

"I'm sorry to bother you, Mrs. Griffis, but do you happen to know Ethan Vansicle? He used to live around here," Jess asked.

"I sure do. He doesn't live too far from here. Let me give him a call for you...right this way," she responded as she led the way around the candy counter to her telephone.

She lifted the phone and spoke to the operator...asking to be connected with him. After a few seconds, she handed the phone to Jess.

Jess had some explaining to do when "Eth" answered his phone. He could hardly believe that Jess was calling from The Griffis Drugstore. After conversing for about three minutes, he told Jess he would come

Mrs. Mary Lee Griffis, owner of Griffis Drug Store, Quinlan, Texas

to the drugstore as soon as possible. Before he hung up, Jess had an important question to ask.

"Say, Eth, do you happen to know of any houses for rent in town? We really need a place to stay," Jess stated.

"Sorry, Jess," Ethan said. "Rent houses are real scarce. Can't think of any, but there's one being built close to the railroad right now, but it's already spoken for. I'll be there in a little while. Can't wait to see you and meet your family."

Jess shook his head in disappointment as he came from behind the counter. Mrs. Griffis, a perky matron with generous bosoms and a smile to match offered to make another call for Jess or provide us with something to drink.

Jess shook his head. He did not know whom to call, as he had been away for many years and had no idea if other friends were still around.

"I guess you could call Helen Finley, if you don't mind," Jess replied.

Mrs. Griffis repeated his request to the operator only to learn that Mrs. Finley did not have a telephone. Once again, she offered to make other calls or provide a beverage. The heat was building, as it was almost ten o'clock on a hot August day.

Lucy and Emma needed to "take care of business" before having anything to drink, so they asked her where they might find the bathrooms, as no signs were posted inside the drugstore.

"Oh, honey," Mrs. Griffis stated, "Just walk to the end of the block and behind Epperson's General Store. The restrooms are right behind there."

Lucy and Emma left the drugstore and followed her directions. All they could see were two wooden square buildings. They thought they had made a mistake or not listened well to her directions given in her lovely Texas drawl, so they returned to the drugstore. When they explained that only two small square buildings were behind Epperson's, Mrs. Griffis smiled.

"Oh, honey, those are 'outhouses' or outdoor restrooms. We don't have indoor plumbing here," she stated.

The girls had no choice, so they returned to the two small square outhouses. As they stepped toward one, a farmer, wearing overalls sauntered out of the one they almost entered. They decided to enter the other one and had their first experience with a Texas outhouse.

᙭

Mary recalled how disgusted Lucy and Emma were with their first experience with a Texas "outhouse." Many thought of the Philippines as an uncivilized country with scantily clad natives living in the jungles. They were not aware that indoor plumbing was more prevalent in Manila than it was in Hunt County. They had much to learn.

CHAPTER 114

Meet the Family

The hot Texas sun beat down on the dusty sidewalk riddled with cracks. We peeked through the glass show window, decorated with the drugstore's name, plus an assortment of small signs advertising the latest items for sale. One small ice cream table and four small chairs, the only seating available in The Griffis Drugstore, was occupied by a farmer's wife and her two young children as they enjoyed their ice cream cone treats, while the woman sipped on a root beer float. We were hot, thirsty, tired, and sleepy, as we had been up since five-thirty this morning…and it would soon be ten. We wanted to go inside and stand under the white ceiling fans whirring lazily around to stir the air, but we knew we must stay outside. We had no money to buy ice cream.

Gradually, farmers and their families came into town to do their shopping. We saw sights we had never seen in Manila. Long trailers pulled by noisy tractors; wagons being pulled by teams of mules (our first to see); women and children riding on the wagons wearing printed cloth bonnets that shaded their faces with long flaps extending from the back of the bonnets to shade their necks; and, young boys, shirtless and wearing overalls, all looked very different to us. They gawked at us as we sat upon our "luggage" placed on the hot sidewalk. We were "strangers" in town, and we looked strange.

Helen Finley, half-sister to Jess, drove the family tractor, with a long livestock trailer attached, and parked on the side of Epperson's General Store. She was in town to pick up cattle feed, when Mr. Epperson told her she had family waiting for her at The Griffis Drugstore.

"Well, who on earth could it be?' Helen puzzled. "I don't know of anyone in my family who said they were coming here today. Wonder who it is and what they want?"

Helen, a twenty-six year old woman with a ruddy complexion weighing about two hundred twenty pounds, brushed her damp golden curls away from her sweaty face by dragging the crook of her right elbow across her forehead. She yanked the bib of her overalls to one side to ease the pressure off her very ample bosoms. Today was going to be a "scorcher" and she had too much to do to "fool with company." There was little or no grass in their pasture and Jim, her husband, told her to pick up several bags of feed for the cattle and hogs. She had brought her largest hog in the front part of the sectioned trailer, hoping to sell it to Mr. Epperson…but that would have to wait. Her curiosity was growing by the minute.

The little kids were perched on some of the "luggage" and the rest were leaning against the brick wall of The Griffis Drugstore when Helen ambled up the sidewalk from Epperson's General Store. None of us had ever seen her before, not even Jess. We had received a small photo of Helen, and her husband, Jim Finley, after they married, but it was before World War II.

"Well, my goodness! Oh, my word! Well, I never expected to see you folks in Quinlan!" Helen squealed and laughed loudly, as she approached us with open arms.

Helen's Texas drawl boomed as if amplified by a microphone and speaker. People across the street at the Quinlan Post Office stopped to stare at the commotion in front of the drugstore. Helen continued her loud pronouncements as she pelted us with questions and smothered us with hugs.

After a few minutes of conversation, Helen decided to move her tractor and trailer to the front of The Griffis Drugstore, so she could take us to the Hodges home place. She insisted there would be room for all of us, our "luggage," plus the hog in the trailer. None of us had ever seen a hog that large before, nor had we ever been transported in a livestock trailer. We stared rather uncertainly at the huge animal. The pigs in the Philippines were miniature copies compared to that very large hog.

With the hog secured in a sectioned area at the front of the long trailer, Junior and Helen placed the "luggage" in the remaining portions so we could use the boxes as seating. Helen, who was accustomed to swinging bales of hay around, had no problem with the "luggage." We were a sight to behold to the crowd of onlookers across the street as Helen started the tractor and pulled this trailer load of "livestock" from the Philippines in a westerly direction to give her mother, Jess' stepmother, a big surprise, as Della had no phone, either.

They arrived at the Hodges home place around noon. The old farmhouse, with a long, rambling front porch, was a welcome sight. We were homeless, and had finally arrived at Jess' home. As Junior and Helen unloaded our "luggage' on the front porch, Della, Jess's stepmother, lumbered out the squeaky screen door. As the screen door slammed behind her, she began to ask questions. I could tell she was not pleased to see us. The screen door opened again. We had a surprise in store. While Jess was introducing the kids and me to Della, her second husband stepped forward. We had no idea Della had remarried. Jess' dad died in 1941, and, within months, Della married Dave Baker. After Dave's curt remarks, Jess felt we were not welcome and began to realize the depth of the many challenges ahead for his family. Jess had survived being a prisoner of the Japs for over three years; he would have to find the strength to endure more.

Mary had mixed emotions. She recalled the many challenges they confronted in starting over in Texas and in becoming a citizen. *I have come through fire and brimstone to become an American, and it has been worth all I have had to endure. I will celebrate my fortieth year in America tomorrow, August 13, 1985. God Bless America!*

Epilogue

Mary was satisfied with writing as much as she remembered of her family's history and many of the experiences they had endured during World War II, along with her family's repatriation to America. She had attained her goal of moving to the United States, but her ultimate goal was to become a citizen of the United States.

Many events caused her to have second thoughts about coming to Texas. They overcame the difficulties of being strangers in a strange land without money, jobs, a home, or friends. The only family members in Jess' hometown were complete strangers, even to Jess. His stepmother and her husband were not happy to see them arrive in Texas.

Advice and a little financial assistance, provided through the state department

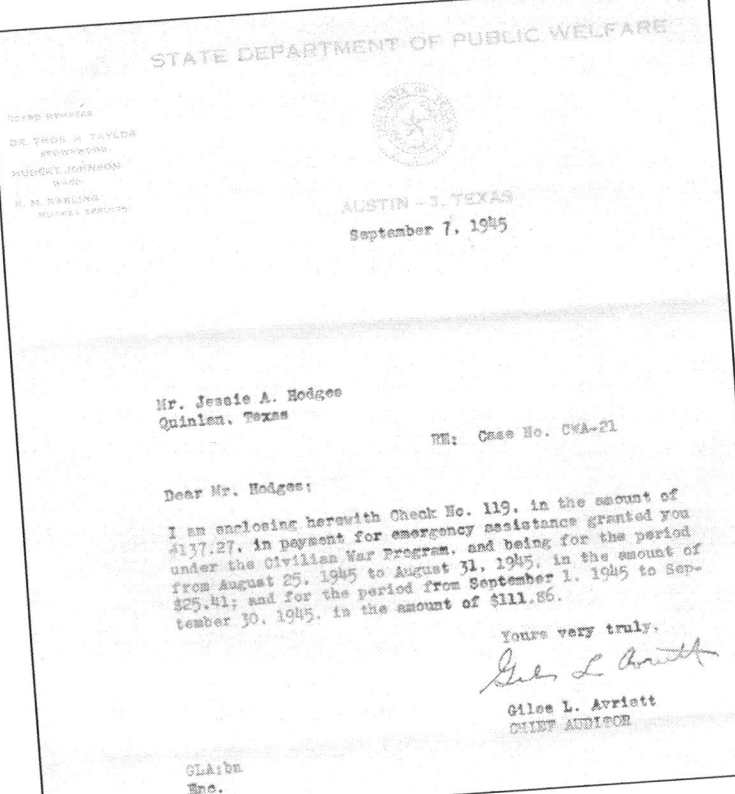

Notice of emergency assistance for the Hodges family after their arrival in Texas following World War II.

of public welfare in Austin, was enough to live as an indigent homeless family with no visible means of support. They had difficulty finding a place to live, and no jobs were available for a fifty-six-year-old man, still recuperating from the rigors of prison camp.

The United States government required the entire family to enter the U.S. Marine Hospital in Galveston for complete medical examinations in September 1945, before they would be allowed to remain in Texas. Jess had still not regained his strength, but he managed to pass the examination. Lucy had to remain in the hospital in Galveston for surgery to remove a cyst on her back, but the others were allowed to return to Quinlan to enroll in public school, which had already begun.

Lucy and Linnie's Certificates of Discharge from the Marine Hospital in Galveston, Texas, where the family underwent mandatory physical examinations.

In reply address not the signer of this
letter, but Bureau of Naval Personnel,
Navy Department, Washington 25, D.C.

Refer to No.

Pers 5323a LHJ
498 54 84

NAVY DEPARTMENT
BUREAU OF NAVAL PERSONNEL
WASHINGTON 25, D. C.

10 November 1945

Mrs. Mary C. Hodges
General Delivery
Quinlan, Texas

Dear Mrs. Hodges:

This will acknowledge receipt of your letter in which you request information concerning your son, Robert Morris Hodges, Seaman second class, United States Naval Reserve.

It is with regret you are advised that your son is being carried on the records of this Bureau in the status of missing as of 6 May 1942, having been serving with the Naval Forces in Corregidor at the time that area capitulated. He was attached to the USS GENESEE. His name has not appeared on any list received from the International Red Cross nor has his name been among those whose liberation has been announced.

Every effort continuously is being exerted to locate or to finally resolve the status of those men who are being carried as missing. Liberated prisoners of war have been interrogated; statements have been secured from survivors of marine and air disasters; and, in addition to these eye witness reports, thorough studies have been made of captured Japanese documents and of reports submitted by the U. S. forces engaged in searches of islands and areas formerly occupied by the Japanese. As this review has progressed the status of many men formerly carried as missing has been resolved. However, such action has not as yet been taken with respect to the status of your son. It is expected that in the near future the review will make final action possible in his case. You will be promptly notified when a decision is reached.

Your change of address has been noted upon the records of your son.

The Navy Department is aware of the anxiety you have suffered and appreciates your patience during this trying period. It is hoped that definite information can be forwarded to you soon.

By direction of Chief of Naval Personnel.

Sincerely yours,

H. B. ATKINSON
Commander, USNR.
Officer in Charge
Casualty Section

One of the many letters Mary received during her search for eldest son Bobby.

The only available house to rent was a shack on Exum Willingham's farm, normally used to house field hands during the cotton harvest, but they rented it so their kids could be close to school. They endured two cold winters in that drafty old shack before finding a livable home across the street from Kenneth and Ann Cannon, plus their son, James, who befriended them.

During the first year, their children, who were quite different from their peers, were teased at school. They had missed three years of schooling during the war and had to enroll in the same grade level as of 1941, making them three years older than their classmates. Thankfully, they met the challenges and were double promoted. Lucy graduated and qualified as Salutatorian, but could not receive the award, as she had not been enrolled for a sufficient number of days. Jesse Jr. was Salutatorian of his class, and Emma ranked in the top five. Mary Jane finished as Valedictorian and eventually earned her doctorate, becoming the first one in the family to earn this honor.

Mary continued her intensive quest to determine the official fate of their son, Robert Morris Hodges, a seaman first class in the United States Navy. A letter was received indicating that Bobby was listed as "Missing In Action." A later notice, a United States flag and a Purple Heart, came in a plain, brown cardboard box that Mary Jane brought from the post office. Mary never gave up searching for her lost son. She even returned to the Philippines to search, only to see his name engraved on a memorial for those missing in action in the American Memorial Cemetery in Manila.

In September 2012, Robert Morris Hodges received the following awards, posthumously: Bronze Star; Purple Heart; World War II Victory Medal; American Campaign Medal; Asiatic Pacific Campaign Medal; Presidential Unit Citation Ribbon; Combat Action Ribbon; and, the Honorable Service Lapel Pin (Ruptured Duck) of the United States Navy.

Mary had an uphill struggle to attain her American citizenship…to the point of responding to a warrant for her arrest as an illegal alien. She fought hard through mountains of paperwork and legal fees to remain in this country she loved. Mary missed her first appearance at naturalization proceedings, because she went into labor and was in the hospital giving birth to James Charles (Jimmy) Hodges on April 25, 1949…the week of her scheduled appearance in court. Her second chance to earn her citizenship came in February 1951. With the help of Emma, and her husband, Carlton D. Smith, Mary appeared at United States District Court, Northern District of Texas, in Dallas, Texas. Carlton accompanied Mary into the courtroom to begin answering the series of questions to become a citizen, while Emma waited in the hallway caring for their son, Barton, wearing his "Dr. Denton's" as he was taken from his crib very early that day, and entertaining two-year-old James (Jimmy). What seemed like an eternity to Emma, taking care of the two little boys, was actually a period of about two hours. As Mary and Carlton exited the courtroom, both were grinning like Cheshire cats. She was officially a Citizen of The United States of America.

Mary and Jess took their family from being a poverty-ridden family to owners of multiple businesses in the Quinlan area. They rose from renting an old cotton

NAVY DEPARTMENT
BUREAU OF NAVAL PERSONNEL
WASHINGTON 25, D. C.

Pers-102H-cor
MM/498 54 84

SEP 1948

Mr. Jesse Allen Hodges
Gen. Delivery,
Quinlan, Texas

Dear Mr. Hodges:

    The Bureau has the honor to inform you of the award of the Purple Heart and certificate to your late son, Robert Morris Hodges, Seaman Second Class, United States Naval Reserve, in accordance with General Order 186 of January 21, 1943 which reads in part as follows:

    "The Secretary of the Navy is further authorized and directed to award the Purple Heart posthumously, in the name of the President of the United States, to any persons who, while serving in any capacity with the Navy, Marine Corps or Coast Guard of the United States, since December 6, 1941, are killed in action or who die as a direct result of wounds received in action with an enemy of the United States, or as a result of an act of such enemy."

    The medal is being forwarded under separate cover. Please acknowledge receipt on the enclosed form.

By direction of the Chief of Naval Personnel.

Sincerely yours,

JOE H. FLOYD
Lt. Comdr., USNR, Director
Enlisted Processing & Transmittal
Medals and Awards

Official notice awarding the Purple Heart posthumously to Robert Morris "Bobby" Hodges recognizing his service during World War II.

U. S. DEPARTMENT OF JUSTICE
IMMIGRATION AND NATURALIZATION SERVICE
SAN FRANCISCO, CALIFORNIA

IN REPLYING PLEASE REFER TO THIS FILE NUMBER
130D-25249

November 23, 1945

Mrs. Mary Gamero Hodges
Route #1
Quinlan, Texas

Dear Madam:

Referring to your application for an extension of temporary stay, you are informed that your departure from the United States on or before February 7, 1946, will be satisfactory.

Kindly inform this office as to the date, steamer and port of your departure in order that your case may be closed.

You should endeavor to adjust your status to that of a permanent resident before February 7, 1946. Information concerning procedure may be secured at any office of this Service.

Very truly yours,

For the District Director

STAN OLSON, Chief,
Entry & Departure Section
San Francisco District.

American Consul,
Nuevo Laredo, Tamps.,
Mexico.

Write him setting forth that your wife is now in the United States; that she is of the Spanish race,; a native of the Phillipines; was admitted at San Francisco Cal. About 8/13/45 as a Transit under Sec. 3(3) of the Immigration Act, 1924; that she is desirous of departing from the United States to secure an Immigration Visa entitling her to reside permanently in the United States. State your name; place of birth; present citizenship; that you have a marriage certificate and your birth certificate; that you own so much land at a certain place; your home; that you do business with a certain bank; that you have so many debts out standing; that you have so many dependents;/that them are employed (or not); that your average monthly income is so much; that you have so much money on deposit with a certain bank; get letter from bank official to substantiate this assertion. Request him to inform you if any other documents are necessary, and if he will issue your a non-quota immigration visa if and when she applies at his office.

(top) Letter from Immigration approving a date for Mary's deportation from the United States as an illegal alien. *(bottom)* The American Consul in Mexico offers assistance toward Mary's quest of US citizenship.

pickers' shack to designing and building their own home next to two of their businesses. Mary managed to operate two of the family's three businesses, care for her family, attend church services regularly in Greenville, Texas, (first at St. Mary's Catholic Church with The Reverend Hugh Smythe, and later at their new building, St. William's Catholic Church), support her children's school and social activities, plus assist in a myriad of school and community projects involving family and friends. Jess operated the Ice House business on the main street of Quinlan and worked the family farm to produce fruit, vegetables, and poultry for the family. He did some construction work on the side. Oh, yes, they managed to have their ninth child, Rose Aline Hodges, who was born on December 27, 1951.

Mary and Jess faced many more trials and disappointments in their struggles to raise their children. They suffered through the multitude of challenges thrown their way and managed to always be thankful to God for their abundant blessings.

Jess had a strong philosophy. He encouraged his children and wife to adopt it as their own. Mary believed his philosophy helped the family to overcome many obstacles, and would always agree, knowing he was right. He also repeated another gem of wisdom to his family. When anyone in the family sought his counsel, he always asked them how much control they had over the situation or problem they faced. When they responded as to their level of control, Jess answered wisely:

First winter in Texas, December 1945, in front of our first car beside the only house (cotton pickers' shack) available for rent in Quinlan, Texas, owned by Exum Willingham. *(L-R)* Jesse Jr. (wearing Jap pilot headgear); Emma, Lucy, Joyce *(front)*, and Mary Jane *(back)* Hodges.

If you have control over a situation or problem, deal with it…take care of it. If you have none, forget about it…set it aside. You cannot change people who do not choose to change.

Those words of wisdom carried our family through many trying times… through marriages, divorces, more children, grandchildren, great-grandchildren, honors, awards, financial losses, illnesses, lawsuits, disappointments, and the ever-present Angel of Death. Mary's strong faith and Jess's philosophy became the pillars upon which their children built their lives.

Mary eventually moved to Greenville, Texas, just one block away from St. Williams Catholic Church. She was able to become more active and attend services regularly, to the point that she and the parish priest were sometimes the only two in attendance. Mary's dedication to her church and family are evidenced by the many hours she spent helping her church to grow, financially and spiritually.

Mary's ultimate goal for her children was to make sure they all had a good education. To this end, she worked many long, hard hours so her children could attain this goal. When this goal was finally reached, Mary fashioned a golden tree from gold metallic paper and arranged the graduation photos of her eight living children in its branches. She wrote the following poem, one of many, which she dedicated to her children.

My Golden Tree

From a distant land with my family I came
With prayer and home I started my aim,
We pointed to our children, where they were bound
Upon my Golden Tree with their cap and gown.

Though my partner is now at rest
Alone I tried to do my best,
I prayed to God day and night
That our last child may reach that height.

So now I have in front of me,
All our children on the Golden Tree
For them I pray The Lord may be
As kind and merciful as He is to me.

I thank The Lord for giving me
This blessed land to raise my Tree
Twenty four years it took in all
For MY GOLDEN TREE to reach its goal.

MARY G. HODGES

On Angels' Wings

Gamero Family Tree

PATERNAL GRANDPARENTS OF MARY OF THE ANGELS

Don José Maria Gamero   *wed*   **Doña Maxima Porras**
bp: Barcelona, Spain   bp: Barcelona, Spain
d: 1879   d: July 1889
dp: Manila, Philippines   dp: Manila, Philippines
Castillian (Spanish)   Spanish/French

Only Child
José Maria Gamero y Porras
    b: June 1, 1835
    bp: Barcelona, Spain
    m: Four Spouses*
    Twenty Children**
    d: November 14, 1908
    Manila, Philippines (Gamero Family Vault)

*Spouse #1: Joaquina Saenz (Spain)
    m: 1855
    d: 1870, Manila, Philippines
  **Child #1: Stillborn, 1858
  **Child #2: Stillborn, 1861
  **Child #3: Stillborn, 1864
  **Child #4: Paz de la Vega Gamero y Saenz
      b: 1868
      m: Antonio Isidorio del Valle
      Child #1: Paz (Pacita) del Valle y Gamero

*Spouse #2: Josepha Boix (orphan) (Spain)   Younger sister
    b: 1853   Pascuala Boix (Lola Lala)
    m: 1872   m: José Rocha (brother of
    d: 1885, Intramuros, Childbirth   Sp. #3 Rosario Rocha)

**Child #5: Mercedes del Carmen Gamero y Boix (Maming)
  b: 1874, Intramuros
  d: January 1958, Intramuros
  (Catholic Nun: Order of St. Augustine)

**Child #6: Maria de la Concepcion Gamero y Boix (Concha)
  b: 1876, Intramuros
  d: Unknown, WWII
  (Lived as a cloistered Dominican nun in the Convent of Santa Clara. Renamed: Mother Tecla de San Antonio)

**Child #7: Maria del Rosario Gamero y Boix (Charing)
  b: 1878, Intramuros
  d: 8-14-1944, Complications of dysentary & pneumonia, WWII

**Child #8: Maria de la Natividad Gamero y Boix (Natting or Nati)
  b: 1880, Intramuros
  m: Capt. Carlos Bores (Stu. of Don José Gamero) Died at sea
  d: 1918, Influenza Epidemic
  Child #1: Angelita Bores y Gamero (Meningitis, Age 3)

**Child #9: Maria del Dolores Soledad Gamero y Boix (Solita)
  b: 1883, Intramuros
  (Entered Dominican Order in 1905: Dolores de San Expedito. Served as missionary to China.)

**Child #10: José Maria Gamero y Boix (Pépe)
  b: 1885, Intramuros
  d: 1940, Antipolo, Pneumonia
  (Jesuit priest at Our Lady of Peace and Good Voyage at Antipolo, P.I.)

*Spouse #3: Rosario Rocha   (José Gamero y Porras' landlady)
  m: September 1887   (Her brother was José Rocha)
  d: 1893 Manila, P.I., Afterbirth infection

**Child # 11: José Agama (Adopted son of José Agama—Don José's student)
  b: 1885

**Child #12: Rosario Agama (Adopted daughter of José Agama)
  b: 1887

**Child #13: Maria del Mercedes Gamero y Rocha (Mercedita)
  b: 1890, Intramuros
  d: 1893, Broken back, Age 3

**Child #14: Maria del Salud Gamero y Rocha (Salud)
  b: 1893, Intramuros
  m: Willi Kursweg (Landsberg, Germany) 1916
  Child #1: Stillborn 1917
  d: 1917 Manila, P.I., Childbirth/spousal abuse

MATERNAL GRANDPARENTS OF MARY OF THE ANGELS

Don Angel Cucullu   *wed*   **Doña Amalia del Valle**

bp: Extremedura, Spain   bp: Madrid, Spain
d: 1890, Manila, P.I.   d: 1910, Manila, P.I.
(Basque) Spanish   (Castillian) Spanish
(Left Spain in 1877 to work in Ilocos Norte, P.I. for *La Tabacalera*)

- Child #1: Francisco Cucullu y del Valle
  - b: 1866
  - m: 1890
- Child #2: Herminia Cucullu y del Valle
  - b: 1869
  - Sp. #1: Eloped 1890 Armando Suarez
    - (Died serving in Spanish Navy)
    - Child #1: Pilar Suarez y Cucullu
  - Sp. #2: Luis Cucullu
    - (Widowed cousin w/two daughters)
  - Stepchild #1: Salvadora Cucullu
  - Stepchild #2: Luisa Cucullu
  - Child #1: Luis Cucullu y Cucullu
    - Killed by Japs, Manila, 1945
  - Child #2: José Cucullu y Cucullu
    - Killed by Japs, Intramuros, 1945
  - Child #3: Angel Cucullu y Cucullu
    - Killed by Japs, Intramuros, 1945
  - Child #4: Alfredo Cucullu y Cucullu
    - Killed by Japs, Intramuros, 1945 (Taft Avenue)
- Children #3/4: Rogelio & Alfonso Cucullu y del Valle (twins)
  - b: 1872
  - d: 1888, San Juan River/Fiesta de San Juan, Beheaded by natives at the fiesta in San Juan

*Spouse #4/Cucullu Child #5:
Maria de la Luz Cucullu y del Valle (Mami)
- b: 10-9-1875, Guernica/Bilbao Spain
- m: 7-6-1895, Church of The Nazarene-Quiapo-Manila, P.I.
- d: 1-31-1958, Manila, P.I.

**Child #15: Maria de la Luz Gamero y Cucullu (Lucing)
- b: 5-17-1896, Intramuros
- m: 5-27-1917 to Francisco (Frank) Gutierrez
- Child #1: Francisco Gutierrez (Jr.) y Gamero (Frankie)
  - b: 1918
- Child #2: Antonio Gutierrez y Gamero (Anthony/Toning)
  - b: 1-19-1919

Child #3: Maria del Carmen Gutierrez y Gamero (Nena)
    b: 8-6-1921
Child #4: José Luis Gutierrez y Gamero (Peping/Pepito)
    b: 1923
    d: 1945, Killed by direct hit to bomb shelter, Baguio, P.I. during WWII.
    (Was with Pilar/Tony Settember)
Child #5: Ramon Gutierrez y Gamero (Pacquito)
    b: 7-7-1926

**Child #16: José Angel Gamero y Cucullu
    b: 1898, Intramuros
    d: 1899, Contracted smallpox from Lucing, Age 18 months

**Child #17: Maria del Consuelo Gamero y Cucullu (Consueling)
    b: 6-14-1900, Intramuros
    m: 2-2-1918
    Sp: Juan Gonzalez y Bailon (Juanito) by Rev. Gamero at The Manila Cathedral
    Child #1: Estephania Gonzalez y Gamero (Fanny)
        b: 6-1-1920 (Fathered by Reyes)
            Child #1: Result of rape Mari Carmen Gonzalez (Negri)
        m: 1935
        Sp: Paulo Santos (Died in 1938)
            Child #2: b. 1936-Son (Adopted by Paulo's sister)
            Child #3: b. 1937-Son (Adopted by Paulo's sister)
        d: During WWII when mental patients were released to roam.
    Child #2: Jose Mari Gonzalez y Gamero (Peping/Bull) (Sorsogon/Bulan)
        b: 1922, Manila, Philippines
    Child #3: Juan Zenon Gonzalez y Gamero (Juaning)
        b: 6-23-1923, Philippines
    Child #4: Maria del Pilar Gonzalez y Gamero (Pilachu)
        b: 11-26-1926, Philippines
    Child #5: Carlos Gonzalez y Gamero (Carlitos)
        b: 1928
    Child #6: Maria Teresa Gonzalez y Gamero (Teresita/Chini)
        b: 1932 (Fathered by Segado)

**Child #18: Maria del Pilar Gamero y Cucullu (Pilachu/Pil)
    b: 10-4-1903, Intramuros
    m: 7-25-1925 Sp. Anthony D. Settember (Tony)
    Child #1: Anthony D. Settember Jr. (Tony)
        b: 7-10-1926, Manila, Philippines

**Child #19: Maria de los Angeles Josefa Gabina Gamero y Cucullu (*Nena*)

b: 2-19-1905, Intramuros
(Three years old when her father died.)
m: 11-10-1923
Sp: Jesse Allen Hodges (Roberts), Quinlan, Texas

Child #1: Robert Morris Hodges (Bobby)
b: 9-22-1924, Manila, Philippines
Missing in Action during WWII in Manila, P.I.

Child #2: Luz Asuncion Hodges (Lucy Ann) (Collins)
b: 8-15-1926, Manila, Philippines
m: 6-3-1947
Sp: Cornelius Collins (Buddy/Bud)
b. 6-12-1920

Child #3: Jesse Anthony Hodges Jr.
b: 6-9-1928, Manila, Philippines

Child #4: Marie Emma Hodges (Smith)
b: 3-1-1930, Manila, Philippines

Child #5: Mary Jane Rita Hodges (Vance)
b: 5-22-1934, Manila, Philippines

Child #6: Joyce Josephine Hodges (Barrow)
b: 11-14-1937, Manila, Philippines

Child #7: Linnie May Hodges (McCormack)
b: ll-23-1940, Manila, Philippines

World War II—Japanese Occupation of the Philippines December 1941-August 1945

Child #8: James Charles Hodges
b: 4-25-1949 (Terrell, TX)

Child #9: Rose Aline Hodges (Strickland/Chieffo)
b: 12-27-1951 (Terrell, TX)

**Child #20: Lorenzo José Gamero y Cucullu
b: 9-7-1907
m: Eloped with Filipina servant (Banished from family.)
d: 1945, Unknown

Resources

Buencamino, III, Felipe. February 1945. "Refugees Salvage Hope, Little Else, From Ruins," *Free Philippines,* Vol. I, No. 6, p. 2, Manila, Philippines.

Grun, Bernard. 2005. *The Timetables of History: A Horizontal Linkage of People and Events.* New York: Touchstone: Simon & Schuster, Inc.

—. 1942. "December 8 Anniversary Rotogravure: Supplement For All Dailies," Published by the Manila Sinbun-sya, Manila, Philippines.

Rice, Barney G. (PFC) (Editor). 1945. *Golden Gate* (A daily newsletter of the S.S. Uruguay published at sea.), Vol. I, Nos. 3, 4, 7, 8, 11, 14, 15, 16, and 17.

Richards, Peter C.. 1945. *Liberation Bulletin of Philippine Internment Camp No. I at Santo Tomas University,* Manila, Philippines.

Robb, Robert Yelton. Feb. 5, 1949. "Nightmare in Santo Tomas." *Collier's,* Vol. 123, No. 6, pp. 34, 64-67. The Crowell-Collier Publishing Co., Springfield, Ohio.

San Francisco News. 1945. "Cruiser Sunk; Carried Atom bomb Cargo—880 Lost on Indianapolis As Two Blasts Rip Her Bow," p. 3.

—. 1945. "A Tired But Empty City—Counts Victory Memories," p. 3.

The Sunday Tribune. November 28,1943, Vol. XIX, No. 216, Manila, Philippines.

—. December 5, 1943, Vol. XIX, No. 222, Manila, Philippines.

The Tribune. May 8, 1942, Vol XVIII, No. 38, Manila, Philippines.

—. May 6, 1943, Vol. XIX, No. 35, Manila, Philippines.

—. December 7, 1943, Vol. XIX, No. 223, Manila, Philippines.

—. December 9, 1943, Vol. XIX, No. 225, Manila, Philippines.

Worcester, Dean C. August 16, 1915. *The Mentor: The Philippine Islands,* Vol. 3, No. 13, published by the Department of Travel, Manila, Philippines.

—. *The World Book.* 1966. Chicago: Field Enterprises Educational Corporation, Vol. 15 and Vol. 17.

Made in the USA
Charleston, SC
29 November 2012